Work, Community, and Power

The Experience of Labor in Europe and America, 1900–1925

Class and Culture
A series edited by Bruce Laurie
and Milton Cantor

Work,
Community,
and
Power

The Experience of
Labor in Europe and
America,
1900–1925

edited by
**James E. Cronin
and
Carmen Sirianni**

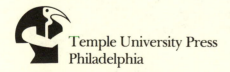
Temple University Press
Philadelphia

Temple University Press, Philadelphia 19122
© 1983 by Temple University. All rights reserved
Published 1983
Printed in the United States of America

Library of Congress Cataloging in Publication Data

Main entry under title:

Work, community, and power.

(Class and culture)
Includes bibliographical references and index.
Contents: Rethinking the legacy of labor, 1890–1925;
Labor insurgency and class formation / James E. Cronin—
The one big union in international perspective / Larry
Peterson—New tendencies in union struggles and
strategies in Europe and the United States, 1916–1922 /
David Montgomery—[etc.]
1. Labor and laboring classes—Europe—History—20th
century—Addresses, essays, lectures. 2. Labor and
laboring classes—United States—History—20th century—
Addresses, essays, lectures. I. Cronin, James E.
II. Sirianni, Carmen. III. Series.
HD8376.W66 1983 331′.094 82-19631
ISBN 0-87722-308-4
ISBN 0-87722-309-2 (pbk.)

Contents

Contributors

JAMES CRONIN is Associate Professor of History at the University of Wisconsin–Milwaukee. He is the author of *Industrial Conflict in Modern Britain*. Currently he is completing a work entitled *Labour and Society in Twentieth-Century Britain*, to be published next year.

GARY CROSS teaches history at the University of Wisconsin–Milwaukee. He is the author of *Immigrant Workers in Industrial France: The Making of a New Laboring Class*. Currently he is engaged in a study of the workday, leisure, and economic change in Western Europe from 1880 to 1950.

MELVYN DUBOFSKY is Professor of History and Sociology at the State University of New York at Binghamton. He is the author of numerous books and articles on American working-class history, among them *We Shall Be All*, on the IWW, *John L. Lewis*, a biography of John Lewis (with Warren Van Tine), and *When Workers Organize*, on New York City in the Progressive Era.

STEVE FRASER is Senior Social Science Editor at Basic Books. He is the author of "Dress Rehearsal for the New Deal," in *Working-Class America*, edited by Michael Frisch and Daniel Walkowitz. Currently he is working on a biography of Sidney Hillman.

DAVID MONTGOMERY is Farnam Professor of History at Yale University. He has written widely on American working-class history, and is the author of *Beyond Equality: Labor and Radical Republicans, 1862–1872* and *Workers' Control in America.*

MARY NOLAN teaches history at New York University. She is the author of *Social Democracy in Society: Working Class Radicalism in Düsseldorf, 1890–1920.* Currently she is working on economic rationalization in Germany in the 1920s.

LARRY PETERSON received a Ph.D. from Columbia University with a dissertation on the labor union policies of the German Communist Party in the 1920s. He has published articles on comparative labor history and the German workers' movement. Currently he is working on international Communist labor union policies between 1918 and 1936. He works for a publishing company in New York City.

WILLIAM ROSENBERG is Professor of History at the University of Michigan. He is the author of numerous books and articles on Russian history, among them *Liberals in the Russian Revolution* and *Transforming Russia and China* (with Marilyn Young). Currently he is working on labor and politics in revolutionary Russia and editing *Bolshevik Visions,* on the cultural revolution.

CARMEN SIRIANNI is Assistant Professor of Sociology at Northeastern University in Boston. He is the author of *Workers' Control and Socialist Democracy: the Soviet Experience.* He has also written articles on the democratization of the state and economy, and on critical problems in Marxist theory. Currently he is working on the dynamics of industrial democracy in the twentieth century from a comparative perspective.

Work, Community, and Power

The Experience of Labor in Europe and America, 1900–1925

Chapter One

Rethinking the Legacy of Labor, 1890-1925

James E. Cronin

I

No variety of historical or sociological analysis is more bound up with politics than the study of labor. Labor movements, if they amount to anything, aim at political power; unions, however much oriented toward economic issues, carry on their work in a thoroughly political context. The structure of governmental power, the framework of law, and the mode of representation all shape the opportunities for working-class organization and activity. More important still, the very existence of the working class in modern society has given rise to major political movements that claim, rightly or wrongly, to represent its interests and that seek its allegiance. It is almost impossible, therefore, to separate the study of workers as a class from politics in general and from labor and socialist politics in particular.

This intertwining of the political and social dimensions of labor has not found an accurate reflection in historical analysis but has instead resulted in two distinct literatures and visions of labor's legacy. The tradition that focuses on politics has provided detailed studies of socialist groupings and leaders of working-class parties and of left-wing thinkers and schools of thought. From this research derives an image of impotence, marginality, and defeat, for—as even the most sympathetic chronicler knows—such movements and ideas have met with more setbacks than successes. The second tradition is what might be called the institutional approach to labor studies—that is, the almost exclusive attention to organized workers, their spokesmen, and unions. To oversimplify just a bit, the dominant impression to emerge from this work is very nearly the direct opposite of the political tradition. It is an image of a labor movement constantly growing in size, strength, and sophistication, becoming increasingly bureaucratic in form and structure and gradually more integrated into the prevailing political order.

Curiously, and despite their differences in method and substance, the two images have often been combined in various synthetic and superficial accounts. The product has been an extremely vague and imprecise but (perhaps because of its vagueness and imprecision) surprisingly powerful composite picture of the working class as bureaucratically and self-interestedly organized within modern industrial society and of socialists as essentially marginal in impact. Even when socialists or communists have held leadership positions and when their rhetoric appears to have achieved a broad resonance, they are seen as incapable of exerting genuine influence upon the largely inert masses they are supposed to lead.

Though this perspective is considerably less fashionable now than it was just a short time ago, it remains resilient. Parts of the model are regularly questioned and rejected, but without an alternative vision to replace it, the old view persists. And the very weakness of the old approach is also its greatest strength. It is clear and simple. Such clarity, of course, is attained at the cost of leaving out what should be the core of labor history—the working class itself. Bringing the workers back in, however, is a difficult process indeed, one that results in the first instance in much greater complexity and, frankly, confusion. In consequence, much of the best recent work on the history of the working class in Europe and America cannot be, or at least has not yet been, synthesized into an interpretation that rivals the prevailing orthodoxy.

The second major source of strength for the conventional historiographical wisdom on labor is that it articulates so clearly contemporary attitudes toward the working class. There is a profound pessimism abroad about both European and American workers, and the dismissive rendering of labor's past fits well with this sentiment. It affects, moreover, as many Marxist or radical scholars as conservative ones, having an apparently equal impact on those who lament the failure of labor and the left, and on those who celebrate it. Since the essential thrust of contemporary analysis is to ask, as Jeremy Seabrook has asked of the British labor movement, "What Went Wrong?", the received historical image of labor is extremely functional.

There is, in short, a strong presentist bias in the analysis of and discourse about the working class, which militates against a more sophisticated reinterpretation. Reinforcing this is the fact that the revision of labor history has begun, as it must, with the late-eighteenth and nineteenth centuries, i.e., with the era of industrialization in western Europe and America. Even in Britain, when labor history has a lengthy record of achievement, scholarship rarely has reached 1914 and virtually never touches upon later events. The enormous advances made by scholars such as E. P. Thompson and Eric Hobsbawm in the understanding of labor during the early years of industrialism have thus had little impact upon the perception of labor in the more recent past, whether in Britain or elsewhere.[1] Their efforts to show the richness and vitality of workers' lives, beliefs, and protests and to locate the workers' politics and collective efforts more precisely in society have for this reason simply not engaged or confronted the much more negative image of labor in the twentieth century.

All of this suggests the need to move decisively into the twentieth century as the key to constructing an alternative reading of the history and present condition of the working class. This volume, which centers upon the era of the First World War, is intended as a first step in that direction. It aims to carry forward the novel techniques and insights developed by the best recent work in the social history of labor and, in so doing, show their import for contemporary analysis. It will also be necessary, however, to shift the focus of research somewhat to deal with certain emergent phenomena of the early twentieth century, such as the increasing role of technology and the state in social and economic life.

Apart from these historiographical concerns, analyzing the story of working-class activity in the first quarter of the century has an intrinsic appeal and significance, for it was an era of great turbulence, of mass insurgency, of feats of organization, and of intense debate. Out of this varied activity, moreover, came critical innovations in tactics and theory: it was the moment of general strikes, of workers' councils and soviets, of syndicalism and industrial unionism; and it was the experience from which emerged the theoretical contributions of Gramsci, Lukacs, Benjamin, the Austro-Marxists, and the Russian Bolsheviks, not to mention those, like Sorel, on the opposite end of the political spectrum. The labor and socialist movements were alive, growing, and hopeful, and they offered a fundamental challenge to the existing order of things.

It is, in sum, a moment well worth capturing, recreating, and studying historically. To do so, however, it is necessary as a preliminary to cut through the thick accretion of opinion sharply critical of the parties and politics of the Second International that also, by implication at least, has hampered the appreciation of the labor movements within which socialists operated. One must, in other words, rethink the problem of Social Democracy as the essential preliminary to the analysis of the working class per se.[2]

II

It is, of course, almost impossible to disentangle the history of workers during the first quarter of the century from that of Socialism and Social Democracy. Social democratic parties grew in step with the formation of the working class and its increasing political activism; they sought to represent the class and succeeded in winning its overt political allegiance; and the trade unions that took root among workers were normally linked to social democratic politics and policies. Most important, the network of local social institutions through which many workers, especially in Germany, Austria, and Italy, led their lives was frequently part of the subculture of Social Democracy. The identification of the history of labor with that of Social Democracy is thus neither foolish nor mischievous.

It is, however, mistaken, and the mistake leads to considerable confusion. For Social Democracy was an explicitly political movement about whose effectiveness and merit it is reasonable to reach narrowly political conclusions, while the evolution of the working class and its collective activity requires a quite different sort of analysis. The specific problem in this case is that the largely negative estimate reached by a variety of judges on the social democratic record has led to a similar general discounting of the effectiveness, richness, and viability of working-class culture, organization, and activity in the very same period.

The process by which the critique of the failures of the Second International passed over into a downgrading of the efforts of working men and women to fashion institutions and a movement was itself a highly political phenomenon. The classic texts, of course, are the contemporary writings of Michels and Lenin. As is well known, Michels' study of the "oligarchic tendencies of organization" focused primarily upon Social Democracy, and he developed a trenchant critique of the bureaucratic, cautious evolution of that movement. To Michels, writing in 1911, the logic of socialist politics in a hostile society was for the party to organize "the framework of social revolution. For this reason it endeavors to strengthen its positions, to extend its bureaucratic mechanism, to store up its energies and its funds." Gradually, however, the preservation of the apparatus becomes not the means but the end of politics; and this organizational imperative is reinforced "by the personal interest of thousands of honest breadwinners whose economic life is so intimately associated with the life of the party." In the end, "the external form of the party, its bureaucratic organization, definitely gains the upper hand over its soul."[3]

Michels' diagnosis was amply confirmed by the decisions of socialists in almost all countries to join with other classes in defense of the national interest in August 1914. In retrospect, these actions seem almost inevitable: all over Europe, the left and the unions were on the defensive; even where they were strongest, the socialists were powerless to prevent war; and the "realistic" logic of maintaining the movement's capacity to defend the workers in wartime easily prevailed over the prospect of futile demonstrations in support of internationalist principles.[4] Still, the betrayal of principle could not be disguised, and it served to break apart the socialist movement. In general, the antiwar forces could trace their roots back to the left oppositions that had surfaced in most parties prior to the war, and the prewar moderates were clearly the core of the patriotic socialists. But there were anomalies, like Ramsay MacDonald in Britain and Eduard Bernstein in Germany, and, in addition, there existed a large body of centrist, pacificist opinion doomed to impotence by the extremism of the situation.

The split in the left rather quickly produced several diagnoses of the "material bases" of reformism, the most penetrating of which was Lenin's. Lenin, together with Zinoviev, argued that imperialism allowed for the creation of an "aristocracy of labor" within the core nations of world capitalism. Imperialism generated the "superprofits" with which it was "possible to bribe the labour leaders and the upper stratum of the labour aristocracy." Most important, "this stratum of worker-turned-bourgeois, or the labour aristocracy, who are quite philistine in their mode of life, in the size of their earnings, and in their entire outlook, is the principal prop of the Second International."[5]

Lenin's critique is of great historiographical significance, for he gave a social basis to the essentially conservative and almost mystical argument of Michels. What for Michels was the inevitable product of organization and bureaucracy became for Lenin the political manifestation of a specific conjuncture and social formation. More materialist than Michels, Lenin's argument implied an even more penetrating criticism of sections of the working class itself. In this early formulation, moreover, Lenin himself was apparently unsure of how broadly his strictures should apply. He slipped casually in his writing from speaking of a "stratum" of the labor aristocracy to discussing the group as a whole and compounded the confusion by attempting to link this material phenomenon with Social Democracy generally. He was obviously willing to contemplate the possibility that the rot had spread far and deep among the working class in the industrial countries.

The Leninist critique was based upon a particular reading of the history of labor and socialism in Europe. Ironically, though, it ran roughly parallel in some of its main contours to the themes of the dominant American school of labor history and labor economics. While Lenin was dissecting the sources of reformism in the European working class, John R. Commons and, later, Selig Perlman were constructing theories and interpretations of labor in America that took reformism as a virtue and, more important, as the almost inevitable product of modern industrial capitalism.[6] Gradually, the Commons/Perlman approach was further transformed, in several stages, into a thoroughly functionalist approach to labor and industrial relations.[7]

Essentially, it came to be argued in the 1950s and 1960s that union organization and, in Europe, Social Democracy as a whole served a useful, functional role in society by providing a mechanism to adjust first-generation proletarians to modern capitalism. There is, to be sure, a genuine correspondence between this notion and the Leninist view of the social democrats as "the principal (social) prop of the bourgeoisie" in the imperialist era. But there was a critical difference, for Lenin's explanation stressed the temporary, contingent nature of the incorporation, while the functionalist view saw integration as normal and pervasive in the modern social order. Moreover, the concept of integration was embedded in a tradition whose assumptions were quite antithetical to Leninism, to materialism and, it may be suggested, to a historical approach more generally. This American functionalist tradition assumed first, the stability of the social formation, and second, a rather close fit between the demands of the system for social control and the institutions and ideas of the society in ordinary circumstances. Social conflict and problems of integration, control, and resistance are thus manifestations of temporary dysfunction caused, in most cases, by the extraordinary pace or unanticipated and indirect consequences of social change. The classic formulation of this view of labor was straightforward and crude: "One universal response to industrialization is protest on the part of the labour force as it is fitted into the new social structure."[8]

It is the transition to industrialism that poses the greatest problem for social integration, according to the functionalist model. But this is also where Social Democracy can play its most useful part, for it is a movement uniquely suited to socializing new recruits to industry to its demands while affording a safe outlet, through its rhetoric and political posture, for discontent. Two historical works have been crucial in arguing for this view of prewar Social Democracy.[9] The first was Gunther Roth's book *The Social Democrats in Imperial Germany: A Study in Working-Class Isolation and National Integration*, which was unabashed in its functionalist orientation.[10] The second was Dieter Groh's massive study of "negative integration" in which the argument was made in great detail:

The process of the negative integration of the Social Democratic worker was . . . enforced through the development of the Social Democratic organization. The strong, internal group integration which underlay the gathering of workers in this organization, eventually led to the formation of an "integration party." [Sigmund Neumann.] This party, in ideal cases, took care of its members from the cradle to the grave, from the workers' kindergarten to the cremation cooperative . . . this contributed in an indirect manner to the integration of the worker into state and society. For the Social Democratic organizations were tied to so many aspects of the existing order that there was not even a need for the government to point out dangers to the organizations in order to prevent any planned action, for the labour movement, as an educational and cultural movement in the broadest sense, possessed an affirmative character in relation to German society. The Social Democrats did not question the accepted cultural, ethical, and moral norms of bourgeois society. Indeed they guaranteed the much discussed "embourgeoisement of the proletariat."[11]

However un-Leninist or un-Marxist the integration argument may be, some at least of its proponents see themselves as continuing and developing Lenin's original critique. Whatever the authors' intentions, the position is profoundly conservative, not simply in its origins and assumptions but also in what it ends up saying about the working class in the first part of the century. It reads back into their wage struggles a petty-bourgeois, consumerist mentality; it views their difficult struggles for organization as the growth of bureaucracy; and it derides their quite considerable achievements in carving out a "social space" for working class culture in the new urban environment as a capitulation to corporate status within bourgeois society. Most important, in interpreting the formation of organizations and formal institutions as an integrating mechanism, it implicitly makes a virtue of weakness and a vice of strength.

The net effect of viewing labor's past in this way has been to downplay and degrade much of the self-activity of workers in waging strikes; establishing unions; elaborating social networks; founding, fighting for, and attending schools; safeguarding their persons; and even participating in politics. And though the argument for integration has been made most forcefully in the German case, it has also come to pervade analyses of British, French, and other experiences. British workers, it has recently been suggested, were simply reinforcing the ties that bound them to their masters in creating their own strong communities, unions, and, ultimately, political party in the years up to 1914. They evolved "a dense inward-looking culture, whose effect," it is said, "was both to emphasize the distance of the working class from the classes above it and to articulate its position within an apparently permanent social hierarchy."[12] Therefore, the effect of activities aimed at creating a socialist world was to reinforce bourgeois hegemony.

Similar arguments have been made for French, Belgian, and other workers, most notably by Peter Stearns.[13] He sees the era up to 1914 as the time when industrial society, and with it the working class, "matured" across Europe. Thus, strikes came to be concerned more with wages than control over the production process, and unions and strikes together came to be viewed instrumentally rather than as confrontations in the class war. Overall, Stearns admits, the integration of workers before 1914 was incomplete, especially in southern and eastern Europe, but there can be no question that the modernization process was working to adjust and integrate workers into the new world of industrial capitalism. Needless to say, such arguments have achieved an even greater currency in America.

Despite the different sources from which the argument for integration has come, the combined effect has been to view the evolution of the working class in much the same terms as that of its institutional embodiments, particularly Social Democracy. In consequence, both have been interpreted as exhibiting the effects of *embourgeoisement* and integration, manifested in the progressive incorporation of the subaltern classes into the smooth functioning of advanced capitalism.

III

In many minds, therefore, the distinction between the history of socialists and that of the workers they attempted to organize and speak for has become blurred, and the critique of the one has implied a cynicism and condescension toward the other. There are signs, however, that this confusion is being recognized for what it is and that a new, more subtle view of both histories is being developed. The authors gathered together in this volume seek to further the process of rethinking the interconnected (but not identical) record of labor and the left in this crucial period of their evolution.

The initial spur to revise the conventional interpretation came, somewhat surprisingly, from historians of politics, war, and diplomacy. During the 1960s, the rather sterile debates on the origins of the Great War and the meaning of the Versailles settlement were transformed by the insight that both phenomena had as much, if not more, to do with internal social developments in different countries as with the imperatives of geopolitics. Building on the inspired interwar writings of Elie Halévy and Eckart Kehr, historians such as Arno Mayer, Fritz Fischer, and others began to look at Germany's drive to war, at the decisions of Britain and Germany actually to declare war in 1914, and at the politics of Versailles as integrally linked to the political and social crises through which Great Britain, Germany, Italy, France, and even the United States were passing, each to a greater or lesser degree.[14]

Logically, such a novel perspective implied reconsideration of the various insurgent movements that had been growing up, particularly within Europe. It also suggested, and quite correctly, that the dominant elites took such movements extremely seriously, even if in retrospect their fears seem to have been misplaced. And one could of course go much further and argue that such fears were actually justified for two historical reasons: first, socialist parties and trade unions were gaining strength rapidly from 1900 in all countries, and workers were beginning to use their collective strength for strike action toward political ends, such as suffrage, and toward purely economic goals; and second, the political systems in which this insurgency was developing were sufficiently archaic in their operation and undemocratic in their structure as to be genuinely incapable of incorporating and absorbing these movements for change.[15]

The second source of historiographical revision has come from within social and labor history. Recent years have witnessed an explosion of interest in working-class history and collective action. While most research in this area has been focused on the early years of transition to industrial society in Britain and Europe, the theoretical results are obviously more broadly applicable. The essential finding of almost all of this work is that working men and women in the past were more articulate and sensible, less traumatized by their environments, and possessed of a much richer culture and set of beliefs than was ever thought before. Historians have come to reject ideas stressing the deprivation and despair of daily life and the desperate character of protest, and to view collective action instead as the product of collective strength, of the interaction between popular mentalities, working people's social networks and relations, and the prevailing economic and political conjuncture.

This perspective has remained implicit in the work of many of the best labor and social historians, such as Hobsbawm, Thompson, and Georges Haupt, and it has been made explicit by the historical sociologist Charles Tilly.[16] Tilly seeks to replace the extant functionalist theory of conflict, with its model of social change producing psychic disruption, alienation, and unrest, by an emphasis upon the mobilization of resources as the key to collective action. Such sociological work is especially important for this volume because, in generalizing about the underpinnings of resistance, it allows for the application of the insights of social historical work on early industrialization to the more recent history of the twentieth century. More specifically, it facilitates reinterpretation of critical aspects of the history of the workers' movement in Europe. For what appears, in the traditional view, to be a factor producing integration may be recast as a source of political strength and opposition. The complex web of union organization, community life, and institutions of social support can be reinterpreted in the mobilization perspective as products of working-class activity and as institutions creating social and political space within a hostile society, rather than as bureaucratic adaptations to the system. Thirdly, one of the net effects of the combined work of social historians and historical sociologists is to direct future research at the nature of work, community, family, and everyday life and at how changes in them affect the capacity and willingness of ordinary people to act together for common ends.

The third tributary to the revisionist stream has a more explicitly political origin. The resurgence of conflict in western Europe in the 1960s among workers and students led, for a variety of reasons, to a renewed intellectual interest in the history of workers' councils and their democratizing potential and in the intellectual justification of councils in anarcho-syndicalist thought or in Gramsci's Marxism. Though the political thrust behind such an interest has begun noticeably to fade, the temporary enthusiasm did serve to launch serious work into a much neglected area of European social history, and a number of important studies have appeared on the shop stewards' and council movements that appeared near the end of the Great War in Italy, Germany, Britain, Austria, and elsewhere.[17]

These movements varied a great deal from one region and industry to another, and their impact was correspondingly differentiated. Yet in every country they showed the enormous potential for working-class action to proceed beyond the bounds set by the structures of union organization and parliamentary politics. Second, and most important, the council-type movements in most cases drew particular strength from those sections of labor involved in armaments, metal working, and heavy industry in general, and attracted especially the new, semiskilled entrants to industry whose position had been curiously elevated during the boom in war production. These correlations indicate that not only could workshop-based organizations be pressed into service during a time of unusual political crisis but that such forms of organization might well be the most effective means of mobilizing workers in those new industrial sectors whose development would loom so large in subsequent dacades.

The focus on the link between the council movement and the workplace has tended more recently to merge into a broader concern for the impact of the labor process upon workers' collective action. Stimulated largely by Harry Braverman's *Labor and Monopoly Capital*, a number of historians, economists, and sociologists have begun to undertake serious work on the manner in which technical development and the changing structure of business enterprise affect the organization of work, the level of skills and the degree of autonomy retained or acquired by the workers, and the shifting potentials for organization and protest. Moreover, since the first major attempt by capital to gain effective control over the details of the labor process appears to have occurred during the period of rapid growth beginning in 1895 and continuing up to the Great War, the issue of work is of great importance in understanding the challenge of labor in this era.[18]

IV

Taken together, these three sets of developments have prepared the way for a new view of the social and political history of labor in the early twentieth century. Such a new synthesis, to be sure, is still inchoate, and much detailed investigation remains to be done in many local contexts before a definitive picture emerges. Nevertheless, we feel that the main contours of such a synthesis can at least be glimpsed and hope that some of them will emerge clearly in the essays gathered in this collection. The authors brought together here can in no way be said to constitute a "school" of thought or interpretation, but they do share an awareness both of the dominant image of labor as increasingly "incorporated" in this period and of the obvious inadequacy of this approach. They are all influenced, in addition, by the new trends in historical and sociological writing that are making this view appear outdated and oversimplified. Most important, they each seek to build upon the insights of recent work in order further to elaborate the complex interactions between economic change, the evolution of social structure, and workers' collective action.

The essays are of two sorts—slightly more than half are comparative analyses of aspects of economic and social change and workers' responses, the rest are more specialized case studies that seek to illustrate the broader comparative arguments as well as provide important local detail. Cronin's essay on labor formation and class insurgency provides a general overview of the structural transformation of the European working class and its social and political consequences. Too much labor history is written as if the subject—the workers—were a stable, easily identified group to whom things happen and that reacts with varying degrees of organization, protest, and acquiescence. What this and several of the other pieces show is that the very nature of the working class was changing during the "long wave" of 1896–1920. Growth was centered particularly in the new industries of the "Second Industrial Revolution"—electricity, chemicals, and steel—rather than in the older textile, iron, and coal industries, which had been pioneered by the British in the nineteenth century.

Inevitably, these new sectors employed different technologies and organized work in quite different ways than the old industries, and the workers in these newer, larger, more technically advanced factories had to submit to new patterns of production and daily life. Skill levels shifted and work routines were altered in such a fashion as to create a labor force that was more homogeneous than before and that tended to be semiskilled rather than skilled and apprenticed on the one hand, or unskilled, casual, and untrained on the other. Thus the internal structure of the working class was greatly transformed. This reshaping occurred in the context of a rapid expansion of the working class, its ranks swelling with rural migrants from the local countryside and from more distant sources like Poland, southern Italy, and Ireland. The mass militancy of the years 1910 to 1925 was, it appears, as much the result of the initial mobilization of this new, reconstituted working class as it was a radicalization of those stable sectors of labor that had been active prior to 1910.

The next two essays, by Larry Peterson and David Montgomery, respectively, explore the strategic and organizational implications of these changed economic and social structures for workers' movements in Europe and America. Peterson shows the vitality and viability of industrial unionism and syndicalism across both continents and documents their direct and indirect influence. While Peterson's emphasis is on the years before the war, Montgomery shifts the attention to the wartime and postwar insurgencies and elaborates the comparison between Europe and the United States. He also seeks to incorporate in his analysis the critical role of community and community formation in sustaining working-class militancy.

It may well be that the aspect of the restructuring of the working class, the implications of which are least well understood, is the way it transformed the social and political life of the major urban centers.[19] What had previously been enclaves of administration, exchange, consumption, and cultural production became the settings for industrial production and class confrontation. Patterns varied from town to town and still more across national boundaries, but everywhere the cities, or rather sections of the cities, became centers of an intense working-class community life and a distinct working-class culture that was at least partially autonomous and freed from direct supervision.

The cultural presence of the working class in these growing urban environments was reflected in the most diverse manifestations—in patterns of residential segregation, in styles and levels of consumption, in architecture and fashion, in leisure and, of course, in local politics—and it can be studied within and through any of these spheres. Several essays in this volume deal indirectly with this urban dimension of class formation; one, by Mary Nolan, does so directly. Nolan, in her essay on Germany during the revolutions of 1918–19, examines the social structure of two Ruhr towns–Hamborn and Düsseldorf—to discover the roots of the insurgencies that swept both areas in the revolutionary years.

After this in-depth study, we move to a rather more general analysis of labor and technology in France by Gary Cross. Cross seeks to explain the paradoxical fact that French workers, whose prewar organizations and ideology were more closely attuned to the rhetoric of syndicalism and "workers' control" than those of other workers, exhibited after the war less enthusiasm for workers' control, and probably less radicalism in general, than workers in virtually the whole of Europe. He finds the answer in the peculiar characteristics of the French economy, in the weakness of union organization, and in the unusual strength of Taylorist and "productivist" tenets among the French left.

Cross' piece reminds us of the truly dramatic nature of the changes affecting industry and its workers in the early twentieth century and the consequent fluidity of industrial structure. This served further to call into question political and social arrangements and the general distribution of power and authority in society. A measure of the flux was the variety of proposals, experiments, and movements for reshaping work and political life in the immediate aftermath of the First World War. The last four essays in the book deal primarily with these responses to the crisis of 1917–20 in Europe and America.

Steve Fraser tells the intriguing story of the collaborative venture in industrial production of the Amalgamated Clothing Workers of America and the Russian Bolsheviks. This unique international exchange allows for a panoramic and revealing portrait of the intellectual and political crosscurrents of the early 1920s. In the following article, Melvyn Dubofsky explains the ramifications of the mass insurgency of the war and postwar years on industrial and labor policy and is able to argue convincingly for the importance of the experience of 1917–20 in shaping subsequent American politics.

In the penultimate essay, William Rosenberg examines the interplay among political democracy, the "democratizing" of social relations, and workers' control on the Russian railroads in 1917. In doing so, he illuminates in fascinating detail the dynamic popular movement that lay beneath the Bolshevik seizure of power. Rosenberg also succeeds in showing the limitations of and contradictions in the Russian situation, thus raising difficult questions about the possibilities inherent in early twentieth century society.

These questions come to the fore more explicitly in the final essay, by Carmen Sirianni, who looks at the outcomes of the various movements for workers' control in Europe during and after the War of 1914–18. Ultimately, labor insurgency runs up against the power of the state, and the result of that contest determines the subsequent ability of workers to control the workplace and most other aspects of their lives. Sirianni argues that the specifics outcomes were shaped by two factors: the relationship between incipient workshop organization and existing trade unions and political parties on the one hand, and on the other, the degree of crisis gripping the political system itself. The latter factor proved critical and has no doubt been underplayed by previous writers on the history of labor and the left, who often write as if the success or failure of insurgency was due solely to the strengths or shortcomings of the movement.

The essays, therefore, cover a wide array of topics and range over much of Europe and America. Though by no means exhaustive, they touch upon a span of experience broad enough to suggest a general analytical usefulness. And, of course, the aim of this collection is only partly to provide answers; it is also to stimulate further research along similar lines by other scholars. Whether that occurs will perhaps be the ultimate testimony to the value of our project.

Notes

1.   This is so despite the evident interest that Hobsbawm, Thompson, and others take in contemporary politics. Cf., for example, E. P. Thompson, *Writing by Candlelight* (London, 1980), and E. J. Hobsbawm, et al., *The Forward March of Labour Halted?* (London, 1981). The latter, because it focuses so directly upon labor, ought to provide more illumination on aspects of working class history than it in fact does.

2.   The process of reinterpreting Social Democracy in its historical context has been begun, but just barely. In the most recent survey of the German experience, for example, the old framework remains intact: W. L. Guttsman, *The German Social Democratic Party, 1875–1933* (London, 1981). Also disappointing in this regard is Adam Przeworski's otherwise thoughtful analysis, "Social Democracy as a Historical Phenomenon," *New Left Review* 122 (1980), 27–58. More helpful are Dan S. White, "Reconsidering European Socialism in the 1920s," *Journal of Contemporary History* 16, no. 2 (April 1981), 251–272; and Geoff Eley and Keith Nield, "Why Does Social History Ignore Politics?" *Social History* 5, no. 2 (May 1980), 249–271, esp. 254–258. Both are better at criticizing the existing interpretation, however, than in outlining a new analysis.

A major factor stimulating the reevaluation of Social Democracy is the recent political successes of "Eurocommunism" and "Eurosocialism." On the former, there is a large but generally quite ahistorical literature. See, however, Carl Marzani, *The Promise of Eurocommunism* (Westport, Conn., 1980); Carl Boggs and David Plotke, eds., *The Politics of Eurocommunism* (Boston, 1980); and Bogdan Denitch, ed., *Democratic Socialism* (Totowa, N.J., 1981).

3.   Robert Michels, *Political Parties* (New York, 1959), 368, 373, 394.

4.   See in particular Georges Haupt, *Socialism and the Great War* (Oxford, 1972), on the context in which these fatal decisions were taken.

5.   V. I. Lenin, *Imperialism, The Highest Stage of Capitalism: Selected Works*, vol. I (New York, 1967), esp. 683.

6.   Maurice Isserman, "God Bless Our American Institutions: The Labor History of John R. Commons," *Labor History* 17 (Summer 1976), 309–329; Selig Perlman, *A Theory of the Labor Movement* (1928; reprint ed., New York, 1949); Mark Perlman, *Labor Union Theories in America* (Evanston, 1958). See also Mike Davis, "Why the U.S. Working Class is Different," *New Left Review* 123 (1980), 3–44.

7.   The boldest, most self-assured statement of this view was probably Abraham Siegel, "Method and Substance in Theorizing about Worker Protest," in *Aspects of Labor Economics*, National Bureau of Economic Research (Princeton, 1962), 21–52.

8. C. Kerr, F. Harbison, J. Dunlop, and C. Meyers, "The Labour Problem in Economic Development," *International Labour Review* 72 (1955), 13–14.

9. We move rather quickly here to the literature of the 1960s for several reasons. First, much of the work on Social Democracy appearing from 1920 through the 1950s either simply rehashed the arguments of Lenin and Michels or else was concerned primarily with explaining the relationship between the failure of the left and the triumph of the fascist right in the interwar years. Though much useful information was unearthed, little new was added in terms of interpretation. Second, although Sigmund Neumann anticipated much of the argument of the late 1950s and 1960s in his work on political parties in Weimar and was, indeed, probably the first to use the term "integration" in describing the Social Democrats as an "Integrationspartei," this particular reading of the past did not really become dominant until the functionalist revolution in American social science, to which its intellectual triumph owes so much. On the state of the debate in the 1950s, at least as it affected German Social Democracy, see W. H. Maehl, "Recent Literature on the German Socialists," *Journal of Modern History* 33, no. 3 (September 1961), 292–306; and Klaus Epstein, "Three American Studies of German Socialism," *World Politics* 11, no. 4 (July 1959), 629–651. On Neumann's views, see S. Neumann, *Die deutschen Parteien, Wesen und Wandel nach dem Kriege* (Berlin, 1932). One rather curious result of this interpretive disjuncture is that the truly seminal work by Carl Schorske, *German Social Democracy, 1905–1917* (Cambridge, Mass., 1955) does not fit easily into either the old interpretation worked out by Michels and Lenin or the orthodoxy of the later postwar period. In fact, its findings are quite compatible with the new directions mapped out in these essays, but it has often been misinterpreted as fitting neatly into the integration perspective.

10. G. Roth, *The Social Democrats in Imperial Germany: A Study in Working-Class Isolation and National Integration* (Totowa, N.J., 1963).

11. D. Groh, *Negative Integration und Revolutionärer Attentismus* (Frankfurt am Main, 1973). English quotation from Groh, "Waiting For and Avoiding Revolution: Social Democracy and the Reich," *Laurentian University Review* 5, no. 3 (June 1973), 98. More recently, Groh's position has been substantially revised. See his "Preliminary Remarks on the Making of the German Working Class," Working Papers of the Research Group on Base Processes and the Problem of Organization, no. 21, Konstanz, 1981.

12. G. Stedman Jones, "Working-Class Culture and Working-Class Politics in London, 1870–1900," *Journal of Social History* 7 (1974), 460–508; S. Meacham, *A Life Apart: The British Working Class, 1890–1914* (London, 1977).

13. P. Stearns, *Lives of Labor* (New York, 1975); and "Measuring the Evolution of Strike Movements," *International Review of Social History* 9 (1974), 1–27.

14. The most explicit and theoretical statement is contained in Arno Mayer, *The Dynamics of Counterrevolution in Europe, 1870–1956* (New York, 1971). On Versailles, see Mayer's *The New Diplomacy* (New Haven, 1959), and *Politics and Diplomacy of Peacemaking* (New York, 1967). Fritz Fischer's work

made a somewhat later impact than Mayer's but it was quite profound. See his *Germany's Aims in the First World War* (London, 1967) and also *War of Illusion* (London, 1975). The latter is especially concerned with internal developments.

Kehr's important work was long ignored but revived and reprinted largely through the efforts of Hans-Ulrich Wehler. His essays were printed under the title *Der Primat der Innenpolitik* in German (Berlin, 1965) and translated as *Economic Interest, Militarism and Foreign Policy: Essays on German History,* ed. Gordon Craig (Berkeley, 1977). Halévy's essay was first written in 1929 and is available as "The World Crisis of 1914–18: An Interpretation," in *The Era of Tyrannies: Essays on Socialism and War* (New York, 1965), 209–247.

15.   On the "backwardness" of political structures in Europe, see Arno Mayer's provocative new book, *The Persistence of the Old Regime* (New York, 1981); and on Russia in particular, see Perry Anderson, *Lineages of the Absolutist State* (London, 1974), 328–360, and Theda Skocpol, *States and Social Revolutions* (Cambridge, 1979), 81–99.

16.   The Tilly argument has been made many times and in many contexts. A most thorough statement is provided in Charles, Louise, and Richard Tilly, *The Rebellious Century* (Cambridge, Mass., 1975).

17.   The literature on both the theory and the practice is by now quite extensive. Among the better studies are James Hinton, *The First Shop Stewards' Movement* (London, 1973); Paolo Spriano, *The Occupation of the Factories: Italy 1920* (London, 1975) and Gwyn Williams, *Proletarian Order* (London, 1975). The extensive German literature is evaluated in W. J. Mommsen, "Die deutsche Revolution, 1918–1920: Politische Revolution und Soziale Protestbewegung," *Geschichte und Gesellschaft* 4 (1978). See also Larry Peterson, "From Social Democracy to Communism: Recent Contributions to the History of the German Workers' Movement, 1914–1945," *International Labor and Working Class History* 20 (Fall 1981), 7–30.

18.   See Richard Price, "Rethinking Labour History: The Importance of Work," in J. Cronin and J. Schneer, eds., *Social Conflict and the Political Order in Modern Britain* (London, 1982), 179–214; and Price's forthcoming review essay on the labor process in the *Journal of Social History*. A second major source of inspiration for such work has been Alfred D. Chandler's *The Visible Hand: The Managerial Revolution in American Business* (Cambridge, Mass., 1977). For an attempt to generalize a theory of worker behavior from such a starting point, see Charles Sabel, *Work and Politics: The Division of Labor in Industry* (Cambridge, 1982).

19.   Several recent studies, however, have added significantly to the historical analysis of the urban aspects of labor organization. See David Crew, *Town in the Ruhr* (New York, 1979); Mary Nolan, *Social Democracy and Society: Working-Class Radicalism in Düsseldorf, 1890–1920* (Cambridge, 1981); John Merriman, ed., *French Cities in the Nineteenth Century: Class, Power, and Urbanization* (London, 1982); and Ira Katznelson, *City Trenches* (New York, 1982).

Chapter Two

Labor Insurgency and Class Formation: Comparative Perspectives on the Crisis of 1917-1920 in Europe

James E. Cronin

The modern working class is not especially noted for its optimism or idealism. Indeed, the industrial proletariat may well have pioneered in the adoption of those secular and cynical life-styles and values that have come increasingly to pervade twentieth-century society and culture.[1] This makes it all the more surprising, then, to rediscover the deep feelings and high expectations with which Europe's workers launched the greatest wave of strikes in their history just after World War I. For a brief moment, the apocalyptic hopes of the left-wing socialists and the fantastic fears of the forces of order seemed about to come true: soldiers deserted en masse and turned against their officers and their governments; workers in almost every industry struck for unprecedented demands; workers' councils were established from Limerick to Budapest; mass strikes broke out in Glasgow, Oslo, Barcelona, Turin, and elsewhere.[2] And if Lenin and Trotsky, Luxemburg, Liebknecht, and Gramsci were wrong in their optimism, they were no more misguided than their panic-stricken opponents, such as Churchill, Lloyd George, the diplomats at Versailles, and the various gener-

This is a revised version of the paper first published in *Social Science History* 4, no. 1 (Winter 1980), 125–152.

als and police commanders charged with controlling and suppressing the volatile crowds of urban workers and discontented ex-soldiers.[3]

Relatively quickly, the hopes of 1919–20 were dashed, popular resistance was crushed, and the established interests were largely restored to dominance. To be sure, the victory of the right was not simply and smoothly achieved, and it remained precarious, particularly in central and eastern Europe, where formally democratic regimes cloaked bureaucratic, military, and economic structures of decidedly authoritarian and anachronistic character. Many factors contributed to this essentially reactionary outcome—the postwar depression and the consequent erosion of shopfloor militancy; the fragmentation of the left; the augmented power and technical competence of armies, bureaucracies, and other elements of the state apparatus; the general level of economic development and class formation; and the international political balance. Conservative stabilization was in this sense "overdetermined," and is thus far less interesting than the origins of the massive, if nonetheless unsuccessful, upheavals.[4]

Most historians offer a straightforward explanation of the great unrest: the privations and frustrations of war led to an outburst of raw anger and revolt. Such an analysis has economy and simplicity to its credit, and possesses some obvious empirical validity—things were tough during 1914–18. But it is marred by one overriding deficiency: it detaches the events of 1917–20 from the general evolution of class relationships prior to the war and is thus incapable of explaining the strong elements of continuity that connect the postwar with the mounting prewar militancy. The aim of this article is to analyze the events of 1917–20 in terms of more long-term processes of class formation. Specifically, it will be argued that the outburst beginning in 1917 was produced primarily by the interaction between the grievances and hardships induced by the war and the enhanced capacity for collective action created by technical changes at the point of production and the simultaneous consolidation of working-class communities in the major urban and industrial centers of Europe.

A brief review of the various national experiences during 1917–20 will establish the basic facts to be probed and analyzed. To begin with, perhaps the most arresting feature of the movements in the different countries was their similarity and simultaneity. The insurgency of 1917–20 was of truly international scope. Paradoxically, the war that at its inception marked the dissolution of internationalism ended with a strike wave of international dimensions.[5] The general strike against the war never materialized in 1914, but it almost happened in January 1918, and this was followed the next November by a widespread revulsion against the war and the war-makers manifest in industrial conflict and political protest. Little in the way of international planning or coordination was behind any of these events, but there was a good deal of emulation of and political inspiration from revolutionary Russia.[6]

The militancy of 1917–20 was also massive and became increasingly so. The movement developed its own momentum: Beginning with some isolated, though symbolically important, strikes and mutinies in 1917, it grew to envelop most of the urban working class in Europe by 1919–20. Participation in strikes is only a crude indicator of involvement, but the increasing number of workers taking part in industrial action between 1917 and 1920 suggests the dimensions of discontent (see Table 2–1). Union membership grew correspondingly, as did the electoral pull of socialist and labor parties.

How many of these strikers and voters were active revolutionaries? We cannot know for sure. The Director of Intelligence at Scotland Yard estimated that as many as 10 percent of the workers in Britain favored violent revolution in January 1920, and admitted further that a clear majority was in favor of some sort of social revolution.[7] In Germany, the victory of the majority Socialists over their Spartacist and Independent Socialist opponents in the elections to the Constituent Assembly in January 1919 has often been cited as proof of the essential moderation of the workers, but the argument is not convincing. Election results seldom reveal the deeper aspirations of voters and are most unreliable at a time of upheaval. In addition, various factors influenced elections on the local level—the degree of organization, the tendency to vote for known quantities, and so on—which in the short run probably worked to the advantage of the right-wing socialists. In places where the radicals developed a strong organization and fielded popular candidates, however, they did quite well. For example, the Independent Social Democratic Party (USPD) gained 27.6 percent of the vote in Berlin, 22.5 percent in Düsseldorf, 38.6 percent in Leipzig, and 44.1 percent in Halle-Merseburg. Most important of all, the dominance of the moderates was short-lived, coming as it did only "at the beginning of a process of radicalization," a process that ultimately involved the establishment of a "soviet" government in Bavaria in 1919, the affiliation of the bulk of the Independents to the Comintern, the general strike against the Kapp Putsch in March 1920, and the ensuing "Ruhr Red Army" revolt.[8]

Questions about the revolutionary zeal of the masses are always hard to answer, in part because they are often incorrectly posed. They tend to assume a relationship between consciousness and behavior that

Table 2-1. *Participation in Strikes, 1916–1920*
(Number of Workers Involved in Disputes)

Year	France	Germany	Italy	United Kingdom	Nether-lands
1916	41,400	14,639	138,508	235,000	18,100
1917	293,800	66,634	174,817	575,000	31,300
1918	176,200	n.a.	158,711	923,000	39,700
1919	1,151,000	n.a.	1,554,566	2,401,000	61,700
1920	1,317,000	1,428,116	2,313,685	1,779,000	64,400

Sources: B. R. Mitchell, *European Historical Statistics* (New York, 1975); W. Kendall, *The Labour Movement in Europe* (London, 1975), 364–378.

is more direct and intimate than seems ordinarily possible to obtain. Workers' attitudes are seldom made explicit enough to judge their precise ideological content; and it would appear that their actions are governed much more by the structured possibilities for resistance than by their desires or discontent. It is not that the sentiments of working people are uninteresting or invariant or that their hopes are not occasionally raised and their horizons lifted; it is rather that for workers the process of radicalization normally involves an increase in mass participation and an escalation of tactical militancy. For the bulk of the working class, the political pendulum swings back and forth between engagement (which is usually of a left-wing or "democratic" variety) and sullen resignation, rather than between left and right. What was most significant and threatening, therefore, about events in Germany and elsewhere throughout 1919–20 was not the slogans and demands of the movement but the sustained level of popular activism.

Insurgency affected equally large numbers in France, Italy, Hungary, and Austria. As Lloyd George explained in a famous passage in March 1919,

the whole of Europe is filled with the spirit of revolution. There is a deep sense not only of discontent, but of anger and revolt among the workmen against prewar conditions. The whole existing order in its political, social and economic aspects is questioned by the masses of the population from one end of Europe to the other.[9]

Thus in France, perhaps the least troubled of European nations, the Confédération Générale du Travail (General Confederation of Labor) (CGT) grew by three times between 1914 and January 1920, and the metal workers' union increased from 7,500 members in 1912 to over 204,000 in December 1918. The new recruits to the labor and socialist

movements were eager and volatile and showed little patience with the
staid politics of a Thomas or a Renaudel. Their propensity for swift,
spontaneous action led to massive strikes and demonstrations, such as
the Paris protest of 6 April 1919 to denounce the acquittal of Jaures's
murderer involving over 100,000 working people, and served to create
what *Le temps* (15 April 1919) called a "ferociously revolutionary
milieu." To the left-wing spokesman Pierre Monatte, writing in *La vie
ouvrier* (11 June 1919), the path ahead in 1919 seemed obvious: "From
discontent to discontent, from strike to strike, from a semi-economic
and semi-political strike to a purely political strike. We're going straight
to the bankruptcy of the bourgeoisie, that is, to the Revolution." Ultimately, the road to revolution was blocked, defeat coming with the
collapse of the general strike of May 1920, the so-called civic battle of
the Marne. Still, from November 1918 until that final failure, the
process of radicalization seemed irreversible.[10]

For the most part, rural France remained calm during 1917–20,
but in Italy conflict engulfed both the cities and the countryside.
Unrest began in May 1917 in Milan, surfaced again in the August
revolt at Turin, and, after a lull during the last year of the war, revived
again in late 1918. The beginning of 1919 witnessed a broad strike
wave and rapid growth of the trade unions, the Socialist Party, the
Catholic unions, and the Catholic Popular Party (Popolari). Strikes,
land occupations, and food riots, particularly during June and July
1919, continued unabated for the entire *bienneo rosso* of 1919–1920,
culminating in the occupation of the factories in September 1920. "A
real class war" raged in both the urban centers and the rural districts,
and probably only the fragmentation of the popular forces prevented
the toppling of the regime.[11]

Hungary was the one place besides Italy and Spain where discontent erupted simultaneously in rural and urban areas; and for a very
brief time the streams of anger fused behind Béla Kun. Kun's soviet
regime arose essentially as a government of national emergency, aim-
ing to "obtain from the East what has been denied to us by the West."[12]
This nationalist component notwithstanding, the real center of revolutionary sentiment was in the Budapest working class, particularly
among the metalworkers, railwaymen, and building workers. The
munitions factories especially were left-wing strongholds, while in the
countryside scattered settlements of miners and steelworkers formed
"communist beachheads." The mass character of the movement was
incontestable and caused the hesitancy with which the powers at Versailles approached intervention. In the end, what sealed the fate of
Kun was not the strength of Horthy's counterrevolutionary forces,

which were quite weak, but the disaffection of the peasantry from the government's land reforms and, in the summer of 1919, the growing hostility of even the urban workers to the regime.[13]

The situation in Austria differed in two major respects from that in Hungary. The Austrian peasants, for all their privations, were a consistently stabilizing force hostile from the beginning to "Red Vienna."[14] As Otto Bauer would later argue, "The peasant proceeded to adopt an attitude of defiance. . . . Peasants' councils struggled with workers' councils for control of the administrative machinery. . . . The peasant knew that he was stronger; he had plenty of food in his cupboard, and he could blockade the town. If it came to civil war, it was not the peasant but the workers who would starve."[15]

The second difference was the Austrian Social Democrats, who were incomparably better organized than their Hungarian counterparts (and much less moderate than their German comrades).[16] In consequence, they were more capable of absorbing the surge of militancy within normal forms of party and trade union activity and organization. On the other hand, the genuine radicalization of the workers probably went further and penetrated deeper in Austria than in any other Western nation. As early as May 1917, the railway workers' journal proclaimed its solidarity with "the heroic Russian proletariat"; in May and June of 1917 the Viennese metal and munitions workers launched a wave of strikes; and in December the workers of Linz elected the first "workers' council." In January 1918, a general strike centered in Vienna swept through Austria and involved over a half-million workers. Led by militant shop stewards operating through local councils, the movement mixed economic and political demands: the restoration of food rations and a democratic peace. Though the strike petered out toward the end of January, it seemed to presage a more thorough and revolutionary outbreak should the Hapsburg regime begin to crumble under the pressures of war and resurgent nationalism.[17]

With defeat and the establishment of an Austrian republic in November 1918, mass mobilization commenced again. To many, a revolutionary outbreak appeared imminent in early 1919, as the Bavarian and Hungarian examples encouraged local communists to think in terms of a Soviet Austria. With some foresight, however, the Austrian Social Democrats headed off the threat by encouraging the growth of workers' councils and by founding a people's army, the *Volkswehr*. By thus co-opting rather than resisting the councils, the party was able to turn the latter against the far left and enlist the support of the bulk of the workers against the attempted communist

risings of 17 April and 15 June 1919. Still, the price of this maneuver
was support for workers' demands and the enactment of a series of
reforms that became a model of social progress during the interwar
years.[18]

Events across the English Channel never approached the dramatic intensity of the social confrontation in central and southern
Europe, but in Britain, too, the years following the war saw a major
challenge from below. The major source of working-class resistance
during the war came from the engineers in munitions, who generated
a fairly widespread shop stewards' movement by 1917.[19] In June of that
year, a coalition of left-wing socialists and shop stewards held a convention at Leeds that endorsed the peace proposals of the Russians and
called for the establishment of workers' and soldiers' councils in
England.[20] Strikes became larger and more frequent throughout 1917
and 1918, and demands became bolder. For all his political astuteness,
Lloyd George could not convince labor that his policies would really
create a "land fit for heroes to live in," and so they took to the streets.[21]
In the lead, once again, were the metal and munitions workers, whose
strike for the eight-hour day in Glasgow during January 1919
approached insurrectionary proportions. The authorities felt their
position was quite precarious, for the troops were mutinous and demanded immediate demobilization. As 1919 progressed, various
groups of workers pressed their demands, particularly the miners,
railwaymen, and dockers, who were formally united in the "Triple
Alliance." The government temporized and sought to break up this
threatening array of forces. The miners got a Royal Commission under
Lord Sankey to study their position; the railwaymen struck alone in
September and won a major victory; and the transport workers, led by
Ernest Bevin, got their own commission under Lord Shaw in 1920.
Tensions remained high throughout 1920, and in the summer the
threat of a general strike dissuaded the government from its contem-
plated action in support of the reactionary Poles. The climax of the
unrest came in April 1921, when it became clear that the miners'
demands were not going to be met and that the mine owners were to be
confirmed in their old positions of power in the industry. The miners
decided to strike and called for support from their erstwhile allies, who
only too gladly found various excuses to back away from the general
strike planned for April 15, 1921. This day, "Black Friday," marked
the effective end of the postwar militancy, although the miners held
out on their own for several long, bitter months.[22]

Industrial protest was truly ubiquitous throughout Europe. Even
the Swedes and the Swiss experienced quite impressive upheavals, and

in most major industrial centers the bulk of the working class was disaffected.[23] This did not, of course, guarantee the success of insurgency. Most important, governments were not only willing, when pressed, to resort to force, but in most regions they had or would have had the support of much of the population. It is often forgotten that even at the end of the war the industrial working class in most of Europe was counterbalanced and outmanned by large numbers of peasants and petty proprietors, both clinging to their tenuous non-proletarian status, and by newly rising middle and lower-middle class elements. This was particularly true in east-central and southern Europe, where industrialization and urbanization had come late and proceeded unevenly, resulting in a state of "partial modernization," as Maier calls it, which called into existence a militant urban working class but which also left the power of preindustrial agrarian and bureaucratic elites at least formally intact.[24] Only in Britain could it be said that a working-class majority existed, but there a long history of parliamentarism guaranteed that social upheaval would not result in a crisis of political legitimacy.[25] In short, the process of class formation under capitalism had created a modern working class but had not yet proceeded to eliminate or "proletarianize" those middle strata of the population that often tilt the balance in revolutionary situations.

In view of this, the mass, sustained character of labor militancy is still more impressive and more in need of analysis. Particularly noteworthy was the apparent spontaneity of the riots, strikes, and demonstrations of 1917–20. Decades of agitation may well have planted the seeds of radicalism, but the socialist parties and trade unions were notoriously ineffectual, first in opposing the war and then in leading the opposition to it. On the contrary, the civic peace—*union sacrée, Burgfriede*—of the early war years led to the entry of socialists into bourgeois governments, the recognition of unions by previously hostile industrialists, and the daily involvement of labor officials in the formulation of policy, the adjudication of disputes, and the administration of economic controls and rationing systems. This absorption of upper- and middle-level leaders of the unions virtually guaranteed that insurgency would be expressed outside the ordinary patterns of party and trade union activity.[26]

Much to their embarassment and dismay, the various left oppositions within the labor and socialist movements were scarcely any closer to the rank and file. Contemporary commentary was nearly unanimous in depicting the militancy near the end of and after the war as spontaneous, at best organized in a loose, informal fashion by relatively unknown leaders, mostly recruited from the shop floor or in working-

class communities. Conversely, both the left-wing and moderate socialists were bypassed at crucial moments.[27] Thus Toni Sender, an Independent Socialist, has described how the November Revolution broke
out in Stuttgart without any planning or leadership, how she and
Robert Dissmann worked overtime giving some sort of form to the
workers' demands, and how, very soon, they began chasing after the
militants in hope of restraining them from inopportune acts of violence. Even relatively hardheaded leaders, such as Luxemburg and
Liebknecht, were carried away against their better judgment by the
workers' apparent readiness to follow the militant slogans of the left.[28]
The apocalyptic tone of so much that was said or written in 1919–20
was a refracted testimony to the elemental nature of the social explosion. It is not surprising, of course, that militants should wish to
circumvent or go beyond the narrow strategies favored by established
leaders; what is surprising and interesting is that they did it so successfully, so massively, and against such odds. That is the real puzzle of
those years. How is all this—particularly the unusual scope and the
mass character of events during 1919–20—to be explained?

Most commonly, "misery and exhaustion" from the war are seen
as sufficient causes of the upheaval.[29] Certainly, ordinary people in all
the belligerent nations became tired of the slaughter after hopes of a
quick victory faded in 1915. By 1916, the implications and terrible costs
of the conflict were becoming clear, and voices of dissension began to
be raised and heard. The various mutinies, strikes, and food riots of
1917 were largely motivated by antiwar sentiments and had definite
political overtones. From the summer of 1917 to November 1918,
however, there was very little mass action of an obviously pacifist
character, certainly not among the workers. In fact, domestic morale in
most countries was distinctly better in the last year of the war. Only
when defeat loomed imminent did the old institutions begin to crumble in the Hapsburg and Hohenzollern domains. No doubt the war
served partially to discredit political leaders and entire regimes, but the
governments of Europe showed a remarkable ability to continue to
wage war against the wishes of their subjects.[30] Pacificism as a political
force remained weak through the end of the conflict.

More important than simple war-weariness and the growth of
antiwar sentiment was the impact of economic hardship. Prices of food,
housing, and coal shot up sharply during the war and wages failed to
keep pace (see Tables 2-2 and 2-3). By the winter of 1916–17, shortages
were severe throughout Europe, especially within the central powers.
In the Dual Monarchy, the Hungarians cut off most grain shipments to
the Austrians, while in Germany efforts to provision the cities foun-

Table 2-2. *Cost of Living in Europe, 1913–1920 Index (1913 = 100)*

Year	Great Britain	France	Germany	Italy
1913	100	100	100	100
1914	103	100	103	100
1915	122	119	129	107
1916	145	134	170	134
1917	174	160	253	189
1918	201	207	313	264
1919	213	259	415	268
1920	247	357	1020	352

Sources: E. H. Phelps Brown and M. H. Browne, *A Century of Pay* (London 1968), 432–452; G. Bry, *Wages in Germany, 1871–1945* (Princeton, 1960), 209–233, 434–456; M. F. Neufeld, *Italy: School for Awakening Countries* (Ithaca, 1961), 540; J. Cronin, *Industrial Conflict in Modern Britain* (London, 1979), 224–227; G. Dupeux, *La société française, 1789–1970* (Paris, 1972), 234–235.

dered on the sullen resistance of the peasants and the temptations of the black market. By the last half of 1918 the Germans were subsisting on a mere 12 percent of the meat, 13 percent of the eggs, and 48 percent of the flour consumed in peacetime; only the consumption of sugar and potatoes was maintained at near normal levels.[31] In England, commissioners toured the country in 1917 hearing complaints on the causes of industrial unrest—everywhere food prices and inequities of distribution headed the list of grievances.[32] Not too surprisingly, working-class protest during and after the war often took the form of consumer actions. Rent strikes occurred in Glasgow and Budapest, and tenants' agitation also sprang up in Vienna.[33] Food riots, which broke out in France, Britain, Sweden, and elsewhere, were a near universal response of workers. In Italy the greatest threat of revolution came in the midst of the food riots of June and July 1919, and the Austrian general strike of January 1918 was touched off by a reduction in the bread ration. The "moral economy" of the preindustrial poor may well have given way to a more calculating mentality among the workers long before 1914, but the deprivations of war served to resuscitate this waning form of popular protest.[34]

The contribution of rapid inflation to the development of class consciousness is difficult to overstress because rising prices did more than simply erode buying power. Inflation tends to break custom, wiping out historical relativities and established differentials and introducing an element of uncertainty and chaos into bargaining. In normal conditions, workers frame wage demands primarily in relation to the

Table 2-3. The Course of Real Wages, 1913–1921 (Index = 100)

Year	France	Germany	Great Britain	Italy	Sweden	U.S.A.
1913	100	100	100	100	100	100
1914	—	96	98	100	—	—
1915	—	90	88	94	—	—
1916	—	83	82	95	—	—
1917	81	76	81	73	—	—
1918	—	76	89	65	—	—
1919	—	85*	98	93	—	—
1920	—	72*	106	114	—	—
1921	140	78*	115	127	112	120

Source: See Table 2-2.
*Refers to skilled workers only.

wages paid to comparable groups of workers in nearby plants or towns. Horizons are limited and expectations exceedingly modest. When prices begin to rise too fast, these stabilizing, conservative habits are altered, and workers are encouraged to expand their "orbits of comparison," a process that leads quite naturally to a spiraling of expectations and demands and, when these are resisted, to an intensification of class antagonism.[35]

All this, to which could be added a wealth of contemporary anecdotes about the hardships of the war, constitutes eloquent testimony to the effect of economic distress, coupled with simple poverty and hunger, in fostering rebellion. Still, it would be a mistake to focus too narrowly on economic distress as a precipitant of militancy. On theoretical grounds alone, hardship is unlikely to spark political and social activism. Numerous recent studies have shown quite the opposite: Revolutions and mass insurgencies seldom take place during periods of acute suffering but tend rather to arise in more buoyant and prosperous times; nor are the participants in such actions ordinarily the most poverty-striken and objectively oppressed sections of the population.[36] More concretely, the timing of protest in 1917–20 was not closely synchronized with the ups and downs of food prices and real wages, at least not after January 1918, and the leading participants were not those worst hit by the dislocations of the war economy.

It is well known, for example, that the most prominent activists in all countries were the metal and munitions workers.[37] Yet because they were deemed essential to the war effort, these were the most favored group of workers, and their wartime earnings rose accordingly. Austrian metal workers received special wage supplements subsidized by the state beginning in June 1918; their English counterparts had received a bonus one year earlier.[38] In Germany the wages of men in the war industries were almost 40 percent higher, relative to prewar levels, than those available to workers in civilian industries.[39] Roughly the same situation prevailed elsewhere in Europe, as the demand for steel, iron, ships, and guns intensified.[40] Nevertheless, these "aristocrats of labor" formed the industrial vanguard of the militancy. Just what other forces propelled them to leadership we shall soon see; suffice it to say here that poverty was not of primary importance.

Nor is the picture of poverty entirely unrelieved for the bulk of the population during and just after the war. The demographic evidence is quite the opposite: Before the war, most countries in Europe were slowly lowering overall death rates, particularly their rates of infant mortality. The war inevitably caused a temporary reversal that lasted through 1918. By 1919, however, the downward trend was reinstituted. Infant mortality was below prewar levels in Austria and Hungary, Belgium, Germany, Italy, Switzerland, and England and Wales; overall mortality was scarcely above normal rates, and by 1920 it too was generally lower. This demographic success, moreover, was achieved despite continuing economic dislocation produced by the extended blockade, demobilization, and political and social conflict.[41]

The point is not to minimize the sufferings borne by the home populations during the war. These were devastatingly real, and left psychological and physical scars as well as demographic asymmetries. But there were countervailing tendencies toward the more effective distribution of necessities. Given the glaring abuses of the black market and the inefficiencies of rationing, it is easy to overlook the substantial improvements that occurred in the lot of the very poor. It is necessary to remember, too, that for many so-called casual workers and their families—and these included almost all dockers, most labor in the building trades, and the majority of agricultural laborers—the onset of war marked the first time in living memory when they could obtain steady work throughout the year. Employment opportunities improved still more dramatically for women, whose earnings now contributed much more substantially than before to family incomes.[42]

The evidence suggests, therefore, that the combination of war-weariness and economic distress, while very important, cannot by itself explain the events of 1917–20. It surely provided plenty of raw material for exacerbating workers' sense of injustice and deprivation, but it did not guarantee the form their anger would take or that workers would find the resources and develop the organization necessary to express their discontent. To be able to launch such massive, insurgent actions, workers needed to formulate their complaints as domestic social and political critique and to devise forms of organization based on new bases of collective strength and identity.

Perhaps the most important factor darkening workers' perceptions of the states and societies in which they lived was the failure of political intervention in the war economy. There was a new visibility to the links between government policy and economic oppression and dislocation. By undertaking to ensure supplies of war materials and vital necessities for the home population and by frequently failing at the task, political regimes and their collaborators at the top of the industry were both seriously discredited. It was only logical for ordinary people to blame the political and economic elites for the shortages, the inequities of the black market, and rising prices, and for material grievances to become transformed into challenges to established authorities in government and industry. In addition, the state's groping attempts to stimulate production almost inevitably appeared to workers as pro-management interventions and virtually guaranteed a hostile response from labor's rank and file.[43]

The specific forms of state intervention applied during the war were thus critical in enabling workers to locate the source of their subsistence difficulties domestically, and gradually to substitute the industrialists and politicians for the external enemy as the targets of their anger. This profound ideological transformation, ultimately a reflection of the long-term centralization of power and the bureaucratization of everyday life in industrial society, created the underlying intellectual justification for the strikes and protests of 1917–20.[44]

If developments at the national level and in elite circles were crucial in changing workers' attitudes, it was a cumulation of changes visible primarily at the local level in the social organization of production and in the nature of working-class communities that, on balance, strengthened worker's abilities to act collectively and to translate grievances into militancy. The roots of these developments go back to at least the 1890s, but they came to fruition under the impact of the Great War. There occurred a structural transformation or reconstitution of the working class that involved both a new type of industry and a new social environment. Economic growth from the 1890s onward was concentrated in the sectors being remolded and stimulated by the "second industrial revolution," the revolution of steel, electricity, and chemicals.[45] The novelty of these industries transcended the products and also encompassed their processes of production, styles of industrial organization, and techniques of labor utilization and control.[46] The factories built after 1890 were bigger, housed more machines of greater speed and efficiency, and required a labor force that was only semiskilled. Ideally, that labor force was also pliable and dependent enough to be fitted in smoothly around the technical requirements of the latest generation of capital equipment. In its very essence, the phase of industrialization that gathered momentum near the end of the nineteenth century was inimical to skilled, craft labor, and tended inexorably toward the creation of a different labor force, typified by the semi-skilled machine tender in mass production. Skilled workers resisted the process with a series of strikes—at Renault's Billancourt works and at the Bosch factory in Stuttgart in 1913, among engineers at Hull and shoemakers in Paris earlier—but only in Great Britain, and even then not universally, were skilled workers sufficiently well organized to resist, or better, deflect for a time, the imperatives of technological change driven on by the quest for profit.[47]

The remaking of the working class conditioned the content, intensity, and expression of protest. The now permanently aggrieved craftsmen, particularly in the engineering industry, became firm supporters of the left. As Hobsbawm argues, "The metal-workers, hitherto rather conservative, became in most countries of the world the characteristic leaders of militant labour movements."[48] This happened in most every center of the new metallurgical industries: Berlin, Glasgow, Milan, Budapest, and, during the war, a host of other cities such as Paris, Hamborn, Merseburg, Mülheim, and, of course, Turin. Thus, Gramsci wrote of the Turin metallurgical workers as the vanguard "who do not have . . . the petty-bourgeois mentality of the skilled workers of other countries."[49] In fact, the restrictive mentality had begun to dissipate elsewhere under quite similar pressures, especially after 1914. The centrality of the metals and engineering industry to the war effort led to an intensified process of rationalization of factory life in metal production, vehicles and armaments, and chemicals. Concretely, the changes involved a suspension of customary work rules and manning regulations and the substitution of female or semiskilled workers for skilled male labor. This "dilution," carried through under harsh conditions and with little subtlety, simultaneously angered the skilled workers and created new job opportunities and possibilities for collective action for the newer laborers in basic industry.[50]

The replacement of craft workers by less skilled recruits to industry was not confined, however, to the metal or munitions industries, or indeed to the war years. Rather, it was the clearest and latest example of a general tendency throughout the economy to reorganize the workplace for maximum profit and efficiency. Even in the absence of major technical change, employers sought by more careful control and supervision, by the elimination of waste, by the abridgement of existing labor prerogatives, and by a general speeding up of machines and the flow of goods to stimulate workers to greater efforts. Even in Europe's oldest industrial center in Lancashire, textile workers faced intensified pressures for production before 1914, and between 1910 and 1914 launched a series of strikes over issues quite unrelated to wages.[51]

The changes were still more dramatic for workers in less modern employments. Economic growth from the mid-1890s transformed one industry after another by mechanizing many trades hitherto conducted on a small workshop basis, such as shoemaking and tailoring, and by imposing more regular work routines and more rational management strategies on previously casual employments, such as dockwork, carting, and brickmaking. The introduction of cranes for dockwork and construction, for example, was a major step in the modernization of those sectors. Gradually the chasm between the old "aristocracy of labor" and the unskilled, underemployed laborers was filled by the rise of the semiskilled and the assimilation of both extremes toward this intermediate position.[52]

The war markedly accelerated this reshaping of the working class. As the new industries were expanded to meet the needs of war production, the proportion of semiskilled necessarily increased. Fiat, for instance, expanded its labor force from 7,000 before the war to 30,000 at its end; Turin, Italy's Petrograd and its center of radicalism, doubled its working-class population.[53] Munich, primarily a cultural, bureaucratic, and commercial center in 1910, acquired a base of heavy industry and with it the raw material for the uprising of 1919.[54] Krupp's at Essen expanded its work force from 34,000 in 1914 to some 100,000 in 1918.[55] Glasgow's engineering factories sucked up thousands of new recruits, leading to the severe housing crisis that culminated in the successful rent strikes of 1915.[56] Comparable shifts occurred in France, where the heavy industries of the northeast were lost to the Germans early in the war and were relocated and rebuilt around Paris and St. Etienne.

During the war, the labor force in building, textiles, and other nonessential industries contracted sharply, while the numbers in the metal industry, armaments, chemicals, and mining grew substantially. This reorientation not only contributed to the long-term shift in the composition of the working class, it also gave more weight in the short run to the younger, more dynamic, and often more radical elements, while eroding the strength of the old bastions of conservative trade unionism and socialist moderation. Particularly in Germany, the contrast between the new and old industries and the new and old insurgents was stark and became the basis for a bitter generational split within the left: Noske, for example, complained crankily that "the most turbulent and disobedient elements in Kiel [during the mutiny] were the very young," and the same point was frequently made about industrial militants.[58] The prewar socialist and labor parties had their social roots among the skilled and the organized not just in France but in England, Germany, Italy, and Austria.[59] The emergent factory proletariat, on the other hand, had remained largely unorganized and unrepresented. When the wartime labor shortage gave these workers some additional social leverage, they organized massively and became the core, if not always the articulate leadership, of the postwar insurgency.[60] Their enhanced bargaining was nowhere more evident than in the drastic narrowing of the gap between the wages of skilled and unskilled workers, as Table 2-4 reveals for Britain and Germany and as contemporary testimony attests to for other nations as well.

The effect of the war, then, was to bring to a head the process by which the gradual accumulation of technological and organizational changes at factory level created a modern proletariat. From this perspective, the explosion of activism from 1917 to 1920 represented the entry into fuller social and political life of this remolded working class, and the shop steward or "works council" organizations were an especially appropriate form of activity. They served as vehicles for the involvement of those "emergent" sections of the working class that had yet to be absorbed by the old union structures and that were best served by organization on the shop floor itself. It seems, in fact, that in most countries a greater proportion of the semiskilled and unskilled, as well as women, workers were organized and active in the postwar insurgency than at any other time in the twentieth century.[61]

With the alteration in the composition of the working class came a dramatic expansion in its size, and this increase ushered in a new phase of urban growth. Between 1890 and 1920, Europe experienced a more rapid urbanization than even before or since; it also was a unique form of urbanization. With the coming of the trolley and tram, the European city extended its limits radially, thus facilitating the dispersion of industry from the central core to the periphery. Still, the rise of mass transport was not sufficient to effect that divorce between workplace and residence that has allegedly come to characterize city life recently.[62] During this intermediate stage of urbanization, workers' quarters remained in close proximity to the newly built plants that produced metal and metal goods, armaments, chemicals, and even some automobiles;

Table 2-4. *Narrowing of Wage Differentials During the War,*
Britain and Germany (Unskilled Rates as Percentage of Skilled)

Country	1913–14	1918
Germany		
Building in:		
Berlin	67.9	93.3
Hamburg	83.3	90.1
Stettin	75.4	89.0
Average	75.0	89.0
Railways	68.6	82.1
Bavaria (all industries)	73.0	79.0
Britain		
Building	66.4	80.1
Shipbuilding	55.2	73.6
Engineering	58.6	75.7
Railways	54.3	78.8

Sources: For Germany, G. Bry, *Wages in Germany, 1871–1945* (Princeton, 1960). Tables 50, A-14, A-39; for Britain, K. G. Knowles and D. J. Robertson "Differences between the Wages of Skilled and Unskilled Workers, 1880–1950," *Bulletin of the Oxford University Institute of Statistics* 13, no. 4, 109–127.

and these quarters became the centers of an intense community life that developed out of the physical overlapping of the spheres of production, consumption, leisure, and collective action.

Between 1890 and 1920 the European working class seems to have envolved a network of social relations in the neighborhoods of the city that eventually thickened into an extremely supportive subculture. Various factors conjoined to bring this about: The peculiarities of early twentieth-century mass transportation and the compelling logic of land values produced about this time a growing segregation of social classes in the urban region; and as workers' neighborhoods became increasingly homogeneous, the local style of life became more distinctly proletarian. Out of the initial chaos of urban and industrial migration eventually came more solid communities, the common locus of friendship, kinship, work, and play. Thus Roberts describes the stabilization of working-class life in Salford, just outside Manchester, before the war:[63]

Throughout a quarter of a century the population of our [urban] village remained generally immobile: the constant shifts of near-by country folk into industrial towns . . . had almost ceased. . . . A man's work, of course, usually fixed the place where his family dwelt, but lesser factors were involved too: his links, for instance, with local kith and kin. Then again, he commonly held a certain social position at the near-by pub, modest, perhaps, but recognized, and a credit connection with the corner shop. Such relationships, once relinquished, might not easily be re-established. All these things, together with fear of change, combined to keep poor families, if not in the same street, at least in the same neighborhood for generations.

Even where substantial migration continued through the war years, there is evidence that working-class communities nonetheless achieved a stability and cohesiveness noticeably lacking prior to 1900.[64] In addition to the increase in the social homogeneity of residential arrangements and the compacting tendencies of the new technology, several other changes seem to have contributed to the formation of more closely knit communities. The progressive nuclearization of the family, so prominent among the nineteenth-century bourgeoisie, seems to have begun to affect working-class family life at about this time, and the decline of domestic service as an occupation for young women and the parallel decay of apprenticeship for boys probably worked in the same direction.[65] Most likely more secure job prospects also discouraged mobility and led to greater local cohesion. Whatever the precise mix of influences, the trend was universal throughout Europe and was reinforced by the war. The onset of war brought to an end a great era of city building, and this cessation of construction meant that existing communities remained intact.[66] Because of the serious housing shortages produced by the forced expansion in certain areas of war-related industries, the influx of labor migrants had to be absorbed into the existing housing stock.[67] Moreover, the strains placed upon individuals and families by mobilization meant an extension of the range of services and supports provided through the informal networks of the neighborhood.

The most detailed study has focused upon the process in Great Britain.[68] "The First World War," it has been argued, "was an event of unparalleled significance in the housing history of British cities." "Changes initiated by the war" caused cities to "diverge radically from the predominating patterns of the previous forty years." The era of industrial and urban growth dating from 1880 and continuing to 1914

had been somewhat contradictory: though there was a marked increase in residential segregation by social class, there remained very
high rates of local and long distance mobility that would have tended to
retard the consolidation of working-class communities. However,
"mobility collapsed during the war and never really recovered after-
wards." As a result, neighborhoods became even more segregated by
class and by the stage in the life cycle of its inhabitants and grew much
more homogeneous and solid.

The actual process of community building inevitably took different forms in various countries. Again, it has been described most
thoroughly in Great Britain, where proletarian social life revolved
around the pub and the music hall, the workingman's club, and, on
occasion, the local union branch.[69] In France, the workers' subculture
was equally apolitical and even less formal, centered on the cafe or
cabaret, the informal links of the immediate neighborhood, and the
small workshop.[70] In Germany, Austria, and, to a slightly lesser extent,
Italy, formal socialist institutions played a greater role. The Austrian
Socialist Party, for instance, had its own schools, choir groups, and
sports clubs as well as the usual array of party and union activities.[71]
Whether explicitly political in form or not, the result was a comparable
strengthening of the network of associations through which workers
led their lives. Upon the grounding of these firm community bonds
arose the characteristic forms of working-class culture and leisure
about which historians are just beginning to become aware.[72]

Everywhere there were political consequences and implications
as well, for it was precisely in these years that the distinctive social
geography of twentieth-century elections was established. The extension of suffrage to the working class occurred first in the towns, and in
this arena working-class political activity blossomed and achieved its
main successes. In the big cities of Europe, working-class communities
began gradually to vote en bloc for one or another left or labor party,
particularly after the war. Entire neighborhoods in London, such as
Hackney and Battersea or Islington, would vote Labor religiously; the
"red suburbs" of Paris made French Communism almost solely "a
Parisian movement," as one of its enemies happily announced in 1924;
and in Vienna the workers' districts formed a solid phalanx of SPD
voters right up to the fascist takeover in 1934. It seems workers voted as
whole communities united around one or another political formation,
not as isolated electors exercising individual choice, as in the classic
bourgeois ideal.[73]

Besides the ordinary and obvious function of enhancing social
interaction and providing psychic sustenance, then, these urban social

networks formed the underpinning of social and political mobilization. This was particularly the case during the crisis years of the war when they served as nodes of organization. Several commentators have noted the specifically urban character of labor militancy during and after the war; but the social, as opposed to the simple geographical, implications of this fact have been overlooked by all but a few writers.[74] In a period such as 1914–18, when normal channels of protest are blocked or atrophied, other less formal linkages between social actors are pressed into service as the basis of new political forms. As one Italian analyst has argued, workers' resistance "was forced everywhere to express itself in new forms, often unorganized and 'spontaneous.' "[75] The web of associations at the workplace represented one such linkage, and as the established union leaderships were coopted into government administration or into active collaboration with the employers, it became the grounding for the emerging shop stewards or works councils. The social networks running through the working-class neighborhoods seem to have played an equally important role in facilitating collection action.

Several facets of the movement of 1917–20 point to this role. Most obvious was the prominent place of women in stimulating and participating in the various actions centered in the community. Whether women were quite so minimally involved in prewar social movements as previous research suggests, it seems nonetheless clear that the peculiar conditions of wartime allowed an explosion of women's acitvity.[76] More closely integrated into local neighborhoods than their husbands, lovers, sons, or brothers, working-class women were more keenly aware of subsistence matters and, because of their extensive networks of support and sociability, readier to move into action over threats to the social resources available to the community. The best documented case is probably Barcelona, where a veritable "women's war" over food and fuel took on insurrectionary proportions in the early part of 1918. The movement was organized and led entirely by women and succeeded in wringing major concessions from the authorities. The defensive character of such struggles may well have limited their long-term impact upon the political system and on the sexual division of labor, as Temma Kaplan has argued, but in the context of the postwar crisis they were extremely significant and undoubtedly enhanced the nature of the working-class challenge.[77]

In fact, on many occasions and in many places during 1919–20, men and women protested jointly over issues of consumption: over prices, rationing, and shortages of food, housing, coal, and other essentials. As noted above, testimony to the British Commission on

Industrial Unrest was unanimous in attributing the mounting unrest to grievances over consumption. Such complaints were at the root of the frequent and violent food riots and the rent strikes that occurred in the most advanced and radical centers, and many of the major industrial actions were precipitated by problems faced by workers as consumers. Characteristically, however, efforts to organize working people as consumers have tended to be launched not in the factory but in the context of the local community. Without the strengthening of neighborhoods and social institutions based on residential proximity, it would seem very difficult to explain the prominent consumerist component in the collective actions of 1917–20.

By a similar logic, the whole style of the postwar insurgency—its apparent disorganization, the frequency of seemingly spontaneous street demonstrations, the tendency for institutions such as the Italian *camera del lavoro* and *casa del popolo*, the German "peoples' house," the Austrian *Volkheim* and the English trades' council to become the centers of agitation instead of the established parties, and so on—suggests that the organizational consequences of urban life were critical ingredients enabling workers to sustain militancy during and after the war.[78]

There would seem, too, to have been a connection between the intense class consciousness of the movement of 1917–20 and its community and consumerist background. Organization at the point of production is notoriously sectional: the stratification of work roles limits the appeal of ideas about "one big union" and one common interest, except in relatively rare circumstances. While such circumstances were becoming more common during precisely this period, the norm was still quite otherwise, and differentials based on skill, sex, and racial or ethnic discrimination remained in force. By contrast, the problems of high food prices, shortages, inequitable rationing, skyrocketing rents, and a deteriorating housing stock transcended the narrowness of purely factory styles of organization and tended to pit all workers in a unified struggle against the rich, the war profiteers, and the bungling bureaucrats. Notions of class solidarity found much more fertile soil in protest over consumption; and the consumerist element imparted a wider sense of class loyalty and class antagonism to the events of 1917–20 than probably would have developed in a more purly industrial situation.[79]

It seems reasonably clear, therefore, that the social consequences of the shifts in industrial structure and in urban spatial arrangements provided the essential preconditions for the wave of strikes and organization that swept over Europe beginning in 1917. Of course, these preconditions had to be combined with the deprivations of the war to produce an outburst of such magnitude, but grievance and anger alone were not sufficient. The expression of discontent required organization, and that necessitated various kinds of resources, opportunities, and ideas. The restructuring of daily life in the factory and in the urban neighborhood shifted every so slightly the balance of collective strengths toward the workers, at least for a time, and enabled them to launch a wave of strikes and insurrections that shook European society to its roots and terrified its ruling classes. It was also this new-found strength and sense of competence that prompted Gramsci and his generation of militants to think through the meaning of working-class hegemony and imagine a future based on vastly different forms of industrial and political organization. The contemporary relevance and potency of that intellectual legacy is reason enough to study those unique conditions that produced it.

Notes

An earlier version of this paper was presented to the Seminar in Twentieth-Century European History at the Institute of Historical Research in London. Comments made there were extremely helpful in preparing the present revision, and I am most grateful for them.

1. E. J. Hobsbawm, "Religion and the Rise of Socialism," *Marxist Perspectives* 1 (Spring 1978), 14–33.

2. J. Kemmy, "The Limerick Soviet," *Saothar, Journal of the Irish Labour History Society* 2 (1975–1976), 45–52; Sten Sparre Nelson, "Labour Insurgency in Norway: The Crisis of 1917–1920," *Social Science History* 5, no. 4 (Fall 1981), 393–416; Bela Kirschner, "Society and Nation in the Hungarian Republic of Councils," in Henrik Vass, ed., *Studies on the History of the Hungarian Working Class Movement* (Budapest, 1975), 125–153; and on Spain, Gerald H. Meaker, *The Revolutionary Left in Spain, 1914–1923* (Stanford, 1974), esp. 158–168.

3. Arno Mayer, *Political Origins of the New Diplomacy* (New Haven, 1959); Albert S. Lindemann, *The Red Years: European Socialism Versus Bolshevism, 1919–1921* (Berkeley, 1974).

4. The best comparative accounts are Charles Maier, *Recasting Bourgeois Europe* (Princeton, 1975), and Arno Mayer, *Politics and Diplomacy of Peacemaking, 1918–1919* (New York, 1967); but see also the essays in Charles Bertrand, ed., *Revolutionary Situations in Europe, 1917–1922* (Montreal, 1977).

5. G. Haupt, *Socialism and the Great War* (Oxford, 1972), esp. 216–249.

6. Mayer, *Politics and Diplomacy*, 284–343; M. Ferro, *The Great War, 1914–1918* (London, 1973), 189–203.

7. Directorate of Intelligence (Home Office), "A Survey of Revolutionary Movements in Great Britain in the Year 1920," PRO, Cabinet Papers, CAB 24/118, C.P. 2455.

8.   G. Feldman, E. Kolb, and R. Rürup, "Die Massenbewegungen der Arbeiterschaft in Deutschland am Ende des Ersten Weltkrieges (1917–20)," *Politische Vierteljahresschrift* 13 (1972), 84–105; R. Wheeler, " *'Ex oriente lux?'* The Soviet Example and the German Revolution," in Bertrand, *Revolutionary Situations*, 39–49; Dick Geary, "Radicalism and the Worker: Metalworkers and Revolution, 1914–23," in R. J. Evans, ed., *Society and Politics in Wilhelmine Germany* (London, 1978), 267–286; and P. Von Oertzen, *Betriebsträte in der Novemberrevolution* (Düsseldorf, 1963); David W. Morgan, *The Socialist Left and the German Revolution* (Ithaca, 1975).

9.   Fontainebleu Memorandum, March 25, 1919, quoted in Mayer, *Politics and Diplomacy of Peacemaking*, 581–583.

10.   Robert Wohl, *French Communism in the Making, 1914–1924* (Stanford, 1966), 117–137; Annie Kriegel, *Croissance de la C.G.T., 1918–1921* (Paris, 1966), 67–97; Kriegel, *Aux origines du communisme français, 1914–1920* (Paris, 1964), 1, 238–247, 408–494; V. Lorwin, *The French Labor Movement* (Cambridge, Mass., 1966), 51–55; M. Gallo, "Quelques aspects de la mentalité et du comportement ouvrièrs dans les usines de guerre, 1914–1918," *Le mouvement social* 56 (July–Sept. 1966), 3–33.

11.   Adrian Lyttelton, "Revolution and Counter-Revolution in Italy, 1918–1922," in Bertrand, *Revolutionary Situations*, 63–73; G. Williams, *Proletarian Order* (London, 1975); P. Spriano, *The Occupation of the Factories, Italy 1920* (London, 1975); Roberto Vivarelli, "Revolution and Reaction in Italy, 1918–1922," *Journal of Italian History* 1 (1978), 235–263.

12.   R. L. Tôkés, *Béla Kun and the Hungarian Soviet Republic* (New York, 1967), 133.

13.   I. Deak, "Budapest and the Hungarian Revolutions of 1918–1919," *Slavonic and East European Review* 46 (1968), 129–140; Kirschner, "Society and Nation," 137.

14.   C. A. Macartney, *The Social Revolution in Austria* (Cambridge, England, 1926); G. Ranki, "Structural Crisis in Agriculture in Postwar Years," in Bertrand, *Revolutionary Situations*, 105–116.

15.   Otto Bauer, "Problems of the Austrian Revolution," in T. B. Bottomore and P. Goode, eds., *Austro-Marxism* (Oxford, 1978), 161.

16.   C. A. Gulick, *Austria: From Habsburg to Hitler* (Berkeley, 1948), I, 15–65.

17.   Ingrun LaFleur, "The Bolshevik Revolution and Austrian Socialism—The January 1918 Strike," *Journal of the Great Lakes History Conference* 1 (1967), 82–96.

18.   See esp. Gulick, *Austria*, I, 69–83, on the co-optation of the insurgents, and p. 175 ff. on the extensive social reforms instituted under Socialist auspices, esp. in Vienna; I. Duczynska, *Workers in Arms: The Austrian Schutzbund and the Civil War of 1934* (New York, 1978); also Ernst Winkler, *Die österreichische Sozialdemokratie im Spiegel ihrer Programme* (Vienna, 1971); and D. Langewiesche, *Zur Freizeit des Arbeiters: Bildungsbestrebungen und Freizeitgestaltung österreichische Arbeiter im Kaiserreich und in der Ersten Republik* (Stuttgart, 1980).

19.   J. Hinton, *The First Shop Stewards' Movement* (London, 1973).

20. S. Graubard, *British Labour and the Russian Revolution* (Cambridge, Mass., 1957).

21. Walter Kendall, *The Revolutionary Movement in Britain* (London, 1969); J. M. Winter, *Socialism and the Challenge of War* (London, 1974).

22. On Lloyd George's role in all this, see Ralph Desmarais, "The British Government's Strike-Breaking Organization and Black Friday," *Journal of Contemporary History* 6 (1971); and Peter Dennis, "The Territorial Army in Aid of the Civil Power in Britain, 1919–1926," *Journal of Contemporary History* 16 (1981), 705–724.

23. On Sweden, see C. G. Andrae, "The Swedish Labor Movement and the 1917–1918 Revolution," in S. Koblik, ed., *Sweden's Development from Poverty to Affluence, 1750–1970* (Minneapolis, 1975), 232–253.

24. A. Mayer, "The Lower Middle Class as Historical Problem," *Journal of Modern History* 47 (1975), 409–436; J. Kocka, "The Problem of Democracy and the Lower Middle Classes in the First Third of the 20th Century: Some Results and Perspectives of Research," XIV International Congress of Historical Sciences, 1975; C. Maier, "Political Crisis and Partial Modernization: The Outcomes in Germany, Austria, Hungary, and Italy after World War I," in Bertrand, *Revolutionary Situations*, 119–130.

25. R. Miliband, *Parliamentary Socialism* (London, 1961).

26. The process was extremely widespread but particularly important in countries or in industries where unions or socialist parties had previously occupied an unrecognized or, in some cases, almost outlaw status. Thus, the legitimacy gained by the trade unions and the SPD in Germany during the war was quite dearly cherished, as was the instant respectability granted in England to the unions of dockers and railway workers. See Gerald Feldman, *Army, Industry, and Labor in Germany, 1914–1918* (Princeton, 1966); P. S. Bagwell, *The Railwaymen* (London, 1963); A. Bullock, *Ernest Bevin* I (London, 1960).

27. W. J. Mommsen, "Die deutsche Revolution, 1918–1920: Politsche Revolution und Soziale Protestbewegung," *Geschichte und Gesellschaft* 4 (1978), 377; N. Papayanis, "Masses révolutionnaires et directions réformistes: les tensions au cours des grèves des métallurgistes français en 1919," *Le mouvement social* 93 (Oct.–Dec. 1975), 51–73; B. Pribićević. *The Shop Stewards' Movement and Workers' Control* (Oxford, 1959).

28. J. P. Nettl, *Rosa Luxemburg*, II (London, 1966), 760–761.

29. R. Rürup, "Problems of the German Revolution, 1918–19," *Journal of Contemporary History*, 3 (1968), 134.

30. P. Renouvin, "L'opinion publique et la guerre en 1917," *Revue d'histoire moderne et contemporaine* 15 (1968); Roland Stromberg, *Redemption by War* (Lawrence, Kansas, 1982), 151–176.

31. G. Hardach, *The First World War, 1914–1918* (Berkeley, 1977), 108–138; Robert Moeller, "Peasants, Politics and Pressure Groups in War and Inflation: The Case of the Rhineland and Westphalia, 1914–1924," Ph.D. dissertation, University of California, Berkeley, 1980, provides a detailed account of the split between rural and urban produces at the end of the war.

32. Great Britain, Reports of the Commission of Enquiry into Indus-

trial Unrest, *British Parliamentary Papers*, 1917–1918, XV (Cd. 8662–8669, 8696).

33.   Hinton, *First Shop Stewards' Movement*, 125–127; Tôkés, *Béla Kun*, 120; Gulick, *Austria*, 421–423.

34.   Lyttelton, "Revolution and Counter-Revolution in Italy," 68–70; Williams, *Proletarian Order*, 71; LaFleur, "The Bolshevik Revolution and Austrian Socialism."

35.   On this more theoretical point, see R. Hyman and I. Brough, *Social Values and Industrial Relations* (Oxford, 1976), 230–246.

36.   Charles, Louise, and Richard Tilly, *The Rebellious Century* (Cambridge, Mass., 1975); Theda Skocpol, *States and Social Revolutions* (Cambridge, 1979), 3–43.

37.   J. M. Cammett, *Antonio Gramsci and the Origins of Italian Communism* (Stanford, 1967), 73–74. See also the personal testaments of the leaders of the Berlin shop stewards: R. Müller, *Vom Kaiserreich zur Republik* (Vienna, 1924), esp. 55–61; and Emil Barth, *Aus der Werkstatt der deutschen Revolution* (Berlin, 1919); and the debate over Russian metal workers: Leopold H. Haimson, "Social Stability in Urban Russia, 1906–1917," *Slavic Review* 4 (1964); G. R. Swain, "Bolsheviks and Metal Workers on the Eve of the First World War," *Journal of Contemporary History* 16 (1981), 273–291.

38.   Gulick, *Austria*, 42; Hinton, *First Shop Stewards' Movement*.

39.   G. Bry, *Wages in Germany, 1871–1945* (Princeton, 1960) 209–212.

40.   In general, see Hardach, *The First World War*.

41.   The data are available in B. R. Mitchell, *European Historical Statistics* (New York, 1975). See also J. M. Winter, "The Impact of the First World War on Civilian Health in Britain," *Economic History Review* 30 (1977), 487–507.

42.   Ferro, *The Great War*, 170–171; Jonathan Schneer, "The War, the State and the Workplace: British Dockers during 1914–1918," in J. Cronin and J. Schneer, eds., *Social Conflict and the Political Order* (London, 1982), 96–112.

43.   See Gerald Feldman, "Demobilization and the Post-War Social Order in Europe," German Historical Institute, Conference on Demobilization, London, May, 1981.

44.   Tilly, et al., *Rebellious Century*.

45.   For a general survey, see David Landes, *The Unbound Prometheus* (Cambridge, England, 1969), chapter 5.

46.   E. J. Hobsbawm, "Custom, Wages and Work-Load," in *Labouring Men* (Garden City, N.Y., 1963), 421–427.

47.   The ambiguities of the resistance of craft workers to the new technologies has been sharply debated by Jean Monds, "Workers' Control and the Historians: The New Economism," *New Left Review* 97 (1976), 81–100; and James Hinton, "Rejoinder," 101–104.

48.   Hobsbawm, "Custom, Wages, and Work-Load," 424.

49.   A. Gramsci, in his report to the Comintern in 1920, cited in Williams, *Proletarian Order*, 87.

50.   The process is described for Britain by Hinton, *First Shop Stewards'*

Movement. For Germany, see Feldman, *Army, Industry, and Labor*; and also Fritz Opel, *Der Deutsche Metallarbeiter-Verband während des ersten Weltkrieges und der Revolution* (Hannover, 1957). For France, see B. Abhervé, "Les origines de la grève des métallurgistes parisiens, juin 1919," *Le mouvement social* 93 (Oct.–Dec. 1975), 75–85; and for other countries, Dick Geary, *European Labour Protest, 1848–1939* (London, 1981).

51. Joseph White, *The Limits of Trade Union Militancy* (Westport, Conn., 1978).

52. P. Stearns, *Lives of Labor* (New York, 1975), esp. pt. II, and "The Unskilled and Industrialization: A Transformation of Consciousness," *Archiv für Sozialgeschichte* 16 (1976), 249–82; A. Levine, *Industrial Retardation in Britain* (London, 1967); J. J. Carré, P. Dubois, and E. Malinvaud, *French Economic Growth* (Stanford, 1975), 162–166; D. Groh, "Intensification of Work and Industrial Conflict in Germany, 1896–1914," *Politics and Society* 8 (1979), 349–397.

53. Williams, *Proletarian Order*, 56.

54. A. Mitchell, *Revolution in Bavaria* (Princeton, 1965); T. Dorst, *Die Münchener Räterepublik* (Frankfurt, 1966), 149.

55. Feldman, "Socio-economic Structures in the Industrial Sector and Revolutionary Potentialities, 1917–22," in Bertrand, *Revolutionary Situations*, 160.

56. Hinton, *First Shop Stewards' Movement*, 109–113, 125–127; S. G. Checkland, *The Upas Tree* (Glasgow, 1975).

57. H. Sellier and A. Bruggeman, *Paris pendant la Guerre* (Paris, 1926); M. Brelet, *La crise de la métallurgie. La politique économique et sociale du comité des forges* (Paris, 1923); A. Fontaine, *French Industry during the War* (New Haven, 1926); Meaker, *Revolutionary Left in Spain*.

58. Noske, cited in Geary, "Radicalism and the Worker," 277, and, on the general point, 276–283. See also R. F. Wheeler, "German Labor and the Comintern: A Problem of Generations," *Journal of Social History* 6 (1974), 304–321.

59. B. Moss, *Origins of the French Labor Movement, The Socialism of Skilled Workers* (Berkeley, 1976); Neufeld, *Italy*, 316–394; Geary, *European Labour Protest*, 91–98.

60. R. Comfort, *Revolutionary Hamburg* (Stanford, 1966), shows this very clearly, esp. 131–147. See also von Oertzen, *Betriebsräte in der Novemberrevolution, 1918–19* (Düsseldorf, 1963); Geary, *European Labour Protest*, 138–140.

61. Conversely, the magnitude of the failure of 1919–20 is perhaps best measured by the drifting away of these newly organized groups from the labor movement and the left after 1920. See, for example, the interesting figures in A. Kriegel, *The French Communists* (Chicago, 1972), 65–70, on female participation in the PCF during the interwar period; also Comfort, *Revolutionary Hamburg*; and J. Saville, "May Day 1937," in A. Briggs and J. Saville, eds., *Essays in Labour History, 1918–1939* (London, 1977), 232–284.

62. J. McKay, *Tramways and Trolleys: The Rise of Urban Mass Transport in*

Europe (Princeton, 1975); Robert Dickinson, *The West European City* (London, 1951), 463–464.

63. R. Roberts, *The Classic Slum* (Harmondsworth, 1973), 29–30.

64. The process by which a distinctively proletarian subculture was formed in the urban environment has been treated very minimally in the history of labor movements. Lately, it has been more often discussed, but usually from one of two equally distorted perspectives. One approach has been to see the strength of the new communities as a force integrating workers into advanced capitalism and reconciling them to a status of permanent subordination. The other approach has been to focus upon the quaint details of everyday life in a romantic view of the warm, friendly social relations common to working-class neighborhoods. Typical examples of the former are G. Roth, *The Social Democrats in Imperial Germany: A Study in Working-Class Isolation and National Integration* (Totowa, N.J., 1963); G. Stedman Jones, "Working-Class Culture and Working-Class Politics in London, 1870–1900," *Journal of Social History* 7 (1974); and, to some extent, S. Meacham, *A Life Apart: The British Working Class, 1890–1914* (London, 1977). The other approach is perhaps most evident in such works as R. Hoggart, *The Uses of Literacy* (London, 1957) and the vast sociological literature on the life-styles and values of the "traditional" worker. See, for example, the articles in M. Bulmer, ed., *Working-Class Images of Society* (London, 1975). For a critique, see Eugene Genovese and Elizabeth Fox-Genovese, "The Political Crisis of Social History: A Marxian Perspective," *Journal of Social History* 10 (1976), 204–220. For more recent approaches, see D. Geary, "Identifying Militancy: The Assessment of Working-Class Attitudes towards State and Society," in R. J. Evans, ed., *The Culture of the German Working Class* (London, 1981), 220–246; Alf Lüdtke, "Cash, Coffee-Breaks, Horseplay: 'Eigensinn' and Politics among Factory Workers in Late 19th and Early 20th-Century Germany," (Davis Center, Princeton, 1982) on Germany; and Victoria de Grazia, *The Culture of Consent* (Cambridge, 1981) on Italy.

65. E. Shorter, *The Making of the Modern Family* (New York, 1975), treats the overall transformation of family styles. The lag in the evolution of working-class patterns is clearly reflected in fertility differentials between social classes that only narrowed after 1900. On these, see J. Knodel, *The Decline of Fertility in Germany, 1871–1939* (Princeton, 1974), chapter 3; M. Livi-Bacci, *A History of Italian Fertility* (Princeton, 1977); and, more generally, G. Z. Johnson, "Differential Fertility in European Countries," in National Bureau of Economic Research, *Demographic and Economic Change in Developed Countries* (Princeton, 1960), 36–72. On apprenticeship and domestic service, see Stearns, *Lives of Labor*, 48–50, 60; T. McBride, *The Domestic Revolution* (New York, 1976); and C. More, *Skill and the English Working Class* (London, 1980). On family structure and class in Germany and France, see L. Niethammer and A. Brüggemeier, "Wie wohnten Arbeiter im Kaiserreich?" *Archiv für Sozialgeschichte* 16 (1976), 61–134; and Jean-Louis Robert, "La CGT et la famille ouvrière, 1914–1918: première approche," *le Mouvement social* 116 (1981), 47–66. Whether changes

in patterns of social mobility correlated in any fashion with the stabilization of working-class communities is not at all clear. In a recent article, H. Kaelble suggests that, after 1900, German rates of social mobility increased slightly, while those of other western nations declined. In consequence, Britain, France, and Germany all exhibited relatively modest and similar rates by approximately 1920. This suggests an overall firming up of the class structure, with a tendency for vertical movements to be of rather short distance: specifically, opportunities for moving upwards in business for workers were replaced by opportunities to enter the white-collar work force. This at least does not contradict the arguments proffered here. See H. Kaelble, "Social Mobility in Germany, 1900–1960," *Journal of Modern History* 50 (1978), 439–461, and *Historical Research on Social Mobility* (New York, 1981).

66. Dickinson, *West European City*, 463.

67. National Civic Federation, Commission on Foreign Inquiry, *The Labor Situation in Great Britain and France* (New York, 1919).

68. R. M. Pritchard, *Housing and the Spatial Structure of the City* (Cambridge, 1976).

69. Meacham, *A Life Apart*, is the most recent analysis—see the literature cited there for earlier work. One important group omitted from Meacham's study is the miners, about whose closely knit communities so much has been said. The first two decades of the century seem critical for this group as well. See C. Storm-Clark, "The Miners, 1870–1970: A Test Case for Oral History," *Victorian Studies* 15 (1971), 49–74.

70. M. Marrus, "Social Drinking in the *Belle Epoque*," *Journal of Social History* 7 (1974), 115–141. Cf. also T. W. Margadant, "Primary Schools and Youth Groups in Pre-War Paris," *Journal of Contemporary History* 13 (1978), 323–36.

71. Gulick, *Austria*, passim; D. Groh, *Negative Integration und revolution-ärer Attentismus* (Frankfurt am Main, 1973); D. Bell, "Worker Culture and Worker Politics: The Experience of an Italian Town, 1880–1915," *Social History* 3 (1978), 1–21.

72. See esp. R. Wheeler, "Organized Sport and Organized Labour: The Workers' Sports Movement," *Journal of Contemporary History* 13 (1978), 191–210; G. Ritter, "Workers' Culture in Imperial Germany: Problems and Points of Departure for Research," *Journal of Contemporary History* 13 (1978), 165–189.

73. H. Pelling, *The Social Geography of British Elections, 1885–1910* (London, 1967); D. Butler and D. Stokes, *Political Change in Britain* (New York, 1969), 247–263; R. Wohl, *French Communism*, 386; F. Goguel, *Géographie des élections françaises sous la IIIe et la IVe République* (Paris, 1970); É. Blanc, *La ceinture rouge* (Paris, 1927); I. Duczynska, *Workers in Arms* (New York, 1978); D. White, "Reconsidering European Socialism in the 1920s," *Journal of Contemporary History* 16 (1981), 251–272.

74. For example, G. Ranki, "Structural Crisis in Agriculture in Postwar Years," and C. Maier, "Political Crisis and Partial Modernization."

75. E. Soave, cited in Cammett, *Antonio Gramsci*, 73.

76. E. J. Hobsbawm, "Man and Woman in Socialist Iconography," *History Workshop*, no. 6 (1978), 121–138; Louise Tilly and Joan Scott, *Women, Work and Family* (New York, 1978).

77. Temma Kaplan, "Female Consciousness and Collective Action: The Case of Barcelona, 1910–1918," *Signs* 7, no. 3 (Spring, 1982).

78. Williams, *Proletarian Order*, 23–24; A. Clinton, "Trades Councils during World War I," *International Review of Social History* (1970), pt. 2. The local context of German events has become increasingly clear with the publication of a number of excellent local studies. Among these, see Comfort, *Revolutionary Hamburg*; Erhard Lucas, *Frankfurt unter der Herrschaft des Arbeiter- und Soldatenräte, 1918–19* (Frankfurt, 1969); Lucas, *Marzrevolution 1920*, 2 vols. (Frankfurt, 1974); Lucas, *Zwei Formen von Radikalismus in der deutschen Arbeiterbewegung* (Frankfurt, 1976); the various studies in R. Rürup, ed., *Arbeiter- und Soldatenräte im rheinisch-westfälischen Industriegebeit* (Wuppertal, 1975); and F. Boll, *Massenbewegungen in Niedersachsen 1906–1920* (Bonn, 1981).

79. Williams, *Proletarian Order*, 24, makes essentially this point in connection with the urban nature of the *camera*. Whereas "unions tended to appeal to the more skilled, prosperous, and sophisticated," the *camera* "tended to breed a populist and communal, sometimes a class, rather than a trade or craft, mentality. It embraced a wider range of workers."

Chapter Three

The One Big Union In International Perspective: Revolutionary Industrial Unionism, 1900-1925

Larry Peterson

During the first decades of the twentieth century, workers in the advanced industrial nations attempted for the first time to organize themselves into industrial unions. Antecedents of modern industrial unionism date to the latter nineteenth century, when workers began to respond to the second wave of industrialization, but the movement to reorganize the labor union movement along industrial lines did not become general until after the turn of the century. Thus, between 1900 and 1925, the *Confédération Générale du Travail* (General Confederation of Labor) (CGT) in France became the first major labor union federation to base itself on industrial unions. Unskilled workers in the United States made persistent efforts to found either single industrial unions, as in steel and mining, or central industrial organizations, as in the American Labor Union (ALU) and the Industrial Workers of the World (IWW). Canadian workers, especially in the West, repudiated their traditional trade unions to join first the IWW and then the One Big Union (OBU). In Great Britain, the general workers' unions expanded phenomenally in the great unrest between 1910 and 1920, and groups of skilled workers in the older craft unions began to advocate

This is a revised and somewhat expanded version of the article originally published in *Labor/Le Travailleur* 7 (Spring 1981).

greater union solidarity in a variety of syndicalist, revolutionary industrial unionist, amalgamationist, and shop stewards movements. Finally, German industrial workers in the largest centers of industry in the Ruhr, the North Sea ports, and Middle Germany reacted to the First World War and the revolution of 1918–19 by repudiating the social democratic free unions in favor of revolutionary general workers' unionism. Common to all these movements were the leadership of revolutionaries and the advocacy of the solidarity of all workers in "one big union."

The purpose of this article is to analyze the movements of revolutionary industrial unionists in five countries. I have chosen Great Britain, France, Germany, the United States, and Canada for comparison because they show clearly the international similarities and national differences of the movement for industrial unionism.[1] The historiography of industrial unionism in these countries has developed to the point at which it is possible to compare the movement for industrial unionism across national boundaries. Indeed, a simultaneous reading of the labor historiography of these countries leads to the inescapable conclusion that industrial unionism after 1900 was a truly international phenomenon. The national focus of virtually all previous studies tends to obscure the general nature of the movement and makes a cross-national comparison all the more urgent if one is to understand the full dimensions and significance of revolutionary industrial unionism in the early twentieth century.

I will not attempt to narrate the general history of these movements, nor will I concentrate on their differences, since the national historiographies of each country already deal in detail with the unique features of each example. Rather, I will employ a method of abstraction from local peculiarities to analyze those features that all five countries had in common, in order to demonstrate the general tendency toward revolutionary industrial unionism.

Much of the existing literature, when it is not devoted to a narrative reconstruction of national industrial unions, concentrates on the problems of ideology and theory. However, one of the cardinal features of industrial unionism after 1900 was its ability to accommodate and pass through a variety of ideologies, none of which ever succeeded in dominating or defining the movement as a whole. British industrial unionism was symptomatic of this trend, for it passed through no fewer than five phases with varying ideologies, even as the movement maintained an integrity all its own. I will therefore say little about the ideology of industrial unionism and will concentrate instead on the social movement of workers. Workers developed their consciousness through this social movement primarily by means of economic action

formal ideology
vs. structured
perceptions

and organization rather than formal ideology. This paper will analyze
those social structural factors that gave rise to revolutionary industrial
unionism and the way in which workers responded to them in the
course of the class struggle.

Economic Change and the Emergence of Revolutionary Industrial Unionism

After 1900, industrial workers responded to the social and economic
changes begun in the late nineteenth century by building a movement
for industrial unionism, and this movement set off a period of renewal
and progress in labor union and socialist organization. It was, in the
first instance, a reaction against the rise of corporate capitalism and the
concentration of industry. The emergence of monopolies in control of
vast industrial complexes underscored the weakness of a divided working class. The concentrated economic power of corporations and their
ability to attack existing craft unions through technological innovation
led to greater aggressiveness of employers against the labor movement.
The need for unity among workers as a precondition for the defense of
even limited economic goals was greatest in the United States and
Germany, where monopolization had advanced furthest, but even in a
country like France, where small-scale production was still predominant, the labor union movement felt the need for the unity of workers
across craft lines. Especially in France, the active intervention of the
state on the side of corporate capital before 1914 reinforced the advocates of a more industrially unified labor union movement. But the
factor of repressive state intervention in strikes was apparent throughout the advanced capitalist countries. Loosely federated unions of craft
workers, which organized only small groups of workers, if indeed any,
in the new mass production industries and which left uncontested the
control of management over the mass of unskilled workers, were no
match for the state-backed resistance of employers.[2]

The growth of large-scale, monopolized industry challenged the
traditional, craft-based labor union movement by undermining or
eliminating the base of unions of skilled tradesmen. This occurred
either through the dequalification of previously skilled labor, through
the creation of entirely new, technologically advanced industries and
factories that relied from the start primarily on unskilled and semiskilled labor, or through the concentration of capital in industries, such
as construction, in which a plethora of craft unions began to face
larger, more powerful employers and unified employers' associations.[3]
Advocacy of industrial unionism was everywhere a reaction to the
inability of the traditional craft unions to defend workers in the newer
industries and to the refusal of these unions to go beyond the defense

of the privileged position of small groups of skilled workers at the expense of the unskilled and the labor movement as a whole. Where monopolized industry was most advanced and the refusal of the existing unions to organize the unskilled most blatant (in Germany, the United States, and the Canadian West) this reaction took the form of a rejection of craft unionism altogether. In France and Britain, where the labor movement had longer traditions, attempts at compromise solutions were made—in Britain, the amalgamation of craft unions and the creation of general unions alongside them; in France, the peaceful transformation of the CGT from local craft-based unions to industrial federations. In both cases, the industrial unification of the working class presupposed the superseding of the existing unions.

Moreover, by the early twentieth century, the state responded to industrialization and labor unrest by attempting to integrate the existing unions into the capitalist system. In addition to overt repression, the state began to experiment with "more subtle forms of social control" including collective bargaining, conciliation schemes, state welfare measures, and union recognition.[4] Some employers and especially liberal state officials began to see the value of defusing worker discontent by recognizing the existing labor unions. In turn, many leaders of the established craft unions eagerly pursued the limited opportunities that opened up in this direction before 1914 and agreed to suppress traditional forms of union struggle and solidarity, such as the sympathetic strike, in exchange for a promise of nationally negotiated contracts and state arbitration services. The incipient integration and bureaucratization of unions in state welfare and collective bargaining institutions led to some material improvements for workers but also to a widening gap between workers and union members on the local level and to an increasingly centralized national union leadership. Industrial unionists reacted to this trend after 1900 by seizing on local dissatisfaction, by appealing to the traditions of militancy and solidarity that many skilled workers still supported, and by trying to organize the mass of unskilled workers, who were largely left out of the new arrangements among state, union leadership, and employers.[5]

All three trends—the concentration and centralization of capital, the undermining of unions of skilled craftsmen, and the reformist intervention of the state—were well under way before 1914. However, it was really the First World War that brought home how pervasive such changes were becoming. To fight the war, the military relied first and foremost on the cooperation of monopolized concerns; the pressures of armaments production and labor shortages undermined the base of traditional craft unions by rapidly diluting skilled labor; and the state, even in Germany, was forced to intervene in labor disputes to arbitrate settlements and recognize national union leaders. All the many little and not so little changes of the previous decades had culminated in undeniably qualitative changes in the functioning of the capitalist system and in the nature of industrial wage labor.[6]

The moves of the state toward intervention, both repressively on the side of corporations in labor disputes and co-optively in social welfare measures, also exposed the political weakness of the labor movement. It did not appear possible to the advocates of industrial unionism after 1900 to break the combined power of the state and employers through parliamentary reform. Nor were they satisfied with the new forms of social control that tamed the existing unions by incorporating reformist laborism into the welfare state. The new industrial unionists were not usually hostile to political action as such. In Germany, they remained active in the political parties, first in the Sozialdemokratische Partei Deutschlands (Social Democratic Party of Germany) (SPD) and later in the Unabhängige Sozialdemokratische Partei Deutschlands (Independent Social Democratic Party of Germany) (USPD), Kommunistische Partei Deutschlands (Communist Party of Germany) (KPD), and Kommunistische Arbeiter-Partei Deutschlands (Communist Workers' Party of Germany) (KAPD); in Great Britain, the organizers of the general unions were early supporters of various socialist parties, in the United States, the ALU and IWW were at first closely associated with socialist politics; in Canada, the OBU was led by members of the Socialist Party of Canada; even in France many socialists were active in the CGT and were probably numerically larger than the syndicalists who controlled the national organization. However, if the difficulties of organizing unskilled workers pushed industrial unionists to support a revolutionary socialist goal, the limitations of parliamentary parties convinced them that political action was insufficient either to defend the short-term economic interests of industrial workers or to achieve the long-range socialization of industry. Parliamentary social democrats ignored the positive role of economic militancy and tended to divide labor unionism from politics through a doctrine of economic determinism.[7]

Industrial unionists added an economic component to socialist revolution. They saw industrial militancy, in the form of direct economic action, as a necessary aspect of the revolutionary takeover of capitalist industry, alongside the overthrow of the bourgeois state, and they assigned to revolutionary labor unions the tasks of transforming capitalist production and organizing socialist industry after the revolution. The addition of an economic component to socialist revolution was the defining feature of all forms of the new industrial unionism. From the cooperative workshop control envisioned by the CGT to the IWW's projected administration of socialist production through industrial unions, to the works councils of German revolutionary unionism after the First World War, general unions on the workshop, factory, and industrial levels were elevated to a position equal to and occasionally above political parties in the revolutionary socialist movement.[8] The new unionists called for the economic solidarity of all workers, which in its most rigorous form culminated in attempts to create "one big union" of all workers. The preponderant power of corporations and the state, which circumscribed the possibilities of economic reform, also led the new unionists to tie the immediate defense of economic interests to a revolutionary economic goal and to see industrial unions as the most appropriate vehicle with which to oppose employers. Finally, the primitive organization and lack of union traditions among unorganized unskilled workers in the new mass production industries encouraged demands for all-inclusive general and industrial unions. Industrial workers reacted to monopolized industry, craft unionism, and the limitations of socialist politics and made a positive attempt to develop new forms of unionism and industrial economic action.

International Similarities and National Differences

Although industrial unionism after 1900 was an international phenomenon, it varied according to different national conditions. There were many instances of industrial unionist ideas being spread directly from one country to another through seamen and labor unionists in port cities, through the international contacts of labor leaders, or through Europeans who carried such ideas back to Europe after a period of activity in North America.[9] However, the spread of industrial unionism only became possible because workers and labor unionists were receptive to foreign ideas. More important, even without foreign influences, forms of industrial unionism developed directly from conditions in each country. Industrial unionism was international in scope after 1900 because of similar conditions throughout the advanced capitalist world.[10]

The movements for industrial unionism in the United States and Britain are familiar to English-speaking audiences, as is the history of the CGT. The Canadian OBU and the German *Arbeiter-Unionen* are less well known; but knowledge of both is crucial in understanding the full range of industrial union movements. Both were founded immediately after the First World War at the crest of working-class radicalism growing out of the wartime experience. The Canadian OBU was founded by labor unionists in the western provinces in opposition to the conservative domination of the established unions by the numerically larger eastern provinces. Its growth was encouraged by the general strike in Winnipeg in 1919 and by strike movements in the extractive and transportation industries of the West. Economically, the OBU was based on an alliance of the unskilled in mining, transportation, and lumber (industries opened up in the West at the end of the nineteenth century) with skilled workers in the rail and metal shops of Winnipeg; organizationally, the OBU leveled the craft distinctions of existing unions to build a broad, unified union of all workers; tactically, it favored militant actions based on mass strikes and worker solidarity; and, politically, it rejected the moderate parliamentarism of eastern unionists in favor of a mixture of socialist politics and advocacy of the general strike. The German *Arbeiter-Unionen* were very similar to the OBU in terms of their economic base, unified organization, militant tactics, and radical politics. Like the OBU, the German *Unionen* started as breakaways from the established unions (primarily the social democratic miners, metal-workers, construction workers, textile workers, and transportation workers unions) before taking on a more positive life of their own. The distinctive features of these unions included their base in the most important centers of German industry and mining (the Ruhr and Lower Rhineland, North Sea ports, Berlin, Middle Germany, and Upper Silesia), their transformation of the works councils movement into the organizational base of industrial unionism, and their extremely close ties to political parties, especially their membership in the Red International of Labor Unions (RILU) and their alliance with the KPD. In addition, many revolutionary industrial unionists in Germany remained active in the established unions and had strong bases of support in some industries, like chemicals, where they favored strong, locally unified, factory-based industrial unions while refusing to affiliate with the independent *Arbeiter-Unionen*. More will be said about the specifics of the OBU and *Arbeiter-Unionen*, but even a brief description serves to point out the similarities in the industrial union movements after 1900 across national boundaries.[11]

Nevertheless, each country produced its own version or versions of revolutionary industrial unionism, and it would be misleading to define the general movement by one model. Rather, there emerged a range of options with related fundamental assumptions, and these options can be analyzed according to a scale of tendencies within the movement. Such a scale can be established according to three major criteria: the period of industrialization and its effect on labor union organization, the type of economic organization adopted in each country to meet national conditions, and the attitude of industrial unionists toward political affiliation.

Industrial Unionism and Industrialization The first major division among industrial unionists can be traced to the period of each country's industrialization and the age of its labor movement. Although some authors have seen the differentiation between industrial unionists as one between Europe and North America,[12] in fact the division occurred between those countries where the labor movement had already been strongly developed in the mid-nineteenth century and those where it grew primarily in response to the second wave of industrialization.[13]

In the older industrial nations with long labor histories—primarily France and Britain—industrial unionists tended to work inside the established unions. This was feasible in part because unions in these countries began to organize unskilled workers at an early date, as was the case with the new "general" unions in Britain from the late 1880s, which were quickly incorporated into the established labor union movement. Moreover, industrial concentration developed more slowly. In Britain, the craft unions adapted themselves to the slower pace of industrial change with fewer internal structural breaks, whereas in France the union movement continued the long tradition of what one historian has called the "socialism of skilled workers."[14] Although there was friction with some of the newer general and industrial unions, the older unions themselves produced strong internal movements toward amalgamation and cooperation with the new unions. Revolutionary industrial unionism developed in an environment of labor union continuity, and the industrial unionist, OBU, and syndicalist groups could act effectively as organized factions within the existing unions. In France, the syndicalists eventually won control of the CGT, having begun as only one of several factions. In Britain, the movement never coalesced into one organization but remained split among numerous radical groups (syndicalists, amalgamationists, industrial unionists, and shop stewards—most of which sought to transform the craft unions) and the general unions (all of which were founded under radical leadership).[15]

In the countries that industrialized largely after 1870—the United States, Canada, and Germany—revolutionary industrial unionism tended persistently toward dual unionism. In these countries industrial concentration, the growth of mass production industries, technological changes, and corporate control all developed in largely virgin territory, preceding, superseding, or breaking whatever labor union traditions had previously existed. In Germany monopolization and industrial concentration were already far advanced when the modern German union movement was founded in the 1890s; in the United States during the period from 1873 to 1900 these same economic forces disrupted the continuity of those older labor union traditions that culminated and then withered away with the Knights of Labor; in Canada the economy of the West grew largely outside of the industrial and union traditions of the East. Thus, in all these countries the gap between craft unions and unskilled workers in the new industries was great, and the craft unions widened the gap by retrenching in the face of corporate capital to defend the special interests of the skilled rather than by adapting union structures to technological changes or by organizing the unskilled. Moreover, in Germany the socialist movement was founded before the labor unions, and the unions were consequently very closely associated from the start with social democratic politics, another aspect of the late, technologically advanced industrialization of Germany. As a result, the movement for industrial unionism grew out of opposition to the subordinate, reformist role to which social democratic politics had relegated the unions.[16] In all these countries, the impact of corporate industrialism was paramount in demonstrating the obsolescence of craft unionism and the need for an entirely new type of union. "Boring from within" appeared—and indeed largely was—futile, and industrial unionists drew the conclusion that new unions had to be created in competition with the craft unions.[17]

Organization The movement for industrial unionism was also characterized by different types of economic organization. Six major types (or degrees) of organization can be delineated.

1. Single local unions comprising all workers in one factory or local industry—what the Germans call a *Betriebsorganisation*—were most commonly breakaway unions that attempted prematurely to reorganize existing unions before union members and workers in other areas were ready to follow the lead of the vanguard. They were founded primarily in Germany after the 1918–19 revolution; they were usually closely aligned with political radicalism (with the KPD or KAPD); and they seceded from existing craft unions because of differences over strike tactics, politics, and industrial organization.[18]

2. Single industrial unions of a national scope were a step beyond revolutionary localism. They were most common in the United

States as an attempt to overcome craft union divisions by uniting all workers in concentrated industries. Thus, Eugene Debs's American Railway Union attempted to bring together all railway and rail shop workers into a single industrial front, while the Western Federation of Miners (WFM) completely bypassed eastern craft unionism by organizing western miners from the start in an industrial union. The British amalgamation movement also worked for the creation of this type of unified industrial union.[19]

3.   Once industrial unionism expanded to several industries or became a more general movement, there appeared a natural tendency to form national union organizations to cover labor in all industries. The classic solution was found by the CGT in France. The CGT subdivided its national federation into a dual organization, horizontally (by geography) as a general union of all workers (united in *unions locales* and *unions départementales*) and vertically by industrial federations. To be sure, the CGT's *unions* were local trades and labor assemblies in which member unions were represented. However, the *unions* originally grew out of the *bourses du travail*, in which union divisions as such had not been recognized; they were never merely federated bodies but have always had a general role and legitimacy of their own over and above individual member unions; and they have consistently acted as the center and mobilizer of the local union movement with an economic and organizational position that goes well beyond the local union federations of the Anglo-Saxon countries or Germany. Thus, the CGT functions in part as "one big union" but also as a federation of autonomous industrial unions.[20]

4.   A second, more radical solution to national organization was adopted by the IWW. Largely because of the concentrated power of American monopoly capital, the IWW wanted to create a centralized union on the national level (as opposed to the CGT's federal organization), which could confront the centralized power of capital. The central union would be subdivided into industrial unions to defend the specific interests of workers in each major industry and to prepare for the eventual takeover of production by the revolutionary unions.[21]

5.   German-American Wobblies carried the IWW model directly to Germany, but once in the German environment of monopolized heavy industry and postwar revolution they reinterpreted this model in an even more centralized manner. Both the *Allgemeine Arbeiter-Union* (General Workers Union) (which was strongest in the North Sea ports and the steel industry of Düsseldorf) and the *Union der Hand- und Kopfarbeiter* (Union of Manual and Intellectual Workers) (which grew out of coal mining and iron and steel production in the Ruhr and

Upper Silesia) placed emphasis on a single, central union of all workers. Such unions were based on works councils, elected by all workers
in each factory or mine in the major monopolized industries, and
attracted lesser categories of workers to this industrial core.[22]
    6.   Nevertheless, the German *Arbeiter-Unionen* maintained sub-
ordinate industrial subdivisions, although they were not given separate
status as industrial unions until forced to by the KPD and Red International of Labor Unions (RILU) in 1924. Revolutionary unionists in
Canada carried centralized organization to its logical extreme by
founding the One Big Union in 1919. All workers were organized in
one union without regard to craft or industry, either in mixed locals or
in central labor councils in larger towns. To be sure, there were strong
movements for separate industrial unions within the OBU, especially
among lumber workers in British Columbia and Northern Ontario.
However, the core of the OBU recognized only general local unions
more radically leveled than, but not unlike, the *unions locales* of the
CGT.[23]
    Important as these differences in national organization were, it
should be remembered that all industrial union movements tried to
balance centralized structures with active local union bodies. For example, an initial step in the formation of amalgamated or original industrial unions in Britain and the United States was often the creation of
shop committees that either represented all unions in an enterprise or
all workers whether unionized or not. The election of shop stewards to
represent all workers in their department was another first step in the
direction of industrial unionism. Shop committees and the organization of shop stewards for the entire factory tended to grow out of strike
movements and became especially prominent in Britain, Germany,
and the United States during the First World War.[24]
    In Germany, the *Arbeiter-Unionen* took earlier forms of labor
union organization, such as the traditional union *Vertrauensmänner*
(liaisons between workers in the factory and union officials), and
generalized them throughout the factory or mine. They also built upon
the shop committees and bodies of shop stewards that grew out of
wartime economic movements by making them part of the structure of
industrial unions. These forms of shop organization were then coordinated with the works councils that workers formed spontaneously
during the revolution of 1918–19. Indeed, *Vertrauensmänner*, shop
committees, and shop stewards were usually the infrastructure out of
which the works councils grew and upon which they built their
strength. The result was a multi-tiered structure within each enterprise
and industry in which all workers were represented. While the union

Vertrauensmänner, shop committees, and shop stewards tended to perpetuate separate representation of skilled and unskilled workers, the works councils represented all workers within an enterprise equally, regardless of skill. When the works councils were regularized after passage of the Works Councils Law of 1920, the *Arbeiter-Unionen* turned their legally elected works councilors into the permanent base and local leadership of their industrial union organization. The novelty of such organization was that it simultaneously equated the union with the factory or mine, through the works councils, *and* integrated the councils into regional or national unions that comprised entire industries. In the event of and in preparation for a revolution such industrial unions were poised to seize control of both local factories and mines and entire industries and to administer both in a socialized economy. The unity of these organizational structures was summed up in the slogan of German revolutionary industrial unionists: one enterprise, one industry, one union (*ein Betrieb, eine Industrie, eine Gewerkschaft*). Thus, if centralization was the key issue of national union organization and the main area of differences from country to country, shop committees, shop stewards, and works councils emerged as the infrastructure of revolutionary industrial unionism and showed greater similarities across national boundaries.[25]

The reasons for national differences in the organization of industrial union movements were varied and complex, and only the most important can be suggested here. First, despite similar international economic trends, there were many social and economic differences between countries. The different pace of industrialization between Britain and France, on the one hand, and Germany, the United States, and Canada, on the other, has already been mentioned and helps to explain the different organizational strategies of industrial unionists in these two groups of countries. In particular, the greater the concentration of ownership in industry and the larger the scale of production, the greater the emphasis on more centralized forms of organization and especially the greater the propensity to found unified national organizations of the OBU type rather than looser union federations. The movements in France and Germany can be seen as contrasting examples. In France, the persistence of more small-scale production lay at the foundation of the *bourses du travail*, which in turn grew into the *unions locales* within a strongly federalized system of autonomous industrial unions; while in Germany the extreme concentration and centralization of heavy industry in a few major areas encouraged the formation of the highly centralized and unified organization of *Arbeiter-Unionen*. Second, national labor traditions contributed to some organizational differences. Thus, in Britain traditions of solidarity among skilled workers transcended craft unionism and lay at the base of much of the amalgamationist and shop stewards' movements; these traditions help to explain the British interest in reorganizing or building individual unions rather than founding a central or national OBU-type organization. In the United States the legacy of the Knights of Labor, a training ground and example for many later industrial unionists, established a model of all-inclusive national unionism that the IWW later tried to modernize in light of industrial changes since the late nineteenth century. Finally, the date of the founding of industrial union movements seems to have had some influence in the choice of organizational forms. The earliest movements tended to create single unions (such as the American Railway Union in the United States or the general unions in Britain) or to concentrate on the transformation of existing unions (as in both Britain and France), while the most centralized and consciously OBU movements (those of Germany and Canada) were founded in the aftermath of World War I. Thus, the years 1900–1925 might be characterized as a cumulative learning process on an international scale: industrial unionists after 1918 drew from the experience and ideas of the pioneers of the years 1900–1910 and consciously set out to found the OBU in its purest forms. The IWW was a sort of middle type both chronologically and organizationally, and its role in the transition from earlier individual industrial unions to the more centralized OBU and *Arbeiter-Unionen* can be clearly documented. On the one hand, earlier movements, like the American Railway Union (ARU) and the Western Federation of Miners (WFM) fed indirectly or directly into the IWW: on the other hand, the IWW was a direct predecessor of the OBU in Canada (the IWW was also a Canadian union before 1914) and a recognized precursor of the *Arbeiter-Unionen* and even a training ground for some individual union organizers in Germany. These examples illustrate some of the more important reasons for organizational differences among industrial union movements and point to the complexity of national differences within international similarities.

Politics and Industrial Unionism The movement for revolutionary industrial unionism exhibited a variety of attitudes toward socialist and labor politics, ranging from rejection of political parties to subordination to a vanguard party.

The industrial unionists of the period after 1900 are often considered to have been opposed to political parties, and this was indeed true of the syndicalists. The CGT, of course, came out openly against

political parties, and the OBU in Canada later adopted a similar position, although it is questionable whether these organizations did so out
of a general repudiation of political socialism or because they wanted to
prevent the disruption of union work by hostile political factions.[26] Still,
the antiparty position of the CGT and OBU merely defined one
extreme and by no means the general sentiment of industrial unionists.
The IWW, for instance, declared its political neutrality in order to
concentrate its efforts on economic action and organization. It wanted
to elevate the importance of industrial action within the revolutionary
movement, but it did not oppose the participation of individual Wobblies in socialist politics. No less a leader than William Haywood made
this point clear.[27] In Britain early leaders of the general unions and in
France and Germany left-wing socialists (and later communists) actively favored the participation of union leaders in labor and socialist
politics.[28] Germany, finally, produced the two most conscious and organized versions of union participation in left-wing politics. In Hamburg,
the *Allgemeine Arbeiter-Union* advocated the creation of what was called
an *Einheitsorganisation*, a single organization of workers, based on the
factory, which united political and economic work in one body. Labor
unions and political party were surpassed by integrating their functions in a single revolutionary organization.[29] The *Union der Hand- und
Kopfarbeiter*, on the other hand, formally endorsed the KPD, belonged
to the Red International of Labor Unions, and eventually (in 1923–24)
came under complete Communist Party control.[30] The syndicalists of
the CGT opposed political parties out of fear that a Marxist party
would win control of and then subordinate the unions and thus hinder
the revolutionary direct action of workers. The counterparts of the
French syndicalists in the revolutionary *Arbeiter-Unionen* of Germany
interpreted the needs of the revolutionary movement in exactly the
opposite way by affiliating with the KPD or KAPD as the necessary
precondition of furthering both the economic and political sides of the
class struggle. In both cases, national conditions determined the options open to revolutionary unionists. Whereas in France the disunity
and divisiveness of the socialist movement made the political neutrality
of the CGT imperative for its successful functioning, in Germany the
long traditions of revolutionary Marxism and the outbreak of a political revolution in 1918 made political commitment seem just as
imperative.

What was common to the political stance of all revolutionary
industrial unionists was not hostility toward political parties as such but
rather a position critical of the dominant wing of labor and social
democratic parties before 1914 and the advocacy of industrial mili-

tancy as a necessary part of the revolutionary class struggle. In particular, revolutionary industrial unionists in general disagreed with the increasing concentration of labor and social democratic parties on parliamentary politics. The corollary of such an electoral strategy was that the workers' movement adhered strictly to bourgeois legality even in countries like Germany, where no democratic system existed, and avoided potentially violent confrontations with the state. Moderate unionism, building upon existing craft unions and restricting tactics to the proven methods of craft union organization and action, was a necessary part of such a strategy. In response, industrial unionists argued—correctly—that electoralism and moderate unionism alone would not bring the mass of unorganized unskilled workers into the labor movement and that the organization of the unskilled would lead ineluctably to major confrontations with the biggest industrialists and through them, the state. The revolutionaries within the industrial union movement went one step further and tried to seize upon the opportunity offered by unionizing the unskilled to build a challenge to the capitalist system as a whole. Some carried this strategy to the extreme of thinking that seizure of the economy was alone sufficient to overthrow capitalism and that the organization of industrial unions was alone sufficient to seize the economy. But a more common position by far was that a militant economic strategy would be complementary to socialist politics. If industrial unionists concentrated their energies on economic organization, it was because they were labor unionists, first and foremost, who wanted to correct the imbalance in the socialist workers' movement, not because they were antipolitical or because they underestimated the role of the state.

In conclusion, it is misleading to define one big unionism or revolutionary industrial unionism according to a single, exclusive model. Though an international phenomenon, it manifested itself concretely in direct relation to national conditions and traditions. The process of industrialization and union traditions were clearly important in deciding the receptiveness of workers to dual unionism. The relative maturity and degree of general support for the movement determined the type of local or national organization that could be created, although in terms of economic organization one can speak of a definite tendency toward "one big unionism." Finally, political traditions—whether of divisiveness (France, Canada and the United States), parliamentary politics (Britain), or revolutionary Marxism (Germany)—affected the attitude of industrial unionists to political parties. The internationalism of the movement grew out of similar economic conditions in the advanced capitalist countries, the critique of social democratic politics, and the common desire to organize unskilled workers in industrial unions, but the specific response of workers in each country varied among numerous alternatives and nuances.

Was Revolutionary Industrial Unionism "Syndicalist"?

Because of the antipolitical position of the CGT and its imitators in other countries, most historians have labeled the revolutionary industrial unionism of the early twentieth century "syndicalist" without necessarily giving this word a precise definition. The syndicalists of the CGT, of course, won adoption of a coherent syndicalist philosophy in the charter of the union. But elsewhere the case is not nearly so clear-cut.

Most historians of the IWW have labeled it "syndicalist" despite the fact that Wobbly leaders consistently called themselves industrial unionists and distinguished themselves from syndicalists. Indeed, the most dedicated syndicalists, like William Z. Foster, left or drifted away from the IWW because of differences of opinion over organization and tactics.[31] Moreover, David Montgomery calls the industrial unrest of the period 1909–22 "syndicalist" without defining what he means by this term or how avowed syndicalists fit into the movement.[32] The major historians of the Canadian OBU repeatedly call this union a Canadian version of syndicalism, but nowhere do they show how the OBU was syndicalist or why this term is specifically relevant in this case. They could easily have left off the label without affecting their overall analysis of the OBU.[33] In Germany, social democrats have traditionally accused the KPD and its left-wing unions of being "syndicalist," but in this case the purpose is patently propagandistic and based upon no analysis of the communist *Arbeiter-Unionen*.[34] In fact, there was a syndicalist union in Germany that briefly won mass support from miners and steelworkers in the Ruhr,[35] but this union failed to keep pace with mass sentiment for revolutionary industrial unionism and was quickly superseded by the communist *Freie Arbeiter-Union (Gelsenkirchen)* and *Union der Hand- und Kopfarbeiter*.[36] Finally, Bob Holton, in an analysis of British syndicalism in the period 1910–14, tries to extend the use of this term from uncontestably syndicalist organizations to the mass industrial insurgency and general labor unrest before 1914.[37] Whereas syndicalists were probably the most influential group of revolutionary industrial unionists in Britain from 1910 to 1914, this had not always been the case, and syndicalist influence declined once again after 1914, in favor of a variety of other organized groups of shop stewards and industrial unionists.

It is necessary first to define what one means by "syndicalism" before one can decide its applicability to revolutionary industrial unionism. Melvyn Dubofsky has offered a general definition that underlies the judgment of many historians. He refers to "syndicalism" as a form of industrial militancy among workers at the point of production that is directed at the takeover and running of industry by the workers themselves, outside the control or influence of political parties.[38] In my opinion, this definition is too narrow. It describes revolutionary industrial unionism in general but not what was specifically (and vocally) advocated by syndicalists, and it applies equally to explicitly nonsyndicalist movements such as works councils and shop stewards.

There are five distinguishing features of syndicalism that must be included in any definition. First, syndicalism favored federalism over central forms of organization and thus emphasized local autonomy. It opposed political parties and replaced political work with economic action and organization. Its supreme revolutionary strategy was the general economic strike, not the overthrow of the bourgeois state. After the general strike, workers would abolish the political state altogether and replace it with a federal, economic organization of society. Finally, this new social organization would be based on *syndicats* (hence the name of the movement), basic local units derived from the structure of craft and industry. Although many syndicalists supported industrial unions, industrial unionism itself was never a universally accepted part of syndicalist philosophy, and many syndicalists continued to envision the *syndicats* of the new society as craft-based (not industry-based) units.[39] And revolutionary industrial unionists, though often in agreement with individual syndicalist positions, never generally accepted the syndicalist philosophy as a whole.

A short digression on the terminology of the labor movement might be instructive at this point. The real terminological unity of the international movement for industrial unionism was not in the use of "syndicalism," but in the use of "unionism" in a new, specific sense. In English, "union" can have two meanings in the labor movement: the first and most common refers to labor unionism in general, whether craft, trade, or industrial, while the second sense denotes the unification of all workers in a single, general organization. This second meaning was that of the OBU after 1900. In French, these meanings are rendered by different words. *Syndicalisme*—not to be confused with *syndicalisme révolutionnaire*, which is usually translated into English simply as "syndicalism"—means labor unionism in general. At the same time the CGT calls its subordinate geographic units *unions locales* and *unions départementales*, bodies that unite all workers without regard to trade or industry, analogous to the OBU of Anglo-Saxon countries. In German, the distinction of meanings is even more explicit. The general term for labor unions in German is *Gewerkschaft*, whereas *Verband* refers to concrete individual unions. *Union*, on the other hand, is a foreign word imported directly from the English after 1918 to denote the OBU. Hence, one speaks in general of the *freie Gewerkschaften* or concretely of the *Deutscher Metallarbeiter-Verband*. But the German counterparts of the OBU were called the *Bergarbeiter-Union*, the *Freie Arbeiter-Union*, the *Allgemeine Arbeiter-Union* and the *Union der Hand- und Kopfarbeiter*. *Unionismus*, not *Syndikalismus*, was the name of the new movement. "Union" is the common international expression of the movement, and one should speak of "Unionism" (with a capital "U") instead of "syndicalism."

If one accepts this definition of terms, syndicalism was only one of several factions within a general movement in favor of industrial unionism. Only in a few albeit major cases like the CGT was this faction predominant, but in the other countries it remained one relatively small tendency among several others. What is really at issue is a movement in favor of revolutionary industrial unionism that arose under specific social, economic, and political conditions after 1900. The term "syndicalism" does not accurately describe this movement.

Bob Holton, although he prefers to call the movement syndicalist or proto-syndicalist, is on the right track when he makes an important distinction between the movement of unrest among industrial workers and the organized groups that tried to lead and influence it.[40] For there is a logical and historical difference between the two that is obscured and confused when one tries to render both as "syndicalist."

For example, Holton calls the mass strikes in Britain between 1910 and 1914 "proto-syndicalist," above and beyond any involvement of committed syndicalist militants. By "proto-syndicalist" he means the unofficial, insurgent, and expansive nature of many of the strikes in mining, transportation, or engineering. In such movements, which union leaders had difficulty containing, Holton points to the "primary importance of direct action over parliamentary pressures as a means of settling grievances, the desirability of industrial solidarity between workers in different industries, and above all at this stage the need for rank-and-file control over industrial policy."[41] He also emphasizes mass support for industrial unionism to oppose employers and further workers' control and to mass sentiment against the union leadership in favor of periodic union elections and the recall of union leaders.

The interesting aspect of Holton's description of British strikes is not their syndicalism but rather their similarity to expansive wildcat strikes in other countries between 1910 and 1925. His description of the water transport, dockers, and railway strikes of 1911, for example, could easily be transferred to the wildcat strikes in Rhineland-Westphalia from 1918 to 1924, and the fluid, flexible relationship of radical leaders and militants to the spontaneous mass unrest was fundamentally the same in Germany as in the earlier strikes in Britain. Yet in Germany, the unofficial movements tended to come under communist leadership. Workers turned to the KPD as the largest, best organized, and most prominent radical force in Germany to give the movement coordination.[42] Just as syndicalists increased their influence in Britain in the years 1910–14, so communists entered the German strike wave as propagandists, agitators, and organizers. But it would be just as wrong to call the German strikes "communist" as it is to call the British ones "syndicalist." What is common to both is the kind of mass unrest and the insurgent, industrial aspect of workers' direct action. National traditions, economic and political conditions, and the general options open to the revolutionary left determined why the influence of syndicalists was on the rise in Britain before 1914 but that of communists more important after the Bolshevik revolution and the founding of the Comintern. But the *mass movement* is the interesting feature of such strikes. This and the relation of organized left-wing groups to it, that is, the structure of such movements, were fundamentally similar in both examples, although the ideologies of syndicalists and communists were themselves different.

All the factions that actively worked for industrial unionism took the raw material of industrial unrest and tried to raise the lessons drawn from it to the level of theory and tactics. They seized in the first instance on the economic grievances of workers, which preceded any coherent political consciousness. These immediate grievances tended to be localized in scope and encouraged opposition to state policies and national union leaders. And such discontent, as it grew, focused quite naturally on the local control of production by workers. Finally, mass unrest tended more and more often to take the form of wildcat strikes as the most effective way to break through the containment policies of the state and national union leaders. And under unstable social and economic conditions (more to be said of this further on), such wildcat strikes expanded spontaneously both geographically and from industry to industry until they took on increasingly general proportions. Not only syndicalists but revolutionary industrial unionists, councils activists, and communists developed their tactics in different, even opposing, directions from the same mass movement of social unrest.

One of the cardinal features of the industrial unrest and the movement in favor of industrial unionism from 1900 to 1925 was the convergence of three forces. After 1900, individual union militants and activists, formal left-wing organizations and propagandist groups, and mass unrest among industrial workers all converged in a general movement in favor of industrial unionism. The role of left-wing organizations lent the movement its revolutionary ideology; the participation of union activists, whether or not members of left-wing organizations, established a vital link between revolutionaries and unions; and the unrest of industrial workers provided the mass force to sustain and extend the movement. This was a real social movement in which the initially spontaneous industrial action of workers (mostly in strikes) opened the way for leaders and militants, and in which industrial workers themselves joined slowly in more organized forms of industrial unionism and direct action as they responded to the leadership and propaganda of union militants. To call this convergence of factors "syndicalist" is to miss the historical forces at work and to replace a process of change and revitalization in the labor movement with an arbitrary (and partisan) definition. Specific groups tried to give organization, leadership, and ideological coherence to this movement among rank-and-file workers, but they could never contain it entirely within one doctrine or organization, whether syndicalist or otherwise.

The Social Composition of Revolutionary Industrial Unionism

The international nature of this movement among workers is revealed by the social composition of workers who supported it or whose industrial militancy served as a spur or context for industrial union militants. Two groups of workers were especially prominent in strikes that led to demands for industrial organization. Unskilled workers in new or rapidly expanding industries were the most visible and characteristic supporters of the movement. Nevertheless, a significant number of skilled, traditionally unionized workers, usually in large industrial settings subjected to technological change, turned to industrial unionism as it became apparent that defense of union standards and adaptation to changes in production required the additional support of the mass of unskilled and semiskilled workers.

By far the most common supporters of revolutionary industrial unionism were miners. Hard-rock miners in the American West formed the core of the WFM, WLU (Western Labor Union), ALU and early IWW in the United States, and hard-rock and coal miners were prominent in both the IWW and OBU in Canada. Syndicalists first won mass influence in Britain among Welsh miners, and the continuing unrest among British miners after 1910 provided a context for the agitation of a variety of radical, industrial union groups. In France, syndicalists won support from miners around Saint Etienne. In Germany, coal miners in the Ruhr, and to a lesser extent in Upper Silesia and Middle Germany, formed the backbone of the *Union der Hand- und Kopfarbeiter* and provided the extensive mass support that made both the KPD and revolutionary one big unionism major economic forces in this most basic and politically sensitive German industry.[43]

Workers in a variety of mass production industries and transportation joined the movement for industrial unionism or responded to the agitation of revolutionary unions. The specific industries varied largely according to the economic structure of each country. After mining, transportation was the most frequent setting of militant strikes and industrial union agitation. Railroad workers were drawn into the movement to a greater or lesser extent in all five countries; dockers supported the movement in parts of the United States, British Columbia, Britain, and Germany; British, American, and German seamen also joined the movement at different times, often carrying revolutionary industrial union propaganda from country to country.[44]

Textile workers in the American East gave support to the IWW, while German textile workers in the region around Mönchen-Gladbach formed a secondary source of support for the *Union der Hand- und Kopfarbeiter* in Rhineland-Westphalia. Also typical of support for the IWW in the eastern United States were the new mass production industries that were later organized by the Congress of Industrial Organizations (CIO): The IWW at its height led major strikes in the steel, rubber, and automobile industries. In Germany, the comparable mass production industries were to be found in the heavy industries developed from 1895 to 1918: Virtually every major steel mill in the Ruhr, the shipbuilding centers of Hamburg and Bremen, and all the big centers of chemical production (especially Leverkusen, Ludwigshafen, and Leuna) supported either one big unionism or revolutionary industrial unionism in one form or another. In Great Britain, the general workers' unions organized the unskilled in these same mass production industries, especially in the period of labor unrest from 1910 to 1920. Lumber, wood, and agriculture formed another center of support where these industries were relevant, that is , in the Canadian West, northern Ontario, the American West and South, and Middle Germany. Indeed, the IWW was perhaps most successful in organizing the lumber industry and migratory agricultural laborers; the strongest group in the Canadian OBU was at first the industrial union of lumber workers; and one of the constituent organizations of the *Union der Hand- und Kopfarbeiter* was the communist *Freier Landarbeiterverband* of Middle Germany.[45]

Common to all these industries were their creation or general expansion in the late nineteenth and early twentieth century and their reliance on vast pools of unskilled, often migratory or immigrant, labor. Unskilled, immigrant, and migratory workers were connected by their common difficulties in organizing unions and the type of union they needed. Unskilled workers in the new mass production industries were easily trained and just as easily replaced, and, as long as there was a steady oversupply of workers (as was generally the case, except at peak periods of demand for labor or in exceptional local circumstances), the unskilled lacked an individual possession (such as a skill) that could be used in bargaining against employers. The steady oversupply of unskilled workers came to a very great extent from immigrants, either from foreign countries or from internal migrations from rural to urban areas. In fact, the role of foreign immigrant workers in supplying unskilled labor was greater than is often assumed; it was by no means limited to the United States and Canada but was of considerable importance in several major industrial regions of Germany and was also a factor in areas of France.[46] By the same token, migratory workers were easily replaced, and while they tended to face smaller, scattered employers (as in agriculture or lumber) than industrial workers, their geographic dispersal, isolation, atomization, and lack of a permanent local base served to strengthen the hand of capital. To be organized at all, such workers had to adopt some form of industrial organization that would comprise all workers in the factory or workplace. The weakness of individual unskilled workers, the concentrated economic power of corporations in many industries, and the atomization and geographic dispersal of migratory workers made the concentration of worker power in industrial unions a precondition for achieving even limited economic goals. Only by organizing all workers in factory and industry could unions hope to control the supply of labor sufficiently to be able to stand up to employers.

The power of corporations was underscored by the industrial settings involved: the list of industrial workers who supported revolutionary industrial unionism and one big unionism contains a disproportionate number who worked in one-industry or company towns where individual corporations or employers' associations controlled economic life. Coal mining, steel, textiles, and chemicals in Germany, mining and lumber in the United States and Canada, coal mining in South Wales, automobiles, rubber, steel, and textiles in the American East all fall into this category. The dual power of corporations and employers' associations on the local and the national industrial level, which made it possible to suppress labor organizations, forced industrial unionists to adopt radical or revolutionary positions in favor of militant resistance to employers and the elimination of privately owned industry. Moreover, workers could and did turn the homogeneity of such towns to their own advantage. Although a dominant industry or corporation could use its immense power to keep unskilled workers atomized and to drive out the craft unions of the relatively small groups of skilled workers, union organizers themselves exploited social and economic homogeneity to make the industry as a whole the focus of the labor movement. Indeed, they went one step further. One-industry settings became a definite spur to one big unionism, a kind of unionism designed to unite all workers on the local level, most of whom worked in the same industry in any case, against the domination of the local economy by one or several large employers.

The unskilled, immigrant, and migratory background of such workers tended to blur the influence of national and indigenous working-class cultures and to underscore the common international conditions behind revolutionary industrial unions. Nevertheless, revolutionary industrial unionism was not confined to the unskilled but also appealed to at least some groups of native, unionized, skilled workers. Most craft workers did not support industrial unions; they remained loyal to the traditional craft-based unions in most advanced industrial nations. Only in France did craft workers in the CGT give their support to syndicalism in significant numbers and agree to the introduction of industrial unions even while they controlled the national union federation. Elsewhere, only very specific categories of skilled workers turned to industrial unionism, in particular, workers in metals and engineering and in construction. In France, metalworkers in Paris, Saint Etienne, and Saint Nazaire gave support to the syndicalists, and workers in metallurgy, foundries, and metal trades had organized industrial unions by 1914. In Britain, many industrial union activists, like Tom Mann, came from metals and engineering, and the amalgamation and shop stewards' movements won their greatest support in old centers of metal production and engineering.[47] The Clyde shipbuilding industry is a particularly interesting case and can be contrasted with the one big unionism of the German North Sea ports.

In Scotland, the impetus for amalgamation and the shop stewards' movement came from long unionized, skilled workers faced with the dissolution of skills during the First World War; such workers were trying to defend the traditional job control of unionized skilled workers by adapting it to changes in technology and production, in the process turning to new forms of union organization, shop committees, and workers' control. In contrast, in Germany, where unionized skilled workers lacked the power and traditions of British metalworkers, revolutionary industrial unionism after 1918 was based directly upon the semiskilled workers that German employers had relied upon to man the shipbuilding industry since the industrialization of the 1890s and 1900s. The industry was the same in both countries, but the constellation of forces behind revolutionary industrial unionism was different.[48]

Another center of support among metalworkers for revolutionary industrial unionism was in railway shops such as those in Winnipeg, the Pullman works in Chicago, and the railway repair shops in Berlin and Opladen. Such skilled workers were no longer isolated craftsmen but worked instead in concentrated industrial settings, alongside a growing number of semiskilled workers, in one of the major transportation industries. Just as railway workers were receptive to industrial unionism, railway shop workers tended to see the advantage of industrial organization.[49]

Construction workers were of secondary importance in the movement for industrial unions, although in some areas they too gave support to the movement. The construction industry was far more decentralized than the other industries in which industrial unionists were active, and much of it remained small-scale and artisan based. However, in the larger urban centers and industrial regions, many of the same trends were at work as in the metal industry. In construction especially, we are concerned with a *tendency* in economic development, not a static or absolute level of concentration. As with skilled metalworkers and engineers, the main factors encouraging industrial unionism in construction were the tendencies toward dequalification of skilled labor, greater employment of unskilled labor, and concentration of capital in larger industrial construction firms and employers' associations. Such factors, to differing degrees, were at work in the Canadian West, where mostly unskilled railway construction workers employed by railway corporations joined the IWW before 1914, and in Great Britain, where syndicalists found some support among construction workers, especially in London.[50] In Germany after 1920, the communists were able to keep most revolutionary construction workers inside the free unions.[51] However, in the Ruhr, where the construction industry was exceptionally concentrated and integrated with coal mining, engineering, and the heavy steel industry, many construction workers defied communist directives and joined the *Union der Hand- und Kopfarbeiter*.[52] In France, Parisian construction workers formed part of the core of syndicalist support, and the individual craft unions in the construction industry united to form an industrial federation between 1906 and 1914.[53]

Thus, both unskilled and skilled workers were prominent in the movements for industrial unionism before 1925, although the former predominated numerically and more often caught the public eye. Relations between these two groups of workers are difficult to assess at this stage of research. Historians have tended to investigate each group separately, concentrating on the big strikes and organizing drives of the unskilled, while linking the skilled primarily to control struggles over the production process. Indeed, wage struggles set off most of the movements of unskilled workers, while the skilled workers who supported industrial unionism tended to do so in response to the restructuring of industry, to technological innovations, and to changes in work processes—all of which tended to undermine existing craft unions by whittling away at skilled workers' immediate control of production through craft knowledge. There can be little doubt that wages were the most important concern of unskilled workers, for their atomization and economic weakness made it possible for employers to keep wages very low and to reduce them further in periods of economic crisis. Skilled workers had much more to defend than wages, and even their relatively higher wage scales were best defended indirectly by fighting for continued control over production processes. This basic division between unskilled and skilled workers found expression in the fact that the former tended to organize new unions around wage movements, while the latter were much more likely to try to salvage forms of craft control through the transformation of existing craft unions into more powerful amalgamated or industrial ones. Still, historians need to investigate possible links between the skilled and unskilled at the workplace and from there in industrial union struggles. One point, however, is clear, even at this stage of research. By 1920 large groups of unskilled workers went beyond wages to raise their own demands for worker control of production, especially through works councils or industrial union structures, while the demands of skilled workers to simplify and consolidate job categories and wage differentials in "rationalized" industries had great potential appeal for unskilled workers and spoke directly to many of their immediate concerns. It is impossible to say whether strong links betwen unskilled and skilled workers conditioned these overlapping demands, but labor historians should begin to look seriously at this possibility.[54]

The role of working-class cultures and their impact on unskilled and skilled workers in the movements for industrial unionism are even harder to discern. The new towns and neighborhoods that grew up with the mass production industries in the decades immediately before and after 1900 were the sites of an entirely new working class, one that for decades was predominantly unskilled, immigrant, and highly mobile (according to fluctuations in employment). At the same time, extremely homogeneous areas—based on one social stratum within the working class, on one industry, and often around one company—could also have a profoundly settling effect and quickly laid the bases for a new working class culture. Nevertheless, there was a strong element of social instability in the new industrial regions, very much related to immigrant labor and the mobility of workers, that existed alongside elements of social cohesion, and this combination of instability and cohesiveness led to a particularly volatile working class after 1900. It affected workers' attitudes toward both mass action and types of organization. In industrial towns with the opposite configuration—long-established industries dependent on a settled class of skilled workers, well-developed working-class cultures tied to the industrial environment, and strong traditional unions growing out of and linked closely with the culture of skilled workers—the workers' movement lacked the volatility of the new industrial regions. Many of these towns were centers of working-class radicalism, but even in one-industry towns where skilled workers were subjected to mechanization and rationalization, the workers often tended to steer clear of the revolutionary industrial unions. They preferred the slower evolution of their stable, traditional union organizations.[55]

The problem of working-class cultures becomes particularly complex when one considers those skilled workers who came to support industrial unionism. Did they live in older towns or neighborhoods but become radicalized at work because of mechanization or rationalization? Were their established routines disrupted by rapid urbanization? Did they, too, move to the newer urban, industrial regions and become subjected to many of the same cultural pressures as the unskilled? Or, even in these newer centers of industry, did they continue to live in socially homogeneous neighborhoods with other skilled workers and merely commute to work at big factory complexes where their fellow workers were mostly unskilled or semiskilled? From what is known of the skilled workers who supported industrial unionism, all these possibilities were true of at least some groups, but it is impossible to point to any definitive trends from the research that has been done so far.

Thus, what is known of the relations between unskilled and skilled workers in the years 1900–1925 poses more questions than it answers. However, a few very general conclusions can be drawn. The movement for industrial unionism from 1900 to 1925 was clearly the expression of workers in two settings, each tied in different ways to the expansion of industry, concentration of corporate power, and technological changes since the late nineteenth century. Moreover, the simultaneous radicalization of the unskilled and of specific categories of skilled workers reinforced the general movement in its tendency to spread from one group of workers to another. Finally, the complexity of the movement, especially the participation of unionized skilled workers, made it a more direct threat to the existing labor movement by creating a general industrial alternative, going well beyond just the unskilled, that challenged existing union structures, practices and politics.

High Point and Decline of the Movement

In the decade prior to 1910 industrial unionists gathered their forces and achieved their initial breakthroughs. The first groups of industrial unionists and syndicalists were founded in Britain at this time; in the United States, the IWW was founded, although it spent its first four years consolidating its organization in a series of factional fights; in Germany, left-wing social democrats began haltingly to reconsider union tactics in the mass strike debate. Only in France were revolutionary unionists successful in winning control of the CGT and in adopting the syndicalist *Charte d'Amiens* in 1906. However, even in France the transition to industrial unionism was only initiated between 1905 and 1910 and did not lead to immediate organizational successes.[56]

After 1910 the movement gained momentum, expanded its organization, and began to penetrate the mass of industrial workers. The exact timing of its growth depended largely on social and economic conditions in each country. Of primary importance in the conjuncture of the movement's development was the impact of inflation. Prices had steadily risen throughout the industrialized world since the turn of the century, and by 1910 the price increases—and the consequent decline in real wages and workers' living standards—began to be generally felt. Holton has pointed to this factor in the outburst of labor unrest in Britain between 1910 and 1914.

Economic trends of this kind produced a massive build up of material grievance among workers. Mass unrest developed because the long-term trend of rising spending power was now checked, and because of the sharp contrast between working-class living standards and the conspicuous luxury consumption of Edwardian rentiers and manufacturers. Economic unrest of this kind did not by itself stimulate syndicalism, but it

did provide a general sense of material deprivation on which revolutionary industrial movements might build. For grievances over wages inevitably created great pressure on orthodox trade unionism and on parliamentary socialism to bring improvement and reform. Any failure here
led the disaffected to look further afield, in particular to the direct action
philosophy of syndicalism which by-passed collective bargaining and
parliament altogether.[57]

It is thus not surprising that industrial militancy and the spread of
revolutionary unionism reached a first peak in Britain just prior to the
outbreak of war, and on the left the syndicalists were the primary
beneficiaries of the strike unrest. French syndicalism grew in an environment of stagnating real wages before 1910. The period from
1909 to the entry of the United States into the First World War was also
the high point of the IWW. The IWW reached its maximum influence
in the American East in these years, when it led a series of major strikes
in the mass production industries, then built its organization of agricultural laborers in the prairie states. Montgomery has also pointed to
the impact of inflation after 1909 on the emergence of what he calls the
"new industrial unionism" among unskilled workers outside the
IWW.[58]
    The First World War made inflation a propelling force behind
industrial unionism throughout the capitalist world. The pent-up
grievances of workers over the decline of living standards, alongside of
the war profiteering of the possessing classes, burst open in the wave of
revolutions and mass strikes after 1918. David Bercuson has clearly
shown the role of wages in the Winnipeg general strike and the mass
movement behind the formation of the OBU. The renewed revolutionization of the CGT after the period of wartime collaboration—a
revolutionization that culminated in the general railway workers' strike
of May 1920 and that contributed to the adherence of the French
Socialist Party to the Comintern at the Congress of Tours—was also
closely bound up with wartime sacrifices and expectations for economic improvements after the armistice. Germany, however, stands
out as the classic example of the impact of inflation in radicalizing
industrial workers. Not only did the decline in living standards lead
directly to the mass strikes of industrial workers in 1918–19 (especially
among Ruhr miners, but also among metalworkers and chemical workers throughout Germany) but the great inflation of the years 1921–23
revived and spread the revolutionary movement after the initial defeats of the 1918–19 revolution and the 1920 Ruhr uprising. It is no
coincidence that the history of the *Arbeiter-Unionen* runs exactly parallel
with that of the postwar inflation.[59]

Groups of industrial unionists seized upon such economic unrest and mass action to organize industrial unions and to coordinate strike movements. They developed a set of tactics to meet the needs of unskilled, previously unorganized workers. Montgomery has succinctly summarized these tactics for the IWW, but his description could be used with only a few changes for any of the groups active in Canada, Britain, France, or Germany.

Agreeing that "trade lines have been swallowed up in a common servitude of all workers to the machines which they tend," the delegates [at the founding IWW congress] decided to organize workers from the bottom up, enlisting first the unskilled and using their enthusiasm and power to pull the more highly skilled workers into action. This meant that the IWW had to replace the craft unions' meticulous caution with dramatic tactics. It would scorn large strike funds, relying instead on mass appeals for aid, on the workers' own spirit of sacrifice and on short strikes. It would reject all reliance on negotiations, labels, written contracts, trade autonomy and benefit funds and it would summon the workers to leave the decrepit "American Separation of Labor" and enlist in the new revolutionary union.[60]

In fact, German communist *Unionisten* spoke in almost identical terms in attempting to build an alternative to reformist trades unionism.[61] Such tactics were not just an abstract ideology but rather grew out of the conditions of industrial workers.

Revolutionary unionists elaborated these tactics in two major directions during and after the First World War. On the one hand, they tried to put their previous advocacy of the general or mass strike weapon into practice. The First World War and postwar period in fact led to a series of mass strikes, industrywide strikes, and general strikes. All types of revolutionary unionists used the industrial militancy of workers to put their ideas in practice: French syndicalists in the general railway strike of May 1920, their American followers in the steel strike of 1919, German communists in the waves of mass strikes in 1918–19, 1920, and 1921–24, and other groups of revolutionary unionists not previously associated with syndicalism, such as those who led the Winnipeg general strike in Canada. And these were only the most spectacular examples. On the other hand, revolutionary unionists introduced new forms of organization, aimed specifically at workers' control of production, during and after the war. Indeed, "control of production" became a major slogan of both the British and German labor movements after the First World War. The shop stewards' movement in Britain and Germany and the revolutionary councils movement in Germany and Italy were the primary examples of this new mode of action. General/mass strikes and works councils/shop stewards together amounted to a revolutionary challenge to capitalist control of the economy: the first was aimed at the eventual seizure of industry as a whole, while the second attempted to establish workers' control at the point of production. Both were predicated upon industrial unions uniting all workers in factory, mine, or workshop organizations.[62]

The movement for revolutionary industrial unionism rose and fell with this industrial unrest. It was defeated everywhere between 1919 and 1925. The reasons for the defeat were complex, but they were closely bound up with the revolutionary nature of the movement. For the movement culminated in an open confrontation with employers and the state, and it relied upon a loose form of organization and upon tactics adapted to mass unrest among industrial workers. If the revolution failed, the industrial unions had no strong organization to fall back on. Once the militancy and dynamism of the movement were checked, the organizational deficiencies became apparent, and most of these unions could not scrape through the hard times that followed. A few survived, but only by discarding their militant or revolutionary orientation. The difficulties in organizing unskilled industrial workers might account for the rapid decline of members after 1920–25, but they cannot explain the overall failure of these unions. The traditional unions, for example, had also gone through early membership crises and cyclical losses of members after major defeats and economic recessions, but while some of these trade unions collapsed, the movement in the long run survived and grew. Moreover, in the first decades of the twentieth century, there were examples of reformist industrial or semi-industrial unions that maintained a fairly tight and stable organization of unskilled workers. Yet the workers who formed OBU-type unions consciously rejected these established industrial unions. Germany is a good example of this: The miners, steelworkers, and construction workers in the Ruhr who joined the *Arbeiter-Unionen* explicitly rejected the traditional unions, even though the old miners' union was already an industrial union and the Metalworkers' Union and the Construction Trades Federation were both amalgamated unions. The major reasons behind this rejection were the reformist politics of the free unions and their bureaucratic organization, both of which inhibited mass action and dynamic organizing of new groups of workers. This does not mean that the leaders of the revolutionary industrial unions (not to speak of the membership) were uncompromising in their advocacy of revolution, but they did tend to see the militancy and dynamism of the movement as their main source of power in extracting material improvements over wages, hours, and working conditions. And such militancy reinforced the movement's revolutionary orientation.

On the other hand, it was not so much the workers or their leaders who were uncompromising (although there are numerous examples of this, and it is not uncommon for newly organized workers, in the first flush of their mass union strength, to be uncompromising in their demands). Rather, the employers, the state, and the traditional unions were the uncompromising parties, unalterably opposed to any sort of recognition of the new unions. Especially after the Russian Revolution—when most industrial unionists initially supported the Soviet regime—the forces of order were bent on destroying revolutionary and industrial unions, for political as well as economic reasons. The confrontations with employers and the state took the form of major strikes, pitched battles in which compromise solutions were rarely possible. The revolutionary intentions with which industrial unionists used direct economic action (and the revolutionary implications of many of the larger unofficial strikes even where there were no revolutionary intentions) made the state and employers defend their positions with all the weapons at their disposal. Moreover, the craft unions fought back to defend their own positions against the industrial unionists, and they found themselves tacit—and often open—allies of employers and the state. The strike confrontations in which the revolutionary industrial unions were decisively defeated were indeed pitched battles: The established powers wanted clearcut victory and threw their power into exterminating the new unions. All of the strikes were eventually defeated by the superior power of these combined forces.

Nevertheless, the crux of the problem was the new unions' reliance on loose, dynamic organization for the achievement of both short-term material improvements and long-term revolutionary goals. The loose organization of the revolutionary unionists could not survive defeat, and one by one the organizations dissolved, split, or declined. The revolutionary strategy and militant tactics of the movement had decisively conditioned the type of organization that developed. To be sure, the new unions often adopted a loose form of organization because of the difficulties in organizing masses of previously nonunionized, unskilled workers. In fact, as it has been pointed out, the leaders of the movement had consciously justified their new form of organization in this way in their polemics against the craft unions. But they refused later to tighten or stabilize their organizations largely because of their revolutionary orientation, because they did not want to deaden the militancy or mass action of the movement.

Finally, the militancy and mass action of workers, upon which industrial unionists based their overall strategy, came to an abrupt end in the early 1920s, when economic conditions changed drastically. The stabilization of the post war capitalist regimes, which was conditioned in large part by the economic and political defeat of industrial workers, brought with it an end to the inflationary cycle. The inflation, which had propelled the workers' movement for two decades, was followed by a deflationary cycle in the mid-1920s. Economic crisis and unemployment, followed by downward pressure on wages and economic stabilization, put an end to the mass unrest and industrial militancy in which revolutionary industrial unionism had grown. It was left for the Comintern to pick up the pieces and to save what was left to be saved. Perhaps the greatest weakness of revolutionary industrial unionism between 1900 and 1925 was its dependence upon the spontaneous movement of unrest among industrial workers. It failed—by and large consciously—to create stable, permanent union organizations because the goal of the movement was not just the reformist defense of limited material demands, but also the socialist transformation of the economy.

■ ■ ■

In a more general sense, I would argue that it is difficult, if not impossible, to maintain a dynamic OBU-type movement over a long period of time. The reliance of the OBU on mass action and mass participation, its class struggle approach to limited demands for material improvements, and its consistent refusal to tighten its organization for fear of deadening its dynamism with bureaucracy were all linked to its revolutionary orientation, and these factors mitigated against the survival of OBU-type unions in periods when workers were neither revolutionary nor militant. By dropping class struggle and revolution, the industrial unions of the 1930s and 1940s were accepted as bargaining partners in a way the OBU movements never could have been. In other words, while the OBU movements were certainly willing to compromise with employers over wages, hours, and working conditions on a short-term basis, they never accepted the idea of binding contracts and would never have entered into the compromise with the capitalist *system* that was at the base of the acceptance of industrial unions by employers and the state a generation later. As long as OBU unions were serious about being revolutionary, they could not stabilize themselves around the more modest objectives of other unions but could only survive as long as a period of great militancy, with an upward movement of mass workers' action, justified the belief in revolution in the relatively near future or when there was a real revolutionary upheaval, as in the years 1918–20.

Nevertheless, from a larger historical perspective, the revolt of the unskilled between 1910 and 1925 was a dress rehearsal for the wave of industrial unionization that overtook the western capitalist world in the mid-1930s and 1940s. Though defeated everywhere, one big unionism fed into both international communism and, later, industrial unionism.[63] Later organizations of industrial unions dropped the revolutionary side of the earlier movement and established in its stead a stable, workable compromise between autonomous industrial unions and general national federations of all industries. The Congress of Industrial Organization (CIO), Canadian Congress of Labor (CCL), CGT, and *Deutscher Gewerkschaftsbund* (German Labor Union Federation) all achieved such a compromise. In one sense, they had learned from the failures of earlier industrial unions and set out to improve conditions for industrial workers by concentrating their efforts on limited material goals that could be quickly won and could solidify the foundation of permanent industrial organizations. Such limited goals included not only wages, hours, and working conditions but also the nationalization of key industries, institutionalization of at least a modest level of union political influence, and the creation of organs, like works councils, for worker participation and at times co-determination in some aspects of the production process. Some of these industrial unions still considered themselves part of a larger socialist or communist movement, but they interpreted this as an alliance with a political party, in which the party carried the burden of revolutionary politics.

The successful creation of stable, officially recognized industrial unions seems to have put an end to the call for "one big union" since 1950. The OBU might thus be called historically specific. In western Europe and North America it was the first stage in the general organizing of the unskilled, the ideology of the unskilled in their first period of revolt. Nevertheless, one should not be too quick to close the book on the OBU. It has, on more than one occasion, been associated with intense working class radicalism and industrial challenge to the wage system; it has given such radicalism a pronounced ideology of class solidarity on the economic front, with the ultimate goal the taking over of industry by workers to be run by workers. Although such movements rarely, if ever, survive defeat, one cannot rule out the possible emergence of similar movements in the future. There is no final formula for organizing workers into unions in periods of great militancy or in revolutionary periods. The OBU offered one way of balancing organization with dynamism, but the problem of economic radicalism will arise anew with each upturn in the class struggle. In a future upsurge of industrial militancy—perhaps around workers' councils instead of industrial unions—the call for "one big union" may be heard again.

Notes

I would like to thank Gregory Kealey and the members of the North American Seminar of the History Department at Dalhousie University for their criticism and suggestions in revising an earlier version of this article.

1.   The movement was not, of course, limited to these countries. It extended to Australia, Latin America, southern Europe, and Scandinavia. However, the movements in these areas introduced no features that did not already appear in the "models" of the IWW in America, the OBU in Canada, or the CGT in France, nor did they add to the politicization and works councils of the German example and the organizational diversity of revolutionary British unionists. Cf. Patrick Renshaw, *The Wobblies* (Garden City, N.Y., 1967), 273–293; David L. Horowitz, *The Italian Labor Movement* (Cambridge, Mass., 1963), 51–87; Gerald H. Meaker, *The Revolutionary Left in Spain, 1914–1923* (Stanford, 1974).

2.   Bob Holton, *British Syndicalism 1900–1914* (London, 1976), 27 ff.; Jacques Julliard, *Clemenceau briseurs de grèves* (Paris, 1965); Melvyn Dubofsky, *We Shall Be All* (Chicago, 1969), 5–56; Larry Peterson, "The Policies and Work of the KPD in the Free Labor Unions of Rhineland-Westphalia 1920–1924," Ph.D. Dissertation, Columbia University, 1978, 1–27; Manfred Bock, *Syndikalismus und Linkskommunismus von 1918–1923* (Meisenheim am Glan, 1969).

3.   See Branko Pribićević, *The Shop Stewards' Movement and Workers' Control 1910–1922* (Oxford, 1959); H. A. Clegg, *General Union in a Changing Society* (Oxford, 1964); Richard Hyman, *The Workers' Union* (Oxford, 1974); Karl-Gustav Werner, *Organisation und Politik der Gewerkschaften und Arbeitgeberverbände in der deutschen Bauwirtschaft* (Berlin, 1968); Helmut Kral, *Streik auf den Helgen* (Berlin, 1964).

4.   Holton, 31.

5.   Holton; Bock; F. F. Ridley, *Revolutionary Syndicalism in France* (Cambridge, 1970); Heinz Josef Varain, *Freie Gewerkschaften, Sozialdemokratie und Staat* (Düsseldorf, 1956); David Montgomery, "Machinists, the Civic Federation, and the Socialist Party," in *Workers' Control in America* (Cambridge, 1979); and Philip S. Foner, *History of the Labor Movement in the United States. Volume V: The AFL in the Progressive Era, 1910–1915* (New York, 1980).

6.   The case of Germany during the First World War has been particularly well studied. See Willibald Gutsche, Fritz Klein, and Joachim Petzold, *Deutschland im erstern Weltkrieg* (Berlin, 1968–69); Werner Richter, *Gewerkschaften, Monopolkapital und Staat im ersten Weltkrieg und in der Novemberrevolution*

(1914–1919) (Berlin, 1959); Gerald Feldman, *Army, Industry and Labor in Germany 1914–1918* (Princeton, 1966); Jürgen Kocka, *Klassengesellschaft im Krieg* (Göttingen, 1973).

7. Holton, 27; Ridley, 53–62, 88–94, 177–179; Walter Kendall, *The Revolutionary Movement in Britain 1900–1921* (London, 1969), 12–13, 28–33; Dubofsky, *We Shall Be All*, 69–76, 91–119, 131–145; Val R. Lorwin, *The French Labor Movement* (Cambridge, Mass., 1954), 43; Vernon H. Jensen, *Heritage of Conflict* (Ithaca, N.Y., 1950), 54–71, 160–196; Joseph R. Conlin, *Big Bill Haywood and the Radical Union Movement* (Syracuse, N.Y., 1969); Philip S. Foner, *History of the Labor Movement in the United States, Volume IV: The Industrial Workers of the World, 1905–1917* (New York, 1965), especially 167–171; Peterson, 28–43; and Carl E. Schorske, *German Social Democracy 1905–1917* (Cambridge, Mass., 1955); Gerald Friesen, " 'Yours in Revolt': Regionalism, Socialism and the Western Canadian Labour Movement," *Labour/Le Travailleur* (1976), 139–157.

8. Dubofsky, *We Shall Be All*, 166–168; Foner, *IWW*, 142–144; Bernard H. Moss, *The Origins of the French Labor Movement 1830–1914* (Berkeley-Los Angeles, 1976); Peter von Oertzen, *Betriebsräte in der Novemberrevolution* (Düsseldorf, 1963); Karl Korsch, *Arbeitsrecht für Betriebsräte* (Berlin, 1922).

9. Renshaw, 273–293; Bock, 77–80, 211–214; C. Desmond Greaves, *The Life and Times of James Connolly* (New York, 1961). Such internationally known labor leaders as Tom Mann, William Z. Foster, James Larkin, James Connolly, and Fritz Wolffheim were at one time or another active in foreign countries, not to speak of international syndicalist conferences as forums for the spread of ideas.

10. Dubofsky, "Origins of Western Working-Class Radicalism," in Peter N. Stearns and Daniel J. Walkowitz, eds., *Workers in the Industrial Revolution* (New Brunswick, N.J., 1974); *We Shall Be All*, 13–56; Foner, *IWW*, 23; Holton, 27; Peterson, passim; David J. Bercuson, *Fools and Wise Men* (Toronto, 1978), 252 ff.

11. See David J. Bercuson, *Confrontation at Winnipeg* (Montreal, 1974); *Fools and Wise Men*; A. Ross McCormack, *Reformers, Rebels and Revolutionaries* (Toronto, 1977); Martin Robin, *Radical Politics and Canadian Labour 1880–1930* (Kingston, Ontario, 1968); Bock; Peterson; and Erhard Lucas, "Ursachen und Verlauf der Bergarbeiterbewegung in Hamborn und im westlichen Ruhrgebiet 1918/19. Zum Syndikalismus in der Novemberrevolution," *Duisburger Forschungen* 15 (Duisburg, 1971), 1–119.

12. Holton, 18.

13. Joseph Conlin also notes the international complexity of the movement, which did not follow European-North American divisions. Joseph R. Conlin, *Bread and Roses Too* (Westport, Conn., 1969), 17 ff.

14. Cf. Moss.

15. See Holton; Clegg; Hyman; Pribićević; and James Hinton, *The First Shop Stewards' Movement* (London, 1973). For the continuity of the French labor movement see Moss.

16. Cf. Schorske; Bock; and Peterson.

17. Dubofsky, "Origins of Western Working-Class Radicalism"; *We Shall Be All*, 57–87; Jensen, 38–53, 54–71; McCormack, 3–17; Bercuson, *Confrontation at Winnipeg*, 1–44; and *Fools and Wise Men*, ix–xvi, 1–28.

18. Peterson, 415–417, 634–663.

19. Almont Lindsey, *The Pullman Strike* (Chicago, 1942); Stanley Broder, *Pullman* (New York, 1967); Dubofsky, "Origins of Western Working-Class Radicalism"; Jensen, 54–71; Pribićević, 65–82.

20. In general, see Jean-Daniel Reynaud, *Les syndicats en France*, Vol. 1 (Paris, 1975); and André Barjonet, *La C.G.T.* (Paris, 1968), For organizational developments, see Moss, 143–153; Lorwin, 23–25; J. A. Estey, *Revolutionary Syndicalism* (London, 1913), 32–48; Ridley, 69–77; Marjorie Ruth Clark, *A History of the French Labor Movement (1910–1928)* (Berkeley, 1930), 24–39.

21. Dubofsky, *We Shall Be All*, 84–85; Foner, *IWW*, 37–38.

22. Bock, 125–126, 195–224; Peterson, 871–883.

23. Bercuson, *Fools and Wise Men*, 166–168. The most informative writer on the OBU's organization is Robin, 187–189.

24. Cf. Montgomery; Foner, *AFL;* Pribićević; Hinton.

25. Cf. Carmen J. Sirianni, "Workers' Control in the Era of World War I: A Comparative Analysis of the European Experience," *Theory and Society* 9, no. 1 (1980), 29–88.

26. Moss, 136–155, especially 141 ff.; Bercuson, *Fools and Wise Men*, 220–227; William Rodney, *Soldiers of the International* (Toronto, 1968), 45–58; Ivan Avakumovic, *The Communist Party in Canada* (Toronto, 1975), 28–31; Robin, 193–197. The OBU was not initially opposed to political parties. Indeed, its leaders in 1919 came almost exclusively from the Socialist Party of Canada (SPC). The anti-party stance of the OBU dates from 1921, when the main issue was adherence to the Third International and RILU.

27. Cf. Conlin, *Big Bill Haywood; Bread and Roses Too*, 27–35, 41–63.

28. Cf. Clegg and Hyman; Kendall, 7; Peterson, passim; Clark for the pro-communist CGTU in France.

29. Bock, 214–224.

30. Peterson, 198–199, 471–473, 640–646, 683–684; Bock, 167–187.

31. Dubofsky, *We Shall Be All*, 169–170; Renshaw; Foner, *IWW*, 19–24, 157–171; Paul Brissenden, *The IWW* (New York, 1919); Conlin, *Bread and Roses Too*, 11–13, 23–24; Foner, *IWW*, 415–434. Conlin, in both *Bread and Roses Too* and his biography of Big Bill Haywood, argues forcefully that the IWW was not syndicalist.

32. Montgomery, *Workers' Control in America*, 91–112.

33. Bercuson, *Confrontation at Winnipeg*, 89; *Fools and Wise Men*, passim; McCormack, 98, 112–113, 143 ff.; Robin, 150–151, 171–177, 275. Robin is perhaps the most explicit, certainly the most insistent, in labelling the OBU syndicalist.

34. This was a standard part of SPD and free union propaganda against the communist opposition in the Weimar Republic. It is repeated by Ossip K. Flechtheim, *Die KPD in der Weimarer Republik* (2. Auflage, Frankfurt am Main, 1971), 122–23, 261, 273; and Hermann Weber, *Die Wandlung des*

deutschen Kommunismus (Frankfurt am Main, 1969), 329; cf. Peterson, 827–837, for a critique.

35. Bock, 118–120, 122–138, 160–161, 167–187; Erhard Lucas, *Zwei Formen von Radikalismus in der deutschen Arbeiterbewegung* (Frankfurt am Main, 1976); "Ursachen und Verlauf."

36. Peterson, 343–345; and Martin Martiny, "Arbeiterbewegung an Rhein und Ruhr vom Scheitern der Räte- und Sozialisierungsbewegung bis zum Ende der letzten parlamentarischen Regierung der Weimarer Republik (1920–1930)," in Jürgen Reulecke, ed., *Arbeiterbewegung an Rhein und Ruhr* (Wuppertal, 1974), 241–273.

37. Holton, 17–21.

38. Melvyn Dubofsky, *Industrialism and the American Worker, 1865–1920* (Arlington Heights, Ill., 1975), 105.

39. Whereas both one big unionism and industrial unionism became central tenets of the CGT (and indeed outlived syndicalist control), the German syndicalists of the *Freie Vereinigung deutscher Gewerkschaften* and the *Freie Arbeiter-Union Deutschlands (Syndikalisten)* never evolved even after 1918 beyond the original syndicalism of craft-based unions. Cf. Bock, 23–24, 109.

40. Holton, 19–21.

41. Ibid., 118–119.

42. Peterson, 117–139, 242–254, 361 ff., 387–411, 476–501, 518–556, 604–626.

43. Jensen; Foner, *IWW*, 14–15, 486–517; Dubofsky, "Origins of Western Working-Class Radicalism"; *We Shall Be All*, 19–56, 120–126, 301–307, 319–383, 366–393, 476–477; Richard E. Lingenfelter, *The Hardrock Miners* (Berkeley-Los Angeles, 1974); Holton, chapter 5; Bercuson, *Fools and Wise Men*, 114–115, 136–146, 188–214, 234–246; McCormack, 36–41, 98–114; Donald Avery, *"Dangerous Foreigners"* (Toronto, 1979), 53–54, 56–57, 80–82; Robin, 179–180 ff., 275; Bock, 160–161; Peterson, 735–743; Peter N. Stearns, *Revolutionary Syndicalism and French Labour* (New Brunswick, N.J., 1971), 39, 98–99.

44. Lindsey; Dubofsky, *We Shall Be All*, 448, 474–475; Montgomery, *Workers' Control in America*, 107; Holton, 89–110; Bock, 160–161; Peterson, 638, 650; Bercuson, *Fools and Wise Men*, 114–115, 155 ff.; McCormack, 44–48, 98–117; Robin, 150–151; Stearns, 50, 70–71; Lorwin, 25; Annie Kriegel, *Aux origines du communisme français 1914–1920* (Paris-The Hague, 1964) 359–547.

45. Foner, *IWW*, and Dubofsky, *We Shall Be All*, go into detail on these sources of IWW support. For Germany, see Peterson, 168, 198, 415–417, 638–639, 743–748, 749–750; and Bock, 160–161. Also Eva Cornelia Schöck, *Arbeitslosigkeit und Rationalisierung* (Frankfurt am Main, 1977), especially 123–141 on the chemical industry; Helmut Gätsch, *Die Freien Gewerkschaften in Bremen 1919–1933* (Bremen, 1969); Richard A. Comfort, *Revolutionary Hamburg* (Stanford, 1966). For Britain, see Hyman and Clegg. For Canada, Bercuson, *Fools and Wise Men*, 134–136, 165–170; McCormack, 98–117; Avery, 80–82; Robin, 179–180 ff., 275. Specifically on the American lumber industry, see Robert L. Tyler, *Rebels in the Woods* (Eugene, Ore., 1967).

46. Lucas, "Ursachen und Verlauf" and *Zwei Formen von Radikalismus*;
Avery; Gerald Rosenblum, *Immigrant Workers* (New York, 1973); and Montgomery, *Workers' Control in America*, 32–47.

47. Pribićević, passim; Holton, 148–154; Stearns, 39, 42, 98–99; Lorwin, 25.

48. Pribićević; Hinton; Kendall, 105–141; Kral; Volker Ullrich, *Die
Hamburger Arbeiterbewegung vom Vorabend des ersten Weltkrieges bis zur Revolution
1918/19* (Dissertation, Hamburg, 1976).

49. Bercuson, *Confrontation at Winnipeg*; Robin, 189 ff.; Lindsey; Peterson, 638.

50. Holton, 154–163; McCormack, 48, 98–117; Avery, 54–55; Foner,
IWW, 227–231.

51. In Germany, the construction unions had already turned to
amalgamated and semi-industrial forms of organization before 1914, so that
the communists could argue against the necessity of forming revolutionary
dual unions. Thus, even when KPD-controlled construction union locals were
expelled from the free unions, the KPD organized a "union of the expelled"
(the *Verband der Ausgeschlossenen Bauarbeiter*) to fight for readmission rather
than an independent revolutionary industrial union.

52. Peterson, 748–749.

53. Stearns, 42, 50–51, 96; Lorwin, 25.

54. For a particularly good discussion of some of these questions, see
Montgomery, *Workers' Control in America*, 113–138, and his article on "Immigrant Workers" in the same volume. In Germany in the 1920s, the German
Metalworkers' Union (before 1918 an amalgamated union dominated by
skilled craftsmen and the largest union in Germany) reorganized itself internally to follow the industrial structure of the works councils and made the
simplification and reduction of wage differentials one of its primary goals in
wage negotiations.

55. By far the best comparative case study of workers' cultures and
their differential impact on the organized labour movement is Erhard Lucas'
study of the Rhenish-Westphalian towns of Remscheid and Hamborn in *Zwei
Formen von Radikalismus*. For the creation of a new working-class culture in the
new industrial regions (especially among the unskilled) and its effect on labor
radicalism, see James E. Cronin, "Labor Insurgency and Class Formation:
Comparative Perspectives on the Crisis of 1917–1920 in Europe," in this
volume.

56. Holton, 39–51.

57. Holton, 28.

58. Stearns, 17–18. For the United States, see Foner, *IWW*; Dubofsky;
and Montgomery.

59. Bercuson, *Confrontation at Winnipeg*, 22–44; D. C. Masters, *The
Winnipeg General Strike* (Toronto, 1950). Kriegel; Peterson, 199–203, 211–226,
347–361, 387 ff., 476–480, 518 ff.; Bock, 87; Jürgen Kuczynski, *Die Geschichte
der Lage der Arbeiter unter dem Kapitalismus*, Vols. 4–5 (Berlin, 1966); Erhard

Lucas, *Märzrevolution 1920*, 2 vols. (Frankfurt am Main, 1970–74); "Zur Ursachen"; *Zwei Formen von Radikalismus*.

60.   Montgomery, *Workers' Control in America*, p. 92.

61.   Peterson, chapter 12.

62.   For the postwar strikes, see the studies by Kriegel, 359–547; Bercuson, *Confrontation at Winnipeg*; McCormack, 158–164; Lucas, "Zur Ursachen"; *Zwei Formen von Radikalismus*; Peter von Oertzen, "Die grossen Streiks der Ruhrbergarbeiterschaft im Frühjahr 1919. Ein Beitrag zur Diskussion über die revolutionäre Entstehungsphase der Weimarer Republik," in Eberhard Kolb, ed., *Vom Kaiserreich zur Weimarer Republik* (Cologne, 1972), 185–217; Gerald D. Feldman, Eberhard Kolb, and Reinhard Rürup, "Die Massenbewegungen der Arbeiterschaft in Deutschland am Ende des Ersten Weltkrieges (1917–1920)," *Politische Vierteljahresschrift* 12 (1972), 84–105. For the councils' movements, see Pribićević; Hinton; Kendall, 142–169; von Oertzen, *Betriebsräte*; Peterson, 871–890; Spriano; Cammett, 19–31; 65–122; Horowitz, 142–153.

63.   Former revolutionary industrial unionists from the years 1900 to 1925 dot the history of the communist movement in the 1920s and 1930s. Although many left the Red International of Labor Unions along with the syndicalists in the early 1920s, an equally large number stayed with the communists and contributed directly or indirectly to the later triumph of industrial unionism, in which communists played a major role.

Chapter Four

New Tendencies in Union Struggles and Strategies in Europe and the United States, 1916-1922

David Montgomery

"For the men who really had the capacity and the organizing power, the men who exercised leadership . . . over the working class in the authentic sense of the term, were the union chiefs," wrote Paolo Spriano of Italy's 1920 factory occupations. "The men of the party, however much they might want . . . to direct the masses toward a violent rupture of the established order, . . . lacked the levers of command, experience, cadres, a rapport with the class which permitted effective leadership." Union leaders, however, even those of the Italian General Confederation of Labor (CGL) who had traveled to Moscow earlier that year to discuss the formation of a revolutionary international of unions, shared "a very rigid conception" of trade unionism, "which erected centralized organization—the discipline, authority, contractual power of the union—into a kind of fetish." They had "fought their most formative struggles against anarcho-syndicalism," so their "natural tendency towards a bureaucratic perspective" on union activity "had been reinforced by their wartime experience."[1]

What was true of Italy was most definitely true of the United

This essay was written on occasion of the conference in Turin November 20–22, 1981, organized by the Instituto Socialista di Studi Storici of Florence.

States, where the leaders of the American Federation of Labor, having repudiated socialism for decades, had collaborated fully in the government's war mobilization.[2] In the United States as elsewhere, wartime experience confirmed the bureaucratic lessons officials had learned from the upsurge of mass strikes during the decade preceding America's entry into the war. Despite the distinctly minority status of the unions within the working class, no other organization had enjoyed an organizational network or experience among workers comparable to theirs. Moreover, the membership of American unions had almost doubled between 1913 and 1920, rising to some 5,000,000 workers. That rate of growth (92 percent) was matched by the unions of Great Britain, which rose from 4 to 8 million members, overshadowed by those of France (143 percent, from 1 to 2.5 million) and Germany (188 percent, from 4.5 to 13 million), and dwarfed by that of Italy (609 percent for the CGL alone, from 327,000 to 2,320,000).[3]

By 1920, therefore, the union, with its unique ties to the routines and needs of working-class life and its distinctive style of operation, was everywhere a power to reckon with. Its growth, however, had taken place in the context of the consolidation of corporate enterprise, imperialism, war, and revolution. That context had generated new forms of local and workplace organization, which often exhibited a "rapport with the [working] class" more intimate than that established by national union officials. Unlike prewar direct actionists, the new militants were as much concerned with building durable governing bodies of workers' delegates in and around the workplace as they were with waging strikes. They thus made a more lasting impression on trade unions and the industrial relations policies of business than had the earlier activities of the *Industrial Workers of the World* (IWW). Unlike the national union officials, however, these local activists had no agency to coordinate their struggles. Their militant but parochial organizations were viewed by AFL leaders as violations of union discipline to be suppressed, by management as a force to be harnessed to company unionism, and by government as a menace to be destroyed.

In order to explore the new tendencies in union strategies and struggles, this paper will focus on the United States between 1916 and 1922 and attempt to determine in what ways patterns of workers' activity there compared with those in England, Italy, Germany, and France. It will examine, in turn, the relations linking business, unions, and the state; new strategies of union leaders; and novel forms of organization at the base. In conclusion, it will attempt some comparisons between the rhythm of evolution of postwar struggles in America and those in Europe.

War, State, and Industry

May 1st allowed me to participate in a real working class Labor Day movement in Minneapolis [reported organizer James Henderson of the International Association of Machinists in 1920,] but as this was an international labor day[,] the object of the meetings the world over expressed the same human greetings. There were 17,000 marchers in line. Machine guns and armored cars, and the State militia mobilized in their armories, made the scene worthy of a moving picture drama. The Department of Deportation agents were everywhere . . . . The parade was led by the World War Veterans, an organization that stands for working-class principles. W. F. Dunn[e], one of the fearless leaders of the Northwest Labor movement [and a founder of the Communist Labor Party, D.M.] . . . was the principal speaker. . . . A mule in the parade carrying a greeting to "openshoppers" received much applause, [and] the banner declaring "The Kaiser lives in a palace in Holland, but Gene Debs lives in an American prison" brought out the true feeling . . . .[4]

The militancy and internationalist spirit that pervaded the ranks of these marchers in a small city previously free of labor organizations typified the labor struggles of postwar years, as did the glowering presence of troops and the reminders of incarcerated comrades. The American government had mobilized for war in the midst of the most extensive and long-lasting strike wave in the country's history. Every year from 1916 through 1922 more than one million workers had participated in strikes, and in 1919 the number had surpassed four million.[5] During 1916 strikes were especially widespread in the munitions industry, just as they were in Britain, Germany, and France. Somewhat of a crescendo of strike activity was reached between April and September 1917 (after the United States had declared war), when machinists, miners, and other workers in extractive and processing industries were especially active. Moreover, there were even more strikes (67) involving over 10,000 workers apiece in 1917 than there were in 1919.[6]

Labor's militancy in America was fueled by many of the same causes that have been identified for Europe: inflation, full employment, and the long-term dilution of skilled crafts and consolidation of working-class neighborhoods. Inflation played a critical role, not because American workers suffered the stark deprivation experienced by their German counterparts in 1918–19 but rather because, as James Cronin argues, it made wage struggles chronic, upset customary standards of comparison of relative earnings (lathe operators turning shells on piece work, for example, often earned more than skilled tool and die makers), and triggered consumers' struggles over the high cost of housing and food, among them the bloody food riots of 1917 in New York and Philadelphia.[7] The labor shortage of 1916–18, though not as acute as that in France or Germany, nevertheless allowed workers to change jobs freely and frequently in search of better earnings, while putting in many more days of work and many more hours of overtime than in normal years. Thus, the largely unskilled workers of Chicago's meat packing plants enjoyed a steady increase in their real earnings from 1916 through the middle of 1919, while the extraordinary rise in the wages that the industry offered women induced thousands of housewives to join their husbands in the packing houses. Only in the year after June 1919 did the cost of living rise noticeably faster than those workers' earnings.[8]

The congested neighborhoods adjacent to the Chicago stockyards stirred with such enthusiasm that 90 percent of the immigrant workers enrolled in the AFL, and the head of the most important fraternal order, the Polish Falcons, provided the union with its most influential leader (John Kikulski). During the major strikes of 1918–22 in textiles, clothing, munitions, and metallurgy, neighborhood benevolent societies of Italians, Poles, Jews, Croatians, and Lithuanians time and again provided bases from which efforts to unionize the factories were launched and sustained.[9] Conversely, the efforts of streetcar and laundry workers to unionize generated such community support as to produce general strikes in Springfield, Illinois, Kansas City, Missouri, Waco, Texas, and Billings, Montana, between September 1917 and April 1918.[10] The vast working-class neighborhoods could make life unbearable for scabs, mobilize massive funerals for slain strikers, and involve various members of the same families in marketplace, as well as workplace, struggles.

Opposition to the war itself often reverberated through these neighborhoods. The Socialist Party of America, like the Italian and Serbian parties, refused to endorse its country's entry into the war. At its Emergency Convention of April 1917, it denounced the government's declaration of war and called for "an even more vigorous prosecution of the class struggle" to protect living standards and civil liberties and to rouse the people against war and conscription. A referendum of the membership upheld that position by almost ten to one, in preference to a minority report that would have recognized the war as a fact and committed the party to seizing "the opportunity presented by war conditions to advance our program of democratic collectivism." The party's firm stand was influenced by the recent departures of socialist ministers from governments in France and Germany, the mounting protests of workers in Europe against the war

and conscription, and the revolution in Russia. Moreover, it was rewarded in municipal elections of 1917 from Elwood, Indiana, to New
York City with the largest votes the party had ever received. Through
the People's Council of America for Democracy and Peace, Socialists
gathered considerable support for a program that demanded immediate peace on the basis of no annexation and no indemnities, self-
determination for all nations, and the conscription of wealth rather
than of men.[11]

The confluence of antiwar agitation and unprecedented strike
activity prompted the government to devote special attention to labor
in its war mobilization measures of the fall of 1917. New espionage and
sedition laws were already on the statute books and the first draft calls
had already been levied by August and September, when the strike
wave reached its peak, and the National Industrial Conference Board
(representing all major employers' organizations) called on President
Wilson to establish an agency with broad powers to settle industrial
disputes. As the government worked out its policy over the ensuing
months, it elaborated two basic principles. First, it would solicit the
cooperation of the existing unions. Second, it would demand that both
industry and labor refrain from using the crisis to "change existing
standards." These decisions were based both on lessons drawn from
the British experience, where the 1915 Treasury Agreement to suspend union rules and shopfloor practices had opened the door to a
militant shop stewards' movement, and on the consistent support that
Samuel Gompers and the Executive Council of the AFL had offered to
defense mobilization agencies since 1916. Although the Executive
Council had repudiated Gompers' adherence in April 1917 to the
ambiguous formula of no efforts to "change existing standards" and
refused to take a no-strike pledge, it did agree to contribute union
representatives to mobilization agencies and to cooperate with those
agencies in preventing strikes. Moreover, in August Gompers and AFL
Secretary Mathew Woll joined with pro-war Socialists in forming the
American Alliance for Labor and Democracy to combat the pacifist
activities of the People's Council. The fury of the final round of
offensives on the Western Front dampened antiwar protest in America, just as it did in France and Germany, and left the labor patriots
facing little effective opposition by the summer of 1918.[12]

Working in close cooperation with Labor Secretary William B.
Wilson, a former vice-president of the United Mine Workers, union
leaders developed a relationship to the state that was much closer in
practice than it was in any formal policy pronouncements. For example, when the IWW led a strike movement among Arizona copper
miners in July, local authorities herded 1,186 strikers onto cattle cars at

bayonette point and shipped them off into the New Mexico Desert. Secretary Wilson rushed an adjustment commission to the scene, and it ordered the reinstatement of all strikers except those guilty of seditious utterances or who belonged to an organization that did not recognize union contracts (i.e., the IWW). It also established grievance committees at each mine and provided for AFL participation in those committees. Simultaneously in the Pittsburgh region a federal mediator reported to Washington that a local Council of National Defense had been formed in response to "Socialist agitators" at the Westinghouse and other machine-building plants, "making speeches against the Government and everyone else." Organizer Andrew McNamara of the Machinists' union and vice-president Philip Murray of the Mine Workers were among the union officials who expressed their willingness to serve on the Council, along with the executives of the Westinghouse company, Mesta Machine, and the adamantly antiunion Pittsburgh Employers' Association.[13]

In both these instances the employers involved subsequently resisted unionization of their own employees despite the government's prodding and the unions' patriotic role. To them, as to most business leaders, the principle of "no change in existing standards" meant that open shop factories and cities would remain that way. Unlike the French and German governments, the United States did not require its suppliers to bargain with unions. Nevertheless, most union officials vigorously supported the war effort. Among them were former Socialists such as Secretary-Treasurer E. C. Davidson of the Machinists, who received a "Tax the Rich to Pay for the War" circular from the People's Council in the mail and forwarded it instantly to the government in case it might prove useful to the state in "breaking up schemes of this kind."[14] Another was John H. Walker, President of the Illinois district of the mine workers, who wrote Secretary Adolph Germer of the Socialist Party: "I want you and your like, who want to bring about improvements for the working people through making the German Kaiser the Emperor of the WORLD . . . to know that there isn't anything I can think of or do, that I won't do, to prevent you from accomplishing your purpose." Indeed, Walker's union agreed to place in the contract covering the highly unionized Central Competitive Field a provision automatically fining any miner who participated in a work stoppage, in order "to protect the great majority of the mine workers against the radical and indifferent element among the employees . . . ."[15]

There was, consequently, little political space in America for anything like England's War Emergency Workers' National Committee, which linked supporters and opponents of the war in the defense of workers' liberties and living standards. Royden Harrison has depicted the majority of that committee as "intelligent patriots," offering reluctant support to the war effort but resisting chauvinism and political repression. Activists who assumed that posture could certainly be found in the United States. Samuel Lavit in Bridgeport and William Z. Foster in Chicago, for example, promoted militant unionism and the sale of Liberty Bonds simultaneously. The only public cause that found everyone from the Wobblies and Gompers on the same side, however, was the struggle to save Tom Mooney from execution. Mooney, a San Francisco syndicalist charged with bombing a 1916 Preparedness Day parade, was also a local officer of the Iron Molders' Union. Even though the AFL's leaders vigorously opposed the 1919 movement for a general strike on Mooney's behalf, they never ceased appealing for his freedom.[16]

This is not to say that AFL leaders asked nothing in return for their loyalty. Quite the contrary. Government arbitration mechanisms stimulated the thorough unionization of Chicago's packinghouses, and after the government took possession of the railroads virtually all employees, except those Blacks whom several union constitutions barred from membership, became unionized. A growth of membership of 111 percent between 1915 and 1920 made transportation the most highly unionized sector of American industry. Unions also expanded their membership by 67 percent in the building trades, 113 percent in clothing (where leaders of the Amalgamated Clothing Workers both spoke against the war and cooperated with war agencies), 280 percent in metal fabricating, and 368 percent in textiles.[17] Moreover, leaders as conservative as William Hutcheson of the Carpenters and James O'Connell of the Metal Trades Department urged aggressive use of this newfound strength to improve conditions. Addressing the Boilermakers' convention in September 1917, O'Connell advised:

Now I want you to get it into your heads . . . to talk about dollars, not pennies. . . . The opportunity is presented for the first time in the history of the United States Government, practically a union contract signed between the government and the officers of the [Metal Trades] Department . . . requiring that the shipbuilders of America come to Washington and put their feet under the tables with labor leaders to settle their troubles. . . . Uncle Sam is paying the expenses of union committees to come to Washington and meet the employers. Isn't that a pretty good union agreement? That is only the beginning. . . . We will come out after the war is over bigger and greater and grander and better understood than ever we were before.[18]

This prospect frightened the leaders of American business as much as it delighted O'Connell. There was no Stinnes-Legien agreement in America because American business feared unions more than it feared revolution. With the defeat and collapse of the imperial government, Jakob Richter of the Union of German Iron and Steel Industrialists (VdESI) had observed: "Allies for industry could be found only among the workers; these were the unions."[19] The situation confronting American industrialists was totally different. Their program of dismantling government regulatory agencies and deflating prices and wages as rapidly as possible, while encouraging the rationalization of industry through scientific management and through voluntary self-organization (called "associational activities" by Herbert Hoover), had been enshrined in the platform of the Republican Party and strongly endorsed by the electorate in 1918 and 1920. Like their French and British counterparts (and unlike the Italian and German business leaders), American corporate executives were encouraged by the results of postwar elections to dig in their heels against union aspirations. Moreover, the American unions, for all their new power, were hardly to be compared in membership, experience, or apparent unity to the British labor movement before "Black Friday" of 1921— i.e., while it could still brandish the threat of the Triple Alliance.

Consequently, the representatives of industry at President Wilson's 1919 Industrial Conference rejected outright the idea of collective bargaining with unions. They also opposed any role for the state in social insurance (though on this point they were largely supported by the AFL). Although both employee representation and welfare programs to benefit the workers might be desirable, business representatives argued, these should be carried out at the level of the enterprise, with no "outside interference" from unions or government.[20] With the war's end, therefore, business demanded the quick end of fuel and price regulations, the return of the railroads to private ownership, and the dismantling of the National War Labor Board. Quite in contrast to the summer of 1917, when the National Industrial Conference Board had wanted such an agency as a defense against strikes, even the business representatives on the Board itself now believed that it was encouraging the spread of unionism and threatening industry with bureaucratic regulations, such as national minimum wages. Furthermore, once private ownership of the railroads had been restored, the American Railway Executives Association, in the face of almost 90 percent unionization of their employees, endorsed the principle of no contracts with labor organizations and abrogated the existing national agreements.[21]

Another tribute to the relative weakness of American unions is found in the failure of American businessmen to forge their own centralized leadership in the way their counterparts in England, France, Germany, and Italy had all done by the end of 1920. The most representative of all employers' associations, the National Industrial Conference Board, had played a major role in the selection of business representatives on wartime government agencies, but after the war, when those agencies were dismantled, the NICB's role became that of a research and publicity agency. Both the NICB and other national industrial associations, save those in bituminous coal and clothing, avoided negotiating with unions on behalf of their members. Each firm jealously preserved its autonomy. Even the Special Conference Committee, formed in April 1919 by ten of the country's largest corporations to discuss questions of labor policy, remained a theater for informal consultations; it made no binding decisions, and it certainly never commissioned its influential secretary, John Hicks of the Rockefeller interests, to enter into contract negotiations with Samuel Gompers.[22]

Corporations and sectoral employers' associations developed their own strategies for combatting unions with little government interference (especially after the dissolution of the National War Labor Board in June 1919). They were greatly assisted by the public policy of deflation, however, and by the repression of radical activities and a governmental strategy of postponing decisions in the face of major confrontations with labor. Wartime restrictions on speech and public assembly remained in force for years after the armistice. By 1921 only 11 of the 88 leading cities of America had removed their wartime bans on street meetings. Post Office censorship of revolutionary publications continued openly until May 1921, and Italy's *Avanti* was still barred from American mails the following August.[23] After the notorious raids and deportations against radical aliens in 1919–20, the Immigration Bureau of the Department of Labor settled into routine scrutiny of foreign-born workers in cooperation with employers, detective agencies, and patriotic societies. In fact, more than three-fourths of the employees of the department dealt with immigration and deportation after 1920, and the number of people they expelled annually rose to more than 38,000 by the end of the twenties.[24]

Presidents Wilson and Harding shared with Lloyd George and Giolitti the talent for delaying decisions when confronted by powerful union demands. Government and business executives alike were convinced that the high prices of 1919 would soon collapse and that to concede wage increases or power to unions would inhibit business' ability to cope with the coming deflation. The art of politics, therefore, became that of postponing the settlement of major disputes from the period of inflation and union strength to the period of depression and union weakness, which began in the summer of 1920 and lasted through 1922. Just as the depression allowed western European businessmen to defy union challenges, so it placed their American counterparts in a position to open a general offensive against unions in meat packing, textiles, railroads, and coal. In the four years following the end of 1920, German unions saw previous gains wiped out and lost more members than the AFL had ever had, French unions shrank to the feeble position they were to know until 1936, and Italian unions were pounded by the *squadristi*. Membership in British unions declined by 34 percent (a loss of 2,842,000) by the eve of the 1926 General Strike. In this context the American loss of roughly 1.5 million members (or 30 percent) was not unusual; but among those lost to the American movement were virtually all the new recruits of the war years. The AFL found itself again shut out of basic industry.[25]

Union Strategies

Rapid growth during the war tempted American unionists to venture into uncharted paths and simultaneously confronted their sense of "discipline, authority, [and] contractual power" with serious challenges from their own membership. Paradoxically, those officials most extensively engaged in innovative forms of struggle—men such as William Johnston, John L. Lewis, Warren Stone, Thomas McMahon, and Sidney Hillman—also wielded disciplinary sanctions against rebellious members most frequently and most draconically. These leaders of coal miners', railroad workers', machinists', and clothing and textile workers' unions were the "progressives" of the labor movement, and their organizations experienced the most spectacular rise and decline of members between 1916 and 1923.

The establishment of the Workers' Education Bureau of America in 1921 (in direct imitation of its British predecessor) was intended to coordinate the many union educational departments and some fifty trade union colleges and schools, which flourished during these years. Its effort to institute formal training of union cadre drew prominent academics, such as Charles and Mary Beard and Paul Douglas, into the service of the unions. Union journals under progressive editorship, most notably the *Brotherhood of Locomotive Engineers Journal*, were filled with essays by prominent intellectuals discussing workers' control, labor parties, imperialism, and union strategies.[26] Britain's movement provided the favorite model for these authors. But some activities of progressive unionists moved in peculiarly American directions, most notably labor banks and union brokerage of trade with Russia and Mexico.

The International Association of Machinists (IAM) led the way into banking, forming the Mount Vernon Savings Bank in 1920 with the dues of its 350,000 members, which providing a year's revenues of $1,728,000. It soon used the bank's funds to induce a Norfolk firm to break ranks with the employers' association and bring a long strike to a successful conclusion for the union. The locomotive engineers followed suit and came to own fourteen banks, eight investment companies, a printing company, and two skyscrapers. The Amalgamated Clothing Workers similarly created seven banks and investment companies, and the Russian-American Industrial Corporation. The last was a truly American form of international solidarity with revolutionary Russia. The Russian-American company served as the primary route for remission of funds between the U.S. and Russia until the 1930s, and it even established several clothing factories in the land of the NEP.[27]

The Machinists also ventured into trade with regimes under the ban of the government, but with less success than the Clothing Workers. The union's trade mission to Russia was turned back at the Polish-Russian border, and an elaborate arrangement with the Mexican government for the purchase of union-made machinery was rudely undercut when the notoriously antiunion Baldwin Locomotive Works outbid the union for the task with an offer to the Mexicans of $2,500,000 credit. More successful were the Machinists' efforts at a commercial alliance with farmers. In the spring of 1921 the IAM encouraged the founding of the All American Cooperative Commission to promote "direct trading between farmer producers and city consumers" and led a movement for union purchase of state bonds of North Dakota, which had been shunned on the stock exchange after that state had created its own state bank and grain terminals.[28]

Working from this imposing institutional base, the progressives sought to convert the AFL to a program including public ownership and worker operation of railroads and coal mines, trade with Soviet Russia, repeal of repressive wartime legislation and release of political prisoners, affiliation with the Amsterdam International Federation of Trade Unions, and collaboration with the British Labour Party on social and international policy.[29] This was a formidable task, because the AFL was essentially a council of national union executives, most of whom supported Gompers in his resistance to this program, and because major progressive leaaders, like Stone of the Locomotive Engineers and Hillman of the Clothing Workers, were not affiliated with the Federation. Although there were 577 delegates at the 1919 AFL convention, 65 union executives among them could cast 82 percent of the votes. Consequently the most dramatic moment of that convention, the address of Margaret Bondfield (the first woman ever to appear as "fraternal" delegate from the British Trades Union Congress) describing the prospects of the Triple Alliance, the shop stewards, the cooperatives, and the Labour Party for replacing Britain's moribund capitalism with a democratic social order, brought the delegates to their feet roaring approval. However, it had no influence on the program enacted by the convention.[30]

During the next two years, however, a close though informal alliance of coal miners, railroad workers, and metal workers lent strength to the progressive program. This coalition overwhelmed the opposition of Gompers at the 1920 convention to commit the AFL to government ownership and democratic control of the railroads (not specifying the Plumb Plan by name, but following a rousing speech by Glenn Plumb to the convention).[31] That was the most that the progressives were ever to win. When Lewis embraced their program and challenged Gompers for the AFL presidency at the 1921 convention, he was easily outmaneuvered. Gompers allied himself with powerful miners' leaders from Illinois and Kansas, whose rebel movements Lewis had tried to crush; wooed the Ladies' Garment Workers away from their fellow Socialists, who backed Lewis; and unceremoniously dumped two trusted colleagues from his slate for Federation officers in favor of leaders of railroad unions, thus shattering the progressive front. From the platform Gompers's supporters alternately denounced Lewis's cowardice in abandoning strikes that had been declared illegal by the governments of the United States and Kansas, and charged his backers with secretly favoring "One Big Union and IWWism."[32]

Nothing like Britain's Triple Alliance appeared in the United States. No successful general dockers' and laborers' union conquered American seaports, and the discussions of alliances that were held among miners and railway workers' unions never bore fruit. Quite the contrary, national craft unions beat back all proposals for treaties of mutual support or even structures for joint campaigns, except the 1920 "wage movement" alliance of railway unions. In their prewar battle with anarcho-syndicalism, the leaders of national craft unions had learned to denounce any proposal for amalgamation of unions or for formal alliances as "IWWism." The various departments established within the AFL before the war—the metal trades, building trades, union label, and railway departments—had been designed to appease members' desire for unity among crafts without limiting or overriding

the exclusive authority of each national union over the craft it represented. The only serious challenge to this principle had been the rise of
system federations, or regional alliances of railroad repair shop workers, which had been fiercely fought by railroad management and
national union executives alike.

During the war, however, several unions involved in the attempt
to organize Chicago's packinghouse workers had combined efforts in
and subordinated their local authority to a Stockyards Labor Council.
Their success inspired the most important nationwide coalition of the
age: the National Committee to Organize Iron and Steel Workers.
Thirty-five unions contributed organizers and funds to this committee,
which enrolled steel workers under its own name, deliberately postponing the question of craft jurisdictions until after recognition had
been won from the companies, and ultimately directed a strike of
350,000 workers under the authority of the Committee itself. Its
secretary and guiding spirit was William Z. Foster, who had earlier led
the Stockyards Labor Council. After the defeat of the steel strike,
however, national executives quickly reasserted their authority and
formed a new alliance of crafts in which the independence of each
union was scrupulously defined. Moreover, in 1921 the Amalgamated
Meat Cutters and Butcher Workmen broke up the Stockyards Labor
Council and put in its place a new structure that rigidly upheld craft
autonomy—the structure that went down to defeat in the strike of
1921–22.[33]

The same spirit of unity that had brought the National Committee to Organize Iron and Steel Workers into being was also evident in
the negotiations undertaken by the United Mine Workers and the
officers of the Big Four railway unions (engineers, firemen, brakemen,
and conductors) during the early months of 1920. None of the unions
involved, however, was willing to commit itself to strike in support of its
allies. The sixteen unions representing railway workers were not even
willing to make that pledge to each other, and indeed during the bitter
nationwide shopmen's strike of 1922, members of the Big Four kept on
driving trains.[34] As far as the national craft unions were concerned, the
much vaunted unity of miners, railwaymen, and metal workers was, at
best, unity for electoral struggles and around a new program for the
labor movement.

Local Militants and Unity from Below

Unity for strikes and joint bargaining did develop at the base, however,
and assumed three forms: the revitalization of city central labor un-

ions, the leadership of local metal trades' councils, and shop committees within the workplace. American labor had no institution like the
Italian *camera del lavoro* or the French *bourse du travail*, whose distinctive
coupling of municipally sponsored hiring hall and other services with
leadership of local workers' struggles implied a life quite distinct from
that of the national trade unions. Between 1890 and 1910 the AFL had
compelled central unions to exclude all groups not belonging to the
Federation, while insisting that affiliated locals adhere to the rules and
discipline of national unions when contemplating strikes or boycotts.
The function of sending workers out to available jobs, which was
important mainly for unions in the building, maritime, and printing
trades, was executed by each union separately. Consequently, central
labor unions were squeezed out of the role of local working-class
leadership, which they had exercised from the 1860s to the 1880s, with
a few notable and defiant exceptions like the Chicago Federation of
Labor.[35]

Starting with the Philadelphia general strike of 1910 and the
attempted general strike of 1916 in New York City, however, central
labor unions began to reassert themselves. In both these instances
strikes of tram drivers had roused such class loyalties that the central
labor unions called out other workers in sympathy. The five general
strikes of 1918 also manifested citywide support of embattled groups
of workers. In Kansas City, Missouri, for example, 146 locals belonging
to thirty different unions and enrolling more than 20,000 workers
struck in violation of their contracts, in order to assist laundry wagon
drivers win a raise and women laundry operatives win recognition of
their union.[36]

The most famous strike of this type occurred in Seattle in February 1919. When shipyard workers struck for a wage increase, the
Central Labor Council conducted a referendum among all the city's
union members (in flagrant violation of national union constitutions),
then called 110 unions out on strike for five days. A committee of 300
delegates, with an executive council of fifteen, organized community
kitchens at twenty-one locations around the city, decided which telephone exchanges, dairies, and hospitals might remain open, and instituted collective butcher shops and laundries. Clearly a network of
effective leadership had been created that enjoyed far greater prestige
and rapport with Seattle's workers than did the national unions. The
city was charged with excitement and as war veterans enrolled by the
strike committee patrolled its streets, shipyard workers insisted that
pay scales must be not only raised but equalized (the greatest raises
going to the lowest paid) and the strike committee boasted loudly that

the workers were "learning to manage." The sense that there was no limit to what workers could do appeared often in Europe between 1917 and 1920, but was fully unleashed in America only in Seattle. Its legacy could still be felt in May 1923, when despite the closing down of many shipyards, police raids on Socialist and IWW halls, and threats and expulsions by national unions, the Seattle Central Labor Council had to be admonished by the AFL Executive Council to rescind its endorsement of Soviet Russia, to deny credentials to anyone attending conventions of the Red International of Labor Unions (Profintern), and to stop referring AFL communiques on politics to the state farmer-labor party.[37]

The shipyard workers of Seattle had been called on strike by a metal trades council, which was comprised of delegates from twenty-one craft unions in the yards. Such councils initiated joint actions so often in 1919 that the Metal Trades Department of the AFL directed a formal warning to all of them:

There seems to have grown up a most serious error in the minds of the delegates making up the local metal trades councils that these councils have the right to order strikes or to approve of them without the laws of our Department and of our affiliated national and international organizations having been complied with. . . . [The constitution of the Department specifies] that no local metal trades council can order a strike unless the local unions affiliated first have received sanction or permission of the internationals . . . and any attempt on the part of any local councils . . . to force a sympathetic strike in any locality is in violation of our general laws.[38]

To prove its point, the Department intervened at the Baltimore shipyards of the Bethlehem and American shipbuilding companies, where metal trades councils were threatening to strike for recognition, and arranged for contract negotiations between the companies and five national unions. Shop committees were reorganized along the lines of craft and no committees that crossed craft lines were allowed.[39]

The desire for unity was often so strong that attempts to repartition workers into crafts under the control of national unions served only to drive them out of the AFL or to contribute to the success of the companies' battles against unionization. To cite but one example out of dozens, under the leadership of a metal trades council the workers at United Shoe Machine Co. had secured recognition of their unions and a 44-hour week in 1919. At the end of the year, however, the company began circulating individual contracts among the workers under which those who agreed to quit their unions and work on the terms specified by the company were evidently guaranteed a year's employment. In

March 1920 the metal trades council struck, with the strong support of the International Association of Machinists. Although some 2,200 workers out of 3,300 left work, the strike was in difficulty from the start. Massachusetts courts ruled the individual contracts legal and a strike against them illegal coercion. Second, the national unions of molders and pattern makers, which had just signed contracts with the company, ordered their members to remain at work. AFL organizer Frank McLaughlin telegraphed Samuel Gompers at the AFL's Montreal convention: "Situation critical. Three thousand men to leave the A.F.L. Outlaw movement strong." The only remedy, McLaughlin advised, was for the Metal Trades Department to order the molders and pattern makers out. That the Department would not do, and the machinists supported the strike alone for four months, until they agreed to return to work on the company's pledge not to coerce anyone to sign an individual contract. By September depression conditions were allowing the company to "reward" its most faithful workers with individual contracts and return to a 50-hour week, while others were discharged.[40]

In short, the initiative of metal trades councils was strangled. Indeed, the Carriage, Wagon, and Automobile Workers Union was expelled by the AFL in 1918 for defying the jurisdictions of other unions and organizing on an industrial basis. That socialist-led union, strong among trimmers and painters in New York, Buffalo, and Detroit, gave plant committees authority to run their own affairs and in general eschewed written contracts. It was one of many small industrial unions of metal workers that flourished before the depression of 1920–22. Among the major AFL unions, however, not one encouraged or utilized the local initiative of the workers as was done, for example, by the Italian Metal Mechanics (FIOM) in the wage struggles of 1920.[41]

Workplace Organization

Hallmarks of workers' struggles in the epoch of World War I were the council of workers' delegates and the slogan of "workers' control." Workplace organization had been nebulous even among unionized workers before the war, and it was resisted as adamantly by American employers as it was by their European counterparts. "Well, we should not have a committee or what they call a steward, an official of the union, in our place to represent the union among our employees," thundered the President of the Western Electric Company in 1900. "We should not have it."[42] Craft workers were expected to enforce union work rules by personally refusing to violate them or to work in the presence of those who did. Walking delegates toured construction sites ready to call all men out if they saw anything wrong. Ad hoc committees of workers often approached employers about grievances, and they would expect the union to come to their defense if they were fired for doing so. The shop committee, in the sense of a body of delegates recognized by the management as speaking on behalf of all its employees, was basically an innovation of the war years.

Precedents had appeared on the eve of the war, with clear syndicalist inspiration, as in Britain or Italy. During 1910, shopmen on the Illinois Central Railroad formed joint committees representing all the metal crafts, clerks and laborers, to combat the introduction of time study and incentive pay. When the railroad's executives ordered supervisors not to treat with such committees, workers sent delegates to Memphis, where they organized a "system federation," then called 16,000 workers out on strike to compel the railroad to deal with the federation rather than with the craft unions separately. The strike dragged on for almost four years before the national craft unions were able to call it off.[43]

During the same years pit committees of anthracite miners began to combine forces into general grievance committees, made up of United Mine Workers' members, but independent of the union. Starting with the negotiation of local wage supplements to the 1912 UMWA contract, they were soon carrying grievances from scattered mines of the large corporations to their main offices and circumventing the elaborate arbitration machinery of the contract. Local strikes under their leadership became common in 1913, prompting the union's district officers to try to suppress the committees and negotiate a more effective grievance machinery under their own control. The strength of the IWW among Italian laborers in the anthracite fields in 1915 and 1916 helped wrap debates over the authority of the miners' delegates in ideological controversy over the basic purposes of the workers' movement.[44]

Starting with the plan of employee representation instituted by the Colorado Fuel and Iron Company among its miners in 1916, employers began to experiment with shop committees under their auspices to combat labor unions. It was the government, however, and especially the National War Labor Board, that encouraged the spread of shop committees. The October 1917 report on works committees presented by England's Whitley Committee to Lloyd George provided the guidelines for the American Board's efforts (though by this time, of course, the governments of France, Germany, and Italy had also formalized systems of works committees). Works committees were envisaged by the Whitley Committee "as the means of enlisting the interest of the workers in the success both of the industry to which they are attached and of the workshop or factory where so much of their life is spent." Its purpose was *not*, Whitley added, to "discourage Trade [union] organization."[45]

During the spring and summer of 1918 the War Labor Board supervised elections for many shop committees in important centers of war production, especially metal and munitions works. Delegates were usually elected by the department in which they worked, rather than by craft, and union membership or nonmembership was scrupulously ignored in the process.[46] The tension between the objectives of representing the workers and interesting them in the factory's success provided the central theme of the drama of shop committees during the next four years.

The AFL convention of 1918 welcomed the establishment "in all large permanent shops" of "a committee of workers" to "regularly meet with the shop management to confer over matters of production," and to carry "to the general manager . . . any important grievances which the workers may have with reference to wages, hours, and conditions." Such organization, in the Federation's view, should be based *both* on "team work . . . for solving industrial problems" and on "collective bargaining" by workers free "to organize and make collective agreements." The next year's convention, however, at the insistence of the National Committee to Organize Iron and Steel Workers, denounced collective bargaining *without* recognized union involvement and agreements as "a delusion and a snare."[47]

During the intervening year many militant unionists had worked within the framework of shop committees, putting themselves forward as candidates and using metal trades councils to coordinate the efforts of craft unionists within the shop committees. This strategy not only linked government-sponsored workplace organization to multi-craft union coalitions (often with revolutionaries prominent in leadership) but also had the great advantage of encompassing many more women than the unions had enrolled (or, in many cases, wanted to enroll), reaching out to unskilled laborers and operatives, and even enlisting office workers. Thousands of stenographers, bookkeepers, and typists had joined AFL federal unions in 1918 and 1919. At the Schenectady works of General Electric, more than 900 office workers were union members by the summer of 1919; they elected delegates to the shop committee, and they participated in the metal trades council.[48]

The case of General Electric illustrates the contradictory tendencies within the movement for shop committees. The company had

57,500 workers in 1917, 40 percent of them in Schenectady and the rest unevenly divided among Lynn and Pittsfield, Massachusetts, Erie, Pennsylvania, and Fort Wayne, Indiana. Schenectady had long been a union and Socialist stronghold, while the other plants had been kept open shop until the war. The War Labor Board had intervened in strikes at Lynn and Pittsfield during 1918, setting up shop committees. Metal trades councils unified the crafts (especially the machinists and electricians) at all the plants, while their delegates on frequent missions to Washington to confer with the War Labor Board opened communication with representatives of other GE plants who were there for the same purpose. Within two weeks of the armistice, the company invited works' representatives from all its plants to Schenectady to form an Electrical Manufacturing Industry Labor Federation in opposition to the AFL. The several metal trades councils convened a rival gathering in Erie on the same day, and formulated demands for recognition of committees elected under union auspices, a 44-hour week, reinstatement of workers at Erie who were being laid off in large numbers, the planned sharing of available work, the release of all political prisoners, and half of every country's delegation to the Paris Peace Conference to be constituted of workers. When the Erie management refused to deal with the metal trades council and rushed ahead with elections for a company-sponsored works council, the Erie workers struck. By the end of December workers at Schenectady, Pittsfield, and Fort Wayne had closed their plants in support of the Erie strikers.

At this point the War Labor Board intervened to end the strike. It threatened to revoke the wage increase and Whitley Council type of organization that had been awarded by the Board to GE workers in Lynn after a local strike in July 1918, if they joined the national strike. It then notified workers at Pittsfield and Schenectady that it would not consider their grievances while they were on strike, just as the company announced it was replacing strikers with returning servicemen. By mid-January the strike had ended amid War Labor Board pledges to send examiners and strengthen shop committees at all the plants. General Electric subsequently declared that there was "no emergency" requiring it to submit to the Board now that the war was over, and that its Federation met all the standards of the Board for collective bargaining and was the only agency with which the company would deal. The company systematically drew into its plan of representation those union activists it termed "the more liberal minded" but withal respected by the workers, while taking advantage of the depression to cut wages and break down workers' defenses against the intensification of work. By 1926 it could truly boast to visiting correspondents that its plan of employee representation had long since ended all union agitation. The General Electric plan had as its sole purpose to enlist "the interest of the workers in the success both of the industry to which they are attached and of the workshop . . . where so much of their life is spent."[49]

In brief, shop committees provided a theater within which struggles for workers' control based on all-grades organization at the point of production clashed with employers' efforts to exclude unions from their works and with the government's quest for a mechanism to mediate industrial disputes and increase productivity. In just the same pattern that Gilbert Hatry discerned at the Billancourt Renault works, the workers first elected as workplace delegates under government plans to mediate and calm industrial disputes included the most militant individuals in the plants. And, as Carmen Sirianni observed, throughout Europe workplace organizations tended to be dominated by skilled male workers who had extensive experience in struggle and who were or had been involved in some revolutionary grouping. Yet those activists came to emphasize the needs and involvement of all the workers, rather than the sectoral needs of their crafts.[50] Moreover, in the public rallies to which they summoned workers, they spoke as much of political questions (freeing Tom Mooney and other prisoners, the Russian Revolution, and combatting the militarization of America, for example) as they did of workplace grievances.

Although experienced skilled males provided the most prominent activists in shop committees and metal trades councils, it was the unskilled workers, immigrants, and women who often took command of the streets during the strikes they called. Typical were the crowds of Lithuanians, Poles, and Italians who waged daily battles against the police in Waterbury, Connecticut, during June 1919, in an effort to force the brass companies to recognize their shop committees. Or the torrents of marchers who filed day afrer day through the streets of Lawrence, Paterson, and other textile centers in early 1919 in support of new industrial unions.[51] Neighborhood solidarities supported workplace organization among these immigrants, just as they did among Chicago's packinghouse workers. It was for this reason that the leaders of the AFL's United Textile Workers (an amalgamation of craft unions) had refused to organize foreign-born workers where, in the words of President John Golden, "they work in a community in large numbers and especially where they are of one nationality." To do so, he explained, was simply to provide recruits for the IWW. The militants from Lawrence, Paterson, and Passaic who met after their 1919 strikes to form the radical Amalgamated Textile Workers of America envisaged such immigrants as their proper constituency.[52]

One strategic objective of company-sponsored employee representation plans was to separate shop committees from such community support and from union involvement as well as from issues other than immediate company affairs (and also from the arbitration of the National War Labor Board before it ceased operations in June 1919). Such plans developed rapidly in heavy industry between 1919 and 1922. Goodyear, Pullman, International Harvester, Westinghouse, and many other firms simply announced dates for the election of representatives from the various departments of their establishments and declared that they would thereafter discuss grievances only with representatives chosen in this way. Commonly they specified that representatives had to be American citizens and have worked in the plant some specified period of time (often a year). Lines of craft were studiously ignored by these plans, and the economist William Leiserson observed that the movement "from the outset was making its greatest strides" among the unskilled and semiskilled who had been neglected by the AFL. Union members, however, were systematically discharged or coopted into the plans, as the postwar wave of labor struggles subsided. By 1924, when the National Industrial Conference Board surveyed 814 plans involving 1,177,037 workers, it found that representatives tended to be married, male, senior employees who were property owners and native Americans. Some managers even complained that they were inclined to "err on the side of being ultra-conservative."[53]

Shop committees organically linked to the union movement survived mainly in the garment industry and in railroad repair shops. In both settings the economic crisis of 1920–22 significantly transformed their functions. The depression cast these progressive-led unions into a war for survival, highlighted by the successful Amalgamated Clothing Workers strike of 1921 and the disastrous railroad shopcrafts strike of 1922. It also broke the upsurge of strike activity, which had encompassed so much of the working class in 1919 and 1920, leaving the progressive unions still strong but isolated. Their lonely, defensive battles tied the shop committees loyally and ardently to the discipline of the unions themselves. But they also made the unions' leaders vividly aware of the vast gap between the wages and hours their members enjoyed and those prevailing in nonunionized sectors of the same industry, let alone in the economy as a whole.

The formula to which the embattled progressives turned for salvation was scientific management. Shop organization, they argued, could be used as a basis for increasing the efficiency of unionized firms so that they could compete successfully with low-wage open shops. The Amalgamated Clothing Workers had turned in this direction as early as September 1919, when shop committees throughout the industry were still battling independently for supplementary wage increases and to ease the intensity of work. Hailing a new agreement with the National Industrial Federation of Clothing Manufacturers for joint councils of management and workers to supervise the terms of work, President Hillman said: "Our organization has demonstrated that labor has nothing to gain by withholding production; on the other hand labor has everything to gain by aiding in increasing production."[54]

As G. D. H. Cole had observed in England during the war, "the existence of comparatively strong workshop organization enabled dilution to proceed more smoothly than it would otherwise have done."[55] Effective workplace organization may have plagued management on the big questions of operating the enterprise, but it had provided a handy vehicle for resolving little ones. Moreover, the revolutionaries who were so prominent in the committees themselves considered many craft practices archaic, and were eager to show, in the words of Clothing Workers' secretary Joseph Schlossberg, that they could "establish order in the industry in the place of the chaos created by the employers when they had things their own way."[56]

Of course, such productivist inclinations were linked to the belief that the industry soon would belong to the workers. When that prospect faded from view, however, and economic crisis threatened the very survival of those companies that had been unionized, the "plant patriotism" implicit in the progressives' thinking flowered. The Ladies' Garment Workers negotiated a far-reaching joint productivity agreement in New York, in order to fend off the spread of piece work and subcontracting in 1921, and the next year actually got a court injunction to force the employers to live up to the agreement. The Clothing Workers promoted time studies and overrode protective craft practices wholesale, even when that led to the dismissal of large numbers of cutters and other skilled workers. The Machinists led other railway shopcrafts into the famous Baltimore and Ohio Plan, under which the structure of system federations was linked with management representatives at every level of command, with the aim of increasing productivity and stopping the railroad from sending repair work out to non-union shops.[57]

Conclusion

The leaders of America's unions in the postwar years had at their disposal those levers of command, experience, cadres, and rapport with the daily patterns of working life that Spriano found put their

CGL counterparts in the decisive role in Italy's labor movement. To American business, however, these attributes appeared not as bulwarks against radicalism but as an intolerable menace to the power of the enterprise to maneuver in an economy characterized first by wartime inflation, then by economic crisis and deflation. AFL leaders liked to depict themselves as fighting a two-front war against reactionary industrialists on one side and mindless revolutionaries who threatened to tear down the "house of labor" by flouting its "tried and true ways" on the other. Indeed, revolutionaries of various persuasions were engaged in revitalizing central labor unions, in developing metal trades councils, and in enrolling all grades of workers into new styles of workplace organization. Their efforts challenged the rigid conception of contracts, discipline, and authority held by union leaders, but they lacked a coordinating center, which might have directed their local activities toward national power. Moreover, they lacked even unionists of national prominence and authority who were prepared to utilize their initiatives in the struggle for national objectives. Only the Amalgamated Clothing Workers mastered the art of tapping the energy and resources of the local radicals rather than attacking them.

Can a pattern of development be discerned amidst all this conflict? Perhaps so. Between the fall of 1918 and early 1920, workers seemed to attack on all fronts at once. Bold organizing campaigns, which spurned the cautious traditions of craft unionism, swept millions of workers into unions in steel, textiles, meat-packing, and metal-fabricating plants. They were joined by typists, telephone operators, government clerks, teachers, policemen, and firemen. Where unions already existed, rebel movements not only mobilized local strikes in defiance of national officers but also struck for freedom for Tom Mooney and an end to arms shipments to Russian counterrevolutionaries. Striking Illinois miners who left the job for Tom Mooney in 1919 then struck again to protest company fines for the first strike and called for the election of worker delegates to an industrial congress, "there to demand of the capitalist class that all instruments of industries be turned over to the working class."[58] Earlier in the year in Pennsylvania a mine union leader reported that anarchist Carlo Tresca had spoken "and aroused the workers so that they would not heed the warnings of . . . the President of the District." Italian miners marched "defiantly through the city bearing the Red flag," infuriating the native-born residents, and then "sent a committee of their own choosing and not composed of union officials, demanding of the company to equalize output at all collieries so that all workers will have some work."[59] Immediate grievances and ambitious political objectives blended in the everyday struggles of workers during these years, and what leadership was evident usually took the form of informal alliances of revolutionaries of varied persuasions and affiliations, rather than the concerted initiative of any one organization. Union authority, discipline, and contractual relations were held in very low esteem.

Then came the hour of union supremacy. Continuing inflation turned the workers' strike militancy overwhelmingly in the direction of wage demands during the first six months of 1920, but that militancy often fueled huge rebellions against the slow-moving bargaining machinery of the national unions, most notably in the strike of railroad switchmen and yard workers that brought out well over 25,000 workers under their own informal leadership in April. It took more than threats and mass expulsions of members to restore the rebels to the union fold; a government board hastily opened formal negotiations for national agreements between the unions (now unified for a general "wage movement") and the reprivatized railroad lines, and for substantial wage increases.[60] As inflation gave way to depression, however, the national authority and discipline of unions became indispensable barriers against wage cuts and ultimate lines of defense of recently won shop committees and eight-hour days. The ranks closed, and experienced officers commanded the type of contractual battle they understood best. The novel element in this contest was the progressives' new strategy: the unions' commitment to make employers who recognized them more efficient, combined with electoral efforts to send friends of labor to Congress and publicity campaigns on behalf of legislation to nationalize the railroads and mines.

What had become of the revolutionaries? As in Europe, they were building parties. Their revolutionary objectives, Vittorio Foa has written, had been separated from the concrete struggles of workers and become entrusted instead to foreign developments: to the success of a socialist fatherland.[61] Had they also been separated from the workers in the physical sense, as James Hinton and Richard Hyman found in England and Dick Geary found in Germany, by being discharged in vast numbers during the depression and living in the world of the unemployed rather than that of the factory?[62] No research has been done to answer that question. We only know that, aside from the garment industry and some western Pennsylvania coal fields, Communists were effectively isolated from union struggles after 1922.

The differences between America and Europe were profound: the revolutionary fervor of Germany and Russia found no parallel in America, nor did the 1919 effort of British unions to use their economic power to win nationalization of the mines and railroads; no Red

Guards bore arms at the behest of factory councils, nor, as I have observed, was there a FIOM, ready to project obstruction and factory occupations as the path to wage gains. These differences attest to the relatively secure position of American business and government, which had only been strengthened by the war.

For all those differences, the rhythm of developments was remarkably similar, just as many of the same forms of struggle appeared on both sides of the Atlantic. American workers may have been out of step with their European counterparts, but they were marching to the same drummer.

Notes

1.   Paolo Spriano, *The Occupation of the Factories: Italy 1920*, trans. Gwyn A. Williams (London, 1975), 34, 28; and A. Losovsky, *The International Council of Trade and Industrial Unions* (New York, 1920).

2.   James Weinstein, *The Decline of Socialism in America, 1912–1925* (New York, 1967); David Montgomery, "Labor and the Republic in Industrial America," *Le mouvement social* 111 (Avril–Juin 1980), 201–215.

3.   *Monthly Labor Review* 14 (Jan. 1922), 203–224.

4.   *Machinists Monthly Journal* 32 (June 1920), 552 (hereafter cited as *MMJ*).

5.   David Montgomery, *Workers' Control in America* (New York, 1979), 91–112.

6.   *Labor Year Book 1919* (New York, 1919), 163–164.

7.   James E. Cronin, "Labor Insurgency and Class Formation," *Social Science History* 4 (Feb. 1980), 125–152.

8.   James R. Barrett, "Work and Community in 'The Jungle': Chicago's Packing House Workers, 1894–1922," Ph.D. dissertation, University of Pittsburgh, 1981, 187. Alexander M. Bing, *War-Time Strikes and Their Adjustment* (New York, 1921), 203–209.

9.   See, for example, the Anthony Capraro Papers (Immigration History Research Center, University of Minnesota) on Lawrence, Massachusetts; and Gladys L. Palmer, *Union Tactics and Economic Change: A Case Study of Three Philadelphia Textile Unions* (Philadelphia, 1932) on the Kensington neighborhood. Cf. the ambivalent image of the role of ethnic organizations in William Z. Foster, *The Great Steel Strike and Its Lessons* (New York, 1920).

10.   Bing, *War-Time Strikes*, 30n.

11.   Alexander Trachtenberg, *The American Socialists and the War* (New York, 1917), 34, 39–45; Weinstein, *Decline*, 124, 127, 134–154; Advertisements of the People's Council of America, R.G. 28, file 50206, National Archives.

12.   Loyall A. Osborne to William H. Taft, May 31, 1918, Records of the National War Labor Board, R.G. 2, Administrative Files E 15, National Archives; James A. Emery, "War Labor Board for Increasing Production,"

New York Times, April 14, 1918; Philip Taft, *The A. F. of L. in the Time of Gompers* (New York, 1957), 343–360. On France, see Gilbert Hatry, "Les délégués d'atelier aux usines Renault," in Patrick Fridenson, ed., *1914–1918, l'autre front* (Paris, 1977), 232; on Germany and elsewhere, see Cronin, 133.

13. Frank J. Warne, *The Workers at War* (New York, 1920), 29–30, 83–84; Melvyn Dubofsky, *We Shall Be All* (Chicago, 1969), 366–375, 384–391; Vernon H. Jensen, *Heritage of Conflict: Labor Relations in the Nonferrous Metals Industry up to 1930* (Ithaca, N.Y., 1950), 411–429. On Pittsburgh, see Clifton Reese to W. B. Wilson, Aug. 3, 1917, Dept. of Labor files, R.G. 280, National Archives.

14. E. C. Davidson to Post Office Department, Feb. 5, 1918, R.G. 28, file 50206, National Archives.

15. John H. M. Laslett, "End of an Alliance: Selected Correspondence between Socialist Party Secretary Adolph Germer and U.M.W. of A. Leaders in World War One," *Labor History* 17 (Fall 1971), 579; Warne, 115. The penalty fine clause was to trigger the large rebel strike of 1919. See Sylvia Kopald, *Rebellion in Labor Unions* (New York, 1924), 74–75.

16. Roydon Harrison, "The War Emergency Workers' National Committee," in Asa Briggs and John Saville, eds., *Essays in Labor History, 1886–1923* (Hamden, Conn., 1971), 211–259; Richard H. Frost, *The Mooney Case* (Stanford, Cal., 1968).

17. Calculations from statistics in *Monthly Labor Review*, 15 (July 1922), 167–169.

18. *Boilermakers' Journal*, Oct. 1917, quoted in V. W. Lanfear, *Business Fluctuations and the American Labor Movement, 1915–1922* (New York, 1924), 87–88.

19. Quoted in Charles Maier, *Recasting Bourgeois Europe* (Princeton, 1975), 59. Cf. Lozofsky, 56: "the bourgeoisie is strong . . . above all because *it relies upon the workers' organizations in its struggle against the workers.*"

20. Haggai Hurvitz, "Ideology and Industrial Conflict: President Wilson's First Industrial Conference of October, 1919" *Labor History* 18 (Fall 1977), 509–524; Marguerite Green, *The National Civic Federation and the American Labor Movement, 1900–1925* (Washington, D.C., 1956), 441.

21. Alexander M. Bing, *War-Time Strikes*, 116–132; Federico Romero, *Il Sindicato come Istituzione: la regolamentazione del conflitto industriale negli Stati Uniti, 1912–18* (Torino, 1981), 196–224. On the minimum wage question, see "Memorandum on the Minimum Wage and Increased Cost of Living" and related correspondence in C. P. Sweeney Files, NWLB, R.G. 2, National Archives. On the railways, see American Federation of Labor, Railway Employees' Department, *The Case of the Railway Shopmen* (Chicago, 1922), 14, 35–37.

22. Clarence J. Hicks, *My Life in Industrial Relations: Fifty Years in the Growth of a Profession* (New York and London, 1941), 136–138. On employers' federations in Europe, see Maier, 86; and also Eugene Rotwein, "Post-World War I Price Movements and Price Policy," *Journal of Political Economy* 53 (1945), 234–257.

23. Editorial, *New York Call*, April 17, 1921; *New York World*, May 26, 1921; *Avanti* file, R.G. 28, Box 20, National Archives.

24. William Preston, Jr., *Aliens and Dissenters: Federal Suppression of Radicals, 1903–1933* (New York, 1966), 181–272; Jonathan Grossman, *The Department of Labor* (New York and Washington, 1973), 23–26; United States Department of Commerce, Bureau of the Census, *Historical Statistics of the United States, Colonial Times to 1970*, 2 vols. (Washington, D.C., 1975), I: 114.

25. Maier, 311–315, 362–386, 427–430, 445–446, 556–572; Henry Pelling, *A History of British Trade Unionism* (Baltimore, 1963), 262.

26. George Soule, *The Intellectual and the Labor Movement* (New York, 1923); *American Labor Yearbook 1919* (New York, 1919), 203–208; J. B. S. Hardman, ed., *American Labor Dynamics in the Light of Post-War Developments* (New York, 1928), 370–372; Harry W. Laidler and Norman Thomas, eds., *New Tactics in Social Conflict* (New York, 1926).

27. Laidler and Thomas, *New Tactics*, 39–41; *Seattle Union Record*, Jan. 19, 1921, p. 3; Mark Perlman, *The Machinists* (Cambridge, Mass., 1961), 114; Harry W. Laidler, *Recent Developments in the American Labor Movement* (New York, 1923), 16–18; David J. Saposs, "Labor Banks and Trade Union Capitalism," *American Review* (Sept.–Oct. 1923), 534–539.

28. *MMJ* 33 (Jan. 1921), 49–50; *MMJ* 33 (Sept. 1921), 759–761, 769. On the IAM's experiences with and changing attitudes toward Soviet Russia, see *MMJ* 33 (Jan. 1921), 18–19; 33 (Sept. 1921), 739–743; 33 (Oct. 1921), 834–839; 33 (April 1921), 293–295; *Seattle Union Record*, March 9, 1921, p. 3.

29. *Seattle Union Record*, Jan. 25, 1921, p. 3.

30. American Federation of Labor, *Report of Proceedings of the Thirty-Ninth Annual Convention . . . 1919* (Washington, D.C., 1919), 269–278. On the voting power of certain delegates and the response to Bonfield, see *American Labor Yearbook 1919*, 150–151.

31. AFL, *Proceedings . . . 1920*, 399–420; JCL, "The A.F. of L. Convention," *Socialist Review* 9 (Aug. 1920), 88–89.

32. AFL, *Proceedings . . . 1921*; *Seattle Union Record*, June 21, 1921, p. 1; June 25, 1921, p. 1; June 27, 1921, p. 8.

33. Foster, *Steel Strike*; report of William Hannon, *MMJ*, 32 (Feb. 1920); David Brody, *Steelworkers in America: The Nonunion Era* (Cambridge, Mass., 1960), 276–278; Barrett, "Packing House Workers," 296–317; William Tuttle, Jr., *Race Riot: Chicago in the Red Summer of 1919* (New York, 1970), 114–142. On the AFL departments before 1914, see Taft, 213–224; Helen Marot, *American Labor Unions* (New York, 1914), 84–111.

34. *Labor Age* 11 (March 1922), 24; David J. Saposs, *Readings in Trade Unionism* (New York, 1926), 135–138. On the 1922 shopmen's strike, see Selig Perlman and Philip Taft, *History of Labor in the United States, 1896–1932* (New York, 1935), 515–524.

35. Little has been written on the subordination of central labor bodies to the AFL, but see the provocative insights in Jacques Rouillard, *Les syndicats nationaux au Québec de 1900 à 1930* (Québec, 1979), 66–84. On France, see Peter Schöttler, "Politique sociale ou lutte des classes: notes sur le syndicalisme 'apolitique' des Bourse du Travail," *Le mouvement social* 116 (Juillet-Septembre

1981), 3–20. Vittorio Foa depicts a subordination of horizontal to vertical organizations in Germany and England, but an unsuccessful effort by the Italian CGL to follow the German model before the war. See Foa, "Corso di storia sociale contemporanea," unpublished manuscript, 50–55, 75.

36.   Montgomery, *Workers' Control*, 95. Melvyn Dubofsky, *When Workers Organize: New York City in the Progressive Era* (Amherst, Mass., 1968), 126–151. On Kansas City, see NWLB files, R.G. 280, National Archives.

37.   History Committee of the General Strike Committee, *The Seattle General Strike* (Seattle, 1919), esp. 5; *Locomotive Engineers' Journal* 57 (July 1923), 558.

38.   *MMJ*, 31 (March, 1919), 233.

39.   John R. Commons et al., *Industrial Government* (New York, 1921), 353–355.

40.   U.S. Department of Labor, Federal Mediation and Conciliation Service records, R.G. 280, file 170/1035, National Archives; *MMJ*, 32 (April 1920), 352, 366–367; *MMJ*, 32 (Aug. 1920), 722–723, 725–726.

41.   Jack W. Skeels, "Early Carriage and Auto Unions: The Impact of Industrialization and Rival Unionism," *Industrial and Labor Relations Review* 17 (July 1964), 566–583.

42.   Quoted in Montgomery, *Workers' Control*, 120.

43.   *Ibid.*, 134–135; Philip S. Foner, *History of the Labor Movement in the United States* (New York, 1980), v: 164–181.

44.   Edgar Sydenstricker, "Settlement of Disputes under Agreements in the Anthracite Industry," in John R. Commons, *Trade Unionism and Labor Problems*, Second Series (Boston, 1921), 495–524. On the IWW, see Patrick Lynch, "Pennsylvania Anthracite: A Forgotten IWW Venture, 1906–1916," M.A. thesis, Bloomsburg State College, Pennsylvania, 1974.

45.   Memorandum, Lieut. F. H. Bird, Office of the Chief of Ordnance to Dr. Lucien W. Cheney, n.d., NWLB, R.G. 2, Administrative File B 56. The Whitley report is in G. D. H. Cole, ed., *Workshop Organization* (Oxford, 1923), 152–155. On the continental countries, see Carmen J. Sirianni, "Workers' Control in the Era of World War I: A Comparative Analysis of the European Experience," *Theory and Society* 9 (1980), 42–49.

46.   See, for example, the elections in Bridgeport. Montgomery, *Workers' Control*, x. According to a survey by the National Industrial Conference Board, 110 of the 225 works' councils established during 1918 and 1919 were instituted by government agencies (86 by the NWLB), and 105 set up by companies independently. Bing, *War-Time Strikes*, 164n.

47.   Commons, *Trade Unionism and Labor Problems, Second Series*, 345–348.

48.   *American Labor Yearbook 1919*, 188–189.

49.   *Employees* v. *General Electric Company*, Erie, Pa., Docket No. 20–127, NWLB, R.G. 2, Administrative Files Box 56; Department of Labor, R.G. 28, file 33/1702 (National Archives); Charles M. Ripley, *Life in a Large Manufacturing Plant* (Schenectady, N.Y., 1919), 43; *New York Call*, Feb. 20, 1919; *MMJ*, 31 (Jan. 1919), 35; "The 1918 Strike at Erie General Electric," *UE 506 News*, Jan., 1980; Robert W. Bruère, "West Lynn," *Survey* 56 (April 1, 1926), 21–27, 49;

[Catherton Brownell] to Owen D. Young, "Report of an investigation into industrial conditions in the several plants of the General Electric Company, together with recommendations of a plan to improve them" [1920], Owen D. Young Papers. I am indebted to Ronald W. Schatz for this document.

50.   Hatry, 221–235; Sirianni, 74–75. Cf., Cecelia F. Bucki, "Dilution and Craft Tradition: Bridgeport, Connecticut, Munitions Workers, 1915–1919," *Social Science History* 4 (Feb. 1980), 105–124; James Hinton, *The First Shop Stewards' Movement* (London, 1973).

51.   Cecelia F. Bucki, *Metal, Minds and Machines: Waterbury at Work* (Waterbury, Conn., 1980), 77–79. On Patterson, see NWLB, R.G. 2, Case File 1123, National Archives. On Lawrence, see David Goldberg, "The Lawrence Strike of 1919," M.A. thesis, University of Pittsburgh, 1979.

52.   Interview with John Golden, Thomas F. McMahon, and James Starr, Feb. 25, 1919, David J. Saposs Papers, Box 21, file 11, State Historical Society of Wisconsin. A. J. Muste, "Sketches for an Autobiography," in Nat Hentoff, ed., *The Essays of A. J. Muste* (Indianapolis, Ind., 1967), 80–150.

53.   Laidler and Thomas, *New Tactics*, 96–111; Stuart D. Brandes, *American Welfare Capitalism* (Chicago, 1970), 131–133. The quotation from Leiserson is in Hicks, 83.

54.   *Survey* 42 (Sept., 1919), 843–846. The quotation is on p. 844.

55.   Cole, 55.

56.   Quoted in Evans Clark, "The Industry Is Ours," *Socialist Review* 9 (July 1920), 59.

57.   On the Ladies Garment Workers, see Jesse T. Carpenter, *Competition and Collective Bargaining in the Needle Trades, 1910–1967* (Ithaca, N.Y., 1972), 323. On the Clothing Workers, see Steve Fraser, "Dress Rehearsal for the New Deal: Shopfloor Insurgents, Political Elites, and Industrial Democracy," in Michael Frisch and Daniel Walkowitz, eds., *Working-Class America* (Urbana, Ill., 1983). A fine account of the B & O Plan may be found in H. Dubreuil, *Standards: le travail américain vu par un ouvrier français* (Paris, 1929), 350–388.

58.   Kopald, 74–75.

59.   Interview with Peter Furrara, Ex. Bd. Member, Dist. No. 2, United Mine Workers, in David J. Saposs Papers, Box 21, State Historical Society of Wisconsin.

60.   Kopald, 124–177; Warne, *Workers at War*, 161–166; "Report of Proceedings in Connection with 1919–1920 Wage Movement," *MMJ*, 32 (March, 1920), 226–240.

61.   Foa, 101.

62.   James Hinton and Richard Hyman, *Trade Unions and Revolution: The Industrial Politics of the Early British Communist Party* (London, 1975), 12–14; Dick Geary, *European Labour Protest, 1848–1939* (London, 1981), 150–155; Geary, "Radicalism and the Worker: Metalworkers and Revolution 1914–1923," in Richard Evans, ed., *Society and Politics in Wilhelmine Germany* (London, 1978), 282–286.

Chapter Five

Workers and Revolution In Germany, 1918-1919: The Urban Dimension

Mary Nolan

In the past decade and a half the German revolution of 1918–1919 has been rediscovered by historians and sociologists. Whereas previous scholars had argued that there was collapse, chaos, and utopian leftism that attracted only weak interest, current writers insist that Germany experienced a genuine if unsuccessful revolution that enjoyed mass support, developed coherent and partially realizable goals, and displayed innovative forms of militancy. Workers' and soldiers' councils, strike movements, socialization demands, and the actions of the Communist Party (KPD) and Independent Social Democratic Party (USPD) have displaced the Provisional Government, parliamentary elections, and the conservative practice of the national Social Democratic Party (SPD) as the objects of analysis. This renewed and reoriented concern with the German revolution of 1918–19 is part of a larger attempt to reinterpret the history of the German working class, which has usually been depicted—with praise or scorn—as thoroughly reformist, negatively integrated, passive, and timid. This new concern also reflects the growing interest in the strengths and limitations of workers' councils, the forms of workers' control, and the possibilities of revolution in more advanced industrial societies.

Three problems have stood in the forefront of recent scholarship. First, the economic and political causes of the moderate revolution of November 1918 and its subsequent radicalization have been explored. Wartime and postwar deprivation, dislocation, and economic reorganization, the lack of political reform despite social democratic collaboration in the war effort, military defeat, the incompetence of the SPD, and the actions of the left have all been explored. Although the complex links between wartime developments and working-class protest have been analyzed, the revolution tends to be viewed exclusively as a product of war. Prewar social, political, and cultural developments have been neglected; the influence of prefigurative institutions and patterns of behavior on workers' consciousness and actions in 1918–19 remains unexamined.

Second, the viability of the various revolutionary programs with their demands for political democratization, partial socialization, and a primary or secondary role for workers' councils has been evaluated in an effort to show that there was a large middle ground between the conservative Weimar Republic, which the SPD established, and Bolshevism, which it eschewed. But a critical assessment of those possibilities by and large remains to be done.

The third focus of current work has been a reassessment of the failure of the revolution. Some scholars blame the SPD and its reliance on the old military and industrial elites, while others give priority to the weakness of the USPD or the lack of a Leninist party, and a third group focuses on the structurally induced reformism of skilled workers undergoing dequalification. While these works have provided a wealth of new information on local and national events, they tend either to overemphasize the role of political parties at the expense of social and cultural developments or to fall back on a sterile reductionism, which precludes an exploration of how workers make sense of and act on their structural situation.

My concern is not with the causes of the revolution, although I shall allude to them in my analysis, but rather with programs and goals, strategies and shortcomings. I am concerned with how and why the German workers who made the revolution in 1918–19 made it in such different ways. These differences have often been ignored in the effort to prove the very existence of radicalism. The historiography is doubly biased—first, toward political as opposed to economic actions, for the former have been better documented, and second, toward metal workers, for they played a prominent role in Germany and had radical counterparts in other countries. The search for broad similarities within Germany and among European countries, however valuable, overlooks the different forms of class consciousness and radicalism manifested by different types of workers. It preempts an investigation of the extent to which diversity was an indication of vitality and a source of strength and the degree to which it weakened the revolutionary forces. An emphasis on the pervasive popularity of workers' control and socialization, while correct on the most general level, blurs rather than clarifies these already murky concepts.

A simple assertion of the prevalence of radicalism frequently leads to a romanticization of the revolt of the less skilled and less organized and limits our understanding of the successes and failures of the German revolution. Historians have not been wrong to place ultimate blame for the failure of 1918–19 on the continued power of the right and on the majority Social Democrats in Berlin, who allied themselves with traditional industrial and military elites, thwarted extensive political as well as economic reform, and used troops against rebellious workers. But a concern with final responsibility must not blind us to the weaknesses within the radical traditions of different regions and occupations. It must not lead us to ignore the limits of workers' goals and strategies or the persistent difficulties they had in merging politics and economics in theory and practice.

The distinction of interest here is not between reformists and radicals or between the more democratic, less industrialized south of Germany and the authoritarian, economically advanced north. Rather, what will be investigated is the differences within radical regions. Even in the most militant areas of Germany, such as the Ruhr and Lower Rhine—where left workers fought from November 1918 until May 1919, where the political order was attacked most strongly and the campaign for socialization most extensive, and where workers' and soldiers' councils and workers' security forces, general strikes, and Communist takeovers proliferated—distinctly different patterns of revolution emerged. Workers in Essen, Dortmund, Remscheid, Elberfeld, and a multitude of other industrial centers played diverse parts in the revolutionary drama, often speaking their own language and pursuing their own course of action with little heed to other actors.

In some cities revolutionaries emphasized political demands and actions and aimed at the seizure of political power locally and nationally. They controlled and worked through left parties and unions rather than ad hoc structures. Having at best a vague notion of workers' control on the shopfloor, they envisioned socialization as a process of nationalization, to be imposed piecemeal and from the top down. They were aware of and tried to coordinate their actions with revolutionaries elsewhere. In other cities and towns revolutionary workers focused on economic demands, ranging from wages to socialization and workers' control. Preferring strikes to political actions more traditionally conceived, and operating through ad hoc organizations with popularly elected leaders, they acted outside of and often against not only the SPD and free trade unions but also the USPD and KPD. They understood workers' control as control of the workplace and wanted to begin socialization from the bottom up. These revolutionaries, who generally worked in mining or basic iron and steel industries, were profoundly isolated from radical workers in other occupations—not only outside the region but within it as well.

Düsseldorf and Hamborn, two Ruhr towns in which workers were singularly radical and active during 1918–19 provide clear examples of the two patterns of revolution, with Düsseldorf adopting what we can call the political model and Hamborn pioneering the economic one. The emergence of different patterns and their respective strengths and weaknesses cannot be understood if we look only at the experience of war and revolution and thereby posit a sharp break between prewar structures and practices and subsequent developments. Nor can we deduce political behavior from different workers' positions in the labor process, looking for threatened skilled workers in one place and alienated, unskilled proletarians in the other. Such reductionism is both simplistic and ahistorical. Instead, we must explore the manifold similarities and differences in the two cities and in the experiences of their workers, similarities and differences that go back to the pre-World War I era.

Düsseldorf and Hamborn represented two typical models of Ruhr urban economic development: the diversified industrial metropolis and the sprawling mining town. Located in the western Ruhr and integrally involved in the mining and metal industries that dominated that region, these cities shared many important characteristics. Both were very much a product of late nineteenth- and early twentieth-century industrialization and experienced not only dramatic economic transformation but also extremely rapid urbanization and high rates of in and out migration. Both towns were predominantly Catholic, a fact of cultural and political significance in Protestant Germany. As a part of Prussia, Düsseldorf and Hamborn were governed provincially and locally by authoritarian political institutions and had a restrictive three-class suffrage that excluded the working-class from representation and power. During World War I both played a pivotal role in the war economy, and their workers enjoyed the leverage accruing from that strategic position. Simultaneously, both towns experienced a dramatic restructuring of their economies and work forces as well as a marked deterioration of working and living conditions.

Despite these similarities the two cities and the experiences of their workers differed in four fundamental ways—ways that created markedly different forms of class consciousness and revolutionary activity. First, the economic structures varied in terms of diversity, skill, occupation, and the organization of work. Second, both the class structures of the two cities and the background and experiences of their working class differed. Third, working-class communities and culture as well as the urban environment in which they were embedded were organized in fundamentally different ways. Fourth, the Social Democratic Party and free trade unions in the two cities did not develop along similar organizational and political lines, and their relationship to their respective working class bore little resemblance to one another. These economic, social, and cultural as well as political differences between Düsseldorf and Hamborn created two distinct patterns of revolution.

Düsseldorf was one of the most important, prosperous, and rapidly expanding cities in Imperial Germany. Situated on the Rhine, north of Cologne and south of the Ruhr mining and basic metal centers, it had been transformed from a sleepy provincial town, without economic or administrative significance, into an industrial metropolis in the last quarter of the nineteenth century. By World War I it had over 400,000 inhabitants. A product of German unification and industrialization, Düsseldorf was a symbol of the economic power and pride of the Empire. It was also a victim of the social problems and political conflicts that plagued an authoritarian society with powerful preindustrial remnants and sharp class divisions.[1]

Industrial capitalism transformed all aspects of Düsseldorf's economy, creating a powerful and modern factory sector, vigorous artisan trades, and thriving commerce. Metal was undisputably king, employing one-third of the work force. Unlike the Ruhr, however, Düsseldorf produced semifinished and finished goods, above all machinery, rather than basic iron and steel. Other factory industries, such as textiles and chemicals, existed but were relatively insignificant. The sector that produced consumer goods for the rapidly expanding population prospered, and both construction and wood workers constituted a major element in the working class and workers' movement. Both within and between sectors of the economy, firm size, the degree of mechanization, and skill levels varied enormously. Machine making, for example, encompassed everything from the sprawling factory of

Rheinmetall, Krupp's main competitor, to the small and specialized artisan shop. While the metal, wood working and construction industries relied heavily on skilled male labor, the highly mechanized, medium-sized chemical and textile factories used unskilled men and women, as did the small-scale, unmechanized food and clothing sectors.[2] Commerce blossomed as well as industry, but it was an appendage to the metal sector rather than autonomous. In addition to being a center for trade and production, Düsseldorf was also the administrative city for the corporations, cartels, and economic interest groups that dominated the Ruhr and Lower Rhine industrial area.[3] Finally, after 1900 the city government, which ran public transportation, gas, water, electrical and sewage works, and a variety of cultural institutions, became the largest single employer in Düsseldorf.[4]

Industrialization fundamentally altered Düsseldorf's precapitalist social order. Economic expansion attracted thousands of migrants, who formed a majority of the population in the prewar years and made Düsseldorf the tenth-largest city in Germany. Most migrants came from towns and cities in the Rhineland and neighboring Westphalia or from the other major cities in Germany rather than directly from the countryside or eastern Germany.[5] Hence, they were acquainted with and committed to urban life and employment in an industrial capitalist economy. Although Ruhr towns, such as Hamborn, were solidly industrial and working class, Düsseldorf was more diverse. Sixty percent of the population depended on industry and two-thirds of the labor force were proletarian, but there was a sizeable old and new lower-middle class, a professional bourgeoisie, and a substantial industrial upper class.[6] As a result, class divisions were sharp and visible, and class conflicts complex.

Whereas neighboring Krefeld had its spinners and weavers, Solingen its cutlery makers, and the Ruhr proper its miners, there was no typical Düsseldorf worker. The work force in metal ranged from unskilled helpers and semiskilled machine operators to skilled factory turners and artisan smiths. Migrant Protestant carpenters, native Düsseldorf painters, and unskilled migrant Catholic helpers all worked in construction. Wood workers and printers were highly skilled, well paid, and well organized, and many had stable family lives and roots in Düsseldorf. Chemical, paper, and textile workers, on the other hand, were transient, semi- or unskilled, and poorly paid. And that was only the male portion of the proletariat. Women workers, low paid and largely single, worked in commercial establishments, the sweated trades, and most frequently in domestic service. Three-fourths of the working class were Catholic, but the Düsseldorf-born and the migrant elements were hardly cohesive and the Protestant contingent was increasing. Although most workers were young male migrants, that fact did not overcome differences in occupation, religion, place of birth, and length of stay.[7] Culture and community, background, and expectations as well as current economic condition all splintered Düsseldorf's proletariat.

Prewar Hamborn presented quite a different picture. Located in the western Ruhr, Hamborn had not been a traditional mining center in the mid-nineteenth century, when mines were state run and miners had a strong corporatist tradition. Instead, like many neighboring industrial centers, Hamborn had been created literally from nothing by the westward expansion of the fully capitalist mining and basic metal industries and the huge migration that it drew in its wake. And the town had been created somewhat later than Düsseldorf. In 1870 Hamborn had a mere 2,000 inhabitants, by 1910 over 101,000. Only at that date was it officially accorded the status of a city, with its own government.[8]

Thousands of German- and Polish-speaking migrants flocked to Hamborn, primarily from east of the Elbe river. For these proletarianized rural laborers, the transition to mining on the other side of Germany was as traumatic as emigration. These migrants, consisting predominantly of men (due to the structure of job opportunities), came to fill the less skilled positions in the three firms that dominated the Hamborn economy, the mines Deutsche Kaiser and Neumühl and the Thyssen steel works, which by 1913 employed 14,000, 6,000, and 11,000 workers respectively.[9] Although these workers were new to urban life and lacked a tradition of industrial employment, they were united not only by a similar background but also by a common work experience in Hamborn. This was especially true of miners, for the nature of mine work created a strong occupational identification and solidarity. Miners worked in groups, whose members had relatively little direct supervision but were heavily dependent on one another for wages and safety. Because mining was expanding rapidly and the hierarchy of skills was rudimentary, most could expect to move through it from hauler to apprentice hewer to hewer.[10]

Working-class solidarity was further reenforced by the overwhelmingly proletarian character of this dual industry town. Hamborn's middle class was miniscule, for the industrial elite preferred Düsseldorf to the dirt, poverty, and unrelievedly proletarian character of Ruhr mining centers. For their part, professionals, civil servants, and shopkeepers found few opportunities in a quasi-company town with a poorly developed urban infrastructure.[11]

In these two industrial centers, wages, working conditions, and the standard of living were remarkably similar despite the differences in the structure of their economies and working classes. Wage differentials were greater in Düsseldorf due to the occupational and sexual heterogeneity of its work force, and weekly earnings varied more in Hamborn due to the variability of different coal seams, but average money wages were unquestionably high in both cities and rose throughout the prewar period. Real wages, however, presented a gloomier picture. Although optimists and pessimists are still debating the national movement of real wages after their undisputed rise in the late nineteenth century, recent scholarship on the Ruhr indicates stagnation after 1900 and actual decline for many workers immediately before World War I. On the one hand, inflation, housing shortages and high rents, and increased agrarian tariffs after 1906 pushed the cost of living steadily upward. On the other hand, employer pressure on the large wage bill of labor-intensive industries and the enormous obstacles to unionization and collective bargaining in the region prevented wages from rising commensurately.[12]

Nor were the life chances and security of workers fundamentally different in the two cities. In a comparison of metal workers in Remscheid, an old artisan town with a highly skilled work force employed in small shops, and miners and factory workers in Hamborn, Erhard Lucas argues that Remscheid workers had significantly better living and working conditions, greater job stability, and predictable life prospects, whereas Hamborn workers lacked all of these.[13] Düsseldorf, with its heterogeneous working class, high rates of in and out migration, and extremely unstable floating population of young workers, resembled the latter more than the former. A 1909 survey of the yearly budgets of better paid, more highly skilled workers in Düsseldorf, for example, showed that between 50 and 60 percent of their income went for food alone and that most families ended the year with no savings or in debt. If the situation was worse in Hamborn, the difference was one of degree, not kind. Unemployment plagued both towns in the recessions of 1901–3, 1907–9, and 1913, and workers in both areas frequently changed jobs, often leaving the city in the process.[14] Work time, an issue of constant contestation between mine owners and workers, ranged from eight to ten hours a day in the Hamborn mines, a figure that compared favorably with the best organized construction and wood workers in Düsseldorf and that represented a marked improvement over many metal workers in both cities who had twelve-hour shifts until 1912 or later. Hamborn workers suffered from more unsafe conditions, especially in the mines, and from the worm disease that

ravaged the Ruhr, but accident and death rates rose steadily in Düsseldorf as well.[15]

The urban environments of Düsseldorf and Hamborn reflected
both similarities imposed by rapid industrialization and differences
resulting from their preindustrial histories and from varied capitalist
strategies. The overwhelming majority of workers in both towns
rented apartments in low-density housing. In Düsseldorf these were
generally owned by speculative builders; in Hamborn, where job turnover was very high and labor shortages frequent, these might well be
part of a company-owned "colony." Such company housing served the
dual purpose of stabilizing the work force and curbing militancy.
Throughout the western Ruhr, government investigators and trade
unionists alike documented housing shortages and high rents for
working-class dwellings from the turn of the century onward and
noted that these made overcrowding and taking in roomers a necessity
for many, especially in towns like Hamborn.[16]

Urban institutions and amenities diverged much more than
housing patterns. Düsseldorf was a multi-class, well-established urban
center before it industrialized from the 1870s on. There was thus a
basic physical and social infrastructure of roads, schools, hospitals,
churches, and pubs, which was expanded, albeit inadequately, thereafter. Moreover, from the 1870s on Düsseldorf had both a rich "high"
culture, centering around theater, concerts, and museums, and an
urban popular culture, built on a social base of craftsmen, small tradesmen, and factory workers. The relative richness of urban life in Düsseldorf by no means integrated workers into the dominant society, but it
did facilitate the socialist and Catholic political and educational organizing efforts and gave them a less work-centered orientation. Hamborn, by contrast, was desolate indeed. Like so many new mining
centers, it lacked a halfway developed urban infrastructure, bourgeois
cultural institutions, and the residues of an older artisan tradition. The
company and the Catholic church filled the resulting gap inadequately,
thus leaving miners to organize many of their recreational and cultural
activities in an informal manner, centering around work groups or
traditional miners' institutions like the *Knappenvereine*, a sort of
friendly society.[17]

Forms of capitalist control were more varied in Düsseldorf than
in Hamborn. Construction, wood, leather, and some metal workers
were employed in small and medium-sized shops with more patriarchal and personal modes of supervision, less hierarchy, more job
control, and less skill dequalification. These conditions facilitated solidarity and organization among such relatively privileged workers but

set them apart from many metal workers, as well as textile and chemical laborers, who worked in large firms with finely graded hierarchies, close supervision, and more anonymous methods of control. Although Düsseldorf's large employers generally preferred authoritarianism to welfare paternalism, several of the largest metalworking and machinery firms, worried about both an adequate supply of skilled workers and potential unionization, did establish a variety of management-run insurance programs, educational courses, and recreational facilities. Such policies fragmented the work force and increased the costs of organization. Workers in the shoe, food, and clothing industries were threatened by mechanization on the one hand and intensification, feminization, subcontracting, and even homework on the other. Municipal workers faced a vigilant city government that rigorously imposed its fiscally and politically conservative policies. One could elaborate still further, but the point is clear: both within and among occupations, Düsseldorf workers faced very different working conditions and capitalist strategies, and there was a corresponding diversity in the tactics and goals they could and did pursue for workplace improvements.[18]

In Hamborn authoritarian mine owners and steel magnates alike insisted on being *Herr-im-Haus*. They combined the power accruing from company housing, stores, insurance programs, and the like with the use at the workplace of ruthless foremen, detailed regulations, firings, and blacklists to assure as far as possible that discipline not be breached and authority not challenged. The situation was particularly stark in mining, where the last residue of state control and with it the privileged position of miners had disappeared after 1865. Throughout the western Ruhr, mine owners sought to increase productivity and cut labor costs by screwing down piece rates, which had to be renegotiated each time a new seam was worked, as well as by zeroing (declaring loads to be unacceptable) and, finally, by undermining the traditional eight-hour day. Such a consistent capitalist strategy generated among miners a community of workplace interests that centered around earnings, hours, and greater worker control of such issues as appraising seams and evaluating coal leads.[19]

Turning from working and living conditions to popular culture and religion, one finds more differences than similarities between the two towns. To begin with, Catholicism, which became a political force in addition to being a religious and cultural one as a result of Bismarck's Kulturkampf of the 1870s, played a much more prominent role in all aspects of life in Düsseldorf than it did in Hamborn. Indeed, Düsseldorf was one of the major cities where political Catholicism made its strongest effort to hold the industrial working class and avoid becoming a party exclusively of agrarian and bourgeois interests.[20]

As even the Social Democrats recognized, the power of political Catholicism was not the result of a clerical swindle, perpetrated on an ignorant populace. There were many reasons, material and cultural, for Catholic workers to look to the Church and its political wing. Catholics mobilized and organized the working class in political associations, Christian trade unions, and educational and recreational clubs. Their cradle-to-grave associational network included welfare services, legal aid bureaus, consumer cooperatives, and labor exchanges as well. Political Catholicism provided a comprehensive ideology, which mixed religion, politics, and economics and promised to harmonize group conflicts. It offered a community that integrated family, religion, politics, and leisure. Finally, the Catholic Center Party controlled the Düsseldorf Reichstag seat until 1911 and exerted a powerful voice in municipal politics throughout the prewar period. In addition to retaining the loyalty of middle and lower-middle class Catholics, political Catholicism was particularly appealing to that one-third of the proletariat who were native-born Catholics. Allegiance to political Catholicism enabled them to satisfy their material, cultural, and political needs without leaving their familial and cultural networks. Migrant Catholics, however, who had broken with traditional authority patterns and social relationships, found neither appeal nor place in Düsseldorf's Catholic milieu.[21]

If political Catholicism dominated the life of many Catholic workers, Social Democracy structured the culture of those Protestants and migrant Catholics who stood outside of the Catholic milieu and found little in their work experience or background to unite them. From the turn of the century the Social Democrats established a rich associational life, centering on singing groups, bicycle clubs, consumer cooperatives, libraries, and legal aid bureaus. They ran educational courses, took workers to the opera and theater, and sponsored a variety of festivals. Special constituencies, such as women and youth, had their own organizations. In the years before World War I a Social Democrat could spend his (or more rarely her) entire life within the ambit of the movement.[22]

The Social Democrats devoted themselves to building this culture not out of aversion to action, love of isolation, or organizational fetishism but rather because the sphere of popular culture in Imperial Germany was thoroughly politicized.[23] Like the workers' movement, the state and the institutions of civil society viewed culture instrumentally and organized actively. The state, fearing that workers would reject the existing order, and political Catholicism, worried that they would defect from the Center, competed directly with Social Democracy by providing many associations for proletarian needs.

Given this competition, the Social Democrats' concern with culture did not represent an escape from action but was part of their active confrontation with the organizations and ideologies of the state and their Catholic opponents. The social democratic cultural, recreational, and service organizations played a crucial role in providing workers, who did not share similar backgrounds, religions, or work, with common experiences and values. It brought the movement into working-class neighborhoods and into daily contact with workers' lives. The creation of a politically oriented, party-mediated culture and community reenforced political principles and taught the political and conflictual character of all aspects of life. The social democratic workers' culture was a means of reaching out to the unorganized and indifferent. By providing the physical and social space in which an alternative community could develop and by offering the experience of practical solidarity, the Social Democrats both attracted migrant workers seeking a place in a new urban environment and lessened the risks of being a dissident in a city dominated by political Catholicism and organized capitalism.[24] In short, the creation of a social democratic culture was central not only to that party's politics but to the very process of class formation in Düsseldorf.

Hamborn also had a rich working-class associational life, but it was not politicized or polarized between Catholics and Social Democrats in the extreme way it was in Düsseldorf. On the one hand, the Church and political Catholicism were institutionally less well developed. In part this resulted from and reenforced the general underdevelopment of the town. In part, it reflected Catholic confidence about retaining the allegiance of miners and factory workers, who came from conservative rural backgrounds and were less receptive to social democratic overtures.[25] On the other hand, the weaker social democratic movement in Hamborn had less success in linking up to existing cultural institutions or creating its own. Class and culture were cohesive in Hamborn, but they had little to do with the organized workers' movements that played such a central role in Düsseldorf.

Hamborn workers built their community and culture around family ties, the work experience, and, if Polish, ethnic identity. They coped with the new urban environment and organized leisure through informal groups, on a subpolitical level. Family played a central role, and family also had a special form. Due to the large number of single miners, high rates of job fluctuation, and a shortage of housing, a "half-open" family structure of kin and roomers was particularly prevalent in the Ruhr. This provided workers with solidarity and support and socialized young men into the miners' way of life. That culture in turn focused on the work group and, to a lesser extent, on traditional miners' associations like the *Knappenvereine*. Informal drinking clubs, composed of members of a particular work team or shift, were especially popular. Indeed, they were necessary for miners who worked odd hours and lived in a town with few public amenities. Familial and cultural life, in short, built on and reenforced workplace identities and interests. Recreation and entertainment, rather than education, politics, or welfare, formed the leitmotifs of Hamborn's workers' culture.[26]

The structure and character of popular culture in the two cities reflected not only the differences in their economies and working classes but also the very different histories of the social democratic movement in the two areas. In both cities the SPD and free trade unions developed relatively late and encountered serious obstacles due to the prevalence of large-scale heavy industry, the power of political Catholicism, and the presence of authoritarian political institutions and limited suffrage systems. Yet in Düsseldorf a large social democratic movement emerged in the decades before World War I, while in Hamborn it was much weaker. In Düsseldorf Social Democracy was a vehicle for mediating working-class diversity, creating class, and directing its concerns in a political direction, while in Hamborn a homogeneous work and community situation served as the basis of class and the arena toward which it directed its concern. Finally, Social Democracy in Düsseldorf was consistently radical and prided itself on being on the movement's extreme left wing, while its counterpart in the western Ruhr was unequivocally reformist.[27]

When the miniscule Düsseldorf social democratic movement emerged from twelve years of illegality in 1890, it entered a decade of frustration and failure. Although they won roughly 30 percent of the vote in Reichstag elections, the Social Democrats were unable to recruit the overwhelming majority of these voters into the party and unions. With unstable and ineffectual leaders, little money, and no aid from the national party, the SPD could not construct viable political organizations, cultural associations, or a press. As a result, it was unable to challenge political Catholicism in the political arena or employer power in the economic one.

From the turn of the century onward, however, Social Democracy in Düsseldorf entered a period of unprecedented expansion, which brought party membership to nearly 8,000 and trade union membership to over 23,000 by 1914.[28] The Social Democrats were finally able to build an efficient party organization, a rich culture, and a viable press. After having gradually gained control of such institutions as the worker-employer mediation courts and the health insurance boards from their Catholic competitors, they finally wrested the Reichstag seat from the Catholic Center Party in 1911 and again in 1912. No one factor explains this reversal of social democratic fortunes. On the one hand, changes in the economy and government policy, continued migration, and the increasing conservatism of political Catholicism laid the groundwork. On the other hand, the emergence of effective local socialist leadership, new forms of agitation and education, and the appeal of the movement's energy and success translated possibilities into actualities.

During the periods of both failure and success the Düsseldorf Social Democrats remained committed radicals—indeed, they became progressively more radical as the war approached. In the 1890s they were radicalized by their isolation from other parties in Düsseldorf and the national movement in Berlin as well as by their inability to defeat political Catholicism or challenge capitalist employers. Between 1900 and 1914, the period of expansion and apparent success, they were radicalized because the limits of reformism remained very narrow and because they could not translate numbers, organizational strength, and visibility into economic and political power. The Social Democrats were unable to win significant material improvements for the working class, unable to gain any representation in the city government or Prussian parliament, and unable to find bourgeois allies. When they finally won the Reichstag seat in 1911, they discovered that the victory had symbolic significance but brought no real power because of the impotence of parliament and the hostility of other parties.

The Social Democrats became radicals by virtue of who they were as well as what they experienced. The bulk of Düsseldorf's Social Democrats were young, skilled, male migrant workers from the metal, wood, and construction industries. At the peak of their earning power, most of these workers joined the movement for the first time upon arriving in Düsseldorf. Their confrontation with an environment that relegated them to a second-class economic, cultural, and political status was mediated by a party leadership that was itself new and young. There was not a generation gap within the Düsseldorf party, nor was there the dominance of vested interests and anxious conservatism that characterized many other locals. Leaders and members alike neither had close ties to the national party nor venerated established organizations and the grand old men of the movement.[29] This distance created the space in which radicalism could develop.

The experience of the Düsseldorf Social Democrats led them to reject theoretical revisionism as well as practical reformism, with its emphasis on short-range gains and collaboration with bourgeois parties. It led them to criticize the bureaucratization and organizational preoccupation of the SPD as a source of caution and strategic error. Throughout the endless debates about revisionism, militarism, and parliamentarism, they urged an unequivocal defense of Marxist principles. From 1910 on they became vociferous proponents of an active strategy of confrontation centering on the mass strike.

The radicalism of the Düsseldorf Social Democrats stressed political goals, such as universal suffrage in Prussia and antimilitarism, and urged political means, such as organization, demonstrations, and the political mass strike. This orientation matched that of the workers, who did not share a common work experience, who encountered extremely strong opposition to their efforts to win union recognition and collective contracts, and who recognized the necessity of organizations that extended beyond the workplace. The working class and the workers' movement alike saw political power and transformation as the prerequisite for social change. It was politics that united Düsseldorf's workers and political reform that they sought first and foremost.

The very factors that promoted radicalism in Düsseldorf, however, limited its effectiveness. Organized capitalism, authoritarian government, and political Catholicism precluded reformism but made organization and mobilization difficult and militant confrontation dangerous. Rapid industrialization and migration provided the movement with ready recruits but undermined organizational stability and educational work. Düsseldorf's isolation from the national movement created a critical distance in which radical ideas could develop, but it also minimized Düsseldorf's influence on Berlin, limited its contacts with leftists elsewhere, and contributed significantly, as will be seen, to the defeat of the postwar revolution. In addition, Düsseldorf workers contributed to the weakening of their prewar radicalism. By catering to the needs of some elements of the working class—above all, young skilled male migrants—they limited their appeal to others, such as women, the unskilled, and native Catholics. Despite their criticism of the national movement, they bowed to its conservative decisions until forced to leave the SPD during the war. Although they created a strongly organized, politically oriented radicalism, they never developed economic organizations, economic protests, and an economic program to match their political ones.

Both the character of Social Democracy and the forms of worker activism were quite different in the western Ruhr. In the late nineteenth century, a very reformist social democratic movement had developed in the traditional mining centers of the eastern Ruhr. The cautious policies of the party and the socialist miners' union, the *Alte Verband*, reflected both the rural and conservative origins of eastern miners, who retained strong vestiges of their corporatist tradition and its elitism, and the relatively stable and prosperous character of communities there. Social democratic reformism was a product of both growing union strength and the *Herr-im-Haus* standpoint of employers, and it continued the tradition of trying to curry favor with a state that had periodically intervened on the behalf of miners.

After the turn of the century the development of the western Ruhr, with its rapid urbanization, high immigration, and deteriorating working conditions, destroyed the structural conditions that had fostered reformism and union strength. Neither the SPD nor the *Alte Verband* spoke to the needs and experiences of workers, such as those in Hamborn, who were new to mining and lived and worked in conditions markedly different from those in the eastern Ruhr. As a result, Hamborn workers were much less involved in political organizations and activism. Instead, like their fellow western Ruhr miners, they engaged in industrial militancy, sometimes sanctioned by the unions, as in 1905 and 1912, but frequently not. They demanded shorter hours, higher wages, and reform of the manner in which the mines were run. These economic struggles over material conditions and control issues were not accompanied by political radicalism. Indeed, the gap between the social democratic movement and the working class widened steadily in the prewar years, and some of Hamborn's more active workers even turned toward syndicalism.[30]

World War I exacerbated the differences between the character of the Düsseldorf and Hamborn workers' movements and their relationship to the working class, even though the war had a very similar impact on economic and social conditions. The outbreak of war temporarily curbed the prewar radicalization and brought prosperity, but its continuation precipitated the disintegration of both the social and political order and the social democratic movement and radicalized the working class in Hamborn and Düsseldorf.

In both cities the war led to a restructuring of the economy and the labor force as well as to a marked deterioration of working and living conditions. The metal and mining sectors were converted to war production and rationalized as far as possible in order to meet the munitions and manpower demands of a two-front war, while nonessential industry was cut to the bone. In both cities, the labor force swelled enormously as women, youths, and inexperienced men were recruited for production.[31] In Düsseldorf alone 30,000 new workers found jobs in the armaments sector between 1915 and 1917, and two-thirds of them were women.[32] Despite extensive government intervention in the economy, munitions production lagged and manpower shortages continued. This, in turn, led to long hours, an intensive work pace, and unsafe conditions in factories and mines. To compound the situation, food shortages became acute in 1916, the first of the infamous turnip winters, and scarcely improved for the remainder of the war.[33] Inflation was rampant, war profits excessive, and real wages fell by nearly one-quarter in war industries and almost one-half in nonessential ones.[34] Finally, even though the national SPD, the Ruhr party, and many unions enthusiastically supported the war effort in the expectation of political and economic concessions, Ruhr employers refused to recognize unions, and government officials and politicians were no more forthcoming on the local level.[35]

In Düsseldorf the wave of social democratic-led mass protests against the war in July 1914 was followed by a tense truce as the national party endorsed war credits and martial law was proclaimed. By early 1915, however, signs of disaffection appeared within the social democratic movement and the working class. The party press attacked war profiteering; the party members publically criticized Düsseldorf's SPD Reichstag deputy Haberland for voting war credits; and, as local leaders made contact with nationally prominent antiwar leftists, nearly all local party and union functionaries signed a letter condemning the SPD for abandoning the class struggle and supporting an imperialist war.[36] By year's end the police predicted that Düsseldorf would split from the right-wing Social Democrats, and two years later that in fact occurred.[37] In the wake of the February revolution in Russia, acute domestic crisis and continued SPD support of the war, 77 of 81 Düsseldorf party functionaries and 561 of 600 members voted to join the newly formed USPD. The Düsseldorf branch of the German Metal Workers' Union and nearly all other organized workers soon followed suit.[38]

Simultaneously, workers were taking to the streets. Acute food shortages precipitated demonstrations and strikes but political demands soon surfaced. According to the police,

the mass of workers, who are very revolutionary, can only be calmed without violent means if political rights are granted and food is supplied.[39]

As the government would not concede the former and could not provide the latter, unrest escalated to the point of extensive looting and property destruction, which could only be stopped by using force and punitive prison sentences and by sending militants to the front.[40]

In 1918 persistent economic crisis, the absence of domestic reform, and continued repression further rebounded to the benefit of the USPD, and SPD influence on the working class all but disappeared. Of equal importance, the Düsseldorf USPD was moving far to the left. It demanded immediate peace and political democratization, applauded the October revolution in Russia, and spoke with increasing frequency of a socialist republic for Germany. As in the prewar period, political goals were given top priority. The vision of the Düsseldorf Independents was as yet vague, their strategy barely worked out, yet their revolutionary aspirations were clear.[41] The workers' movement thus moved in step with the working class—at times it moved even more quickly to the left—and the ties between workers and their institutions remained close.

A very different situation developed in Hamborn. There, as in most areas of the Ruhr, the Social Democrats continued to support the war to the bitter end, even distributing a prowar pamphlet written by the army as late as 1918.[42] In Hamborn the relatively weak social democratic organization virtually ceased to function, while the *Alte Verband*, which unlike the metal workers' union had few dissidents, cooperated willingly with the state and employers.[43] What little contact had existed between the social democratic movement and the working class was destroyed when miners and factory workers in Hamborn moved from a critical wait-and-see attitude toward the war to a stance of active opposition.

As the war progressed, wages and working conditions, inflation and food shortages, owner intransigence, and trade union weakness radicalized workers.[44] Protests first involved food issues, then wages, and finally political demands, albeit of a poorly articulated kind. Unlike in Düsseldorf, the newly emerging left groupings—the USPD and the Spartacists—could not capitalize on this radicalization. On the one hand, there were no functionaries or institutions that switched allegiance and provided leadership and structure for a leftist political movement. On the other hand, Hamborn workers remained concerned primarily with local economic issues. A few joined the syndicalist Free Association of Miners, just as they had in the prewar years, but most shunned formal organizations.[45]

The revolution, which began in Düsseldorf on November 8, 1918, with wide popular support and strong USPD leadership, gave the Düsseldorf working class the long-awaited chance to put its radicalism into practice. The revolution intensified the close ties between the working class and the organized workers' movement and heightened the concern with political goals. But it also illustrated the limits of such a political strategy. It revealed the workers' inability to develop a conception of workers' control and to wage a struggle for socialization that went beyond rhetorical support for the plans of workers elsewhere.

There were three phases to the revolution in Düsseldorf, and with each successive one the working class had more radical political and economic aspirations and less real power. In November and December the revolution was run by the USPD-dominated Workers' and Soldiers' Council, which began to democratize the government, build alternative institutions, and initiate economic reform while maintaining order and broadening its base of support. Understanding the necessity of thoroughgoing political change, the Council suspended the city council, established control over the bureaucracy, and established a 1,500-man security force to supplement and curb the police.[46] The Council and its USPD and Spartacist supporters demanded that the middle and upper classes be more heavily taxed and that unoccupied houses be given to the poor. They condemned the SPD's plans to call a National Assembly, arguing that such a strategy would subvert the revolution and "save capitalism." They enthusiastically endorsed the regional Workers' Council's call for partial socialization, beginning with the mines. In so doing, they recognized both the need for economic transformation and the inevitability of strong bourgeois opposition to it. But such socialization was to apply elsewhere, be implemented from above, and not entail shopfloor workers' control.[47] Although the SPD left the Workers' Council by early December, the USPD and unions, especially the metal workers', continued to support it.[48] Although works councils were formed in the larger factories, they cooperated closely with the unions and were subordinate to the Workers' Council. Thus old and new institutions were merged, and traditional leaders and forms of action and organization were perpetuated.

Despite great determination and some success, it was clear by late December that the USPD and working class were unsure how to advance the political revolution or initiate the social one of which they spoke with increasing frequency. Their failure and the growing conservatism of the SPD national government opened the way for a Communist-led council government with strong USPD participation.[49] Workers endorsed the Spartacist takeover and street tactics because organization and mobilization alone had neither sustained the momentum of the revolution nor prevented the broad socialist alliance from disintegrating and because control of the administration had not brought sufficient democratization. They favored council rule because they were convinced that a National Assembly would restore the old order.

The Communists held power for two months, despite several armed battles between workers and the police and despite two strikes by civil servants. But the form and style of their rule distinguished itself little from that of the USPD. Political parties continued to play the leading role and major decisions were made by the leaders of formal organizations. Of greater importance, the Communists engaged in demonstrative actions, such as renaming the elegant Königsalle Karl Liebknechtstrasse, but failed to implement revolutionary measures.[50] They lacked not only a positive political program but an economic one as well. They called on the national government for unemployment funds and government contracts—hardly radical measures—but the SPD leaders predictably refused the requests.[51]

Neither the left political leadership nor the rank and file initiated a socialization campaign that would affect local industry. They supported the socialization demands of the Ruhr miners but did not consider Düsseldorf's industry, even its metal sector, ripe for transformation.[52] The diverse structure of industry, the complex and varied character of the labor process, and the heterogeneity of the working class and its lack of experience with shopfloor militancy all militated against any spontaneous socialization movement from below. Düsseldorf workers, like their leaders, regarded city hall and Berlin— not the factory—as the center of action despite Düsseldorf's isolation from Berlin and from the USPD elsewhere. The more skilled workers, who led the revolution, channeled not only their own militancy but also that of the unskilled into political actions and to a lesser extent into a political demand for socialization from above. To be sure, the Düsseldorf working class wholeheartedly supported the February 1919 general strike called by Ruhr miners to demand socialization and an end to the military occupation of parts of the Ruhr. And they stayed out even longer than their comrades elsewhere.[53] Their action was born out of solidarity with other workers and a commitment to revolutionary change. But it also reflected defensiveness, frustration about recent failures, and confusion about the most appropriate goals and strategies for the revolution in Düsseldorf.

Of equal importance, the strike intensified social democratic and bourgeois opposition to radicalism in Düsseldorf and precipitated national government intervention. On February 28 the Free Corps Lichtenstrahl marched into the city and the last, defensive phase of the revolution began. Despite militant working-class resistance to the military and the national SPD, which had sent it, and despite growing support for the USPD and KPD and a second general strike in April, the tide of counterrevolution could not be turned.[54] Although the revolution in Düsseldorf was floundering by late February owing to political isolation and the lack of an economic strategy, it was military repression that dealt the death blow.

The revolution took an entirely different, although no less radical course in Hamborn. The revolution exacerbated the conflicts between the SPD and free trade unions on the one hand and the working class on the other. It led to an intensification of industrial protest, but that protest continued to lack a political component. It illustrated the strengths and limits of a spontaneous, economically focused revolution from below.

The November revolution in Hamborn proceeded relatively peacefully under the auspices of an SPD-dominated Workers' and Soldiers' Council, which demanded democratization, the eight-hour day, a National Assembly, and socialization. Although the party leaders took few concrete actions in subsequent weeks, trade union functionaries immediately began negotiating with mine owners. Clinging to its previous cautious reformism, the miners' union asked only for union recognition, a moderate wage increase, and slightly shorter shifts, thereby both ignoring the more extensive wage and work demands of the miners and attempting to exclude all syndicalist influence.[55] Although the miners were relatively unconcerned with the Social Democrats' political passivity, they were angered and radicalized by the unions' attempt to quell the revolution with inadequate reforms. From late November to January the Hamborn miners demanded an eight-hour day, which included the travel time of the entire shift, substantial wage increases, a one-time payment of 500–600 marks per worker, and more control over working conditions. Instead of working through the *Alte Verband*, they formed works commissions, which were elected by the various shafts and responsible to the mass of workers. Although some syndicalist spokesmen encouraged the movement, it was largely spontaneous but not, however, unorganized. Instead of negotiating with employers, miners struck and staged militant demonstrations, which marched to the mine directors' homes and to mines in neighboring towns. These tactics did extract more concessions than the bargaining of the unions had, even though they failed to achieve the miners' ambitious program.[56]

But the miners' vision did not extend beyond the pithead. They wanted economic improvements and workers' control but had no political program. Due to the continued isolation of mining communities, the weakness of political parties, and the ineffectiveness of the regional Workers' and Soldiers' Council, miners had little knowledge of conditions and developments elsewhere. Neither the USPD nor the Sparticists gained more than a foothold in Hamborn during the most militant months of the revolution, and works councils remained at the heart of the movement.

From January through April 1919 the Hamborn miners supported broader struggles for socialization going on in the Ruhr, even though their understanding of the implications of these struggles was limited. They came to the direct aid of their fellow miners in nearby towns during strikes and demonstrations. They endorsed the work of the Essen socialization commission, which advocated multi-level councils and nationalization from above, even though this commission, with its painfully slow deliberations and complete lack of influence on the national government, had the effect of defusing militancy. Finally, when the SPD government's determination to reject socialization and pacify the Ruhr by force became clear, the Hamborn miners struck en masse in February. After the late February military occupation of the city, they struck again in March and for a third time in April.[57] As in Düsseldorf, the actions were both defensive and futile.

The failure of revolution in Düsseldorf and Hamborn had first and foremost to do with the continued power of the army and bureaucracy, the collaboration of the SPD with the old industrial and military elites, and its willingness not only to oppose the left politically but also to attack it militarily. Isolated local action, even uncoordinated regional uprisings, could not survive in such a hostile national environment. But the problems of revolutionary change in capitalist societies and the potential and limitations of council movements cannot be understood if we stop the analysis there. The two patterns of revolution that have been explored testify to the depth of the radical tradition among many German workers. But they also testify to the shortcomings, imbalances, and contradictions of different strands of that radicalism.

Düsseldorf workers created strong organizations, effective and responsive leaders, and a clear political analysis and goals. But they were unable to find a strategy for economic reform, let alone revolution, and were unable to overcome the diversity of their work situations in economic, as opposed to political and cultural, ways. Hamborn workers excelled at ad hoc industrial protest, which was spontaneous but not unorganized, which covered not only material demands but control questions, and which was extremely responsive to rank-and-file sentiment. But they had no political vision, organization, or strategy.

The very particularity of their economic concerns made it difficult for them to unite with other workers. Düsseldorf workers could sustain action but not give it adequate direction, while Hamborn ones suffered from the opposite problem. Düsseldorf workers sought to solve the problem of economic power by seizing control of the state, while those in Hamborn sought economic power as an end in itself and ignored the state. Each pattern of revolution was the product of distinct economic structures, working-class experiences, and political histories. The strength of each was also its weakness. Neither was able to overcome the German working class' longstanding inability to merge economic and political action. Neither was adequate to the task of transforming the economy and state in capitalist society.

Notes

1.   Mary Nolan, *Social Democracy and Society: Working-Class Radicalism in Düsseldorf, 1890–1920* (New York, 1981); Hans-Arthur Lux, *Düsseldorf* (Düsseldorf, 1921–22); and Hugo Weidenhaupt, *Kleine Geschichte der Stadt Düsseldorf* (Düsseldorf, 1968), 131.

2.   Josef Wilden, *Grundlage und Triebkräfte der Wirtschaft Düsseldorf* (Düsseldorf, 1923), 12, 20. *Mitteilungen zur Statistik der Stadt Düsseldorf, Nr. 3, Industrie und Handelsgewerbe in Düsseldorf nach der Betriebszählung von 12. Juni 1907*, ed. Otto Most (Düsseldorf, 1908), passim.

3.   Lux, 56, 206, and Wilden, 33.

4.   Weidenhaupt, 129–131, and Otto Brandt, *Studien zur Wirtschafts- und Verwaltungsgeschichte der Stadt Düsseldorf im 19. Jahrhundert* (Düsseldorf, 1902), 403. *Mitteilungen, Nr. 3*, 20.

5.   Wolfgang Köllmann, "Industrialisierung, Binnenwanderung und die 'soziale Frage,'" *Vierteljahresheft für Sozial- und Wirtschaftsgeschichte* 46 (1959), 53, 66. *Mitteilungen zur Statistik der Stadt Düsseldorf, Nr. 4, Die Nichteinheimischen in Düsseldorf nach der Volkszählung von 1. Dezember 1905* (Düsseldorf: Statistisches Amt, 1912), 10*, 18*–19*.

6.   Köllmann, 66. *Statistik des deutschen Reiches*, neue Folge, Bd. 108, p. 183; Bd. 207, Part II, p. 477.

7.   *Statistik des deutschen Reiches*, neue Folge, Bd. 108, p. 183. *Mitteilungen, Nr. 4*, 10*, 18*–19*.

8.   Jürgen Tampke, *The Ruhr and Revolution: The Revolutionary Movement in the Rhenish–Westphalian Industrial Region, 1912–1919* (Canberra, 1978), 3–7; Klaus Tenfelde, *Sozial Geschichte der Bergarbeiterschaft an der Ruhr im 19. Jahrhundert* (Bonn, 1977), 164–170; Erhard Lucas, *Zwei Formen Arbeiterradikalismus in der deutschen Arbeiterbewegung* (Frankfurt, 1978), 29–36.

9.   Lucas, 29–36. Tenfelde, 230–231. Klaus Bade, "Massenwanderung und Arbeitsmarkt im deutschen Nordosten von 1800 bis zum ersten Weltkrieg," *Archiv für Sozialgeschichte* 20 (1980), 277.

10. Stephen Hickey, "The Shaping of the German Labour Movement: Miners in the Ruhr," in Richard Evans, ed., *Society and Politics in Wilhelmine Germany* (London, 1978), 221. See also Tenfelde, 340–342.

11. Lucas, 24–28. Wilden, 50.

12. Tampke, 13–14, 27. Hickey, 221–222. Kenneth P. Barkin, *The Controversy over German Industrialization, 1890–1902* (Chicago, 1970), 267. Gerhard Bry, *Wages in Germany, 1871–1945* (Princeton, 1960), 71–74. *Jahresbericht des Statistischen Amts Düsseldorf*, 1907, p. 15; 1909, p. 20; 1912, p. 27.

13. Lucas, 21–109, passim, 249–256.

14. *Beiträge zur statistischen Monatsberichten der Stadt Düsseldorf*, July 1909, XL–XLIII. Lucas, 57–70. Georg Renard, *Struktur- und Konjunkturtendenzen im Düsseldorfer Wirtschaftsraum* (Essen, 1939), passim. Franz J. Brüggemeier and Lutz Niethammer, "Schlafgänger, Schnapskasinos und schwerindustrielle Kolonie," in Jürgen Reulecke and Wolfhard Weber, eds., *Fabrik, Familie, Feierabend* (Wuppertal, 1978), 150–151.

15. Tampke, 7–12. Hickey, 220–223. "Statistik des Jahres 1906 über Lohn- und Arbeitsverhältnisse der Arbeiter in Düsseldorf," *Bericht des Gewerkschaftscartell*, 1906. Nolan, 237–238.

16. Tampke, 14–15. Brüggemeier and Niethammer, 135–148. Franz J. Brüggemeier, "Ruhr Miners and Their History," in Raphael Samuel, ed., *People's History and Socialist Theory* (London, 1981), 330. Nolan, 24, 66–67, 220.

17. Lutz Niethammer, "Wie wohnten Arbeiter im Kaiserreich?" *Archiv für Sozialgeschichte* 16 (1976), 101–107.

18. See Nolan, 106–110 for a detailed discussion.

19. Lucas, 119–130. Hickey, 227–231. Tampke, 6–12. Hans Mommsen, "Die Bergarbeiter an der Ruhr," in Jürgen Reulecke, ed., *Arbeiterbewegung an Rhein und Ruhr* (Wuppertal, 1974), 278.

20. For discussions of political Catholicism, see Michael Berger, *Arbeiterbewegung und Demokratisierung* (Freiburg, Ph.D. dissertation, 1971); August Erdmann, *Die christliche Arbeiterbewegung in Deutschland* (Stuttgart, 1909); and Ronald Ross, *Beleaguered Tower: The Dilemma of Political Catholicism in Wilhelmian Germany* (Notre Dame, 1976).

21. Nolan, 42–52, 113–114.

22. Information on the cultural activity of the Düsseldorf SPD was drawn from the social democratic papers, *Niederrheinische Volkstribune* and *Düsseldorfer Volkszeitung*, the *Bericht des Gewerkschaftscartells*, 1902–6, 1911–12, and police reports, Stadtarchiv Düsseldorf, III 6918–33, 1890–1910.

23. For the standard interpretation of the SPD culture as passive, isolationist, and integrative, see Peter Nettl, "The German Social Democratic Party, 1890–1914, As a Political Model," *Past and Present* 30 (April 1965), 66, and Guenther Roth, *The Social Democrats in Imperial Germany* (Totowa, N.J., 1963), 203–231.

24. See Patrick de Laubier, "Esquisse d'une theorie du syndicalisme," *Sociologie du travail* 10 (1968), 364–366. Nolan, 134–145.

25. Although there was an active Catholic miners union in the Ruhr, the Center Party was much less prominent than in Düsseldorf. Tampke, 26–27.

26.   Lucas, 92–109. Brüggemeier and Niethammer, 154–165. Robert Giebisch, "Miners and Workers' Control in the German Revolution of 1918–1919," senior thesis, Harvard University, 1980, chapter 2.

27.   Nolan, parts I and II.

28.   At the time of the last prewar occupational census in 1907, there were 63,833 blue-collar workers in Düsseldorf. *Statistik des deutschen Reiches*, neue Folge, Bd. 207, part II, 478–481. Movement statistics are from the *Düsseldorfer Volkszeitung*, November 21, 1914, April 23, 1915.

29.   The analysis of the party membership is from information on over 4,000 new male members that was collected by the police from lists that the party submitted. Stadtarchiv Düsseldorf, III 6929–33, 1896–1908. For information on the leadership, see the police files in Staatsarchiv Koblenz, 403 6867, n.d. and 403 6870, n.d.

30.   Tampke, 19–27. Hickey, 223–233.

31.   Tampke, 34–5. Jürgen Reulecke, "Der erste Weltkrieg und die Arbeiterbewegung im rheinisch-westfälischen Industriegebiet," in Reulecke, *Arbeiterbewegung*, 205–239.

32.   Adelbert Oehler, *Düsseldorf im Weltkrieg* (Düsseldorf, 1927), 243.

33.   For a discussion of the war economy and its impact on social conditions, see Gerald Feldman, *Army, Industry, and Labor in Germany, 1914–1918* (Princeton, 1966); Jürgen Kocka, *Klassengesellschaft im Kriege, 1914–1918* (Göttingen, 1973); and Oehler.

34.   Kocka, 18.

35.   Susanne Miller, *Burgfrieden und Klassenkampf* (Düsseldorf, 1974).

36.   Staatsarchiv Düsseldorf, Regierung Düsseldorf 15985, March 5, 1915. Institute für Marxismus-Leninismus beim ZK der SED, ed., *Dokumente und Materialien zur Geschichte der deutschen Arbeiterbewegung*, Reihe II, Bd. I, 157–159 (referred to hereafter as *Dokumente und Materialien*).

37.   Staatsarchiv Düsseldorf, Regierung Düsseldorf 15985, May 1915.

38.   *Dokumente und Materialien*, Reihe II, Bd. I, 582–583.

39.   Stadtarchiv Düsseldorf, III 4604, April 1917.

40.   Ibid. *Volkszeitung*, July 14, 1917. Oehler, 363.

41.   Stadtarchiv Düsseldorf, III 4604, November 17, 1917, September 23, 1918, October 18, 1918.

42.   Tampke, 48–51.

43.   Lucas, 146–149.

44.   Mommsen, 280–281. Tampke, 33.

45.   Tampke, 39, 55–66.

46.   Reinhard Rürup, ed., *Arbeiter- und Soldatenräte im rheinisch-westfälischen Industriegebiet* (Wuppertal, 1975), 15–16, 21–23. *Volkszeitung*, November 11 and 14, 1918.

47.   *Volkszeitung*, November 1918, passim. Stadtarchiv Düsseldorf, Arbeiter- und Soldatenrat, XXI 332, November 29, 1918. *Dokumente und Materialien*, Reihe II, Bd. 2, 511.

48.   Oehler, 560.

49.   Ibid., 653. *Dokumente und Materialien*, Reihe II, Bd. 3, 440–441.

    50.   Stadtarchiv Düsseldorf, XXI 333, January 9 and 14, February 4,
1919.
    51.   Stadtarchiv Düsseldorf, January 14 and 30, February 4, 1919.
    52.   *Volkszeitung*, January and February 1919, passim.
    53.   Stadtarchiv Düsseldorf, XXI 334, February 21, 1919. *Wochenschrift
der Handelskammer zu Düsseldorf*, Nr. 9/10, March 15, 1919, 86–87.
    54.   The Düsseldorf general strike demanded the resignation of the
SPD national government and the formation of a council republic. *Volkszeitung*,
April 15, 16, and 18, 1919.
    55.   Mommsen, 286–288.
    56.   Lucas, 155–192. Tampke, 102–107.
    57.   Ibid.

Chapter Six

Redefining Workers' Control: Rationalization, Labor Time, and Union Politics in France, 1900-1928

Gary Cross

I

Since the days of the *sans-culottes*, the French labor movement has been identified with direct action and the ideals of self-management. The tradition of J. J. Proudhon and the survival of craft industry into the twentieth century helped to create and preserve a pattern of labor militancy peculiar to France; workers' control not only permeated the thinking of the communards of 1871 but survived the repression of this urban insurrection to revive among the skilled workers who gathered around the labor exchanges (*bourses du travail*) in the 1890s. Along with the vision of autogestion came the notion of workers' self-emancipation and autonomy from the state and socialist politicians. The syndicalist formula of direct action and the general strike emerged as a dominant theme in 1888 and after the local unions and trade federations were united in 1902, these ideas dominated union congresses. With a militancy unparalleled in Europe, the General Confederation of Labor (CGT) in its famous Charter of Amiens (*Charte d' Amiens*) in 1906 called for self-liberation through direct action and preparation for workers' unmediated control of production.[1]

Yet by December 1918, that same CGT had adopted a strikingly different posture. Its Minimum Programme for postwar France advocated social amelioration through legislation and collective bargaining, and union participation in national economic councils. The Programme distainfully labeled the tradition of direct action as "street riots."[2] An insurgent movement emerged during the war and blossomed in 1919 and 1920. It revived the syndicalist ideal of direct action and identified the soviets of Bolshevik Russia with the French idea of union control of production. However, control of the CGT eluded the insurgents and with the failure of the strikes of 1920, the left minority abandoned syndicalism for the political unionism of the communist-controlled United General Confederation of Labor (CGTU). What brought this eclipse of syndicalism and workers' control in France where it had been so deeply rooted before the war?

Many French labor historians have skirted this problem by ending their studies at 1914 or earlier, confining their attention to the "golden years of French syndicalism."[3] Others, such as Peter Stearns, have argued that the French labor movement in the decade before the war was not nearly so militant as the Charter of Amiens suggests.[4] After the large but unsuccessful strikes of 1906 for the eight-hour day, the CGT stagnated and slowly drifted toward collective bargaining and alliances with the socialist parliamentarians. Others claim that the union leadership's participation in the *Union Sacrée* during the war led it to abandon a class and revolutionary perspective for a national corporatist approach—relying on a partnership with the "progressive bourgeoisie" to bring about a modern economy and collective bargaining system.[5] Still others argue that the weak impulse toward workers' control after the war is a result of the adaptation of French labor, long wed to ideas appropriate for a declining craft-based industry, to the reality of mechanization and industrial concentration.[6]

All three perspectives declare that a large share of the French labor movement became integrated into the bourgeois state and economy. Whether seen as an inevitable acceptance of "modernization" or as a betrayal of the revolutionary élan, all three arguments interpret this history essentially as a passive response of labor to external economic and political exigencies. Rather, I shall argue that the trend toward reformism in the prewar CGT was an effort to widen and deepen the organizational strength of labor. The shift of the CGT leadership during the war was not an abandonment of ideals of labor self-emancipation but an attempt to ameliorate working conditions and living standards and to prepare workers for assuming control over production. Finally, the apparent adaptation of the CGT to economic rationalization, or Taylorism, was not made in the face of widespread mechanization; rather, it advocated increased productivity in opposition to a French *patronat* that was reluctant to pay the price of innovation.

The CGT had adopted a strategy appropriate for an economy entering a more mechanized and rationalized phase; nevertheless, it failed to mobilize a social base to correspond with this strategy. The CGT's membership remained in the craft and government/service sectors long after its strategy had shifted. Furthermore, during the war, the leadership isolated itself from the rank and file by its dogged commitment to the war effort, which alienated a large minority of workers and split the movement in 1920–21. The loss of unions to the communist-led CGTU in 1921 greatly diminished the power of the CGT to press for structural reforms.

However, we must reassess the history of this transformation of the CGT's ideology by going beyond the dichotomy of reform versus revolution and the presumption of embourgeoisement and passive adaptation. The CGT reformists obviously failed after the war to build an effective movement, but their ideological shift over the issue of workers' control and economic rationalization nevertheless was an integral part of the struggle for an improved labor standard and a step toward the social control of a modernized economy. In fact, the communist unions, which later proved to be more successful than the CGT in organizing the new industrial sectors, essentially adopted the CGT's position.

II

Revolutionary syndicalism was the dominant but not unchallenged theme of the CGT from its foundation in 1895 until 1910. Beyond its obvious militancy (a theoretical rejection of collective bargaining, opposition to legislative amelioration, insistence on raising revolutionary as well as wage and hour demands, and advocacy of sabotage), revolutionary syndicalism was, essentially, a movement for a decentralization of power. According to Fernand Pelloutier, Emile Pouget, Victor Griffuelhes, and other syndicalist leaders, local unions were to struggle against the state and the political leadership of the socialists and remain autonomous even from the CGT bureaucracy. Local unions were to organize the direct self-emancipation of rank-and-file workers and thus make possible the transformation of the *syndicats* into organs of production and distribution. This was a vision of an enterprise-based workers' control, which assumed the efficacy of localized action and the capacity of rank-and-file workers to manage production on the shop floor. Its craft origins are obvious. That the vision was largely inapplicable to large-scale mechanized industry operating in a national economic context was starkly revealed by the failures of the CGT after 1906.

The massive wave of general strikes in May 1906 for the eight-hour day was a culmination of revolutionary syndicalist tactics. They not only failed to meet their objectives, but offered decisive proof of the weakness of autonomous and spontaneous action. Many unions acknowledged their impotence by concluding a separate peace with their employers (for example, the printers, who settled for a nine-hour day); more broadly, the ill-coordinated movement was isolated and repressed by the government.[7] The increasingly harsh stance of the state and the growing effectiveness of employer associations after 1906 contributed to the further decline of syndicalism.[8] Moreover, the narrow base of the CGT in the skilled sector of the French working class limited its appeal and ability to organize workers in the modernizing and unskilled industries. CGT membership stagnated, growing a mere 15 percent from 1906 to 1914, compared with the 70 percent growth between 1900 and 1906. Numbers of strikes and strikers also stagnated. Most important was a trend toward strike failures after 1906 (see Table 6-1).

These defeats both reflected and accentuated the instability of membership. This was especially true in the modernizing sector. Despite the high participation of smelting and metal-working labor in the 1906 strike (31 percent and 8.6 percent respectively, compared with a national rate of 2.1 percent), the CGT made little permanent headway in organizing these sectors.[9] Christian Gras shows that while between 1909 and 1913, 174 new local unions were formed in the Metalworkers' Federation, some 104 disappeared.[10]

CGT membership remained heavily concentrated in the artisan, government, and service sectors; trade unions had hardly penetrated beyond mining into the "proletarian" industrial sector (see Table 6-2). This stagnation and narrow base of organized labor in France was hardly lost on CGT leaders. Already in 1906, in recognition of the declining importance of craft industries, the CGT refused membership to additional craft unions and promoted the merger of existing craft federations. The national committee (Comité confédéral national, CCN) in turn attempted to coordinate and prepare strikes. The CGT, under its new leadership of Léon Jouhaux (who replaced the syndicalist champion Victor Griffuelhes in 1909), formed alliances with the socialists in order to broaden its base of support. The syndicalist strategy was no longer effective and the leadership recognized the need to centralize and broaden its appeal.[11]

Table 6-1. *French Trade Union and Strike Data; 1900–1914*

Year	Number of union members	Number of Strikes	Number of Strikers	Percent Success and Compromise	Percent Failure
1900	492,000	890	215,700	63	37
1901	589,000	541	110,800	59	41
1902	614,000	571	212,400	58	42
1903	644,000	642	120,300	61	39
1904	714,000	1,087	269,900	67	33
1905	781,000	849	175,900	62	38
1906	836,000	1,354	437,800	66	34
1907	896,000	1,313	197,500	59	41
1908	957,000	1,109	123,800	47	53
1909	945,000	1,067	177,000	59	41
1910	977,000	1,517	287,000	60	40
1911	1,029,000	1,489	228,200	54	46
1912	1,064,000	1,150	270,700	52	48
1913	1,027,000	1,099	226,400	52	48
1914	1,026,000	685	161,400	52	48

Source: Charles Tilly and Edward Shorter, *Strikes in France* (New York, 1974), 151.

The syndicalist goal of skilled workers' control began to recede at the same time. In part this was a response to new managerial methods and mechanization. The pressure of competition, especially in the new automobile industry, forced managers to attempt to reduce the control of skilled labor over the methods and pace of work. This offensive, usually identified with the doctrines of Frederick W. Taylor, was a direct attack on the traditional concept of workers' control. Although craft workers opposed these changes, unions quickly recognized that the new methods could not be defeated. The CGT did not simply capitulate to industrial progress; rather the unions made an ideological leap. The CGT recognized that it had to cast its net beyond the declining craft sector and to appeal to the economic needs of the mass of French workers—especially those entering the growth industries—if it were to regain momentum. This required a new definition of workers' control, one based not on an opposition to but on a participation in an effort to mechanize and to increase the productivity of the French economy.

Taylor's ideas for enhancing managerial control over production were hardly new to France,[12] and thus he found there, as early as 1900,

Table 6-2. French Union Members as a Percentage of Work Force by Sector

Sector	1884–1897	1921–35
Industries		
Mining	12%	20%
Glass	11	6
Printing-paper	9	11
Ceramics	6	14
Metals	4	3
Chemicals	4	1
Construction	4	4
Leather	4	4
Textiles	3	7
Food	2	3
Garments	1	1
Ports/docks	1	6
Services/Government		
Tobacco/matches (state monopoly)	55	71
Utilities	44	72
Railways	18	37
Transport	9	16
Postal/telephone	0	30

Source: Charles Tilly and Edward Shorter, *Strikes in France* (New York, 1974), 151.

a receptive audience.[13] Taylor's system of scientific management in France was often broadly identified with mechanization, the continuous production line, and a greater division of labor in general. Yet Taylor's personal contribution was largely confined to time and motion studies designed to analyze work methods and to enable the employer to set a piece rate that encouraged workers to increase their productivity. He also advocated a complex reorganization and specialization of management in order to maximize employer control of the production process and with it to increase productivity.[14]

Despite the active support of Henri Le Chatelier and other academic engineers, French industries were not quick to adopt these methods. The earliest support for Taylorism came from the auto industry, and it was hardly unequivocal. In response to the crisis of overproduction in 1907, Louis Renault hired Georges de Ram to

Taylorize a shop of 150 workers.[15] However, not only did supervisors resist the innovations of this outsider, but Renault himself was reluctant to invest his profits in factory reorganization rather than style and model changes.[16]

For Renault the key innovation was the time study, a rather crude attempt to speed up individual output. Renault hired "demonstrators"—young, strong, and experienced workers paid a special rate—and timed their output over short intervals. Their output was used to determine the piece rate. The time study from its first experimental appearance in 1907 was criticized by the syndicalist press. By 1912, it had provoked a number of automobile strikes, the most important of which was the strike precipitated by the introduction of the stopwatch to one-quarter of Renault's shops.[17] A thousand of the 4,000 affected workers walked out on December 12. After an interim settlement failed to quell workers' dissatisfaction, a second strike broke out on February 12, 1913. This strike soon turned into a lockout when an intransigent Renault refused to negotiate with workers.[18]

This strike prompted a national debate in the popular as well as the business and syndicalist press over Taylorism.[19] The Metalworkers' leader A. Merrheim and anarcho-syndicalist Emile Pouget presented the CGT's position. They attacked Taylorism as a threat to skilled workers' control. Pouget claimed that motion studies "stifled the ingenuity of the worker" and placed a premium on brute strength and manual dexterity rather than intelligence. Taylor's claim to know the "one best way" of work and assumption that "the best mechanic is incapable of working efficiently without the daily aid of his instructor" was an insult to the workers' dignity.[20] Taylorism also threatened the sense of solidarity and cooperation between workers, for Taylor's piece rate stimulated a selfish "appetite for gain."[21] Merrheim declared that Taylorism reduced the worker to "an automaton ruled by the automatic movements of the machine" and weakened the "market value" of professional or skilled workers.[22] Merrheim somewhat earlier had lamented that job specialization and new machines had reduced apprenticeship and threatened to replace the autodidact with the "ignorant masses."[23]

This defense of artisan values, along with its undercurrent of disdain for and fear of the unskilled machine operator, could be interpreted as a last ditch stand of the militant craftsman in a losing battle against economic progress. Yet, in spite of these "reactionary" sentiments, the CGT leaders clearly recognized the inevitability of economic rationalization and with it the decline of the skilled mechanic.[24] Moreover, many French syndicalists were keenly aware of the backwardness of French industry and began to see innovation as the only means of raising the French workers' standard of living. As early as 1910, Victor Griffuelhes claimed that French production could compete only if French manufacturers adopted the innovative management of the Americans. It was the *patronat*, according to Griffuelhes, rather than the workers who resisted innovation.[25] Léon Jouhaux in 1912 blamed long working hours and low wages on the industrialists' failure to modernize. In 1913, he specifically blamed the reluctance of both labor and management in the French fishing industry to "modernize their form of work" for France's inability to compete with Norwegian and Spanish fisheries.[26]

Ervin Szabo went so far as to argue in 1913 in *Le mouvement socialiste* that economic rationalization could improve working conditions because it would replace the "bourgeois lord" with the "producer" as manager who had learned the "scientific knowledge of efficient production." In France, this Saint-Simonian faith in the productive engineer and condemnation of the "feudal" bourgeois was, of course, a long-established tradition. Furthermore, Szabo envisioned in the prospect of factory-trained workers an elimination of the old chasm that divided the apprenticed craftsman from the common day laborer. This essentially Marxist view of capitalist development held that labor's power would grow because of its unity and prosperity despite the strength of big capital.[27] This was a dialectical as opposed to the syndicalists' ahistoric view of the future. It depended, however, on whether rationalization was used for or against the worker.

The core of the Metalworkers' opposition to Taylorism was not based on their fear of economic rationalization but rather on how it affected labor. Pouget, for example, held that Renault's brand of rationalization was merely a speedup, with no provisions made to protect the health or safety of the worker. The "time-study men," said Merrheim, were less interested in economizing labor, making it more efficient, than in a crude effort to increase output.[28]

During the Renault strike, Merrheim himself indicated the new direction the CGT would take:

[A] rational organization of work is absolutely necessary for the progress of industry. . . . As for me I think that the Taylor system adapted to the French mentality will be introduced more and more in industry. . . . [T]he interest of workers is to supervise this process and to favor all those efforts in the degree that they do not harm their moral, economic, or physical interests.[29]

This was not merely a grudging and defensive acceptance of a fait accompli. After all, only a handful of French factories had adopted

Taylorism. Rather it was an outline of a new concept of workers' control, one that discarded the old defense of the craft tradition and instead advocated labor's "supervision" of economic innovation as part of the struggle for the benefits of increased productivity.

Any ambiguity about CGT goals was eliminated by the result of the Renault strike. With only fifty CGT members out of the 4,000 employed at the Renault Billancourt plants, the strikers lacked effective organization. After one month of the strike, participation had dropped more than two-thirds to 390. Only a hard core of skilled workers held out defending a craft tradition isolated from the new young proletarianized work force. Moreover, Renault had no difficulty ignoring workers' demands for "supervising" the time study. He refused to negotiate and accepted the return of workers only on his terms.[30] Surely if the old form of artisan control was a dead letter, the new model of workers' control of a more productive economy was far from realized.

In the aftermath of the failure at Renault, the Metalworkers faced an impasse. As Gras has shown, all but a rightist trade-union minority wanted to expand into the new sector of unskilled production workers. Yet the union was divided over how to undertake this difficult project. While the Federation leadership, especially Merrheim, advocated patient organization of industrial workers around a concrete economic program, a syndicalist wing, mostly from Paris, proposed a wave of strikes to mobilize the unorganized workers. The CGT never abandoned mass organizing. However, its historic weakness in the proletarianized sector and its inability to expand beyond local municipal coalitions and to organize whole industries greatly limited its effectiveness.[31]

It is not surprising, then, that the leadership sought allies among friendly industrial engineers and the progressive bourgeoisie, at least as a tactical measure, in its struggle over productivity. The CGT embraced engineers who, like Jules Amar and J. M. Lahy, sought not only to increase output but also, through studies of the physiology of work, to reduce fatigue and nervous exhaustion. Lahy held that workers must be consulted before innovations are made and thereby be given a measure of control over industrial change.[32]

The CGT even found in Taylor himself ammunition for their demand that the French economy must be rationalized to the benefit of workers. While Taylor, in his popular work *The Principles of Scientific Management*, berated workers for their "soldiering" on the job and declared that management alone has the knowledge to determine the "one best way" of doing a job,[33] he was obliged to soften the antilabor bias of his program in 1912.

In that year, when Taylor faced opposition to his methods from workers in the naval shipyards of Massachusetts, he defended his innovations before a well-known congressional investigation. Scientific management, far from being antilabor, he claimed, was a "mental revolution," the best means of overcoming class conflict in the factory; it benefited both sides, providing high wages through wage incentive plans for the worker and increased output for the employer. In addition, the consumer got a more plentiful supply of cheaper goods. Even management's control over work methods had its redeeming aspect: at least, this control was to be based on scientific principles, rather than the arbitrary will of the boss.[34]

While Taylor's "mental revolution" essentially offered no more than management's promise of higher wages in exchange for labor's ceding control over production, French labor drew quite different conclusions: Taylorism could increase the standard of living of workers and consumers, and could be equitably applied. Most important, the CGT would use these ideas as a stick to beat the noninnovative French *patronat* who was responsible for France's poverty and the country's increasingly noncompetitive position in the world market.

While the CGT's new approach to productivity and innovation was surely appropriate, its weak base among proletarianized workers resulted in a tactical shift away from mass organizing and an alliance with elites. The war accelerated this movement toward cooperation with engineers and a progressive bourgeoisie, a trend that would split the French labor movement. Yet the war period also led to a clarification of the new ideology, which despite these war-generated distortions in tactics would permanently replace the old syndicalist formula.

III

The war afforded French engineers, the CGT, and business a unique opportunity to rally around the flag of Taylorism as well as the tricolor. Because the profits of the war industries were not limited by the market but only by their capacity to produce, employers were keenly interested in engineers like E. Nussbaumer and Charles de Freminville, who experimented in Taylorizing munitions factories.[35] French trade unionists embraced Taylorism as they collaborated in the war mobilization. As a *délégué à la nation*, Jouhaux joined a number of commissions that provided manpower needs for the war economy.[36] Not only did these offices coordinate manpower procurement, but they "encouraged all necessary modifications of work and facilitated the rapid adoption of new work methods."[37]

The CGT found at least temporary allies who shared its commitment to the modernization of postwar France. Albert Thomas, a rightwing socialist deputy and proponent of class collaboration, took a position similar to Lahy and other humanistic engineers.[38] From May 1915 to September 1917, Thomas achieved a unique and ironical position for a socialist, by becoming Undersecretary of State for Munitions. During his tenure he became an energetic proponent of Taylorism. He not only favored piece rates and bonus systems but also motion studies, division of labor, and vocational screening.[39] Also for the sake of social peace and uninterrupted production, he proposed, like humanistic engineers, that psychological and social factors should be taken into consideration. He insisted that piece rates should "reflect average ability in the factory and the average productivity of the machine rather than the fastest worker and machine."[40] In April 1917, in his bulletin, *Usines de guerre*, Thomas summarized his position on Taylorism:

No longer will the worker be content with fixed salaries which he gains for a week of non-strenuous work. No longer will the employer be content with the careless methods of the past. The employer now wants a greater productivity; the worker wants the highest salary; and they give each other perfect satisfaction when they reach their goals by a method of payment for work based on results.[41]

This view, although linked to a patriotic concern with munitions production, had a broader meaning. It was almost identical with the "mental revolution" advocated by Taylor in 1912 and was a prescription for reform after the war. Fundamentally, he advocated a trade-off between labor and management.

Thomas's commitment to postwar economic rationalization was shared by the *Societé d'encouragement pour l'industrie nationale*, an agency of heavy industry.[42] Louis Renault, who had used Taylor's method in arms production during the war, advocated that France produce the greatest amount in the least time with the least effort, stating that "If we do not maximize production, we will remain a tributary power to other lands."[43] In 1918, André Citroën proposed that a national industries ministry be established to encourage postwar factory specialization and increased efficiency.[44]

Nevertheless, the application of Taylorism in war production was quite limited, largely owing to the prevalence of small workshops.[45] Moreover, as both Aimée Moutet and Richard Kuisel have shown, cartelization rather than the introduction of new technology was the key to French business strategy. Nor did business social policy recognize the need to share the benefits of growth, much less accept labor input in innovation; rather, they stressed an only slightly modified form of traditional paternalism. Renault, for example, advocated social programs (workers' gardens and better city services to improve the moral environment of workers). More substantial social reform measures, including a shorter workday and improved wages, were to follow, not parallel, increases in productivity.[46] The "progressive bourgeoisie" thus shared with Thomas and the CGT little beyond a willingness to modernize, and even this goal was held only by a small group of large employers.

While the CGT had worked with business representatives during the war, it would be incorrect to label it as simply reformist or class collaborationist. The Minimum Programme adopted by the *Comité confédéral national* (CCN) one week after the Armistice was certainly opposed to prewar anarcho-syndicalism; but it went far beyond business plans for enlightened, paternalistic capitalism. Its opening sentence was, "We must direct ourselves to take control of production." As a first step, it advocated the preservation of the organizations "installed in the course of the war," in order to forestall a revival of the "Oligarchy" whose private interests had been "strangling industry and consumers," and to end "sterile and destructive conservativism." A program of "incessant progress of production" and developing "all new inventions and discoveries" was to make possible a number of social reforms (improved social insurance, education, and the eight-hour day). These reforms were to prepare the worker for the "ultimate goal of emancipation." The package of reforms included the nationalization of railroads, mines, shipping, banking, and electricity, to be administered by committees of producers (labor and technicians), consumers, and deputies.[47] To be sure, the CGT leadership sought to expand its base of support beyond the worker, but it was more interested in reaching out to consumers and the new working class of technicians than to the employer class. Like Thomas, Jouhaux supported the incentive wage, however, not as a trade-off between business and labor but to "link the interests of the producers to those of the consumers." As Jouhaux declared at the 1918 Congress of the CGT, "We must strive to realize this formula, the maximum production in the minimum of time, for the maximum salary with the general increase of the buying power for all." Also, after the CGT's plan for a National Economic Council was rejected by the Clemenceau government, the CGT established between 1919 and 1921 a National Council of Labor with representatives of labor, consumers, and technicians.

The goal of postwar CGT policy was not compromise with capitalism but a strategy of economic democracy in and through a modernized and productive society.[48]

This trend is most obvious in the stance of the union most affected by rationalization—the Metalworkers' Federation. At its congress in July of 1918, A. Merrheim and R. Lenoir approved of "new methods of work and renumeration" and denied "neither the inevitable specialization nor useful intensification of production either in war or peace." In sharp contrast to its prewar defense of craftsmanship, the Metalworkers declared themselves "no longer isolated from the general spirit of the population" and willing to "contribute toward the achievement of general abundance."[49] In September 1918, Lenoir wrote that a rationalized consumer-oriented economy would bridge the gulf that divided France into two societies, one of "subsistence" and the other of "arrogant excess."[50]

The Metalworkers' leadership was not oblivious to the psychological costs of rationalization. "The machine," said Lenoir, "changes the worker from being the practitioner who directs something himself . . . to the servant resigned to the moving machine which commands the rhythm of work." Yet, if less interesting work is inevitable, it must be rewarded, declared Lenoir, not merely with higher pay but also with labor's participation in the process of change.[51]

Surely the most important prerequisite for the CGT's acceptance of economic rationalization was the eight-hour day. On April 23, 1919, the French parliament, facing massive May Day strikes and demonstrations, accommodated workers and veterans by passing an eight-hour day law. The act generally reduced the workday from ten to eight hours with significant exceptions for delays, temporary exemptions, and seasonal fluctuations.[52] In collective bargaining, the Metalworkers', Clothing, and Construction Federations agreed to increase productivity in order to smooth the transition to a shorter work day.[53] Yet despite the CGT's willingness to increase productivity, employers resisted the reduction of the workday from the start. Jouhaux defended the eight-hour day by challenging business to increase productivity rather than production time, an argument repeatedly made throughout the 1920s.[54] In this context, the CGT's acceptance of Taylorism was hardly a capitulation to the needs of capitalist accumulation nor an adaptation to business unionism *à la americain*. Rather it was an integral part of the political and ideological struggle for a shorter workday, improved wages, and the social control of production.

IV

This trend toward democratic control over innovation was blown off course after the war. The CGT's weak base in growth industries and its failure to develop a strategy to win it left the leadership seeking allies among the French elite, a shift that contributed to the split of the rank and file and the failure of the new orientation. This trend became obvious when, in August 1914, instead of attempting to organize a general strike against the war, the CGT joined the *Union Sacrée*.

The power of federation officials increased as they worked with government and employers in the war economy. Despite the rank-and-file dissatisfaction with the *Union Sacrée* during the spring strikes of 1917 against the war, the leadership supported Thomas's program of shop stewards, compulsory arbitration, and no-strike pledges. Even though the *Union Sacrée* dissolved in September 1917 with the socialists (including Thomas) leaving the government, the CGT leadership remained unwilling and probably unable to take charge of the growing restiveness among the workers. The result was local strikes (e.g., the Metalworkers in the spring of 1918) and the election of antiwar radicals (e.g., Gaston Monmousseau as secretary of the Railway Workers' Federation in April 1920). By early 1918, the leadership (*majoritaires*) faced within the federation a growing antiwar movement led by Pierre Monatte, Raymond Pericat, and Gaston Monmousseau (*minoritaires*), who hoped to emulate Lenin's smashing of the Russian state and to establish soviets of workers out of the French unions.[55] Merrheim denounced the *minoritaire's* call for a "catastrophic" political revolution. Whereas Bolshevism was "incomplete," merely a destruction of the bourgeois state, Merrheim proposed an economic revolution that promised true "emancipation" through "general abundance."[56] In the midst of this Bolshevik challenge, the CCN confidently declared that the new work methods would force management into employing "our technical and administrative staff" who "will be ready to organize a new society" based on the "law of progress."[57] Such statements indicate an elitist approach to the struggle for control over innovation and implied cooperation with the "progressive bourgeoisie." This is confirmed by the CGT leadership's participation in the Association for the Struggle Against Unemployment and their support for the weekly *Information ouvrière et sociale*, both of which were forums shared by industrial and technical elites as well as labor. I have already argued that there was no real possibility for class collaboration; nor did the CGT leadership intend to abandon class struggle or workers' control but only to redefine them. Yet the CGT *minoritaires* could easily have read this intent in their leadership's words and deeds.[58]

One disastrous but symptomatic result of this mistrust was a strike of Metalworkers in June and July 1919. Organized by a "Committee of Action" from the Parisian Metalworkers' union, it was directed against the settlement that Merrheim and Lenoir had made with the employees in April 1919. By this agreement, which established the eight-hour day, the wages of hourly workers were increased to account for the shortening of the work day, but the piece rate workers won no such increase. Instead the union leaders simply agreed that they would encourage an increase in productivity. This arrangement meant a real wage cut during a period of inflation and postwar decline in jobs. The strike against this policy quickly took on a revolutionary political character. Leadership devolved to the local level and without the support of the Federation organization it soon disintegrated in complete failure.[59]

The well-known strikes of May 1920 followed a similar pattern. After the failure of management to implement a settlement to a successful strike of railway workers in February 1920, the Railway Federation, under the newly elected leadership of the pro-Soviet Gaston Monmousseau, narrowly approved of a general rails strike in late April, which the *minoritaires* hoped to build into a revolutionary movement. This poorly organized plan for a walkout (perhaps one-half of the railworkers participated) forced a reluctant CGT leadership into joining it with a general sympathy strike for May. It was staggered into three "waves" of strikes in the first three weeks of May. With lackluster coordination from the top, absentions were widespread, especially in the north and east. The results were worse than a disappointment: by May 20, the CGT voted for a return to work as the ex-socialist president Alexandre Millerand won a temporary court-ordered dissolution of the CGT and 20,000 railway workers were fired. It showed the final collapse of the syndicalist strategy of the revolutionary general strike.[60]

During the next eighteen months the CGT lost half of its membership and split into two bitter factions. A militant wing supported the International Red Trade Unions (created by the Communist International) and formed *comités syndicalistes revolutionnaires* or Revolutionary Syndicalist Committees (CSR). At the CGT Congress of July 1921, the revolutionary faction was a large minority (losing 1,325 to 1,572 on a vote for the CGT's leadership). When the CCN subsequently demanded that the unions dismantle factions (the CSR), the result was the succession of the revolutionaries and the creation of the CGTU in

December 1921, which joined the Communist International's trade union arm.[61]

Without mass support, the CGT's dreams of "economic revolution" soon faded. In the midst of the May 1920 strikes, Robert Pinot, president of the Iron and Steel Committee (*Comité des forges*) declared that the CGT could not be trusted to control the working masses, thus signaling a stiffer resistance of French employers. In January 1921, the Union of Metal and Mining Industries broke off negotiations with the Metalworkers' Federation over introducing shop stewards.[62] Except for the eight-hour day, none of the objectives of the Minimum Programme of 1918 was won.

The issues that split the CGT were essentially political—the position of the leadership on the Soviet Union and its collaborationist role during the war. Significantly, the question of workers' control and Taylorism played no important part. Indeed, the CGTU quickly was purged of adherents to anarcho-syndicalism and with it the old tradition of skilled workers' control. Yet the impotence of labor, partially resulting from the split, blocked any effective policy on economic innovation.

V

The French labor movement was in an anomalous situation in the 1920s. The unions had adopted an ideology that was appropriate for an industrialized economy, but they were constrained by two barriers: (1) the French *patronat* had only an ambiguous commitment to innovation—hardly fulfilling the historic progressive role of the bourgeoisie, and (2) organized labor lacked a large base in growth industry. Neither confederation was able to broaden its base beyond the craft and service sectors (see Table 6-3). This produced a movement that exhorted business to innovate and idealized foreign models of economic rationalization (the United States and the Soviet Union). At the same time, the labor movement in the 1920s demanded a share of the benefits of increased productivity—the eight-hour day and increased wages—but because of their weak bargaining position, the demand for labor's control over the introduction of new methods receded into the background. Despite the great differences between the CGT and CGTU, both converged on these points, leaving a rear guard of syndicalists to defend the old model of skilled workers' control.

The CGT pursued its strategy of the Minimum Programme in the highly adverse circumstances of the 1920s—defending the eight-hour day and advocating a vague program of social control of a more

Table 6-3. *Occupational Distribution of French Trade Union Membership in 1926, by Sector*

Sector	CGT	CGTU
Industry		
Metal	4.5%	9.8%
Textiles	8.5	7.5
Construction	4.0	10.7
Mining	13.7	5.4
Ports and Docks	3.5	2.2
Books/paper	3.3	2.8
Miscellaneous industries	3.8	4.4
Services/Government		
Railroads	8.9	26.4
Transport	5.9	4.7
Public Services	14.4	10.0
Government establishments	3.8	3.9
Postal/telecommunications	6.5	3.6
Education	9.2	1.2
Miscellaneous services	4.5	4.4
Others	5.0	3.0

Source: Antoine Prost, *La CGT 1934–1939* (Paris, 1964), 201–204.

productive economy. Capital resisted the demand for the eight-hour day arguing, for example, in a government commission of March 1919 that it would threaten postwar recovery and that a shortened workday was possible only after economic modernization.[63] Employers accepted the eight-hour day only in the face of the strike threat of May 1919. Thus, when the labor movement disintegrated in 1921, the employer press led by the *Comité des forges* and the *Groupe des intérêts économiques* called for a rollback to a longer workday. The short day, they claimed, led to inflation, made France uncompetitive, and prevented the country from modernizing for lack of capital. The eight-hour law, claimed the conservative deputy Paul Messier in 1920, was passed only to give the workers "a little rest" after the war, but was unthinkable as a permanent policy.[64]

In response to a coordinated effort of conservative deputies to suspend the law, the CGT organized a petition drive in the summer of 1922 that brought nearly two million signatures in favor of the eight-hour day. The refusal of leaders of the governing *Bloc nationale* to support the industrialists (fearing social disorder if the law were abandoned) temporarily quelled this attack on the eight-hour day.[65]

The issue of the eight-hour day, which smoldered throughout the early 1920s, was enflamed in late 1925. The International Labor Office, (ILO), an outgrowth of the League of Nations directed by Albert Thomas, campaigned throughout that year to induce the industrial nations to ratify the Washington Convention of 1920, which sanctioned the eight-hour day. This effort met a setback when, in the spring of 1926, Fascist Italy reinstated the nine-hour day. The business press in other European countries clamored to follow suit, presumably to prevent Italy from winning a competitive advantage.[66]

Against this attack on labor's one lasting victory after World War I, the CGT and its allies in the ILO defended the eight-hour day as the norm for modern industrial society. It promised, according to Thomas, to restore family life, led to a decline in alcoholism and promised a development of general and professional education.[67] A "change of machine and methods of work rather than an increase in work time" said Francis Millon of the CGT, was the solution to labor productivity.[68] Union leaders, close to the rank and file, criticized how economic rationalization was applied, complaining that it led to fatigue and the discharge of older and less robust workers, and softened the labor movement by reducing the scarcity of skill. Nevertheless, the central leadership felt compelled to ignore the long-term issue of democratic control over innovation and repeated its advocacy of increased productivity as an alternative to the conservative pressure for a longer workday.[69]

Despite its inability to control the rationalization process, the CGT also continued to support Taylorism as the only way of increasing French standards of living. Toward this goal, the CGT even adapted the ideas of American welfare capitalists, especially Henry Ford, who was presented in Europe as a champion of increased productivity, high wages, and a mass consumer economy.[70] This image of American Taylorism was a kind of wish fulfillment for the CGT leadership, the hope of "general abundance" that Lenoir in 1919 had identified as the "economic revolution."

An instructive if extreme example of this seemingly unnatural embrace of American capitalism by French labor can be seen in the case of Hyacinthe Dubreuil. A machinist for over twenty years, by 1920

Dubreuil rose through the ranks of the Metalworkers' Federation to become secretary of the CGT in the Seine. Noted for his strong anti-communism, he drew the attention of Albert Thomas. In February 1927, through the good offices of Thomas and the Industrial Relations Council (an affiliate of the Rockefeller Foundation), Dubreuil began a fifteen-month tour of model factories in the United States. As a former machinist, Dubreuil was a credible advocate of Taylorism to a working-class audience. Thus upon his return to France, Dubreuil wrote a series of books praising the new methods of production in the U.S.[71]

Dubreuil found in the scientifically run American factory the rule of technique and objective procedure rather than the arbitrary privilege of status or wealth. Because of this "scientific" procedure, cooperation replaced the old pattern of "discord and of class war." Both the "aristocratic pride" of the French factory owner and the "excessive individualism" of the French worker were superseded by a "democratic" supervisor and a worker whose "remarkable trait" was a "natural placidity" in receiving orders and accepting change. Most important, Dubreuil saw the American factory as a solution to mass want through mass production. For Dubreuil all of this was a sign that the U.S. was moving "toward some form of socialism."[72] Obviously Dubreuil was holding up an idealized image of how industrial society ought to be—a Saint-Simonian meritocracy and consumer economy. But the core of his praise for America was a trenchant critique of French capital in the 1920s.

Despite considerable growth, French business remained backward in the 1920s. Jean Carré has calculated an annual increase of man-hour productivity in France of 5.5 percent between 1921 and 1929 (the same as between 1946 and 1953 and considerably higher than the average of 2 percent between 1896 and 1913). Yet this growth was concentrated only in a few industries (electricity, chemicals, and mechanical goods).[73] Moreover, even the comparatively innovative sector of automobiles lagged far behind that of the United States. Citroën calculated that French autos were produced in 300 man-days, compared with the 70 man-days of the American car.[74] Further, in a government survey of the impact of the eight-hour day on productivity, conducted between 1921 and 1927, only one of sixty-six factories reporting had adopted the key component of Taylorism, time and motion studies. Although twenty-eight introduced new or more machines, most relied on rather crude means of increasing productivity, including fifteen who increased machine speeds, fourteen who increased discipline, and twenty-seven who simply introduced piece work (some firms reporting several innovations). [75] Given this evidence, plus the persistent cry from business for a longer workday, it is not surprising that Dubreuil had an audience among workers.

Despite the deep ideological divisions within the French labor movement, the CGT's rivals in the CGTU and Communist Party held a position on economic rationalization only cosmetically different from that of the CGT. They strongly criticized the CGT, claiming that it had accepted capitalism as long as it was productive and renounced the class struggle. Yet the communists and the CGTU did not criticize scientific management itself nor did they generally defend the traditional values of skill and the profession autonomy of labor. Probably more than the CGT, the CGTU found itself in an anomalous situation: it shared with the CGT a belief in the progressive function of technological innovation (derived from Marxism). However, in order to avoid class collaboration and, more important, to win new union members, the CGTU also attacked the "consequences" of capitalist innovation. The CGTU reluctantly defended both those opponents of Taylorism, who wanted innovations but demanded that they be democratically controlled, as well as those who defended traditional skills against economic change. By failing to distinguish between these two critiques, the CGTU, like the reformists, obscured the new model of workers' control in which labor "supervised" innovation.

The communists held that technological innovation was not only inevitable but an aid in organizing because it created a more "homogenous worker" replacing the parochial skilled workers with a "base for a large and general class movement."[76] The CGTU's position was also colored by Lenin's advocacy of Taylorism in April 1918 as a solution to Soviet Russia's massive economic problems. Indeed, scientific management institutes, which Lenin had established in 1920–21, were expanded in 1928 on the eve of Stalin's First Five-Year Plan.[77]

Central to the CGTU's doctrine was its distinction between capitalist and socialist rationalization, which emerged in 1926 in response to the CGT's campaign for scientific management.[78] In contrast to capitalist rationalization, socialist rationalization did not waste energy in class exploitation but rather realized the dream of the eight-hour day, whereas under capitalism it was only advocated.[79] While the CGT used an idealized image of Fordism to criticize the failure of French business to modernize, the CGTU posed an equally unrealistic picture of Soviet economy for essentially the same purpose.

Unlike the CGT, which increasingly abandoned the struggles on the shop floor for interest group politics, the CGTU was committed to organizing new workers, especially those in the larger and more concentrated industries. The Communist International in February 1928 advocated organizing "the new ranks of workers, especially the semi-skilled machine operators." Attempts of the CGTU to penetrate innovative industries such as the automobile industry obliged them to attack the new work methods.[80] During the boom years of 1929 and 1930 communist labor organizers filed dozens of reports in *L'humanité* condemning the new factories. For example, the Michelin rubber workers were pictured as a "vast army of 18,000 people making the same mechanical movements under the watchful eyes of the company's band of young and loyal 'stooges.'" Complaints of the breakup of small cohesive work groups with the introduction of piece work, the stopwatch, and the greater division of labor were very similar to the opposition of Taylorism in the auto plants before the war.[81] Moreover, the CGTU also defended the skills of artisans such as Breton fishermen, Parisian metal workers, and construction workers whose immediate economic interests were threatened by innovation.[82]

Like the CGT, the communist unions demanded that the benefits of increased productivity be shared by those workers forced to submit to more intense production. The CGTU's program stressed the need for vacations and the 44-hour week for the "recuperation of energy" dispensed by workers in rationalized plants and higher wages for the "general improvement" of the standard of living.[83]

However, by 1929, under pressure from the rank and file, whom they hoped to organize, the CGTU was forced to go a step further, demanding workers' control over innovation on the shop floor.[84] It advocated the suppression of time study and "dangerous machines" (as determined by workers' delegates), and demanded rest breaks for conveyor workers and even a reduction of the speed of the belts by "collective action" where needed.[85] This policy was clearly a concession to organizers just as was the defense of the craft skills of metal workers and fishermen the year before. It was not an integral part of CGTU strategy; the communists defended, although reluctantly and inconsistently, both the progressive and conservative demands of workers against the consequences of Taylorism. They failed to distinguish between workers' control of innovation and craft defense of traditional skills and thus did not develop a goal of democratic economic innovation.

The French communists in the 1920s faced an untenable problem: they wished to affirm the necessity of the rationalization of work and yet avoid supporting those capitalists who controlled it. They rejoiced in the emergence of the mass production worker, and yet they defended the immediate interests of the French laborer in a painful transition to a modern economy. They encouraged shopfloor agitation against the new work methods. Yet the main thrust of their policy was hardly distinguishable from the "reformist" CGT—higher wages and shorter hours in compensation for Taylorism and mechanization.

The only proponent of the anarcho-syndicalist tradition of workers' control was the small and ephemeral *Ligue syndicaliste* (Syndicalist League). Organized by a small group of largely ex-communist radicals, under the guidance of Pierre Monatte and Maurice Chambelland, the *Ligue syndicaliste* attempted within both federations to organize a revolutionary trade unionism independent of the communist party and thus to recreate the CGT of the Charter of Amiens.[86] Against the reformists' acceptance of Taylorism, which they held to be only a speedup, the league advocated that workers "go slowly." They also rejected the communist distinction between capitalist and socialist rationalization: "let the workers in no case abandon absolute control over working conditions in either a bourgeois or workers' state," Max Emile declared in 1927.[87]

How did the *Ligue syndicaliste* advocate exercise of workers' control? Principally by regulating the speed of work. The productivity movement was management's "revenge" on labor for winning the eight-hour day, an attempt to force workers to do ten hours worth of labor in eight hours. If workers accepted this, one member wrote, they would have "gained nothing" from the shortened workday. He proposed that workers impose a general slowdown, a boycott of the most Taylorized plants, and generally "fix the work rate for all."[88]

For the *Ligue syndicaliste* work was not a means toward general prosperity but an embodiment of personal value and autonomy, which scientific management threatened. However, in contrast to the anti-Taylorism of the prewar period, these independent radicals did not defend traditional skills. Their concern was merely with the quantity of work, an obvious reflection of the rise of a totally quantifiable pattern of repetitive labor.

As a viable strategy of French labor, anarcho-syndicalism was dead by 1906. With the Renault strike of 1913, if not sooner, the goal of skilled workers' control had also been abandoned. To the extent that the syndicalist tradition survived World War I, it surely failed in May 1920, while the ideal of artisan management of production persisted in the 1920s only in the episodic and pale form of the *Ligue syndicaliste*.

Shortly before the war the mainstream of French labor moved away from a decentralized and craft-based syndicalism and toward an organized movement committed .to mobilizing the industrial work force. Recognizing the need for a more productive economy, the

French labor movement abandoned the defense of craft skills and sought means of making economic innovation serve the long-term interests of labor. Lacking an ability to organize the new unskilled industrial workers until 1936, and facing a *patronat* that failed to innovate, the French labor movement confronted an ironic situation: it advocated an ideology appropriate for a labor movement that it could not organize and for an economy that did not yet exist. Despite the obvious differences between Dubreuil and the communists, not only did both extremes favor innovation but they saw in it the future of French labor. The central problem—one that the division of the left and the poor organization of labor made impossible to solve—was how workers were to use innovation to improve their material conditions and ultimately to control the production process.

Notes

1. For studies of prewar French syndicalism, see Val Lorwin, *The French Labor Movement* (Cambridge, Mass., 1954), Edouard Dolleans and Gerard Dehove, *Histoire du travail en France*, vol. I (Paris, 1953), Georges Lefranc, *Histoire du mouvement syndical français* (Paris, 1937), and Robert Goetz-Girey, *La pensée syndicale française* (Paris, 1948). More recent works include Peter Stearns, *Revolutionary Syndicalism and French Labor: A Cause without Rebels* (New Brunswick, 1971), Harvey Mitchell and Peter Stearns, *Workers and Protest: The European Labor Movement, the Working Classes and the Origins of Social Democracy* (Ithaca, 1971), F. F. Ridley, *Revolutionary Syndicalism in France* (New York, 1971), and Jacques Julliard, *Fernand Pelloutier et les origines du syndicalisme d'action direct* (Paris, 1971).

2. The Minimum Programme is published in Léon Jouhaux, *Le syndicalisme et la CGT* (Paris, 1920), 205–213.

3. A recent example of this approach is Bernard Moss, *The Origins of the French Labor Movement, 1830–1914* (Berkeley, 1976).

4. Stearns says that the theory of syndicalism embodied in the Charter of Amiens was a product of the French intelligentsia and not the workers who were indifferent to theory. The syndicalist "image lives in the minds of those historians who wish that workers had been what they were not." Stearns, *Revolutionary Syndicalism*, 102.

5. See Martin Fine, "Toward Corporatism: The Movement for Capital-Labor Collaboration in France, 1914–1936," Ph.D. dissertation, University of Wisconsin, Madison, 1971, especially 4–129, and "Albert Thomas: A Reformers' Vision of Modernization, 1914–1932," *Journal of Contemporary History* 3 (July 1977), 545–564. See also Alfred Rosmer, *Le mouvement ouvrier pendant la guerre*, 2 vols. (Paris, 1936 and The Hague, 1959), John Godfrey, "Bureaucracy, Industry, and Politics in France during the First World War," Ph.D. Dissertation, Oxford University, 1974, and Michael Delucia, "The Remaking

of French Syndicalism, 1911–1918: The Growth of the Reformist Philosophy," Ph.D. Dissertation, Boston University, 1971.

6. See Alain Touraine, *Workers' Attitudes Toward Technical Change* (Paris, 1965); Michel Collinet, *Esprit du syndicalisme* (Paris, 1950); and Georges Friedman, *Industrial Society* (Glencoe, Ill., 1956). See also Charles Tilly and Edward Shorter, *Strikes in France* (New York, 1974), 180–184 and Serge Mallet, *La nouvelle classe ouvrière* (Paris, 1963).

7. See Georges Lefranc, *Le mouvement syndical sous la Troisième République* (Paris, 1967), 125–146.

8. Stearns, *Revolutionary Syndicalism*, 79–85. See also Jacques Julliard, *Clemenceau, briseur de greves: L'affaire de Draveil-Villeneuve-Saint-Georges (1908)* (Paris, 1965).

9. Tilly and Shorter, 119.

10. Christian Gras, "La Fédération des Métaux en 1913–1914 et l'evolution du syndicalisme revolutionnaire française," *Le mouvement social* 77 (October–December 1971), 87–88.

11. For background on the prewar shift in organizational strategy of the CGT, see Bernard Georges and Denise Tintant, *Léon Jouhaux, cinquante ans de syndicalisme*, vol. 1 (Paris, 1962), 65–101. See also Christian Gras, "Merrheim et le capitalisme," *Le mouvement social* 63 (April–June 1968), 143–163, Michelle Perrot, "Grèves, grèvistes, et conjoncture: Vieux problème, travaux neufs," *Le mouvement social* 63 (April–June 1968), 109–124, Stearns, *Revolutionary Syndicalism*, 85–93 and Lorwin, 145–179.

12. See Bernard Mottez, *Systèmes de salaire et politiques patronales*, (Paris, 1966) for an account of experiments in bonus and piece rate systems in late nineteenth-century France that were very similar to those of Taylor. See also Michelle Perrot, "The Three Ages of Industrial Discipline in Nineteenth-Century France," in John Merriman, ed., *Class Consciousness and Class Conflict in Nineteenth-Century Europe* (New York, 1979), 149–68.

13. J. M. Laux, "Travail et travailleurs dans l'industrie automobile jusqu'en 1914," *Le mouvement social* 81 (October–December 1972), 14–23.

14. The literature on F. W. Taylor is immense. A concise analysis of Taylorism in the European context is Charles S. Maier, "Between Taylorism and Technocracy," *Journal of Contemporary History* 5, no. 2 (1970). An excellent bibliography is in Aimée Moutet, "Les origines du système de Taylor en Fance, le point de vue patronal (1907–1914)," *Le mouvement social* 93 (October–December 1975), 17. See also Maurice Levy-Leboyer, *Le patronat de la second industrialisation* (Paris, 1979).

15. Georges de Ram, "Quelques notes sur un essai d'application du système Taylor dans un grand atelier de mechanique française," *Revue de métallurgie*, September 1909, 929–33. See also Patrick Fridenson, *Histoire des usines Renault* (Paris, 1972), 71–72 and E. Riché, *La situation des ouvriers dans l'industrie automobile* (Paris, 1909), 54–91. See also J. P. Bardou, J. J. Chanaron, P. Fridenson, and James Laux, *La revolution automobile* (Paris, 1977).

16. Moutet, "Origins du système," 35–37.

17. Sources on the Renault strikes of 1913 include Direction du Travail, *"Statistique de grève pendant l'année 1913* (Paris, 1914), 234–235. Contemporary trade union accounts are in *La bataille syndicaliste*, February 11, 1913, and March 23, 1913, and Alphonse Merrheim, "La méthode Taylor," *La vie ouvrière* 5 (1913), 210–211, 226, and 301–306.

18. Analysis of the strike is found in Michel Collinet, *Esprit du syndicalisme*, 41–47, Fridenson, *Histoire des usines*, 73–78, Laux, "Travail," 25–26, Moutet, "Origines du système," 40–41, and G. Hatry, "La grève de chronométrage," *De Renault frères á Renault Régie nationale*, December 1971, 73–81.

19. For the debate on Taylorism in the French press see *L'auto*, February 12, 1913, and *Le matin*, March 4, 1913. See also Moutet, "Patronat français," 43.

20. Emile Pouget, *L'organisation du surmenage* (Paris, 1914), 53–54.

21. A. Merrheim, "Le système Taylor," *La vie ouvrière*, March 5, 1913, 309.

22. Ibid., February 20, 1913, 214 and 224.

23. Merrheim at the 1908 Congress of the CGT lamented that new machines allowed metal workers to be trained in one week. See Georges and Tintant, 1: 145. Pierre Coupat of the *Fédération de mécaniciens de la Seine* in 1906 had also denounced the increasing specialization of work and the decline of long apprenticeships. See P. Coupat, "L'enseignement professional," *Revue syndicaliste*, December 1906, 224.

24. Adophe Loyau, "Les conditions du travail dans la mecanique," *Revue syndicaliste*, August 1907, 84.

25. Victor Griffuelhes, "L'inferiorité de capitalisme française," *Le mouvement socialiste*, December 1910, 329–333.

26. Léon Jouhaux, *La bataille syndicaliste*, July 3, 1911. See also Georges and Tintant, 72–77.

27. Ervin Szabó, "Principes d'organisation scientifique des usines," *Le mouvement socialiste*, January–February 1913, 128–132.

28. Pouget, 4, and Merrheim, "Le système Taylor," *La vie ouvrière*, April 5, 1914, 306.

29. Quoted in André Viellerville, *Le système Taylor* (Paris, 1914), 139–140.

30. Collinet, 44–45.

31. C. Gras, "La Fédération des Metaux," 98–101.

32. J. M. Lahy, "Le système Taylor et l'organisation des usines," *La revue socialiste*, August 1913, 126–138 and "L'étude scientifique des mouvements et le chronometrage," *La revue socialiste*, December 1913, 501–520. See also J. M. Lahy, *Le système Taylor* (Paris, 1916).

33. Frederick Taylor, *The Principles of Scientific Management* (New York, 1967), 19–24.

34. Ibid., "Testimony before the Special House Committee" in *Scientific Management* (New York, 1947), 24–30. See also Milton Nadworny, *Scientific Management and the Unions* (Cambridge, Mass., 1955).

35. B. Thumen, "Organisons la production," *Cahiers du redressement française* 2 (Paris, 1927). See also Bertrand Thompson, *Le système Taylor* (Paris, 1916) and *L'organisation des usines* (Paris, 1926), especially the foreword. The engineering journal, *Le génie civil*, became a vehicle of Taylorism in France during the war; see, for example, the issues of November 4, 1916, p. 315 and November 10, 1917, p. 307.

36. The labor commission of the Seine, for example, set up seven committees that were directed to solve problems related to job placement, foreign labor, unemployment, and apprenticeships. See Roger Picard, *Le mouvement syndical durant la guerre* (Paris, 1928), 59.

37. "Rapport sur l'action générale de la CGT depuis Août 1914," *La voix du peuple*, December, 1916, 7. Léon Jouhaux, *Les travailleurs devant la paix* (Paris, 1918). See also Georges and Tinant, 153–185, and Picard, 58–72, for CGT cooperation in the war effort.

38. For background on Thomas, see Fine, "Albert Thomas," 545–564; Patrick Fridenson and M. Reberiou, "Albert Thomas, pivot du reformisme," *Le mouvement social* 87 (April–June, 1974), 85–98; Thomas Schaper, *Albert Thomas, trente ans de reformisme social* (Assen, 1959); Guy de Lusignan, "Albert Thomas et la justice sociale," *L'actualité de l'histoire* 24 (July–August, 1958), 2–28.

39. William Oualid, *Salaires et tarifs* (Paris, 1929), 90 and 97. For two studies on Thomas' role in the war industries see Alain Hennebicque, "Albert Thomas et le régime des usines de guerre, 1915–1917," 111–144 and Gerd Hardach, "La mobilisation industrielle en 1914–1918: production, planification, et ideologie," 81–109, both in Patrick Fridenson, ed., *1914–1918: l'autre front, Cahiers du mouvement social* 2 (1977).

40. Oualid, 97.

41. *Bulletin des usines de guerres*, April 4, 1917, 273.

42. *Le génie civil*, February 8, 1919, 177–181; February 15, 1919, 137; and October 18, 1919, 379–380.

43. Louis Renault, *Bulletin des usines Renault* (August 1, 1918), quoted in Fridenson, *Histoire des usines*, p. 57.

44. Andre Citroën, "L'avenir de la construction automobile," *La revue politique et parlementaire*, May 10, 1929, 241.

45. Henri Le Chatelier, for example, claimed in 1919 that "there is no industrialist in France . . . rigorously applying the Taylor system." *Information ouvrière et sociale*, September 14, 1919. See Aimée Moutet, "Patrons de progrès ou patrons de combat? La politique de rationalisation de l'industrie française au lendemain de la Premiere Guerre mondiale" in Leon Marard and Patrick Zylberman, eds., *Soldat du travail*, special issue of *Recherches* (Paris, 1978), 454–455.

46. Ibid., 476–486.

47. Le Comité Confédéral National, "Le programme minimum de la CGT," (December 15, 1918), in *La Confédération générale du travail et le mouvement syndical* (Paris, 1925), 165–171.

48. CGT, *Congrès national corporatif, compte rendu* (Paris, July 1918), 234, 184–192, and see *Information ouvrière et sociale*, January 11, 1920, for a descrip-

tion of the National Labor Council. A good recent analysis is in Richard F. Kuisel, *Capitalism and the State in Modern France* (New York, 1981), 59–69.

49. *Information ouvrière et sociale*, July 28, 1918.

50. Ibid., November 7, 1918.

51. Ibid.

52. Legal background on the application of the eight-hour day and an interesting survey of business and labor opinion about the economic and social effects of the shortened workday can be found in Jean Beaudemoulin, *Enquête sur les loisirs de l'ouvrier français*, Thèse par le Doctorat, Université de Paris (Paris, 1924).

53. The agreement was published in the *Bulletin du Ministère du Travail* 31 (April–June 1924), 98. For an analysis of this accord see Bertrand Abherve, "Les origines de la grève des métallurgistes parisiens, Juin 1919," *Le mouvement social* 93 (October–December, 1975), 75–85.

54. See the report of the CCN meeting of January 14, 1920 in *Voix du peuple*, February, 1920, 89.

55. The best source on the split of the French labor movement during the war is Anne Kriegel, *Aux origines du communisme francais 1914–1920*, vol. I (Paris, 1964), 193–351. See also Robert Wohl, *French Communism in the Making* (Stanford, 1966), Max Gallo, "Quelques aspects de la mentalité et du comportement ouvriers dans les usines de guerres, 1914–18," *Le mouvement social* 56 (July–September 1966), 3–33, and for a view from the extreme left, see the collected papers of Pierre Monatte in Colette Chambelland and Jean Maitron, *Syndicalisme révolutionnaire et communisme* (Paris, 1968).

56. A. Merrheim, *Information ouvrière et sociale* May 4, 1919. Jouhaux stated this distinction between political and economic revolution even more explicitly, claiming the idea "that one ought to produce intensely only in victorious revolution and when capitalist society has been abolished as false and useless." *Voix du peuple*, November 1919, 343. In place of revolutionary abstentionism, Jouhaux advocated an economic revolution which in a "slow process of evolution . . . little by little penetrates the system, which saps the regime and which in the very midst of the established order creates a new organism." *Le bataille syndicaliste*, July 23, 1919.

57. *Information ouvrière et sociale*, November 7, 1918.

58. See Fine, "Toward Corporatism," 35–45 and 70–79.

59. Abherve, 75–81. See also Nicholas Papayanis, "Masses révolutionaires et directions réformistes: les tensions au cour des grèves de métallurgistes francais in 1919," *Le mouvement social* 93 (October–December, 1975) 52–73.

60. Kriegel, *Aux origines du communisme*, vol. 1, 359–547.

61. The brief account of the split of the CGT is found in Lorwin, 47–67, Georges Lefranc, *Le mouvement syndical sous la Troisième République* (Paris, 1967) and Anne Kriegel, *La croissance de la CGT, 1918–1921* (Paris, 1966).

62. Fine, "Toward Corporatism," 76 and 115.

63. Moutet, "Patrons de progrès," 476.

64. See *l'intransigeant*, December 28, 1920. *Archive nationales de la France*

F²² 405 and 422 contain press clippings documenting this offensive against the eight-hour day. Business requests especially from the leather and shoe industries for special exemptions from the law are in F²² 411. Examples of this literature are the booklet by Andre François Poncet and Emile Mitreaux (from the Comité des Forges), *La France et les huit heures* (Paris, 1921) and articles in *La journée industrielle*, January 25, February 2 and 24, April 12, 20, and 24, June 2, 1922, *Le temps*, November 17, 1921, and *L'oeuvre*, April 17, 1922. Evidence of a continued attack on the eight-hour day in 1924 and 1925 are also in these cartons.

65.   Conservative deputies including Daval-Arnould, chairman of the Commission du Travail, proposed a bill to allow the suspension of the eight hour day by ministerial decree in January 1922. *La journée industrielle*, January 25, 1922. Against this threat, the CGT mobilized its forces during the spring. Its daily, *Le peuple*, devoted twenty-six major articles to the subject between May 6 and October 30. The eight-hour day was repeatedly defended as a workers' right and with the claim that if employers would only modernize, the shorter workday should not hurt productivity. On October 9, 1922, large demonstrations for the eight-hour day were held in Nantes, Bordeaux, and Marseilles. In fact, in November talks were held between the CGT and CGTU for a common program of defense. *La journée industrielle*, November 24, 1922. By November, not only had the Minister of Labor, Albert Peyronnet, come to the defense of the eight-hour day but he was also joined by the centrist *parti republicain democratique* and the Radical Party, thus signaling the defeat of the business-inspired offensive. *Le peuple*, October 30 and November 6, 1922.

66.   A. Thomas feared that the Italian action would spark a "race for the longest working day" among the industrial powers. See Albert Thomas, "The Eight Hour Day," *International Labour Review*, 6 (August 15, 1926) 154. See also Fine, "Toward Corporatism," 141.

67.   *Le peuple*, November 25, 1926.

68.   Ibid., August 15, 1926. Between November 12, 1926, and March 15, 1927, the CGT published twenty-six lengthy reports on the benefits of the eight-hour day in *Le peuple*. They were also published in E. Morel, *La production et les huit heures* (Paris, 1927).

69.   Examples of these critiques of the CGT position are found in *Le peuple*, January 11, 1927, May 12, 1928, November 20, 1928, and January 14, 1929.

70.   Bertram Austin and W. F. Lloyd, *The Secret of High Wages* (London, 1926). For enthusiastic reviews of this book see *Le peuple*, March 30, 1926, and *L'information ouvrière et sociale*, April 15, 1926.

71.   See *L'information ouvrière et sociale*, May 28, 1925 and July 10, 1930, as well as H. Dubreuil, *Standards* (translated as *Robots or Men*) (New York, 1927), 78. Additional background on Dubreuil can be found in Martin Fine, "Hyacinthe Dubreuil: le témoignage d'un ouvrier sur le syndicalisme, les relations industrielles et l'evolution technologique de 1921 à 1940," *Le mouvement social* 106 (1979), 45–63, and G Truillier, *Pour la connaissance de Hyacinthe Dubreuil: ouvrier, syndicaliste, sociologue* (Paris, 1971).

72. Dubreuil, *Nouveaux standards* (Paris, 1931), 48, 200, and 213. See also Dubreuil, *Standards*, 48 and 192.

73. Jean-Jacque Carré, et al., *La croissance français* (Paris, 1972), 109–111 and 138.

74. Andre Citroën, "L'avenir de la construction automobile," *La revue politique et parlementaire*, May 10, 1929, 224.

75. This study was a collection of reports published in the *Bulletin du Ministère du Travail* under the title "L'adaptation des conditions de production et de travail à la loi du 23 April 1919 sur la journée de huit heures," which appeared in the issues from April to December 1924, January to March 1925, and July to September 1927.

76. A. Losovsky, "La trustation, la rationalisation, et nos taches," *L'international syndicate rouge* (November 1926), 947–54. See also Jane Degras, ed., *The Communist International, 1919–43, Documents*, (London, 1960), 44, for a similar statement by the Executive Committee of Comintern in a session held November 22 to December 6, 1926.

77. V. I. Lenin, "The Immediate Tasks of the Soviet Government," (first published in *Pravda* [April 28, 1918]), in *Selected Works II* (Moscow, 1967), 663–664. See also Jermey Azrael, *Managerial Power and Soviet Politics* (Cambridge, Mass., 1966); James Bunyan, *The Origins of Forced Labor in The Soviet State, 1917–1921* (Baltimore, 1967); J. G. Crowther, *Industry and Education in Soviet Russia* (London, 1932), Jean Querzola, "Le chef d'orchestra à la main de fer. Leninisme et taylorisme," in *Soldat du travail*, 57–94, Kandall E. Bailes, *Technology and Society under Lenin and Stalin: Origins of the Soviet Technical Intelligentsia, 1917–1941* (Princeton, 1978), and Rainer Taub "Lenin and Taylor, The Fate of Scientific Management in the (Early) Soviet Union," *Telos* 37 (Fall 1978).

78. F. Fontenay, "A propos Fordisme," *Les cahiers du bolshevisme*, October 9, 1926, 1862. See also, "Qu'est à qui la rationalisation?" *Les cahiers du bolshevisme*, January 15, 1927, 49.

79. See *La vie ouvrière*, July 19, 1929, 2, and September 3, 1929, 1.

80. Degras, vol. 2, 433. According to the CGTU's *Report d'activité* prepared for the 1929 Congress, not only the metalworkers' but the miners', textile, construction, and wood workers' unions made studies of rationalization for use by their locals to organize the semiskilled machine operator. See *La vie ouvrière*, June 28, 1929, 3.

81. *L'humanité*, January 4, 1928; see also July 4, 1928, July 8, 1928, July 11, 1928, July 26, 1928 and August 7, 1928.

82. Ibid., December 5, 1928 and March 15, 1929.

83. CGTU, *Congrès national ordinaire, compte rendu* (September 19–24, 1927) 508 and CGTU, *Congrès national ordinaire, compte rendu* (September 15–17, 1929), 527–529.

84. See *L'humanité*, April 15, 1929, and *La vie ouvrière*, May 1, 1929, for evidence of a greater shopfloor militance within the struggling Metalworkers' Federation.

85. CGTU, *Congrès* (1929), 529.

86.   See John Gerber, "Dissident Communist Groups and Publications in France during the Interwar Period," *Third Republic/Troisième République* 9 (Spring 1980), 1–62.

87.   *La révolution proletarienne*, September 1926, 22 and March 15, 1929, 84–85.

88.   Ibid., November 1928, 275–281.

Chapter Seven

The "New Unionism" and the "New Economic Policy"

Steve Fraser

In 1922, the Amalgamated Clothing Workers of America (ACW) concluded an agreement with the Supreme Council of National Economy of the Soviet Union (the Vesenkha) and with the All-Russian Cothing Syndicate to jointly operate and modernize nine clothing and textile factories in Moscow and Petrograd. Lasting only a few years, this joint venture, the Russian-American Industrial Corporation (RAIC), eventually employed more than 15,000 workers in twenty-five plants in eight Russian industrial centers and accounted for 20 to 40 percent of the new capacity of the Soviet clothing industry created during the initial phase of the New Economic Policy (NEP). By itself, the episode was critical neither to the long-term development of the ACW nor, of course, to the history of Bolshevism. It was nevertheless an exemplary experience, encapsulating a systematic response to those historic problems of culture, organization, and political economy confronting the whole of the industrial world in the aftermath of World War I.[1]

■ ■ ■

Everywhere the crisis of state and society that accompanied and followed the war erupted with particular force across the contested terrain of the industrial workplace. If the disturbance was most profound in Russia and perhaps least severe in the United States, it was nonetheless true that the unsettled and unsettling issues of industrial authority and authority over industry ranked high on the social and political agendas of both countries. Throughout Europe and even in the U.S., revolutionary parties, trade union bureaucracies, and political and business elites reexamined and struggled over the customary prerogatives of management and the "rights" of the managed. The relationship between democracy and industrial organization, between public institutions of the state and the private institutions of the economy, were subjected to an unprecedented social inspection and criticism.[2]

"Workers' control" and "industrial democracy," two enormously evocative and equally imprecise formulations, aptly express the era's sense of possibility and uncertainty and its attempt to domesticate the energies released as the old order disintegrated. "Workers' control" was a concept subject to numerous interpretations depending on the historic context in which it emerged. When most parochial and essentially conservative, it involved the reassertion by localized work groups of traditional and exclusivist prerogatives over particular skills and workshops. In other circumstances, it was associated with the revitalization of the movement for workers' cooperatives. Where revolutionary solutions were seriously debated, it implied the democratic mass management of particular industries or even a reconstituted polity and political economy. Often enough, it meant a complex combination of these and other plans and practices.

"Industrial democracy" was also a complex metaphor whose meaning varied according to the social grammar into which it was incorporated. For those networks of militant shop stewards organized in works councils and factory committees, it suggested a system of syndicalist management of the shopfloor by the rank and file. Trade union elites, momentarily allowed into the corridors of power during the war, saw in "industrial democracy" a scheme for the co-management of particular enterprises or whole industries by democratically constituted bureaucracies representing management, trade unions, and the public power. Corporate managements, anxious about democratic enthusiasms and seeking ways to restore authority on the shopfloor, invented elaborate democratic charades that sometimes came complete with mock industrial parliaments, and described these "employee representation" plans as another form of "industrial democracy."[3]

Europe experienced the most radical and prolonged challenge to its prevailing institutional structure. However, plans to reconstruct the foundations of politics and economics, including every sub-species of industrial democracy, were mooted about in the U.S. as well.

Memories of pre-war unrest and the aggravated antagonisms that accompanied the period of global war, revolution, and reconversion caused severe anxiety, not only among radicals and social reformers, but among industrial and political elites as well. The erosion of managerial authority on the shopfloor, the undermining of commercial and industrial stability by an unregulated marketplace, and widening inequities in the distribution of the national wealth, all serious in themselves, together comprised a political crisis for the future of liberal democracy in America. How was it possible to restore managerial authority, regulate the market, and redistribute income in the interests of mass consumption while preserving the formal institutional framework of a democratic politics. Faced with this crisis of legitimacy, social liberal businessmen, social engineers and social workers, and progressive political reformers had begun to experiment with methods of redeploying authority, sometimes through coercion, but more often through mechanisms of compliance that would complement the embryonic system of state directed capitalism.[4]

Recasting the relationship between work, the economy, and the state was, however, not simply a straightforward matter of substituting manipulative for authoritarian modes of social control. Erecting a new kind of rational-bureaucratic and administrative institution, charged with the responsibility of resocializing the experience of work, depended on the active collaboration of worker elites otherwise interested in shifting the balance of political power on the shopfloor away from the centers of managerial autocracy. Plans and programs, some quixotic, some not, proposing various forms of social "partnership" and "participation" entailed, to a more or less significant degree, the delegation of authority and the real sharing of power, albeit within the accepted groundrules of capitalist enterprise. But if "industrial democracy" thus at times implied more than a piece of tactical cleverness imposed from above, it also envisioned an internalized system of self-restraint and an indigenous structure of authority capable of commanding obedience to the precepts of productivity and efficiency.[5]

The *New Republic*, a forum for social liberalism, was well aware that democracy was being subjected to "tests of unprecedented severity throughout the world," and concluded that its future "depends . . . upon the capacity of employers and workers to harmonize democratic ideals of freedom with the voluntary self-discipline essential to efficient production." The editors could happily report that "no group of men in America has a keener appreciation of this fact that the ACWA."[6]

Indeed, during its brief history the ACW had emerged as a social laboratory in which the organizational and political chemistry of "industrial democracy" was perfected. By the end of the war, this "new unionism" had managed to orchestrate an alliance between the informal traditions of "workers' control" from below and the rational bureaucratic procedures of co-management from above. The union's leadership expressly associated the practice of co-management and workers' participation with the wartime fascination with workers' control, suggesting that the innovative grievance procedures and apparatus of impartial arbitration pioneered by the ACW were, in part, designed to equip the rank and file to assume direction of the industry itself, perhaps in partnership with the state.[7]

ACW President, Sidney Hillman, along with other ideologues of social liberalism, viewed "industrial democracy" as a kind of political prophylaxis and therapeutic. He warned that if the nearsighted opposition to "industrial democracy" continued, the recent revolutionary turmoil in Russia would be repeated elsewhere. Initially pessimistic about the Bolshevik seizure of power, Hillman favored the "evolutionary road" opened up by the British Labour Party.[8]

However, as much as Hillman might have hoped to quarantine the union against the contagion of revolution, it was irrepressibly infectious. The overthrow of the Russian autocracy was welcomed with delirious enthusiasm by the heavily Jewish and socialist membership as well as by vocal clusters of Italian syndicalists and Slavic nationalists. A crescendo of stoppages, slowdowns, and other forms of shopfloor rebellion was sparked by the Bolshevik triumph.

At the union's May 1920 convention, delegates wildly applauded socialist Charles Ervin's fraternal greetings to the Soviet Revolution and called on the General Executive Board (GEB) to mobilize public opposition to the Western blockade of the Soviets, which it proceeded to do with enthusiasm throughout the civil war. In addition to its political support, the union provided a continuous stream of food, clothing, and medical supplies during the period of economic paralysis and famine that followed the war.[9] Writing in the *Liberator*, Mike Gold, soon to join the American Communist Party, described this convention as a "soviet of the sweatshops," and concluded that the union was "bringing in the social revolution in America as fast as it can be brought."[10]

The union leadership, however, was not contemplating "social revolution," and Hillman sometimes worried publicly about the more extravagant rhetoric of union cadre, especially as the Red Scare shifted the balance of power decisively against the surviving circles of social reform. But in general, membership and leadership continued to speak the same language, albeit with diverging intentions. They shared, for example, an enthusiasm for the cooperative movement. This was perhaps the last time that the cooperative ideal presented itself as a serious historical alternative to the political economy of liberal, industrial capitalism. From the vantage point of the rank and file, notwithstanding some opposition from the left, the cooperative idea was an included feature of a broader urban populist antipathy to industrial capitalism. It had been part of the vocabulary of Jewish radicalism since the late nineteenth century, and cooperative undertakings, run by skilled craftsmen, had always found nourishment in the protean sea of small-scale enterprise characteristic of the garment industry. A traditional, if anticapitalist, ideology whose values, styles, and nostalgic tone remained disconnected from the new processes and institutions of modern industrial society found in the cooperative movement a congenial ally.[11]

From the standpoint of the union elite, cooperatives—whether in the realm of manufacturing, distribution, or finance—opened up another avenue along which to advance the material interests of the membership while pursuing the possibilities of collaborative economic management with enlightened businessmen, technocrats, and social reformers. Drawing on the union's successful experience operating seven cooperative commissaries during the protracted New York lockout of 1920, Hillman began advocating the creation of large cooperative enterprises as a central feature of the "new unionism." Impressed by the success of consumer cooperatives in Britain and Scandinavia, and at the same time sensitive to the messianic mood of the membership, Hillman presented the cooperative idea as a device for training workers to control production with the ultimate objective of assuming full responsibility for directing the social economy.[12]

Together, then, the élan of postwar rebellion, the special sympathy for the Russian revolution, the still live hopes for class detente, and the specific tactical initiatives represented by the "new unionism" and the cooperative movement, constituted the historic environment in which the RAIC was born and matured.

Plans to undertake a joint manufacturing venture originated in a series of consultations between Hillman and the Bolshevik leadership, including several discussions with Lenin as well as Trotsky, Radek, Kamenev, and various trade union officials. The General Secretary of the International Council of Trade and Industrial Unions, Losovsky, had earlier sent a message congratulating the union on the settlement of the bitter New York lockout. The message invited the ACW to join the new Red International of trade unions and suggested Hillman visit Russia.[13]

Hillman first conferred with Kamenev. The latter headed the All-Russian Committee for Relief and the two men discussed the immediate need for emergency aid. The ACW was already providing such help and Hillman pledged continued assistance.[14] More important, Hillman met with Lenin at the end of September when the ACW relief ship arrived and at the same time attended a session of the Supreme Soviet of Labor and Defense at which the NEP was debated. Hillman was impressed by the NEP's committment to planning, technological advance, efficiency, and above all its "realism." Lenin and Radek explained that "war communism" was but an interlude, necessary to destroy the vestiges of feudalism and to consolidate the revolution. Lenin emphasized the NEP's critical need for technical knowledge and skilled workers. At the same time, he argued that NEP did not contradict the fundamental purposes of the revolution: "We are willing to pay out to foriegn capital hundreds of millions or even billions of dollars in order to get them to develop Russia economically for us. We are willing to pay for technical knowledge, technical skill, and for anything that will help us build up Russia."[15]

Hillman returned to America a staunch defender of the Bolshevik revolution against the "small imperialistic clique" that sought to destroy it. He carried with him greetings from Lenin, "one of the few great men that the human race has produced, one of the greatest statesmen of our age and perhaps of all ages."[16]

On his way to and from the Soviet Union, Hillman traveled throughout western Europe, which he described as a political and economic insane asylum on the verge of collapse. It was, he reported to the overflow audiences that came to hear about the heroic Bolsheviks, hopelessly corrupt and selfish, its population demoralized and without the most elementary democratic rights. By contrast, the Soviets represented the only truly stable regime in all of Europe and the Bolsheviks the only vehicle of political and social cohesion preventing the sort of political dismemberment that was then well under way in China. He especially admired the Bolsheviks' practicality and flexibility, their concern for efficiency and respect for the "facts"—qualities frequently cited by others to characterize Hillman.[17]

Most of all, Hillman was pleased with the Bolsheviks' new approach to economic reconstruction and reported the apparent widespread support for the NEP's departure from the practices of "war communism." He noted that the policies of "war communism," including the suppression of the free market, rationing, and the centralization of employment, had generated great discontent and proved un-workable. The NEP, on the other hand, provided economic incentives for all classes and thereby held out real hope for economic revival.[18]

Privately, Hillman mentioned to the GEB the possibility of entering into a partnership with the Russian government to operate its clothing industry. He told his colleagues the Russians had great confidence in the ACW, that they were in desperate need of capital as well as technical and managerial experience, and that they were prepared to make guarantees with respect to preferential access to raw materials, export licenses, and special banking relations. Hillman had spent part of his visit inspecting clothing factories in Moscow and Petrograd, and apparently it was he who first broached the idea of a cooperative manufacturing venture in his meetings with the Bolshevik leadership. Indeed, in an interview published in *Izvestiia* shortly before his departure Hillman remarked that the ACW was not only interested in the already established Soviet clothing industry: "Our aims are much higher; we will begin with this industry and then grant credits to the other trusts."[19]

Back home, preparations for the formal creation of the RAIC coincided with the union's initial venture into the business of labor banking, in which Hillman saw the "germs of a new cooperative commonwealth." The RAIC too was designed as a cooperative enterprise. Under the guidance of American experts, Soviet clothing factories were to be reorganized along the most modern lines of technology and labor organization. The ACW had pioneered in these areas, often in active collaboration with the largest American clothing manufacturers as well as the leading exponents of the scientific management movement.[20]

Hillman unveiled the actual plan for the RAIC near the end of the 1922 convention. Hillman's speech captured the delegates' prevailing sense of revolutionary determination. He accused the Allies of "attempting to starve the Russians into submission to the rule of international financiers" and argued that disaster would result if "the masses were prevented from determining for themselves the course of economic reconstruction." Cooperation with the Soviets was not a question of being "for Bolshevism or against Bolshevism, but of being for or against the slaughter of millions of people." He expressed his confidence in the Bolshevik approach to labor organization and in the work ethic and "iron discipline" of the Russian proletariat. The latter, together with the great natural wealth of the Soviet Union, made it perhaps the most promising place to invest in all of Europe.[21]

Hillman concluded by outlining the concrete plans for the corporation, emphasizing that Soviet assurances respecting preferential access to raw materials and government contracts made it a sound business as well as fraternal undertaking. In fact, Hillman was well aware that from the Soviet point of view as well, the venture was principally an industrial experiment, ideological promissory notes notwithstanding. Lenin and Hillman "did not discusss the revolution in the U.S. or even in Russia. We did not discuss any theories. . . . It is much more important to have a proper policy than a great deal of noise." The union president told his GEB that "If Russia believed our tendency was to become a communist organization the real government would not make the arrangements with us." He furthermore reassured GEB members worried about the riskiness of the investment that Lloyds of London felt confident enough about the arrangement to insure it.[22]

Once the convention voted its general approval, Hillman returned to Russia in the late summer of 1922 to negotiate specific contractual arrangements. The Corporation was to issue stock selling for $10 a share with the expectation of raising $1 million, although in the end subscriptions never amounted to more than $300,000. Arrangements were codified in three contracts: a general agreement with the Council of Labor and Defense authorizing the RAIC to do business in the Soviet Union and underwriting the RAIC's contracts with other Soviet agencies; an agreement with the Vesenkha pledging a minimum annual dividend of 8 per cent and the return of the principal should either party choose to dissolve the venture after an initial three-year period; and a profit-sharing arrangement with the All-Russian Clothing Syndicate that included a provision for the reinvestment of all earnings over 10 per cent.[23]

The agreements established a Control Board composed of representatives of the RAIC and the Soviet government, with voting power proportional to the size of each party's investment in the enterprise. In a formal sense, this meant the ratio of voting strength was 7 to 2 in favor of the Russian Clothing Syndicate. But because the Soviets were above all interested in securing the technical and administrative experience of the Americans, actual management was quickly turned over, in large measure, to ACW personnel. In fact, the ACW even supplied skilled workers and industrial engineers to plants functioning outside the Syndicate.[24]

The RAIC agreement established fifteen branches around the country that channeled capital equipment, managerial expertise, and skilled labor from RAIC to various clothing and textile plants.

Although the original negotiations covered plants in Moscow and Petrograd only, the final arrangements included factories in Kazan, Nizni, and smaller industrial centers, and established operational procedures quite similar to ones set up with other Western corporations, as for example between the Soviet government and General Electric.[25]

RAIC plants were valued at between $2.5 and $5 million and were equipped to manufacture suits, coats, shirts, underwear, caps, gloves, and overcoats, as well as certain textile products. Hillman was sanguine about the RAIC's commercial prospects, especially given the fact that it would not have to contend with the problems of seasonality that chronically disrupted the American industry. He anticipated an annual turnover of $40 million and was supported in his judgment by financial adviser Leo Wolman and legal advisers Max Lowenthal and Maxwell Brandwen, all of whom had come to work for the ACW on the recommendation of Felix Frankfurter.[26]

The assistance of Lowenthal and Wolman was indicative of the broad support offered this newest innovation of the "new unionism" by those circles of progressive reformers with whom the ACW had established close working relations over the previous decade. The *New Republic* editorialized on behalf of the RAIC.[27] Earl Dean Howard, labor manager for Hart Schaffner & Marx, who had collaborated with Hillman on installing the first impartial arbitration machinery after the great strike of 1910, accompanied Hillman on his second trip to Russia. Although the company maintained that Howard's trip was for strictly personal reasons, he did meet with people associated with the RAIC, and it is reasonable to surmise they explored the contribution of the "new unionism" to efficient factory administration. George Soule of the *New Republic* went to work promoting the RAIC. And Felix Frankfurter, who had privately expressed to Hillman his support for the project, allowed Soule to publicize that fact. Indeed, before it was announced publicly, the plan for the RAIC was examined and approved by Frankfurter, Florence Kelley of the National Consumers' League, Frank Walsh, who chaired the Industrial Commission of 1914, before which Hillman had testified, and Grace Abbott, Chief of the U.S. Children's Bureau.[28]

There were of course those who denounced the venture, among whom, not surprisingly, was Samuel Gompers, whose anxiety about the shadows of Bolshevism in the American labor movement was further aggravated by the outlaw status of the ACW in the eyes of the AFL. Much displeasure was also expressed from within the union by elements associated with the Jewish *Foward* and those circles of right-wing

Jewish socialism that had by this time become resolutely anti-Soviet, although it was delivered in voices muted by the overwhelming rank-and-file sentiment favoring aid to those who had overthrown the tzar.[29]

That the union weathered this opposition and the country's pervasive anti-Bolshevik mood suggests that its commitment was, however pragmatic, not merely expedient. If Hillman could befriend the Bolshevik experiment and communists do likewise for the ACW, it was also due to a more basic if temporary affinity between Bolshevik policy during the period of the NEP and that of the "new unionism." While Hillman had long since given up the revolutionary enthusiasm of his youth, his anomalous position outside the legitimate precincts of the American labor movement provided space within which to maneuver and experiment programmatically on behalf of the social aspirations of the "new unionism." Moreover, the grammatical substructure of the "new unionism" was, in certain essential respects, akin to the lingua franca of Bolshevism.

To begin with, the ACW elite was firmly implanted in those socialist traditions that affixed the tempo and timing of socialism to the inexorable rhythms of industrial and social development under capitalism. While continuing to declare itself at war with contemporary society, this "scientific" socialism increasingly shared a set of operating assumptions with currents of social liberalism that sought to meliorate the crisis of industrial society. Thus "history" and its "progress" were to be the ultimate arbiters of the class struggle. Sophisticated technologies, the concentration of capital, the rationalization of the labor process were as necessary to the socialist future as they were hallmarks of advanced capitalism. Collaborations with business and political reform elites were scripted prologues in an unfolding socialist or cooperative drama, epilogues to capitalism's denouement. As the ideology of "progress" came to be more comfortable with and in need of the perspicacious observations of Marxism, much of Marxist practice unambiguously expressed the premises of 'modernization."[30]

As part of this general historical perspective, the ACW elite had during its formative years made its peace with Taylorism. Just as the liberal wing of the scientific management movement was committed, by the time of Taylor's death in 1915, to the perspective of achieving shopfloor discipline and efficiency by "consent," Hillman was prepared to embrace scientific management so long as greater efficiency was accompanied and accomplished by mechanisms of democratic—i.e., union—control.[31]

This accommodation with Taylorism, occurring a decade before most of the rest of the organized American labor movement made a similar adjustment, need not be interpreted as an acquiescence in the inevitable. While in other industries and in other countries trade unions often had little choice if they were to survive the new rigors of domestic and international competition, in the case of the ACW the initiative lay as much with Hillman as it did with industrial engineers and businessmen. Indeed, this "democratic Taylorism" was often fiercely resisted by the mass of petty entrepreneurs whose tiny, technologically primitive, and commercially marginal shops continued to occupy much of the clothing industry.

As it turned out, the situation was broadly similar in the new Soviet state. Bolshevism of course did not share the more fatalistic predispositions that otherwise dominated the Second International, and it is furthermore true that before the revolution Lenin bitterly denounced Taylorism as the "scientific method of extortion of sweat." As early as 1916, however, Lenin had made extensive notes on Taylor's experiments in rationalizing work and in particular studied Gilbreth's motion studies, which he came to see as a means to enhance the technical transition from capitalism to socialism. Shortly after October the exigencies of the civil war and acute economic distress produced a fundamental shift in orientation converging on the politically sanitized approach to Taylorism already adopted by the ACW. Increasingly, Lenin chose to emphasize the virtues of centralized management, efficiency, and labor discipline, and the critical importance of productivity and the intensification of labor if the revolution were not to perish. "We must organize in Russia the study and teaching of the Taylor system and systematically try it out and adapt it to our purposes." Very much like Hillman, Lenin avoided becoming the prisoner of theoretical pronouncements made for other times and purposes.

It is therefore arguable in the Soviet case, given the drastic loss of skilled workers to the civil war and to the new state institutions and where industry had to be developed with some considerable speed just to reestablish exchange with the countryside (especially in industries like clothing and textiles), that efficiency methods imported from the West were vastly superior to anything then available in Russia. All discussions and struggles over the form and extent of "workers' power" could only ignore these historic constraints at their peril. The adoption of "democratic Taylorism," whether by the ACW or in the Soviet Union, would accelerate the disintegration of preindustrial craft and workers' control traditions and on occasion prompt serious resistance. Yet, however much their passing was mourned, such practices scarcely represented a realistic organizational and political strategy either in the United States or in the Soviet Union. Indeed, at least during the early period of the NEP, as compared with subsequent developments, importing a version of the ACW's union-supervised Taylorism may have democratized production practices more than might otherwise have been the case.

In any event, Taylorism in Russia was thus reassessed, and its "scientific" discoveries, including the "analysis of mechanical motion during the work process . . . the elimination of superfluous and awkward motion . . . [and] the introduction of the best systems of auditibility and control," were systematically applied to the reconstruction of the Russian economy, subject to the harmonizing influence of Soviet direction. Both Lenin and Trotsky were, moreover, prepared to override the objections of the trade unions, the factory committees, and "left communists" especially opposed to the piece-work norms associated with Taylorism. By April 1918, the Central Council of Trade Unions had assumed some of the responsibility for this drastic change in labor policy, so that beginning with the period of war communism, production norms and piecework became standard features of Soviet industrial organization. The Bolshevik elite came to view such innovations as the only way to establish modern labor discipline among a proletariat still attached to the more traditional rhythms and "incentives" of peasant life. So too had the ACW elite found it necessary to disrupt the preindustrial structures of behavior and belief characteristic of its Jewish, south Italian, and Slavic membership.[32]

Bolshevik commitment to scientific management continued into the period of the NEP, especially since two-thirds of new Soviet industry was built with the aid and guidance of American engineers and businessmen familiar with its methods. A new technical elite began to share political and administrative power in the factories with less technically expert "Red Directors." Under the guidance of the Russian "bard of Taylorism," Alexei Gastev, scientific management became a kind of messianism of the machine. Gastev founded the Central Institute of Labor, whose researches into the reorganization of work were expressly aimed at creating a culture of work that would include a "severity, a postponement of immediate satisfaction which may be called conditioning for work" and that would create a "Soviet Americanism." The Institute operated under the auspices of the All-Russian Central Council of Trade Unions (and at the same time was responsible to the Gosplan), so that Russian trade unions, despite some internal opposition, found themselves shouldering the responsibility for instilling the new labor discipline—a role already familiar to the ACW.[33]

It is true that under the NEP, as part of its general policy of loosening statist controls of the economy, the state functions of the trade unions were reduced. However, while the latitude for collective bargaining as a legitimate trade union function had thus been extended, this did not mean any lessening of trade union responsibility for maintaining order on the shopfloor or increasing productivity. The labor code of 1922 called for a guaranteed minimum wage in return for a guarantee with respect to output, with quotas to be fixed jointly by factory management and trade union representatives. The latter procedure closely resembled the prevailing arrangements for determining "production standards" in those portions of the men's clothing industry supervised by the ACW.

As the NEP developed, the trade union bureaucracy more and more became the mediating agency between the state and factory administration on the one side and the shopfloor on the other. Because light industry recovered most quickly under the NEP, collective bargaining concessions in that sector, in particular wage rates, were considerable. This was the case in the trade unions in the clothing and textile industries in the Soviet Union. However, although strikes were permissible, they were to be avoided, in favor of conciliation and impartial arbitration, as was also the case in the U.S. Conciliation courts and "comradely disciplinary courts," composed of representatives of the factory administration and the trade union, were established to adjudicate shopfloor grievances and handle violations of work rules, including lateness, absenteeism, rudeness and failure to meet group and individual production quotas. Both the kinds of grievances and violations and the methods of resolving them resembled the work of grievance boards and boards of impartial arbitration inaugurated by the ACW.[34]

The Bolshevik elite was also coming to terms with the marketplace. NEP was designed in part to promote cooperative enterprise, especially in the realm of trade. Lenin envisioned, at least as an interim arrangement, a "cooperative capitalism," distinct from private commercial institutions and at the same time a species of state capitalism under Soviet control. Industrial cooperatives were encouraged, granted some autonomy from direct state regulation, and provided with credits. Moreover, because the NEP was conceived in part to repair the complete breakdown of exchange between town and country, it particularly emphasized the consumer goods sector of industry. The most viable enterprises in specific industries were assembled together in trusts and operated according to commercial principles, which included a rigorous rationalization of the production process. Trusts were not governmental but economic units operating on the basis of contractual arrangements with the state, although their man-

agements were appointed by the Vesenkha. The largest such organization was the textile trust employing 54,000. In general, the NEP enjoyed its greatest successes in light industry.[35]

Economic paralysis also caused the Bolsheviks to look to the West
for fresh infusions of capital. By 1921, the first experiments with
"mixed companies," formed jointly by foreign capital and agencies of
the Soviet state, had begun to supply the vital capital equipment and
technical help necessary to develop Russian resources as well as produce items for mass consumption.[36]

The formation of cooperative trusts and "mixed companies" was
accompanied by the return of U.S. emigrees who reportedly organized
"American Departments" that used the "last work in efficiency
methods" in order to create "a genuinely American attitude to work."
Thus, for example, a group of thirty-six American tailors joined the
Moscow Tailoring Combine, originally established during the revolution by a returned Baltimore garment worker, Borgrachov. *Pravda*
noted that they "have raised its work to such a level of efficiency that
the Combine has become a model establishment . . . there are now six
cutters to 150 machines, where as formerly there were 50 cutters when
hand machines were used." After the RAIC was established, the ACW
supplied this experimental factory, which included its own cooperative
stores, with an experienced manager from a unionized plant in
Rochester. Another group of 120 U.S. deportees, armed with 200
sewing machines, took over an old clothing factory and established the
Third International Clothing Works. [37]

NEP thus encouraged the institutional and economic environment in which an industrial experiment like the RAIC could flourish.
And the RAIC, in turn, crystallized a perspective on policy amenable to
both Bolshevik and ACW elites. That perspective included the elabora-
tion of a system of rational and formally democratic labor relations and
the invention of machinery for the co-management of the industry in
the interests of planned production and consumption. The union
leadership was as receptive to strategies for rationalizing an underdeveloped clothing industry as the Bolsheviks were attracted by Western
administrative and technical practices that promised to modernize an
underdeveloped country. In a sense, the Bolshevik RAIC and the
ACW's "new unionism" were each other's mirror image: the RAIC as
the embryo of what Hillman characterized as "state" and "cooperative"
capitalism germinating within the womb of war communism; and the
"new unionism" as the kernel of state capitalism concealed within the
husk of free enterprise.[38]

Moreover, the actual operating experience of the RAIC further confirmed this historic convergence. As it turned out, even more valuable than the modern machinery transported to the Soviet Union was the accumulated expertise in industrial engineering, technological innovation, and personnel relations that Hillman had pledged to make available. Skilled cutters from the most advanced factories in Rochester, Chicago, Baltimore, and Philadelphia were sent to Russia to provide technical advice and training. They reported to scientific management expert Otto Beyer that in every essential respect the revitalized Societ clothing factories resembled modern, unionized plants in the United States. Not only was the machinery up-to-date but so was the system of resolving shopfloor grievances through arbitration. Workers' representatives participated in the fixing of rates and poured over books by Taylor and Gannt on industrial efficiency.[39]

Garment manufacturer Abraham Cohen also visited the Russian clothing syndicate and observed that most of the critical skilled positions were manned by Americans from companies like Hart Schaffner & Marx, Sonneborn & Co., and Snellenburg & Co., which had pioneered, in collaboration with the ACW, the introduction of scientific management reforms in the men's clothing industry. Cohen noted that piece work and the eight-hour day were the rule in all RAIC factories.[40]

Paralleling Hillman's ideal scenario for the American clothing industry, RAIC plants were supervised by joint union-management councils that cooperated in fixing "scientific" standards of production and rates of pay. Ultimate authority, however, resided in the Vesenkha, a scheme of which Hillman approved—since he acknowledged that trade unions by themselves were too parochial and stubborn to take into account industrywide and general economic needs. At the same time, Hillman was pleased to report that strikes were not uncommon, as he considered them a positive sign of "democratic vitality."[41]

The latter issue concerning the extent of trade union autonomy and freedom of action continued to interest Hillman throughout the life of the RAIC. At the end of 1925, when the RAIC was coming to an end, he was still sanguine about the prospects. He reassured the GEB that "fundamentally . . . there is trade union control. Nothing can be done without the support of the trade unions. In five years there will be a live trade union with responsibility for production. It is to be expected that cooperative and government control will remain."[42]

Whether or not Hillman was whistling in the dark in this case, his concern about the position and power of Soviet trade unions serves as a cautionary note about exaggerating the degree and significance of the resemblances between NEP and the "new unionism." By 1924, Soviet trade unions had become in many essential respects the creatures of state and party labor policy. That is to say, their very conditions of existence and their role in the political economy were both more fundamental and at the same time far less independent than those of the ACW or, for that matter, the labor movement at large in the United States. While Hillman had every reason to underestimate if not ignore the inherent tension between workers' control and scientific management, it is also true that the unique relationship between party and trade union in the Soviet Union was only just then emerging, and it would take some time to make clear the special consequences of party domination. Nevertheless, the similarities are illuminating and perhaps none more so than the historic resistance encountered by both the RAIC and the ACW as they attempted to introduce rationalized methods of industrial management and labor relations.[43]

Skilled American workers, on loan to the RAIC and charged with importing a modern sense of industrial work discipline, reported that the Soviets had to overcome the same artisan and preindustrial traditions of work confronting proponents of "industrial democracy" in America. Given that the population of factory-employed, male clothing workers in Petrograd, for example, had been decimated (perhaps by as much as 90 percent) by the revolution and civil war, it is not surprising that the re-manning of the industry necessarily called upon a reserve of village workers still enmeshed in the prewar craft traditions of custom tailoring.[44]

The "new unionism" confronted a similar milieu, composed mainly of skilled work groups accustomed to regulating the pace and quantity of production informally and semiautonomously. Still surviving precariously in tiny shops and under factory roofs, but mortally threatened by a degrading standardization of tasks, these artisan-syndicalist groupings sought to preserve their independence and skills and an older law of shopfloor discipline. However, the practices and procedures initiated by "industrial democracy" threatened the integrity of artisan democracy. They depended on the workers' willingness to accept new work rules, technical innovations, standards of performance, disciplinary procedures, and new codes of shopfloor behavior that were designed first of all to maximize efficiency, regardless of whether or not that disrupted the internal hierarchies and moral codes of artisanal solidarity. Above all, the "new unionism" called upon work groups to relinquish their customary "right" to strike whenever they felt justice or self-interest demanded they exercise it. [45]

Shopfloor militance on behalf of traditional rights to regulate the pace of production, to control the level of expected output, to police the introduction of new machinery, and so on was not in itself irretrievably inimical to management and union objectives. In fact, the creation of the ACW helped to reinforce and formalize many such prerogatives. However, the behavioral and even characterological change sought by "industrial democracy" demanded that such popular sentiments be rechanneled, transformed, and encoded in a new rhetoric of workers' demands and perceptions emphasizing economic self-interest, contractual obligation, and industrial equity.[46]

This struggle, in large measure a protracted process of linguistic socialization, was inevitably fought out in the political arena as well. In Russia, the left "Workers Opposition" carried on the workers' control movement, many of whose leading militants dispersed after 1917 into the new institutions of the state and economy. It tried to protect both the trade unions and the revolutionary factory committees against encroachment by the state and party. Although the early revolutionary decrees on workers' control had, at least formally, left the proprietary position of managements largely untouched, in practice it was not at all uncommon for workers to assume operational control of local factories, even in defiance of directions from the central organs of the Soviet economy. The NEP, however, accelerated the elimination of the last vestiges of workers' control, while simultaneously augmenting the authority of factory managements. This process paralleled the struggle within the more circumscribed circles of the technical intelligentsia over the issue of Taylorism. For a technical elite committed to a policy of rapid industrial modernization, the aversion to industrial discipline and the persistence of seasonal and rural work habits and religious inhibitions among Russia's newly proletarianized peasantry was an intolerable obstacle to the application of time-and-motion studies, incentive pay systems, and other methods of labor intensification. While the "Workers' Opposition," elements of the trade union movement, and even a minority of technocrats denounced the pampering of the specialists, the political victory of the latter was ensured first of all by Lenin and later by Stalin.[47]

The political struggle in the Soviet Union was of course more complex and extended across a broader range of issues than is indicated here. Nevertheless, it does suggest the nature of the tension between the modernizing elite directing the RAIC and at least some of its workers recruited from the towns and villages of the Russian countryside. Syndicalist currents particularly were opposed by the Bolshevik majority as profoundly conservative. While this was not an entirely implausible judgment, and one to be expected from a vanguard whose announced purpose was to bring Russian society forward into the twentieth century, it also functioned as a rationalization for making alternative methods of industrialization ideologically and socially illegitimate. It is in any event apparent that a party ostensibly committed to a specific kind of modernizing project still contained within its ranks a cadre with a historically divergent view of the future.

Hillman fully agreed that the syndicalist animus was essentially nostalgic and conservative. Interestingly enough, so did the leadership of the newly formed American Communist Party. Moreover, the American party's position was not simply a knee-jerk reaction to impulses from abroad but grew out of the experience of a sizeable fraction of the leadership during the previous decade of socialist politics. It is not surprising therefore, that alongside the Bolshevik faction fight there developed an internal political struggle in the ACW that joined together the RAIC and the question of Taylorism and created a temporary alliance between the union elite and the American equivalent of the Bolshevik inner circle. The latter, like the Russian Bolsheviks, found itself at odds with its own rank and file.[48]

During the same conventions of 1920 and 1922, when fraternal sympathies and more practical gestures toward the Russian Revolution were exhibited freely, the union leadership faced the most concerted resistance to its policy of cooperation with scientific management. While the forms of factional opposition were diverse, eventually the Socialist Party cadre in the union directed this struggle against Taylorist "production standards" and combined it with an attack on the close working relationship established between the Hillman group and the Communist Party's trade union organization, the Trade Union Educational League (TUEL).[49]

It is true that until the middle of 1924 an alliance between the ACW leadership and the TUEL cadre within the union delivered tactical advantages to both sides. Not only did Hillman provide political and material support for the Bolshevik revolution, he also extended the union's administrative protection to the TUEL caucus then under attack by the Socialist Party right. In return, the party leadership assisted in the introduction of "production standards" by disciplining those segments of its own shopfloor membership that were otherwise inclined to oppose the further rationalization of the industry.

Just as the Bolshevik and ACW cadres in Russia found themselves at odds with surviving artisan practices and attitudes, so too the leadership of the American Communist Party stood outside the social and cultural universe of its own constituency. While party propagandists argued that "production standards" were not a concession to antilabor Taylorism, TUEL members on the shopfloor considered it a kind of counterfeit piece work and a return to an "old slavery." The American party, together with Hillman, made deliberate and successful use of the RAIC to morally embarass these TUEL cadre into muting their instinctive hatred of "production standards" at a decisive moment in the union's internal life. Thus, while the issues and alignments were by no means identical, there emerged a substantial similarity in the political dynamics set in motion by the RAIC and the "new unionism."[50]

For all intents and purposes, the RAIC experiment was over by the end of 1925, as was the union's alliance with the American Communist Party. Hillman remained optimistic about the prospects of doing businesss in the Soviet Union. During his last trip to Russia in 1925, the Bolsheviks offered new investment opportunities despite their intentions to liquidate the RAIC. Hillman wrote from Moscow that despite the fact he was not any longer "personna gratta politically [sic]," business relations were excellent, notwithstanding the death of Lenin, "without whom I could not have gotten anything done on my last two visits." In fact, as late as 1928, ACW banks—which during the life of the RAIC had been used to transmit dollars to the Soviet Union for the purchase of raw materials and machinery for the clothing trust—were involved with the Chase Manhattan Bank and the Bank of Italy in an effort to float a Soviet bond issue in the United States. The State Department ultimately thwarted the attempt.[51]

However, Hillman did lose all interest in collaborating with communists in the United States once the American party broke with the LaFollette presidential campaign, which Hillman had helped to organize. As a social and industrial experiment, the RAIC hardly lasted long enough to prove much about the future of "cooperative" or "state" capitalism. The Russians, who were in any event about to revamp the administrative and political structure of all the industrial syndicates, eventually returned the original investment as promised and the agreement was terminated amicably. Indeed, so long as the business relationship with Hillman lasted (through most of 1925), the Bolsheviks assiduously avoided discussing with the ACW president the nasty details of Hillman's falling out with the American party—much to the displeasure of the U.S. communist leadership.

Thus the RAIC was decidedly not the victim of an otherwise extraneous political struggle, and on the part of the ACW its dissolution may have had more to do with the depletion of the union's treasury by the protracted International Tailoring strike of 1925. An ephemeral episode, the RAIC was significant, however, insofar as it reflected more fundamental processes reshaping the world of work, politics, and labor organization in the decade before the Great Depression.[52]

Notes

For their valuable suggestions and criticisms I want to thank Jill Andresky, Melvyn Dubofsky, Stan Engerman, Joshua Freeman, Herb Gutman, Paul Milkman, Joan Scott, and Carmen Sirianni.

1.   Anthony C. Sutton, *Western Technology and Soviet Economic Development, 1917–1930* (Stanford, 1968), 225–238.
2.   Charles S. Maier, *Recasting Bourgeois Europe* (Princeton, 1975), passim; Carmen Sirianni, "Workers' Control in the Era of World War I: A Comparative Analysis of the European Experience," *Theory and Society* 9, no. 1 (1980).
3.   Maier, passim; Sirianni; James Hinton, *The First Shop Stewards' Movement* (London, 1973); Larry Peterson, "The One Big Union in International Perspective: Revolutionary Industrial Unionism, 1900–1925," in this volume. There is a considerable amount of literature on industrial democracy and labor relations policy in the U.S. in this period including the following useful selection: Norman J. Wood, "Industrial Relations Policies of American Management, 1900–1933," *Business History Review* 34, no. 4 (Winter 1960) James R. Green, *The World of the Worker: Labor in the 20th Century* (New York, 1980); David Brody, *Workers in Industrial America* (New York, 1980), especially chapter 2; David Montgomery, *Workers' Control in America* (New York, 1979), especially chapter 4; Irving Bernstein, *The Lean Years* (Boston, 1972).
4.   Louis B. Wehle, "War Labor Policies and Their Outcome inPeace," *Quarterly Journal of Economics* 33, no. 2 (February 1919); Morris Cooke, "Modern Manufacturing: A Partnership of Idealism and Common Sense," *Annals of the American Academy of Political and Social Science* (hereafter cited as *Annals*), Sept., 1919; Robert D. Cuff, "The Politics of Labor Administration during World War I," *Labor History* 21, no. 4 (Fall 1980); Paul Douglas and F. E. Wolfe, "Labor Administration in the Shipbuilding Industry during World War I," *Journal of Political Economy* 2, no. 3 (March 1919); Brody, chapter 2; James Weinstein, *The Corporate Ideal in the Liberal State, 1900–1918* (Boston, 1968), 214–241; Haggai Hurvitz, "Ideology and Industrial Conflict: President Wilson's First Industrial Conference of October, 1919," *Labor History* 18, no. 4 (Fall 1977), John S. Smith, "Organized Labor and Government in the Wilson Era, 1913–1921: Some Conclusions," *Labor History* 3, no. 3 (Fall 1962); *Waste in Industry*, a study prepared by the Committee on the Elimination of Waste in Industry of the Federated American Engineering Societies, 1921. The two industrial conferences sponsored by the Wilson administration and the conference on unemployment and on waste in industry organized by Commerce Secretary Hoover were indicative of this continuing interest in reform.

5.   Steve Fraser, "Dress Rehearsal for the New Deal" in Michael Frisch and Daniel Walkowitz eds. *Working-Class America*, (Champaign, Ill., In press); "Works Councils in the U.S.," National Industrial Conference Board (NICB) Report no. 21, October, 1919, and "Experience with Works Councils in the U.S.," NICB report no. 50, May, 1922; Cooke, "Modern Manufacturing"; James Gilbert, *Designing the Industrial State* (Chicago, 1972); Milton Derber, *The American Idea of Industrial Democracy, 1865–1965*: Urbana, Ill., 1970); George Bell, "Production the Goal," *Annals*, Sept. 1919; Morris Cooke, Samuel Gompers, and Fred J. Miller, eds., "Labor, Management, and Production: An American Industrial Program," *Annals*, Sept., 1920; Willard E. Hotchkiss, "The Bases of Industrial Stability," *Annals*, Sept., 1920; William E. Leiserson, "Collective Bargaining and its Effects on Production," *Annals*, Sept. 1920; Sidney Kaplan, "Social Engineers as Saviours: Effects of World War I on Some American Liberals," *Journal of the History of Ideas* 17, no. 3 (June, 1956); Felix Frankfurter, "Social Unrest," *Current Affairs* 10, no. 35 (1920); *Bulletin of the Taylor Society*, December, 1919.

6.   *New Republic*, Feb. l, 1919.

7.   Fraser, "Dress Rehearsal"; Morris Cooke to Sidney Hillman, June 18, 1919, Oct. 10, 1922, June 7, 1919, Sept. 10, 1919, April 5, 1920. Morris L. Cooke Papers, Box 9, Files 73–90, Franklin Delano Roosevelt Library; "Hart, Schaffner, and Marx Labor Agreement—Cases Decided by the Board of Arbitration" (HSM Cases) and "Men's Cothing Industry Board of Arbitration—Chicago Market" (Chicago Cases); Ray Stannard Baker, "Shop Council Plan Covers the Entire Clothing Industry," *N.Y. Evening Post*, Feb. 14, 1920; *New Republic*, May 6, 1920.

8.   *New Republic*, Feb. 1, 1919; *The Advance*, Feb. 8, 1918 and March 22, 1918—Hillman speech to Montreal workers; *The World*, July 27, 1919; Sidney Hillman to John E. Williams, Jan. 2, 1918, Jacob Potofsky Papers, Martin P. Catherwood Library of the New York School of Industrial and Labor Relations at Cornell University; Hillman speech to Annual Convention of the Industrial Relations Association, May, 1920, ACWA Papers, Cornell.

9.   Hillman testimony before the Chicago Arbitration Board, Dec. 13, 1919, Chicago Cases; William Z. Ripley to Hillman, Sept. 4, 1918 and Sept. 20, 1918 and Nov. 18, 1918, Sidney Hillman Papers, Cornell; William Z. Ripley, "Loading the Olive Branch," *The Survey*, Sept. 1, 1922; William Z. Ripley, "Bones of Contention," *The Survey*, April 29, 1922, *Proceedings of the 4th Biennial Convention of the ACWA* (Conv. Proc.), May 1920; Hillman appeal to ACW membership, Nov. 10, 1920; Hillman telegram from Berlin, Aug. 16, 1921, and from Moscow, Sept. 17, 1921, to the General Executive Board; Soloviev, President of the Russian Red Cross to the ACWA Convention, May 8, 1922; Lenin to Hillman, Oct. 13, 1921—all reprinted in Sidney Hillman, "Reconstruction of Russia and the Tasks of Labor," an address before the 5th Biennial Convention, May 11, 1922; *Documentary History of the ACWA* (hereafter cited as *Doc. Hist.*) 1920–22.

10.   *Conv. Proc.*, 1920; *Syndique communiste*, 1921, Red Books clippings file, ACW Papers; Mike Gold, *The Liberator*, July, 1920, and June, 1922.

11.   Hillman to Joseph Schlossberg, April 16, 1920, Hillman Papers; Matthew Josephson, *Sidney Hillman: Statesman of American Labor* (New York, 1952), chapter 9; Fraser, "Dress Rehearsal"; Irving Howe interview with Paul Novick, March 29, 1968, YIVO Archives; Trade Union Educational League leaflet in Charles S. Zimmerman Records, ILGWU Archives, Box 40, file 5; Melech Epstein, *Jewish Labor in the U.S.A.*, 2 vols. (New York, 1950), vol. 1; Irving Howe, *World of Our Fathers* (New York, 1976).

12.   Josephson, chapter 10.

13.   Losovosky's message and invitation was actually transmitted through William Z. Foster, then in Russia discussing his TUEL; FBI File no. 61-9899, Internal Security File on Sidney Hillman, released under an FOIPA request, including "Report from D. M. Ladd to J. Edgar Hoover," June 26, 1946 and George J. Starr report to the FBI, Nov. 14, 1922.

14.   *Doc. Hist.* 1920–22.

15.   Josephson, chapter 9; *N.Y. Call*, Nov. 22, 1921.

16.   *Daily News Record* (hereafter cited as *DNR*), Nov. 18, 1921; Hillman speech on his Russian trip at Carmen Hall, Nov. 18, 1921.

17.   *Doc. Hist.* 1920–22; *DNR*, April 18, 1921. Many years later, J. B. S. Hardman recalled the deep affinity Hillman felt for the Bolsheviks in this early period of the revolution. Just before he left for Russia, when asked what he wanted to discover there Hillman explained to Hardman and to the Bolshevik head of the Jewish section of the Russian Communist Party (then visiting in the U.S.) that "If I can find out that it can hold power, I don't care very much what you are telling this man [Epstein, the Bolshevik representative] about his party. I'm not interested in his party. But if it can't hold power, even if the party is perfect, what use do I have for it." J. B. S. Hardman Papers, Box 6, file 47A, Oral History, p. 67, Tamiment Library.

18.   *N.Y. Call*, Nov. 22, 1921; *DNR*, Nov. 18, 1921.

19.   General Executive Board Minutes, December, 1921; *DNR*, May 13, 1922; Sutton, 227.

20.   Josephson, chapter 10; Draft of "The Labor Banking Movement in the U.S." by Sidney Hillman, ACW Papers.

21.   Fraser, "Dress Rehearsal"; *Conv. Proc.*, 1922.

22.   *Conv. Proc.*, 1922; Hillman, "Reconstruction of Russia"; General Executive Board Minutes, January, 1923; FBI File no. 61-9899 contains a RAIC circular noting that "Investments will bring you dividends in hard cash and also dividends in the health and happiness of the Russian people."

23.   *Chicago Daily News*, Nov. 11, 1925; *Doc. Hist.*, 1922–24; FBI File no. 61-9899; "Certificate" issued by the Chief Committee of the Council of Labor and Defense in Matters of Concessions and Limited Companies, Nov. 4, 1922, "The Decision of the Council of Labor and Defense," Nov. 4, 1922, signed by Acting President L. Kamenev and Secretary L. Fotieva, "Memorandum of Agreement entered into between the Supreme Council of Public Economy of the Russian Socialist Federative Soviet Republic and the Russo-American Industrial Corporation," all in ACW Papers; *DNR*, Sept. 1, 1922; *The Chronicle*, Nov. 3, 1923.

24. Hillman, "Reconstruction of Russia"; *DNR*, Nov. 29, 1922; Sutton, 229; *Nation*, Nov. 7, 1923.

25. Sutton; *DNR*, Nov. 5, 1922.

26. Hillman, "Reconstruction of Russia"; *Wall Street Journal*, June 8, 1922; *Doc. Hist.* 1922–24.

27. *New Republic*, May 31, 1922.

28. *New York Globe and Commercial Advertiser*, Nov. 4, 1922; Felix Frankfurter to Hillman, June 6, 1922 and George Soule to Frankfurter, June 26, 1922, Box 103, Felix Frankfurter Papers, Library of Congress; FBI File no. 61–9899.

29. Fraser, "Dress Rehearsal"; *The Survey*, May 20, 1922; General Executive Board Minutes, August, 1922.

30. *Conv. Proc.*, through 1924; Biographical sketches of founding union members in ACW Papers; David Saposs interviews with ACW leaders in Saposs Papers, Wisconsin State Historical Society.

31. Fraser, "Dress Rehearsal"; Gilbert, Samuel Haber, *Scientific Management in the Progressive Era, 1890–1920* (Chicago, 1964); Derber, pp. 134–136, 244–245; Milton J. Nadworny, *Scientific Management and the Unions, 1900–1932* (Cambridge, 1955), 98, 105, 110, 118–119, 126–128, 133, 135.

32. Rainer Taub, "Lenin and Taylor: The Fate of Scientific Management in the (Early) Soviet Union," *Telos* 37 (Fall 1978); Judith Merkle, *Management and Ideology* (Berkeley, 1980), 107, Lenin as quoted pp. 113, 114, 115, 119; Kendall E. Bailes, *Technology and Society under Lenin and Stalin*, (Princeton, 1978), 37–38, 50, 59.

33. Merkle, 122; Bailes, *Technology and Society*, 62; Kendall E. Bailes, "Alexei Gastev and the Soviet Controversy over Taylorism, 1918–24," *Soviet Studies* 29, no. 3 (July 1977), 62.

34. E. H. Carr, *The Bolshevik Revolution, 1917–23*, vol. 2 (London, 1952), 207, 220, 228, 319–320, 325–326; Margaret Dewar, *Labour Policy in the USSR, 1917–28*, (London, 1956), 83–84, 90–92, 97, 102–104, 110.

35. Peter G. Filene, ed., *American Views of Soviet Russia, 1917–65*, (Homewood, Ill., 1968), 56–60; Sutton, 279; Carr, *Bolshevik Revolution*, vol. 2, 299, 302, 304–310, 335–337, 342; Eugene Zaleski, *Planning for Economic Growth in the Soviet Union, 1918–32*, trans. and ed. Marie-Christine MacAndrew and G. Nutter (Chapel Hill, 1971), 14, 20–21, 29.

36. Carr, *Bolshevik Revolution*, vol. 3, 279, 281, 351, 353.

37. Sutton, 227, quoting *Pravda*, Aug. 6, 1922; *The Liberator*, December, 1923; *Nation*, Nov. 7, 1923.

38. Hillman's Carnegie Hall speech, Dec. 1, 1922, and Hillman's speech before the Foreign Policy Association, Feb. 3, 1923, ACW Papers.

39. Mary Agnes Hamilton interview with Hillman in *Contemporary Review*, February, 1927; Hillman's Carnegie Hall Speech, Dec. 1, 1922; *New York Globe and Commercial Advertiser*, Nov. 18, 1922; *Soviet Russia Pictorial*, April, 1924.

40. *N.Y. World*, Oct. 20, 1922. *DNR*, Nov. 26, 1923.

41. Hillman's Carnegie Hall speech, Dec. 1, 1922. In this talk, Hillman

also noted the ease with which the union in Russia could have officers of the trust recalled, as well as its attempts to provide the workers with free housing and day care services; *Christian Science Monitor*, Dec. 2, 1922; *DNR*, Nov. 26, 1923.

42. General Executive Board Minutes, December, 1925.

43. Bailes, "Alexei Gastev"; Dewar, 102, 120.

44. George Soule article in *New York Globe and Commercial Advertiser*, Nov. 8, 1922; *DNR*, Nov. 18, 1921; *Soviet Russia Pictorial*, April, 1924.

45. Fraser, "Dress Rehearsal"; HSM Cases and Chicago Cases.

46. Fraser, "Dress Rehearsal."

47. Carr, *Bolshevik Revolution*, vol. 2, 220, 226; Bailes, *Technology and Society*, 37–38, 59, 62; Zaleski, 15; Bailes, "Alexei Gastev"; Taub, "Lenin and Taylor."

48. Carr, passim; Daniel Bell Collection, Boxes 2, 3, and 9, Tamiment Library.

49. *Conv. Proc.*, 1920 and 1922; Fraser, "Dress Rehearsal"; Theodore Draper, *American Communism and Soviet Russia* (New York, 1960), 65–66, 70–71; Daniel Bell Collection, Box 9, Bell interview with Earl Browder.

50. Daniel Bell Collection, especially précis of J. B. S. Hardman article, "Needle Trades–1920's," Box 3, written in 1922, and Bell's interview with Browder, Box 9, and Bell's "Notes on TUEL Minutes, 1923–27," Box 3, especially March 7, 1924, and Browder's minutes, May 1, 1924. Epstein, *Jewish Labor*, vol. 2, 64–66, 110–111, 115, 123, 130–131, and passim; Author's interview with Samuel Liptzin, Feb. 2, 1980, transcript in possession of author; Oral History Collection, Charles Zimmerman file, Box 6, Nov. 13, 1964, YIVO Archives; Samuel Liptzin, *Tales of a Tailor* (New York, 1965), 167–172; "Amalgamated Clothing Workers of America," Box 5, Bell Collection; Melech Epstein, "Profile of Sidney Hillman," Bund Archives of the Jewish Labor Movement, Atram Center for Jewish Culture.

51. *Doc. Hist.*, 1924–26; Hillman to Jacob Potofsky, Oct. 3, 1925, Hillman Papers; Sutton, 290–291.

52. "National Committee of the TUEL Box 5, Bell Collection; Report to the Red International of Labor Unions," Sept. 27, 1924; Trade Union Committee of the Box 3, Bell Collection; Central Executive Committee telegram to Losovsky, Sept. 30, 1925, *Brooklyn Daily Eagle*, Sept. 12, 1924; *Chicago Daily News*, Nov. 11, 1925; *The Advance*, Nov. 27, 1925; *DNR*, Nov. 25, 1926.

Chapter Eight

Abortive Reform: The Wilson Administration And Organized Labor, 1913-1920

Melvyn Dubofsky

Fashions in history sometimes seem as fashionable as those in dress. In the 1950s and early 1960s the Progressive era was an exciting intellectual frontier for scholars, and was still largely interpreted as the "age of reform." More recently, however, a growing number of historians have perceived Progressive reforms as the limited triumphs of a group of emerging professionals and bureaucrats who were seeking to rationalize and stabilize a turbulent society. For such scholars, Frederick Winslow Taylor and John B. Watson serve as the chief surrogates for the age. In a somewhat similar, if partially divergent, interpretive vein, the "new left" historians of the late 1960s and 1970s portrayed the Progressive era as the moment when "monopoly capital" (to use the term that they were usually loath to apply) used the national state to solidify its dominance in the marketplace. For them, corporatism emerges as the central reform motif, and George W. Perkins (J. P. Morgan's "right-hand man"), Ralph Easley (secretary of the National Civic Federation), and ultimately the National Industrial Conference Board appear as the era's "brain trusts." In all these interpretations, however, labor-capital conflict at best lurks in the background.[1]

To slight the centrality of labor-capital conflict in Progressive America and the role of the labor movement in the era's history seems to me a mistake. We would do better to recall the contemporary judgment of an ardent Wilsonian, Ray Stannard Baker, who in a series of magazine articles published in 1904-1905 described labor-capital relations as the central national political issue of his time. For of all the questions that embroiled politics in the early twentieth century, the labor question was the most sensitive and divisive and the least amenable to compromise. Indeed, the issue was so contentious that most politicians preferred to evade it. Nevertheless, as Bruno Ramirez has observed, the battle between labor and capital, workers and employers, dominated the hidden agenda of progressivism. At no time was this more true than during the presidency of Woodrow Wilson, the subject of this essay.

Many aspects of the political struggle among trade unionists, employers, and Democrats in the Wilson years presaged comparable events during the turbulent 1930s.[2] Let me try to explain briefly why this was so. First, the labor movement challenged fundamental American traditions from two directions. Radicalism, whether of socialist or syndicalist variety, was a vital presence among organized workers during the Progressive years. Either form of working-class radicalism threatened the established order. Yet, however threatening labor radicals may have been, they represented only a minority of organized workers. But it is a grave mistake to see the nonradical majority as domesticated citizens in an emerging corporate-liberal system. If Samuel Gompers, John Mitchell, and the workers they represented rhetorically defended private property and free enterprise, their actual practices conflicted with established principles of property rights and circumscribed entrepreneurial freedoms. As David Brody has written, " . . . power and interest can be issues of deadly conflict even in a system in which men agree on the fundamentals."[3] American business *never* willingly conceded any of its prerogatives to workers and unions.

Second, in the early twentieth century organized labor for the first time in American history represented a durable mass movement. Between 1897 and 1903 the unions affiliated with the American Federation of Labor (AFL) grew more than sixfold, from 400,000 members to almost 3 million, as also did many independent unions. An aggressive employer counterattack as well as the business contraction of 1907–1909 thwarted the advance of unionism but failed, unlike similar conjunctures in the nineteenth century, to paralyze it. Then, in the years 1910–13, unions grew again and succeeded in organizing workers hitherto thought unorganizable, setting the foundation for the remarkable growth in membership during World War I. This increase was linked directly to a rising intensity in industrial warfare.[4]

Third, what was happening in the United States must be understood in the context of the entire Atlantic economy, if not the globe. Similar forces and events were sweeping Italy, France, Germany, the Lowlands, Britain, Scandinavia, and even eastern Europe and Russia. This was indeed the age of the mass strike. It was also the golden age of working-class internationalism and its institution, the Second International. The rise of the European working classes and the waxing power of socialist parties did not pass unnoticed in the United States.[5]

Fourth, American unions and workers became more active in national politics than ever before. As unions grew in size and industrial conflicts spread over a larger arena, federal policies and actions often proved decisive to the success or failure of the labor cause. John Mitchell, one of the nation's more moderate labor leaders, put the case well when he wrote in 1903: "The trade union movement in this country can make progress only by identifying itself with the state."[6] In fact, his union, the United Mine Workers (UMWA) had just benefited from the actions of Theodore Roosevelt.

But it was not until the presidency of Woodrow Wilson that the labor question became a persistent, inescapable national issue. Wilson's predecessors, Roosevelt and Taft, occasionally grappled with the problem of labor. Yet their administrations lacked well-defined labor policies, built and maintained no regular, systematic relationship with the labor movement, and, in the case of Taft especially, opposed labor's primary political goal: relief from legal injunctions and exemption from the Sherman Act. All this changed with Wilson's election. From 1913 through 1920, labor had direct access to the White House and the cabinet, achieved its most desired legislative goals, and gained a share, however small, in national political power.

Before analyzing Wilsonian labor policy in detail, we should consider briefly what might be defined as its general dynamics. It is essential to keep in mind that at no point between 1913 and 1920 was there a clear, consistent federal policy toward workers and trade unions. The structural separation of power at times resulted in conflicting policies adopted by the executive, legislative, and judicial branches of government. Even within the executive branch, bureaucratic competition proved the rule, as different cabinet officers and their departments contended for supremacy—especially during World War I. Despite the confusion and conflicts among Democrats in Washington over policy, however, by the midpoint of the Wilson presidency a firm political alliance had been built between the AFL, most of its affiliated unions, and the Democratic party. Wilsonian labor policy divided into three quite distinct stages. The first ran from the creation of the Department of Labor through the publication of the *Final Report* of the United States Commission on Industrial Relations. It included the enactment of several laws dear to the hearts of labor lobbyists. The second stage occurred during the World War I years when the government provided organized labor with opportunities for growth hitherto unimaginable to most labor leaders. In the last stage, the federal government retreated from its advanced position on the labor-capital front and policymakers diluted their previous solicitude for independent trade unionism.

The political alliance between labor and the Democrats did not emerge suddenly with the election of Woodrow Wilson. Despite conventional notions concerning the AFL's apolitical traditions, the Federation had in fact originated to defend and advance labor's political interests. That was why when unions expanded so rapidly between 1897 and 1903 the AFL moved its headquarters from Indianapolis, a center of trade unionism, to Washington, the locus of national politics. The issue for such labor leaders as Gompers and the chiefs of the independent railroad brotherhoods was *never* whether or not labor should be active politically. Rather, it was to find a mode of political action that would produce the fewest divisions among the rank and file. Labor leaders had to maintain loyalty and solidarity among a membership split three ways: the Federation comprised traditional Republicans and Democrats plus a growing number of independents and socialists. It is difficult to estimate in what proportions organized workers split among the three, but it would seem that the great majority of workers (70 to 80 percent) preferred either Democratic or some form of independent labor/socialist politics and that the remainder, mostly American-born Protestant workers whose allegiances derived from a political culture formed during the Civil War and Reconstruction, leaned toward Republicanism.[7]

Whatever the political inclinations of the rank and file, leaders realized that federal policies and actions vitally affected the security of trade unions. Railroad union leaders had learned that lesson by 1900 after almost three decades of industrial warfare punctuated by federal intervention.[8] As the economy continued to nationalize, many unions found their actions coming under federal scrutiny. The boycott, the secondary strike, and the sympathetic strike—essential weapons in labor's arsenal—were all at one time or another declared illegal by federal courts. Sections of the Sherman Antitrust Act, the Interstate

Commerce Act, and federal proscription of common law conspiracies in restraint of trade combined to imperil the future of trade unionism.[9]

A comparable situation in Britain had pushed workers and their unions toward more independent forms of political action and ultimately to the founding of the Labour Party. American union leaders were aware of British developments and were made more so by pressure from their followers. Not only was socialism making substantial inroads among workers, especially in such core unions as the mine workers, the machinists, and the brewery workers, but city centrals and state federations of labor were also flooding headquarters with petitions and letters demanding the creation of an American labor party and often citing the British example.[10]

In response, Gompers and his associates devised a political strategy that would mollify their followers while causing the least political dissension. First, AFL officials in 1906 drew up Labor's Bill of Grievances and presented it to leaders of both parties in Congress for action. They then established a Labor Representation Committee (patterned after the British model) to seek the election of trade unionists and union sympathizers to congress. They even targeted specific members of the House, all Republicans, for defeat. Finally, Gompers went to the 1908 conventions of both major parties demanding that they incorporate labor's primary goals into their platforms.[11]

The AFL's political assertiveness served primarily to forge an alliance between labor and the Democrats. In Congress, Democrats responded more sympathetically to the Bill of Grievances. The trade unionists elected to the House were mostly Democrats (of fifteen elected in 1910, thirteen were Democrats). And in 1908, the Democratic party agreed to incorporate the AFL's demands into its platform. As a consequence, Gompers and other labor leaders cooperated with the Democratic National Committee in campaigning for Bryan. For their part, the Democrats had good reason to seek union support. As a minority party nationally, they needed allies wherever they could be found. Moreover, as a party whose strength was concentrated in the South and West, Democrats shared labor's antagonism to big capital. Thus political calculation and sentiment increasingly bound Democrats and labor together.[12]

Ironically, however, the emergence of Woodrow Wilson as a national political figure at first threatened the Democratic-labor alliance. Though Southern-born, Wilson was "discovered" and promoted politically by what remained of the old northern Democratic financial community, the "gold bugs." Wilson brought to Democratic politics a distaste for organized labor and the principles it personified.

A "Credo" written by the future president in 1907 defended the
absolute right to freedom of contract from its union critics, whom he
defined as men "who have neither the ideas nor the sentiments needed
for the maintenance or the enjoyment of liberty." Only two years later
he declared to an antilabor banquet audience, "I am a fierce partizan
[sic] of the Open Shop and of everything that makes for industrial
liberty." Not surprisingly then, when Wilson ran for governor of New
Jersey in 1910, the state's labor movement united against him. To quiet
the voices of his trade union critics, Wilson in 1910 changed his line. "I
have always been the warm friend of organized labor," he assured
trade unionists, and he defended their right to organize independent
unions.[13]

Still, at the 1912 Democratic convention, labor held firm in the
anti-Wilson camp, much preferring the candidacy of Missouri's
Champ Clark. Once the nomination was his, though, Wilson had little
choice but to further his rapprochement with labor. Nor did Gompers
have much choice other than to accept Wilson's overtures, unless he
preferred to see the labor vote move more swiftly toward Debs and the
socialists or Roosevelt and the Progressives. For in 1912, the Democratic party once again incorporated the AFL's primary demands into
its platform. Although in his 1925 autobiography, Gompers asserted
that he played no active role in the 1912 election and the public record
in fact shows only circumspect labor support for Wilson and the Democrats, the AFL national office served as a clearing house for Democratic
National Committee efforts to woo the labor vote. The Party Chairman
contacted Gompers about sending AFL organizers to different parts of
the country on behalf of the Wilson campaign. John L. Lewis, for
example, campaigned for the Democrats in New Mexico and Arizona.[14]

AFL assistance surely did not harm Wilson's prospects. Although
it is impossible to apportion a labor vote among the parties and candidates, circumstantial evidence suggests that union endorsements
brought Wilson a good many votes. He owed his victory primarily, of
course, to the split within the Republican party; but the election re-
turns proved how vital labor would be for future Democratic successes.
The Taft Republicans, the only party among the four major ones
contesting the election that offered nothing to workers and unions,
received less than 25 percent of the popular vote. Wilson could interpret the results as well as anyone. It was not only the influence of Louis
Brandeis that encouraged Wilson to show more sympathy for organized labor. What Brandeis did perhaps was to accelerate the speed at
which Wilson was already moving owing to political realities and elec-

toral calculus.[15] In any event, after his election the new president worked to solidify the Democratic-labor alliance.

Unlike any previous chief executive, Wilson opened his administration wide to the leaders of trade unionism. Cabinet officials, especially the Secretary of Labor, conferred regularly with the AFL executive council. Gompers and other labor leaders corresponded often and at length with the President, who made them feel their counsel was sought. Wilson made sure to appear personally at the July 4, 1916, dedication of the new AFL headquarters building and to say the proper ceremonial words. He also sought the AFL's advice of pending judicial appointments, up to and including the Supreme Court, a matter of no small importance to organized labor. Finally, a year after his reelection, in November 1917, Wilson became the first president to address an annual convention of the AFL. Surely, American labor now had a friend in the White House.[16]

Organized labor reciprocated Wilson's attentions. At no time was this clearer than in the election of 1916. The reunification of the Republican party boded ill for Democratic chances that year. Thus Gompers called out the troops for Wilson and himself campaigned publicly for the Democrats. Such unions as the United Mine Workers (UMW) and the International Association of Machinists, which had leaned toward socialism before 1916, now fell in line behind Wilson. The railroad brotherhoods, special beneficiaries of Wilsonian largesse, were perfervid in their support for the President. In the western states, which were to prove so decisive in Wilson's reelection, labor united behind the President, and its votes were probably critical to his victory. By November 1916, organized labor had become a core constituency of the Democratic party.[17]

That connection, however, was built on more than symbolism. The Department of Labor, which was established as a cabinet-level agency in Wilson's first term, advocated trade unionism's case within the administration. The Secretary, William B. Wilson, an ex-UMWA officer and former Democratic congressman from Pennsylvania, considered himself and acted as a partisan of trade unionism. As he wrote to Gompers after eight years of service as secretary, the most important of the Labor Department's many duties was " . . . to have someone as its directing head who can carry the viewpoint of labor into the councils of the President." That was a task to which Wilson dedicated himself. As he told the 1914 AFL convention, "If securing justice to those who earn their bread in the sweat of their faces constitutes partisanship, then count me as a partisan of labor." A year earlier he had informed the same audience, much to the consternation of many conservatives, that absolute rights in private property did not exist. Society, he explained, has a perfect right to modify such rights " . . . whenever in its judgment it deems it for the welfare of society to do it."[18]

In staffing the new department, Wilson acted on these principles. Whenever possible, he chose officials sympathetic to labor or drawn directly from trade unions. The newly established federal conciliation service selected many of its mediators from the UMWA. In their capacity as mediators/conciliators, these Labor Department agents not only sought to eliminate the sources of industrial conflict; they also promoted the recognition of AFL and other unions.[19]

Equally positive in its effects on the development of organized labor was the field work, public hearings, and final report of the United States Commission on Industrial Relations (CIR). Originally conceived in the waning days of the Taft administration as a federal response to labor-capital violence, the CIR functioned as an advocate for the poor, the oppressed, and the unorganized. That was primarily because of the person Wilson chose as chair, Frank P. Walsh, a Kansas City attorney and left-wing Democrat. Otherwise balanced among representatives of enlightened capital, responsible labor (the AFL and the railroad brotherhoods), and the public at large, the Commission was driven to the left by Walsh and his lieutenant, Basil Manly.[20]

For more than two years, the CIR conducted public hearings across the nation at which witnesses from management, labor, and the community testified about industrial violence, labor relations, and exploitation. Almost invariably, the public hearings, whether concerned with the 1913 Paterson silk strike, labor policy in the Chicago packinghouses, or the shopmen's strike on the Illinois Central Line, offered unions a friendly forum in which to state their case. In dealing with capitalists, however, Walsh played the prosecutor. He pilloried John D. Rockefeller, Jr., and held him personally responsible for the company policies that had resulted in the infamous Ludlow, Colorado, massacre. While castigating capital, Walsh publicly and more so privately extended a comradely hand to radicals—not only such "respectable" socialists as Morris Hillquit but also such notorious Wobblies as Vincent St. John and William D. Haywood. While the CIR held its public hearings, scores of field investigators filed unpublished reports. These, too, generally made the case for organized labor. Equally important, these unsung investigators later played prominent roles in implementing World War I and New Deal labor policies.[21]

Walsh's radicalism ensured that the CIR would divide internally when the time came to issue a final report and recommendations, which was precisely what happened. The Commission split three ways. The representatives of capital essentially leaned to a middle way. They condemned equally irresponsible capital and radical labor, calling upon enlightened businessmen and responsible trade unionists to bargain reasonably. They also defended the open-shop principle and drew no distinction between independent and company unions. The public representatives, John R. Commons and Mrs. J. Borden Harriman, stood midway between the representatives of capital and the Walsh majority. More sympathetic to independent trade unions than the employers on the Commission, Commons and Harriman found the majority too condemnatory of business, too soft on labor radicals, and too favorably inclined to positive state action. They preferred to have "experts" chair impartial joint labor-management boards that would bring law and order to the anarchy of industrial relations. If "corporate liberalism" existed anywhere in Wilsonian America, it was among such people, whose recommendations were rejected by both capital and labor. The majority report, by contrast, prepared by Manly and signed by Walsh and the three labor commissioners, was perhaps the most radical document ever released by a federal commission. It blamed industrial violence and exploitation on the gross maldistribution of wealth and income, the ubiquity of unemployment, and corporate denial of workers' human rights, especially the right to organize unions of their own choosing. "Relief from these grave evils cannot be secured by petty reforms," declared the majority. "The action must be drastic." Among the drastic reforms proposed were federal laws and agencies to protect the rights of workers to organize and bargain collectively. Independent unionism was to be made a central objective of federal policy, as was a panoply of measures aimed at securing working people against unemployment, illness, and indigent old age. As Walsh himself wrote to a UMWA leader after the CIR submitted its final report, it was "more radical than any report upon industrial subjects every made by any government agency."[22]

Trade unionists and radicals were much impressed. A railroad brotherhood journal proclaimed that the Report "will go down in history as the greatest contribution to labor literature of our time." The socialist *Appeal to Reason* described it as peeling the hide off capitalism, and the *Christian Socialist* compared it to the Declaration of Independence and the Emancipation Proclamation. Finally, the *Masses* saw it as " . . . the beginning of an indigenous American revolutionary movement."[23] Indeed so, for the Walsh-Manly recommendations of July 1915 incorporated a labor program that encompassed every reform of the New Deal and others that have never been enacted. In fact, the combination of a split Commission and a radical majority report ensured that nothing substantive would come immediately from the CIR's work. But less than three years later Frank Walsh would serve as co-chair of the National War Labor Board (NWLB), a position from which he sought to implement many of his 1915 proposals.

Strangely enough for an administration that otherwise did so much for organized labor, the Wilsonians stocked the barest of legislative cupboards. On no issue was this truer than on the one closest to the heart of labor, relief from legal injunctions and antitrust legislation. Rather than describe in detail the complicated legislative politics and history of the Clayton Act controversy and its labor clauses, let me simply conclude that on the issue of injunctive relief, Wilson refused to defer to labor's requests or even to compromise. In his view, any statute that exempted labor from judicial review was a form of class legislation alien to the American way.[24] Nevertheless, for exigent political reasons, Wilson did in the summer of 1916 endorse an effort to abolish child labor through federal legislation (the Keating-Owens Act) and recommended passage of the Adamson Act to award operating railroad workers the basic eight-hour day at their previous ten-hour wage. This legislation proved an essential element in Wilson's 1916 political strategy and his electoral coalition.[25]

What had been mostly tendencies or halfway measures toward a new labor policy became a reality during World War I. One part of that reality, the AFL's cooperation in Wilsonian diplomacy, has been described and analyzed by Ronald Radosh and Frank L. Grubbs, Jr.[26] The other and far more important part—domestic labor policy—has received no comparable treatment. James Weinstein touches several vital aspects of the subject in his book *The Corporate Ideal in the Liberal State*, as does David Kennedy in *Over Here*. But Weinstein forces Wilsonian labor policy into the Procrustean bed of his "corporate liberal" interpretation of American history, and Kennedy deals with it largely from the perspective of corporate planners and those members of the administration least sensitive to organized labor.[27]

Wartime labor policy was shaped by two distinct factors: the new realities of social and economic power, and the absence of a uniform, central direction in administration policy. The demands of war magnified labor's power. With unemployment eliminated, workers and unions felt free to press their claims against capital, whether through voluntary quits or collective action. Both labor turnover and the number of strikes reached unprecedented levels in 1917.[28] As for policy, what Robert D. Cuff has shown to be true for the War Industries Board—the existence of bureaucratic infighting and the absence of any accepted central plan—was also true for labor policy.[29] By and large, the president allowed subordinate officials, departments, and boards to make policy. Except for the heavy-handed repression of labor and political radicals, he rarely tried to coordinate actions on the labor front. The Labor Department under William B. Wilson and the war department under Newton D. Baker generally favored trade unionism, as did the NWLB and the War Labor Policies Board (WLPB). The Commerce, Agriculture, and Justice Departments as well as the separate military branches, the WIB, and corporate dollar-a-year men often equated unionism with radicalism (subversion) and sympathized with open-shop principles. Added to this confusion, the federal judiciary handed down several decisions that conflicted with vital aspects of Wilsonian policy. In February 1918, the journalist Robert Bruere succinctly noted these contradictions. "Here were three branches of the Federal Government," he wrote,

pursuing three radically divergent and hopelessly conflicting policies towards the wageworkers at the very moment when the nation was making a patriotic appeal to the workers to get out a maximum production . . . . The United States Department of Justice was arresting them, the President's Mediation Commission was telling them that they must organize into unions, and the United States Supreme Court was announcing that if they attempted to organize under certain conditions they would be guilty of contempt of court.[30]

Despite the confusion in Washington, trade unionism clearly gained from the prevailing drift in federal policy. In this sense, David Kennedy is wrong to assert that federal labor policy did not alter the existing lines of power in society but instead scrupulously followed them and set them more rigidly in place. He is equally wrong in insisting that reformers and labor leaders had little success in winning federal support for trade unionism, or that Gompers himself perceived such a goal as unrealistic by agreeing to an unpublished Council of National Defense (CND) statement stipulating "that employers and employees in private industries should not attempt to take advantage of the existing abnormal conditions to change the standards which they were unable to change under normal conditions."[31]

The evidence suggests a far different reality than the one limned by Kennedy. Of course, if one focuses primarily on the policies of Bernard Baruch, Walter S. Gifford, Louis B. Wehle, and Colonel Brice P. Disque, unions seemed to get short shrift in wartime.[32] But if one examines the records of the labor department, the President's Mediation Commission, the NWLB, the WLPB, and union leaders' own role in setting wartime policies, a quite different picture emerges. For example, on the CND statement concerning the maintenance of standards during the war, Labor Secretary Wilson interpreted that as applying only to working conditions and not to the question of unionization. He defined the right to organize as the "burning issue" of the day, and asserted " . . . that capital has no right to interfere with working men organizing. . . ." And he convinced the President to write as follows to the director of the antiunion Alabama coal operators' association: "It is generally acknowledged that our laws and the long established policy of our Government recognize the right of workingmen to organize unions if they so desire."[33]

Moreover, many officials in Washington found labor more amenable to federal policies and goals than capital. President Wilson told unionists publicly at the 1917 AFL convention, "you are reasonable in a larger number of cases than the capitalists." More revealingly, War Secretary Baker confided to the President: "I confess I am more concerned to have industry and capital know what you think they ought to do in regard to labor than to have labor understand its duty. In my own dealings with the industrial problem here, I have found labor more willing to keep step than capital."[34]

As unrest swelled in the summer of 1917 and strikes disrupted war production, employers and patriots demanded they be suppressed. The administration, however, preferred a different prescription for quelling the eruption. As the Labor Department defined the situation, unrest was primarily an expression "of revolt at low wages and hard conditions in industry and impatience with the slow evolution of economic democracy through the organized labor movement." The Labor Department seconded Gompers's advice to the President that if employers recognized bona fide AFL unions, the labor unrest would diminish. The problem was that capital refused to keep step with federal labor policy. And capitalist resistance to unionism grew as employers increasingly expected assistance from their many friends in Washington, whose policies were seldom directly overruled by the President.[35]

To overcome employer antiunionism and also to define more clearly a federal labor policy, Secretaries Wilson and Baker joined with Gompers in August 1917 to urge the president to appoint a special commission to investigate the wartime upheaval and make recommendations for its resolution. The result was the appointment in September of the President's Mediation Commission. Chaired by Secretary Wilson and composed of two AFL representatives and two employers, the Commission was in fact dominated by Felix Frankfurter, who shared his friend Walter Lippmann's conviction that the war provided an unsurpassed opportunity to reform American society.[36]

Even before the Commission began its task, Frankfurter laid down its guiding principles. He agreed with the Wilson-Gompers diagnosis of the labor troubles, that is, that most strikes resulted from a combination of real material grievances and employer antiunion practices. Frankfurter thus proposed that the mediators conduct in-depth investigations of working conditions in the troubled industries, that they recommend the creation of formal conciliation machinery to ameliorate grievances, that they urge employers to deal responsibly with their employees, and that they convince American workers that the war was not only to defend democracy abroad but also to establish industrial justice at home. Like Gompers and Wilson, Frankfurter believed that these objectives could best be accomplished through peaceful bargaining between employers and AFL unions.[37]

Guided by Frankfurter's principles, the Commission investigated disputes in the southwestern copper industry, the Pacific northwest woods, the West Coast telephone business, and the Chicago packing houses. In January 1918, it recommended that (1) a form of collective relationship between management and men is essential and that the recognition of this principle by the government should form an accepted part of the national labor policy; (2) employers should immediately establish grievance machinery to handle real problems equitably before they precipitate strikes; (3) the eight-hour day be established as national policy; and (4) unified direction of wartime labor policy be established.[38]

Acting on the Commission's recommendations, President Wilson charged his Labor Secretary with directing labor policy. Secretary Wilson promptly invited representatives of capital, labor, and the public to meet as a War Labor Conference Board to devise a program to govern labor-management relations. In March 1918 the Board approved recommendations comparable to those of the Commission, defending the principle of workers' right to form trade unions unimpeded by employers. But it still equivocated by also recommending that management be required to bargain with shop committees not with union representatives, and that unions coerce neither workers to join nor employers to grant the union shop.[39]

In April 1918 the President created the NWLB, which was patterned after the composition of the War Labor Conference Board. As important as the policy principles enunciated and implemented by the NWLB were the practices of the co-chairs, William Howard Taft and

Frank P. Walsh, especially the latter. Walsh convinced Taft that the right of workers to organize should be sacrosanct and free of all employer interference. The Board, as a matter of policy, ordered reinstatement and back pay for employees discharged for union activities. It also ruled that a whole host of traditional employer antiunion tactics were in violation of federal labor policy. Walsh, moreover, privately cooperated with labor leaders seeking to unionize the meatpacking and steel industries. Paradoxically, he also offered what assistance he could to labor radicals (mostly Wobblies) whom the federal government sought to put "out of business."[40]

The NWLB instituted a minor revolution by making the right to unionize real. Some of its specific orders introduced a whole new concept of property rights consonant with those William B. Wilson had enunciated before the 1913 AFL convention. As one business journal said of an NWLB order: "We know of no legislation authorizing the [NWLB] . . . to require private business concerns to revolutionize their business methods. We cannot see that the War Labor Board or the War Department has any more right to prescribe collective bargaining instead of individual bargaining than it has to prescribe red ink instead of black ink for the firm's letterheads."[41]

This legal revolution also was endorsed by another agency created in the spring of 1918 to implement labor policy: the War Labor Policies Board. And no wonder, for its head was Felix Frankfurter. Indeed, an unpublished document in the files of the WLPB proposed " . . . to create in industry a condition of collective bargaining between employer and employee. It contemplates, and is based upon the existence of unions of employees and unions of employers."[42] Together these agencies were responsible for transforming labor-management relations from a totally private arena to a semi-public one and, in the process, upsetting the historical balance of power in many industries between workers and bosses. As William Z. Foster, the leader of the meat-packing and steel organizing campaigns, observed about the spring-summer 1918, " . . . the Federal administration was friendly; the right to organize was freely conceded by the government and even insisted upon. . . . The gods were indeed fighting on the side of Labor. It was an opportunity to organize the [steel] industry such as might never again occur."[43]

Labor took full advantage of the opportunity. The growth in membership was truly remarkable, increasing by over 2 million between 1917 and 1920, a gain of almost 70 percent. For the first time total union membership approached 20 percent of the civilian nonagricultural labor force, a level more than twice as high as any previous peak. Along with this growth went steady rises in wage rates and the general achievement of the eight-hour day.[44]

Union advances could be seen wherever the federal government intervened directly and regularly, and wherever effective labor organizations or aggressive organizers functioned. In the men's clothing trade, which prospered on wartime federal contracts, Sidney Hillman, the president of the industry's union, the Amalgamated Clothing Workers of America, established excellent relations with federal contract administrators. As a result his union, barely two years old when the United States entered war, more than doubled its membership.[45] In two industries controlled by the federal government during the war (one, the railroads, directly and the other, coal, indirectly), unions also flourished. The United Mine Workers won equal participation with employers on the wartime Fuel Administration and used its influence there to advance the union into the previously nonunion Southern Appalachian coal fields. By war's end, the UMWA claimed over 500,000 members, making it far and away the nation's largest union.[46] The story was much the same on the railroads. William McAdoo, federal railroad czar, put out the welcome mat for labor leaders. Federal Railroad Administration orders increased wages, standardized work rules, and improved conditions. Unions grew rapidly, especially the previously smaller nonoperating unions. Between 1914 and 1920, for example, the Brotherhood of Railway Carmen expanded from 28,700 to 182,000 members. "A worker . . . with a union card in his pocket," reported one carman, "will be looked after and has been assured by the government of this great country of ours that he will get a square deal."[47]

The most surprising gains occurred in industries with strong traditions of antiunionism: meat packing and steel. In both cases, the labor organizers (the same people, John Fitzpatrick and William Z. Foster, were primarily responsible for initiating both campaigns) looked to the federal government for support and received it. Between September 1917, when the Stockyards Labor Council was created in Chicago, and January 1918, organized labor succeeded in increasing dues-paying membership from about 8,000 to 28,229, and claimed between 25 and 50 percent of the industry's workers. Unable to stop their employees from joining the union, the packers drew the line at recognition and collective bargaining. But federal pressure compelled the packers to negotiate with union representatives if not to recognize unionism. At the end of January 1918, the packers conceded union demands on employment and shop conditions, leaving other issues to be resolved by formal federal arbitration. In the arbitration hearings,

Frank Walsh, soon to serve as co-chair of the NWLB, represented the unions. On March 30, 1918, the arbitrator, Judge Samuel Alschuler, handed down his award. He granted workers a basic eight-hour day with ten hours' pay, substantial wage increases, and overtime premiums. The union took credit for the award and, in its wake, unionization swept across the meat-packing industry. Beginning in April, the NWLB delivered specific rulings and awards, which added impetus to the union drive. By November 1918, the Amalgamated Meat Cutters reported 62,857 dues-paying members, over twice as many as nine months earlier, and over ten times as many as three years earlier. "I think the foundations of unionism have been laid in the packing industry for a long time to come," Foster informed Walsh. Although the companies still refused formally to recognize the unions, in David Brody's words, "under the Alschuler administration, the unions assumed an important role both for the employees and management."[48]

A similar story repeated itself in steel. There too, as the journal of the Amalgamated Association of Iron, Steel, and Tin Workers reported, "The Government stands firmly behind the organized labor movement in its right to organize, and that is why it [the union], is going to push its work of organization into the steel industries." Foster transferred his attention from meat packing to steel and took command of an AFL-sponsored joint union organizing campaign (modeled after the multi-union Stockyards Labor Council). In the summer and fall of 1918, steelworkers joined the unions by the thousands. Foster claimed between 250,000 and 350,000 members. The balance of power in steel had surely shifted. Judge Elbert Gary of United States Steel recognized as much when he observed that the best that employers could hope for was that labor questions be evaded until the war was over.[49]

To summarize the impact of the federal war labor policies, wherever unions had real strength or solid footholds before the war crisis, they made enormous membership advances and often won *de facto* recognition, bargaining rights, and even the union shop. Where able and dedicated organizers worked to spread the union gospel, as in meatpacking, steel, and the railroad shops, labor's gains were equally substantial. Only where unions had been absent in the prewar period, fought among themselves, or lacked able organizers did the employers prevail. In those cases, war and federal intervention caused no fundamental alteration in relations between labor and capital. But even there, the war produced some changes. Nonunion workers won the eight-hour day, vastly improved working conditions, and formal grievance procedures. The *New Republic* was not far off when it observed at the war's end: "We have already passed to a new era, the transition to a state in which labor will be the predominating element. . . . The character of the future democracy is largely at the mercy of the recognized leaders of organized labor."[50]

Federal wartime labor policies and Wilsonian democratic rhetoric had fired the imagination of labor leaders. "What labor is demanding all over the world today," asserted Sidney Hillman, "is not a few material things like more dollars and fewer hours of work, but a right to a voice in the conduct of industry." In January 1918, Hillman was moved to write to his young daughter: "Messiah is arriving. He may be with us any minute—one can hear the footsteps of the Deliverer—if only he listens intently. Labor will rule and the world will be free."[51] In more prosaic language, Harold Ickes described the postwar situation thus: "The chief issue is likely to be the relationship between capital and labor. . . . We sense disturbances way down underneath our social structure."[52]

Ickes was right; so was Hillman. In 1919 both labor and capital awaited "the Deliverer." For radical trade unionists, Messiah appeared in the guise of the Bolshevik Revolution, or the British Labour Party's plan for a New Social Order, or more simply as the triumph in America of trade unionism and industrial democracy. For employers, Messiah came as the armistice with its promise of the restoration of the *status quo antebellum*. Of such conflicting visions was industrial warfare made.

The year 1919 was one like none other in American history. Industrial conflict reached unprecedented levels as more than 3,000 strikes involved over 4 million workers. Even police walked out. Race riots and bomb scares proliferated. Not one but three American communist parties were formed. The world had been turned upside down. So thought Warren G. Harding, who wrote to a friend in the fall of 1919: "I really think we are facing a desperate situation. It looks to me as if we are coming to a crisis in the conflict between the radical labor leaders and the capitalistic system under which we have developed the republic. . . . I think the situation has to be met and met with exceptional [sic] courage."[53] So, too, thought Joe Tumulty, President Wilson's close and confidential adviser, who observed of the February 1919 Seattle general strike: "It is clear to me that it is the first appearance of the Soviet in this country."[54]

In this highly charged and tense situation, American labor faced a new set of economic and political realities. Fears abounded of labor-made surplus in a depressed economy. Yet wartime inflation continued unabated, sparking consumer resistance to union wage demands. Wilsonianism seemed discredited politically. The Republicans had swept into control of Congress in the 1918 election, and their triumph flowed as much from disenchantment with Wilson's domestic policies, especially his alleged truckling to labor, as from his diplomacy. The 1920 election seemed destined to confirm Republican national political dominance, a dominance now more threatening than ever to organized labor. Small wonder then that during the spring and summer of 1919 all the federal agencies that had governed wartime labor policy were dismantled. Trade unionists could no longer look to a Frank Walsh or a Felix Frankfurter to defend their interests in Washington.[55]

These new realities quickly made themselves felt in the Wilson administration. Tumulty, for one, advised that high wages were bad for consumers and hence for Democrats. As workers walked off their jobs by the millions, Tumulty suggested that "One way labor can help is to increase production." The new Attorney General, A. Mitchell Palmer, sounded a similar note. During the autumn 1919 coal strike, he recommended against any concessions to the miners' unlawful behavior because " . . . concessions . . . will insure unreasonably high prices in all commodities for at least three years to come." And Tumulty spelled out the political implications lucidly for the President. Wilson had already assured the Democrats of labor's political support through enactment of the Clayton and Adamson acts as well as wartime labor policies. If the administration continued to befriend unionists, advised Tumulty, "The country at large would think that we are making a special appeal to labor at this time. If there is any class in this country to which we have been overgenerous it has been labor. I think that this class owes us more than they have been willing to give."[56]

This is not to say that the Wilson administration completely deserted its friends in the labor movement. Quite the contrary. Administration officials still believed in the right of workers to organize unhindered by employer coercion and in basic trade union principles, and they still encouraged employers to recognize unions and bargain with them. But now they also feared labor radicalism, took the AFL's support for granted, and declined to pressure or compel employers to deal with unions.[57]

With the war over and Republicans in control of Congress, Judge Gary and other corporation leaders could now deal with the labor question—and on the terms they preferred. In the packinghouses and railroad shops employers refused to extend recognition or bargain collectively. In both places, the unions were unable to perfect the organization begun during the war. And they could no longer turn to

Washington for support. If unions in the two industries did not collapse absolutely in 1919–20, they were much weakened by 1922.[58]

Even more revealing was what happened in steel and coal. In the former, the union suffered a stillbirth; in the latter, the largest and most powerful union in the country bore the full brunt of a federal antistrike campaign. In steel, union leaders had believed, in the words of John Fitzpatrick that ". . . the Government would intervene and see to it that the steel barons be brought to time, even as the packers were. . . . President Wilson would never allow a great struggle to develop between the steelworkers and their employers." Wilson indeed sympathized with the unions' plight in steel and desired to avert a strike. But he would neither rebuke steel management publicly nor compel it to meet with labor. For with the war over the President lacked the law or precedent to do so. Thus, the strike came on September 22, 1919, federal troops helped break it, and the unionization of steel failed.[59]

The situation in coal was both more complicated and less decisive in its outcome. Unlike in steel, unexpired wartime federal legislation still governed the industry and the UMWA had a friend in the Secretary of Labor. Also the UMWA, unlike the steel unions, had a large and loyal dues-paying membership with a long union tradition. Yet when the miners actually left the pits, the administration officials most involved in the situation, William B. Wilson excepted, defined the strike "as not only unjustifiable but unlawful." They insisted that the walkout was directed against the government, not the mine owners. "I am sure," wrote Tumulty, "that many of the miners would rather accept the peaceful process of settlement . . . than go to war against the Government of the United States." But go to war the miners did. As a result, the administration sought and obtained a stringent antistrike injunction. It also readied troops for duty in the coal fields, tapped the phones of union leaders, sent federal agents to spy on the union, and threatened alien strikers with summary deportation. In the end, union leaders had no choice but to call off the strike. Because the UMWA was a large, stable union, it ultimately won a compromise wage award through the assistance of William B. Wilson. Yet as a result of the 1919 struggle, it lost most of its footholds in Southern Appalachia, a precondition for its subsequent national collapse in the 1920s.[60]

The record of the immediate postwar years confirms David Brody's observation that "depending on their own economic strength, American workers could not defeat the massed power of open-shop industry. Only public intervention might equalize the battle." In two years the labor movement lost 1.5 million members and was forced to retreat to its prewar bastions. After 1919, the great mass-production industries again operated without unions.[61]

How great a distance remained in 1919 between the aspirations of organized labor and the desires of corporate capital was revealed by the Industrial Conference that President Wilson convened in October 1919. Conceived to resolve the postwar labor-capital upheaval and to avert the steel strike, Wilson's First Industrial Conference did neither. It deadlocked over irreconcilable union-management positions. The AFL unionists in attendance sought an equal role with management and government in the control of industry. The business delegates, on the contrary, advocated the extirpation of unionism root and branch. It was the union movement, not the spectre of violent revolution, that frightened most businessmen. Hence they wanted the government to curb the unions' drive for industrial power. And the essence of the open-shop principle, which remained their benchmark throughout the conference, was in Haggai Hurvitz's words, "the 'utmost freedom' of management to act without outside interference and not labor's freedom to be employed without discrimination."[62] In the absence of a countervailing government presence on behalf of labor, management's principles and programs prevailed throughout the 1920s.

All in all, however, the Wilson years had provided a full dress rehearsal for the labor program of the New Deal. The political coalition between organized labor and the Democrats, constructed from 1912 to 1916, was perfected and strengthened in the Roosevelt years. The recommendations contained in the Walsh CIR report bore fruit in the advanced New Deal reforms of 1933–37. The labor policies the Wilson administration implemented during a war crisis the Roosevelt administration set in place in peacetime. Even the political dynamics of the two eras bore striking resemblances. By 1938, Roosevelt's advisers were warning him that the labor question had become political dynamite, that the administration had already granted labor too much, and that the Democrats had the labor vote in their pocket. But 1938 was not 1919. War was yet to come, and when it came it lasted more than twice as long and necessitated many more elaborate and stringent domestic regulations. That, in many respects, was the fundamental difference in labor politics between the Wilson and Roosevelt years. The great labor reforms of the Wilson era occurred in the midst of war and collapsed in the disillusionment of peace. Roosevelt's reforms were introduced in peacetime, were stabilized and routinized during the war, and then developed enough resiliency to enable organized labor to survive the postwar retrenchment.

Notes

1. For these themes see, among other works, the following: Robert Wiebe, *The Search for Order, 1877–1920* (New York, 1967), chapters 5–8; Gabriel Kolko, *The Triumph of American Conservatism* (Glencoe, Ill., 1963); James Weinstein, *The Corporate Ideal in the Liberal State* (Boston, 1968); Harry Braverman, *Labor and Monopoly Capital* (New York, 1974), chapters 4 and 5; Daniel Nelson, *Managers and Workers: Origins of the New Factory System in the United States, 1880–1920* (Madison, 1975), and *Frederick W. Taylor and the Rise of Scientific Management* (Madison, 1980); James B. Gilbert, *Work without Salvation* (Baltimore, 1977), passim; and Martin J. Sklar, "Woodrow Wilson and the Political Economy of Modern United States Liberalism," in James Weinstein and David W. Eakins, eds., *For a New America* (New York, 1970), 46–100.

2. Ray Stannard Baker, "Parker and Theodore Roosevelt on Labor," *McClure's* 24 (Nov. 1904), 41; Bruno Ramirez, *When Workers Fight: The Politics of Industrial Relations in the Progressive Era, 1898–1916* (Westport, Conn., 1978).

3. David Brody, *Workers in Industrial America* (New York, 1980), 127.

4. Graham Adams, Jr., *Age of Industrial Violence, 1910–1915* (New York, 1966).

5. Cf. Georges Haupt, *La Deuxième Internationale, 1889–1914* (Paris, 1964), and *Socialism and the Great War: The Collapse of the Second International* (Oxford, 1972).

6. Cited in Marc Karson, *American Labor Unions and Politics, 1900–1918*, (Boston, 1965 ed.), 90.

7. For the historical and cultural roots of working-class politics see Alan Dawley and Paul Faler, "Working-Class Culture and Politics in the Industrial Revolution: Sources of Loyalism and Rebellion," *Journal of Social History* 9 (Summer 1976), 466–480; Richard Jensen, *The Winning of the Midwest* (Chicago, 1971), Paul Kleppner, *The Cross of Culture* (New York, 1970), and Samuel P. McSeveney, *The Politics of Depression* (New York, 1972).

8. Gerald Eggert, *Railroad Labor Disputes* (Ann Arbor, 1967).

9. Charles O. Gregory, *Labor and the Law* (New York, 1946), chapters 4–6, 8, 10; Karson, *American Labor Unions*, 29–41; Bernard Mandel, *Samuel Gompers* (Yellow Springs, Ohio, 1963), 263–283.

10. See AFL Papers, Office of the President, File A, State Historical Society of Wisconsin (hereafter cited as SHSW) for the many boxes of correspondence and petitions concerning political action. See also John H. M. Laslett, *Labor and the Left* (New York, 1970); and David Montgomery, *Workers' Control in America* (New York, 1979), 48–90.

11. *American Federationist* 12 (May, 1906), 293–296; (Aug. 1906), 529–531; 15 (Aug. 1908), 589, 598–605; Karson, *American Labor Unions*, 42–70; Mandel, *Gompers*, 284–295.

12. Dallas Lee Jones, "The Wilson Administration and Organized Labor, 1912–1919," Ph.D. Dissertation, Cornell University, 1954, 1–33.

13. Arthur S. Link, *Wilson: The Road to the White House* (Princeton, 1947), 112, 127, 158–159.

14. Ibid., 470–471; M. Karson, *American Labor Unions*, 70–73; Mandel, *Gompers*, 295–297; J. J. Keegan to Samuel Gompers, Oct. 11, 1912; Gompers to Keegan, Oct. 14, 1912, and Keegan to Gompers, Oct. 15, 1912, all in AFL Papers, Office of the President, File A, Box 17, SHSW; Samuel Gompers, *Seventy Years of Life and Labor* (New York, 1925), 2: 282–283.

15. Jones, "Wilson Administration," 50.

16. Ibid., 312–320; John S. Smith, "Organized Labor and the Government in the Wilson Era, 1913–1921," *Labor History* 3 (Fall, 1962), 267–268, 272; Memorandum, R. Lee Guard, July 14, 1916, AFL Papers, Office of the President, File A, Box 22; Gompers to John L. Lewis, Nov. 19, 1916, Lewis to Gompers, Nov. 20 and 21, 1916, and Gompers to William B. Wilson, Nov. 23, 1916, all in AFL Papers, Box 23.

17. This led Cyrus McCormick to criticize the President in a letter to his brother Harold: ". . . he has alienated almost the entire business community because of the way he openly espoused the cause of labor and yielded to the threats of labor leaders." Cited in Robert Ozanne, *A Century of Labor-Management Relations at McCormick and International Harvester* (Madison, 1967), 114.

18. For the letter to Gompers see Jones, "Wilson Administration," 88; for the two quotations, John Lombardi, *Labor's Voice in the Cabinet: A History of the Department of Labor from Its Origins to 1921* (New York, 1968 ed.), 104–107, and 75–95 on William B. Wilson.

19. The files of the United States Mediation and Conciliation Service, Record Group 280, National Archives, show how Wilson used former union colleagues; cf. J. S. Smith, "Organized Labor," 276, and Jones, "Wilson Administration," 85–90.

20. The best history of the Commission remains Adams, *Age of Industrial Violence*; a brief, more tendentious summary is in Weinstein, *Corporate Ideal*, chapter 7.

21. In 1916 the Commission Hearings and final report were published in eleven volumes as "Final Report and Testimony Submitted to Congress by the Commission on Industrial Relations," *Senate Document No. 415* (1st Session, 1916). More material can be found in the Frank P. Walsh Papers, New York Public Library, the reports of the investigators in the National Archives, Department of Labor Record Groups 1 and 174, and the CIR records at the SHSW, as well as twenty separate publications based on the field reports.

22. CIR, "Final Report," 1–91; Adams, *Age of Violence*, 215–217; Weinstein, *Corporate Ideal*, 188, 190–191, 208–210; John R. Commons, *Myself* (Madison, 1964), 166–167, 172–173. Weinstein nevertheless concludes that Walsh had no intention of transforming social relations.

23. Adams, *Age of Violence*, 219–220.

24. Arthur S. Link, *Wilson: The New Freedom* (Princeton, 1956), 428–431; Link, *Woodrow Wilson and the Progressive Era, 1910–1917* (New York, 1954), 69–70; Mandel, *Gompers*, 297–300; Gompers, *Seventy Years*, 2: 298–299.

25. A. S. Link, *Wilson and the Progressive Era*, 235–237; Edward Berman, *Labor Disputes and the President of the United States* (New York, 1924), 106–125; K. Austin Kerr, *American Railroad Politics, 1914–1920* (Pittsburgh, 1968), 33–34.

26.   Ronald Radosh, *American Labor and United States Foreign Policy* (New York, 1969), Frank L. Grubbs, Jr., *The Struggle for Labor Loyalty* (Durham, N.C., 1968).

27.   Weinstein, *Corporate Ideal*, chapter 8; David Kennedy, *Over Here: The First World War and American Society* (New York, 1980).

28.   Montgomery, *Workers' Control*, 95–98.

29.   Robert D. Cuff, *The War Industries Board* (Baltimore, 1973).

30.   Robert Bruere, "Copper Camp Patriotism: An Interpretation," *Nation* 106 (Feb. 1918), 236; Robert D. Cuff, "The Politics of Labor Administration in World War I," *Labor History* 21 (Fall 1980), 546–569; E. Berman, *Labor Disputes*, 126–153; J. Lombardi, *Labor's Voice*, 228–259.

31.   Kennedy, *Over Here*, 266–267.

32.   Kennedy's interpretation seems drawn heavily from three articles by Louis B. Wehle: "The Adjustment of Labor Disputes," *Quarterly Journal of Economics* 32 (1917), 122–141; "Labor Problems in the United States, ibid. (1918), 333–392; and "War Labor Policies," ibid. 33 (1919), 321–343. Bernard Baruch succinctly stated Kennedy's view: "While I am in favor of making every possible concession, at the same time we certainly should preserve the *status quo* and not permit anything to be used as a leverage to change conditions from the standpoint either of the employers or the employees." Baruch to William B. Wilson, June 30, 1917, Department of Labor, Record Group 280, File 33/493.

33.   Jones, "Wilson Administration," 343; Mandel, *Gompers*, 366–368.

34.   Lombardi, *Labor's Voice*, 238; Jones, "Wilson Administration," 350–351.

35.   Gompers to Wilson, Aug. 10, 1917, Gompers Letterbooks, 5: 237, Library of Congress; Newton D. Baker to William B. Wilson, Aug. 1, 1917, and Wilson to Baker, Aug. 3, 1917, Department of Labor, Record Group 280, File 33/574; *Survey* 38 (Aug. 11, 1917), 429.

36.   Gompers to Baker, Aug. 22, 1917, Gompers Letterbooks; Gompers to W. B. Wilson, Aug. 27, 1917, W. B. Wilson, memo to President Wilson, Aug. 31, 1917, Woodrow Wilson to N. Baker, Sept. 19, 1917, and Woodrow Wilson to W. B. Wilson, Sept. 19, 1917, Department of Labor, Record Group 174, File 20/473; cf. Meyer H. Fishbein, "The President's Mediation Commission and the Arizona Copper Strike, 1917," *Southwestern Social Science Quarterly* 30 (Dec. 1949), 176ff.; Weinstein, *Corporate Ideal*, 214; Ronald Steel, *Walter Lippmann and the American Century* (Boston, 1980), 112–115.

37.   F. Frankfurter, memo to the Commission, Oct. 5, 1917, Department of Labor, Record Group 174, File 20/473.

38.   *Report of the President's Mediation Commission to the President of the United States, January 9, 1918*; the unpublished hearings and reports of the Commission can be found in Department of Labor, Record Group 280, File 33/517; for more on Frankfurter's role, Harlan B. Phillips, *Felix Frankfurter Reminisces* (New York, 1960), 117–121.

39.   David Brody, *Labor in Crisis: The Steel Strike of 1919* (Philadelphia, 1965), 53; Jones, "Wilson Administration," 363–370.

40.   Jones, "Wilson Administration," 372; Weinstein, *Corporate Ideal*, 248; H. F. Pringle, *The Life and Times of William Howard Taft* (New York, 1939),

2: 916; see Walsh Papers, Box 18; Bureau of Labor Statistics *Bulletin No. 287*, "National War Labor Board" (Washington, 1922).

41. Jones, "Wilson Administration," 381.

42. Brody, *Labor in Crisis*, 58; Lombardi, *Labor's Voice*, 265–292.

43. Brody, *Labor in Crisis*, 61.

44. *Historical Statistics of the United States* (Washington, 1960), Series D 735–740, p. 97; Montgomery, *Workers' Control*, 95–101; Brody, *Labor in Crisis*, 50–51, 60–61; Stanley Shapiro, "The Great War and Reform," *Labor History* 12 (Summer 1971), 334–335.

45. Matthew Josephson, *Sidney Hillman* (New York, 1952), 162–176.

46. United Mine Workers *Journal*, June 21, 1917, 4, Aug. 30, 1917, 6; Melvyn Dubofsky and Warren W. Van Tine, *John L. Lewis* (New York, 1977), 35–37, 42.

47. *Railway Carmen's Journal* 23 (June 1918), 347–348, cited in Stephen Freedman, "The Union Movement in Joliet, Illinois, 1870–1920: Organization and Protest in a Steel-Mill Town," unpublished paper, p. 20; K. Austin Kerr, *American Railroad Politics*, 91–92.

48. David Brody, *The Butcher Workmen: A Study of Unionization* (Cambridge, Mass., 1964), 76–83.

49. Brody, *Labor in Crisis*, 60–61, 63–77.

50. Cited in Shapiro, "The Great War and Reform," 340.

51. Josephson, *Hillman*, 190–193.

52. Cited in Kennedy, *Over Here*, 287.

53. Warren G. Harding to F. E. Scobey, Oct. 25 and Nov. 3, 1919, Harding Papers, Reel 21, Ohio Historical Society.

54. John Morton Blum, *Joe Tumulty and the Wilson Era* (Boston, 1951), 206.

55. Berman, *Labor Disputes*, 154–209; Lombardi, *Labor's Voice*, 306–315; Jones, "Wilson Administration," 436–440.

56. A. Mitchell Palmer to Chamber of Commerce, Moberly, Missouri, Dec. 1, 1919, Department of Labor, Record Group, 174, Box 207; Blum, *Tumulty*, 148–149.

57. On this point see Brody, *Labor in Crisis*, 103–104, 127–128.

58. Brody, *Butcher Workmen*, 85–91; Robert Zieger, *Republicans and Labor, 1919–1929* (Lexington, Ky., 1969), 129 ff.

59. Brody, *Labor in Crisis*, 102–103, 147–178.

60. Dubofsky and Van Tine, *Lewis*, 53–61.

61. Brody, *Workers in Industrial America*, 45.

62. Haggai Hurvitz, "Ideology and Industrial Conflict: President Wilson's First Industrial Conference of October, 1919," *Labor History* 18 (Fall 1977), 516–517, 518–519, 521–522; for a more benign view of the conference, Brody, *Labor in Crisis*, 127–128; on a second Wilson Industrial Conference and its failure, see Gary Dean Best, "President Wilson's Second Industrial Conference, 1919–1920," *Labor History* 16 (Fall 1975), 505–520.

Chapter Nine

The Democratization of Russia's Railroads in 1917

William G. Rosenberg

In explaining the failure of democracy in Russia during the 1917 revolution, Western historians have long emphasized the weakness of representative institutions and traditions and have stressed such influences as the enormous social and economic dislocation brought on by the war, Bolshevik disdain for legality, and Russia's general cultural backwardness, particularly in the countryside. Recent research, some of it contributed by Soviet historians, has allowed these matters to be treated with considerable sophistication.[1] New attention has also focused on aspects of popular (mass) mobilization and the ways in which "bureaucratization from below," especially through networks of popular councils like the soviets, accentuated social polarization, undermined government legitimacy, and helped create a civil war mentality that Lenin's supporters used to great advantage.[2] Still, the prevailing explanation for the failure of democracy remains closely tied to the views of well-known contemporaries like Vasilii Maklakov, the Provisional Government's ambassador to France, or Alexander Kerensky,

Reprinted, with permission, from *American Historical Review* 86, no. 5 (December 1981), 983–1008. An earlier version of this essay was presented at the Second World Congress for Soviet and East European Studies, held in Garmisch-Partenkirchen, West Germany, September 1980.

its last prime minister, who were convinced that Russia received prematurely "more freedom than it could manage" and that "only conspiracy and treacherous armed struggle broke up the provisional regime and stopped the establishment of a democratic system."[3]

This view is both conceptually and analytically weak. To be sure, the institutional weakness of the provisional regime—by now, surely, well enough known to require no rehearsal—played a vital role in the transition to October. So did the war, Bolshevik organizational strength, Russia's economic condition, the social and cultural isolation of the peasantry, and the absence of strong democratic political traditions. But, to understand democracy's failure in 1917 (as well as to comprehend, incidentally, the major contours of the early Bolshevik state), one must recognize that democracy was not merely—perhaps not even largely—a matter of representative politics or civil liberties in the Russian revolution but concerned mass participation in social affairs, popular initiative in resolving a wide range of issues, and the assault on what might be called the social corollaries of autocratic politics: status differentials, privilege, income and welfare inequities, the power of social elites, and, above all, the arbitrariness with which this power was often exercised. As such, democracy or, more precisely, the process of democratization involved decentralized, popular supervision over all aspects of social and public administration by new, mass institutions, which were not necessarily electoral or even formally representative. In the language of the revolution itself, to be a "democrat" was to support popular authority (control by "the democracy") over the dominance of Russia's traditional elites (control by "the society").

The question of democracy's "failure," therefore, needs to be conceptualized and explored not so much in terms of elections, political legitimacy, or Bolshevik conspiracy but in terms of how "democratic" mass organizations performed, the psychology and social objectives of their members, and the ways in which these groups may or may not have been recognized in various quarters as proper components of a new revolutionary order. Most important is a range of issues touching the relationship between democratic mass institutions and the government's formal commitments to democracy in the more common political sense of the term. What, for example, did the end of political authoritarianism imply for authoritarianism in other areas of Russian life? What was the democratic way to organize the workplace in Russian industry? Was it an unwarranted extension of equality to allow employees a voice in factory administration, or did limiting their role to welfare matters simply reinforce a lack of interest and subservience that contributed to low productivity and enhanced authoritarian traditions?

The range of questions can, of course, be expanded, but I focus on labor and industry because my aim here is to explore in some detail the process of democratization as it emerged during 1917 in one vital industrial sector, the railroads, and to examine the relationship between this process and the values and institutions that the Kerensky government struggled unsuccessfully to defend. In doing so, I hope to test the hypothesis that a regime more sympathetic to democracy in the sense of mass participation, perhaps one in which Petrograd Soviet leaders, rather than liberals, were vested early on with full power, might have prevented the failure of political democracy at high levels and facilitated a different revolutionary outcome. I think that it would not; indeed, the very "success" of workers' control on the railroads weakened resistance in this crucial sector to the Bolsheviks' coming to power. More generally, and most importantly, I hope to demonstrate that the failure of democracy in 1917 can only be properly understood in terms of broad conceptualization of Russia's democratic experience.

■ ■ ■

I concentrate on the railroads for several reasons. First, the railroads constituted Russia's most important industry in 1917, both economically and politically. Stretching over some sixty thousand kilometers of track and employing somewhere in the neighborhood of one million people, railroads were the lifeline of Russia's army, the crucial supply link to its cities, the lynchpin in the system of distributing industrial goods and raw materials, and a nerve system of telegraphic and other communication. When not in service, all significant political and economic activity came to a grinding halt. In 1905, a massive general railroad strike amounted to just that, and the strike was one of the decisive steps in forcing the tsar to issue his October Manifesto, promising a constitutional regime. No regime could survive for long if Russia's trains were not running, as Lenin himself recognized. Even armed force could not compensate for the special skills required in railroad operations.

Russia's railroads also epitomized the process of workers' control in 1917. In no other industrial or social sector was there a more dramatic proliferation of influential mass organizations—workers' committees, line congresses, trade unions, craft organizations, and more. By early April there was hardly a depot, shop, station, or administrative office that did not have its own workers' committee. Every one of the country's major private and state-owned lines had "line executive committees" supervising the operation of central administrative offices. On some lines, the committees personally selected new administrative officers (*nachal'niki*) to replace those appointed by the company or those (on state lines) who resigned with the tsar's abdication. On virtually all others, administrative effectiveness depended on the committees' sanction. As many as twenty-five different railroad lines throughout the months between February and October even held representative workers' congresses that established railroad policy, organized workers into additional "democratic" committees, and issued specific directives on railroad operations.[4] Examining the railroads thus permits the exploration of a full range of "democratic" activity "from below."

Third, all Russian railroads in 1917, state-owned and private, were legally under the full control of the government, specifically the Ministry of Transport.[5] And, unlike the situation in other branches, transport officials even in Prince Lvov's first cabinet were committed to extensive employee participation in industry affairs and were strong partisans of a regime closely allied with soviet leadership. From March through July, the transport post was held by the left Kadet, Nicholas Nekrasov, a bitter enemy of conservative liberals even within his own party and a champion of workers' control.[6] Working closely with Kerensky and especially with George Plekhanov, the venerable elder of Russian Marxism whom he appointed to head his most important ministerial commission, Nekrasov strove to create precisely the responsive administration envisioned by those in favor of a popular, worker-oriented regime. Studying the railroads thus permits rather careful testing of the "alternative model" hypothesis.

Finally, railroad workers as a group were not politically radical in 1917, despite the vital role they had played in precipitating the constitutional reforms of 1905. On the contrary, many leftists thought they displayed overwhelmingly a "petty bourgeois" mentality. Bolsheviks had substantial influence in major repair shops, but even here railroaders seemed far less militant than their comrades in other metalworking industries. The vast number of clerks, trainmen, station officials, baggage handlers, engine personnel, and the like appeared solidly behind the Socialist Revolutionaries (SRs), whose supporters also dominated the all-Russian union's executive committee (*Vikzhel'*). Railroaders were, in short, "loyalists" in 1917. Kerensky and others expected them to fight tooth and nail against any unilateral Bolshevik seizure of power. Many have believed this did not happen because Lenin immediately entered into negotiations with *Vikzhel'* leaders and for a time seemed ready to accept their demand for a coalition regime.[7]

But the very range of antagonisms and problems associated with railroad democratization more than likely made a general strike on the lines highly improbable in October, even had one been called. Thus, exploring this particular aspect of the Russian revolution closely should facilitate a clearer understanding of the full dimensions of Russia's democratic experience as a whole.

■ ■ ■

Russia's democratic experience began in the February Revolution with extremely widespread support for a change of government and the creation of some form of representative rule. The strikes and demonstrations in the streets of Petrograd and the crucial decision of garrison soldiers not to suppress the disorders were popular reflections of the deep disaffection running through virtually all levels of Russia's highly stratified social order. Even many monarchists, shocked by the tsar's abdication, recognized the need for a government "commanding everyone's confidence and able to exalt Mother Russia."[8]

This general enthusiasm for change tended to obscure the fact that the nature of the disaffection characterizing Russian society was actually of quite different sorts. Among industrial leaders, Duma representatives, leading gentry elements, and even many state and army figures—that is, "privileged Russia" in general—concern focused on Russia's ability to prosecute the war. Victory was vital to Russia's national interest. The February Revolution's importance to Russia's elite, then, centered on the expectation that the political and administrative impediments to military success could now be overcome. This required both able people in responsible positions and the rationalization of Russia's political and economic apparatus, long the goals of such groups as the War Industries Committees and the Union of Towns and Zemstvos.

Quite a different range of disaffection, however, characterized "ordinary" Russians in early 1917. The impact of the war on the cost of living, on the availability of foodstuffs, and on the cohesion of family life was compounded initially by the indiscriminate mobilization of skilled workers and peasant heads of household and later by the autocracy's inability to manage effectively Russia's transport system, the distribution of scarce materials, or even the proper supply of troops. All such problems produced real privation as well as a growing sense of insecurity. Even temporary factory closings and lockouts threatened workers' well-being (particularly that of the older men and the women), just as orders to the front threatened and frightened garrison soldiers.

Popular disaffection also stemmed from the virtually unlimited powers that many foremen, factory administrators, and other officials held over their employees, paralleling in many ways the power of army officers over their troops. Authoritarianism in the workplace was as little bound by judicial or other restraints as that in the army or government. On the railroads, closely regulated because of their strategic and economic importance, an especially broad range of arbitrary sanctions was used to keep order. On one line, employees were "strictly forbidden to bring charges of any sort in a civil court," since the "resolution of all grievances" was the prerogative of line officials; on another, employees were "strictly forbidden to go into debt," since indebtedness was "immoral" and indicated that "an employee cannot live within his means."[9] Violations brought immediate dismissals. There were also fines, detention, and even imprisonment, all imposed by petty autocrats whose decisions could not be appealed. During one week in January 1917, for example, twenty-six workers on the Riazan-Urals railroad were jailed for an entire week for lateness; forty-eight others were held from one to fourteen days for "negligence on duty and failure to follow regulations."[10] The threat of such sanctions also pressed many railroaders to take dangerous chances—switching and coupling cars on the run, shortcutting road repair work in order to finish it on schedule, running engines without proper repairs. Railroad work, particularly in the yards and shops, was one of Russia's bloodiest occupations, a fact many workers tied directly to the arbitrary powers of their *nachal'niki* ("bosses"), whom they derisively referred to as *tsar i bog*—"caesar and god."

Consequently, among ordinary Russians, especially in urban centers like Moscow and Petrograd, revolution at first had little to do with the question of military victory and only partly concerned the establishment of democratic political institutions in the Western sense. Rather, concern here focused overwhelmingly on ending the power of arbitrary authorities and on taking control, in one form or another, over whatever seemed directly to affect popular welfare. If institutions like the Petrograd Soviet set themselves such supervisory tasks in terms of Provisional Government policies, creating the familiar pattern of "dual power" at the national level, equally consequential was the simultaneous and spontaneous creation of literally thousands of local workers' and soldiers' committees to secure new social relations, material benefits, and individual security.[11]

Moreover, while government-soviet relations became immediately problematic, particularly on the question of war aims, the ways in which these mass organizations reflected differences in the meaning of democracy and revolution were at first barely perceptible. Indeed, workers' committees were initially welcomed by Prince Lvov's cabinet as the appropriate organs for resolving labor-management conflicts and bringing new harmony to Russian industry.[12] This was especially the case with the railroads. The Kadet transport minister, Nicholas Nekrasov, a well-known Central Committee member and spokesman for the party's left wing, had long been an advocate of workers' rights. He believed not only that the revolution "dictated a basic transformation of all institutions" but that this transformation also had to involve popular participation at all levels. Nekrasov saw the roots of railroad deficiencies in excessive centralization, bureaucratic isolation, and *proizvol*—the arbitrary and capricious behavior of railroad officials. "Democratization" was thus the "first task of the new regime," while "democratizing the entire railroad structure," by which Nekrasov meant involving workers directly in line operations, was the "primary means for renewing Russian transport."[13] The result of both of these processes, Nekrasov hoped, would be cooperation, mutual respect, and "a government enjoying the confidence of the people who have called us to power" as well as an improvement in railroad operations.[14] In his view, and in that of Soviet leaders like Nicholas Chkheidze, Michael Skobelev, George Plekhanov, and others, the danger of the new government becoming isolated from popular opinion was as threatening to the success of political democracy as the danger of anarchy or political extremism.

Support for administrative decentralization and employee participation in railroad affairs was shared by the widely respected Conference of Railroad Engineers, which argued in its journal for a shift of responsibility for day-to-day operations to local branch and section organizations, and by the All-Russian Trade Industrial Congress, which met in Moscow on March 19 and passed a resolution endorsing representative "supervisory organs" on the railroads. Responsible local committees of informed, competent employees were seen as the basic answer to "excessive and unworkable central control."[15] General S. A. Ronzhin, a leading railroad specialist, thought reorganizing railroad operations was "absolutely and unconditionally needed"; even a meeting of railroad supervisors in Moscow on March 5 endorsed the idea of local committees to help unsnarl transport problems.[16]

Such a view was certainly compatible with the outlook of Russia's thousands of railroad workers themselves, who in the first weeks of March seized the revolutionary moment to organize literally hundreds of workers' committees in virtually every major junction, depot, or administrative center. As early as March 3, workers on the showcase

Nikolaev line (between Moscow and Petrograd) organized a "Temporary Line Committee" and issued telegrams calling for worker organizations throughout the system.[17] Their example was followed elsewhere almost at once, as news traveled to every corner of the country on the railroad telegraph service. In Ekaterinoslav on March 4, employees of the vital Ekaterininskaia railroad, serving the Don coal basin, issued their own "Order Number One" to announce the formation of a "Provisional Line Committee" with responsibility for controlling railroad operations and convening a workers' congress to organize permanent mass organizations.[18] In Kharkov, Southern railroad workers held their first "Provisional Line Committee" meeting on March 6, and, on the same day in Riazan, workers of the Riazan-Urals railroad committee dispatched "agitators" up and down the line to help organize similar groups and secure support for the government.[19] By the end of March, according to one observer, the drive for organization "so overcame the masses of railroad workers throughout Russia that there did not seem to be a single line, district, or service that remained unorganized."[20]

That this remarkable, spontaneous "democratization" of the lines, as it was heralded at the time, did not initially appear to be at variance with the government's own objectives is a fact of considerable importance in understanding later conflict. Railroad committees seemed to be staffed on the whole with responsible employees committed to "maximum labor productivity," "complete dedication to work," and "strict labor discipline" (Omsk line). They insisted on law and order, and many organized workers' militias to protect the lines in place of the tsarist militia (Moscow-Vindavo-Rybinsk, Riazan-Urals, Moscow-Kursk, Southern, and other lines). A few worked with central line administrations in removing immediate traffic bottlenecks (Northern, Chinese Eastern, and Omsk lines). Committees often appointed persons to replace tsarist administrators who had fled their posts, sometimes in conjunction with management (usually private lines), sometimes not (Moscow-Kazan and other state lines).[21] Most important to those in high places, the railroads seemed institutionally and ideologically committed to close soviet-government relations, the solution Nekrasov and others sought to the problem of dual power. "We consider the Soviet the true representative of the revolutionary proletariat," delegates to the first "Line Congress" of the Moscow-Vindavo-Rybinsk railroad resolved in late March, for example, "but we pledge full support and solidarity to the Provisional Government as well while it fulfills its obligations to the country and works closely with the

Soviet."[22] Similar declarations came from other congresses of railroad delegates, which began to convene line by line on a number of roads in late March and April to organize "permanent" central line committees, confident of government support.[23]

This support was, to be sure, somewhat circumscribed. Nekrasov telegraphed railroaders that "the degree and manner of employee representation in railroad administration" could not be resolved officially until the nation elected a permanent government and asked that "no steps be taken immediately that might interfere with regular railroad operations."[24] Others, like the engineers, stressed workers' participation but not supervisory control. The significant point is not, however, that support "from above" was qualified but that railroaders presumed broad backing for their efforts and saw in this an apparent unity between government and soviet leaders. As Ekaterininskaia railroad workers wired enthusiastically back to Nekrasov, "not only" would they "refrain from independent steps," but their own newly elected soviet of line deputies would also "pass a special resolution to this effect!"[25] And, as the *Izvestiia* of railroad workers in Moscow reported, "even our supervisors on private lines as well as those under state control" recognized the necessity for organization, "and so we have organized."[26] On the Southern line, workers even declared strikes to be an "unacceptable" method of resolving grievances "before the successful completion of the war."[27]

There was also some indication that employee participation was helping to ease the transport crisis. The number of freight cars hauled in daily service increased from an average of sixty-six thousand in February to seventy-three thousand in March, seventy-five thousand in April, and seventy-six thousand in May. Statistics on car loadings showed increases of 14 and 19 percent for March and April in comparison to the figures for February. The number of locomotives in service also increased.[28] What seemed most impressive about this process, moreover, was not merely the level of cooperation between government and labor but also the manner in which personnel at all levels apparently functioned well under the supervision of representative workers' committees, despite the incredible number of these organizations that had sprung up on the lines. "Democratization" in the sense of broad worker participation in railroad industry affairs thus seemed capable of achieving both what the upper reaches of society undersood as the goals of a democratic Russia (the successful prosecution of the war, responsible government, and the rule of law) and what most workers on the railroads and elsewhere saw as a democratic solution to the root causes of their own disaffection (material deprivation, personal insecurity, and the extensive and arbitrary powers of officials).

■ ■ ■

Appearances can be—and were—misleading. Beneath surface unity, powerful countervailing pressures were already moving to disjoin this "loyalist" labor army from supporting government and soviet leaders alike. At the outset, these pressures had little to do directly with national politics. The first major crisis of the revolutionary period—in April, over dual power and the war—led to a redefinition of Russia's war aims and the formation of a liberal-socialist coalition. But these changes, if anything, seemed to strengthen the position of men like Nekrasov and their hopes for a responsive, popular regime. What was happening instead was twofold:

First, the proliferation of workers' control organizations was creating what might be called a broadly based "syndicalist mentality" on the part of committee members, who were reluctant to yield to any outside authority and increasingly willing to countenance popular actions without regard to normative judicial or governmental processes. With Lenin's return to Russia in early April, the Bolsheviks played an increasingly important role in stimulating these attitudes, but such views were not of their making. At the first Conference of Petrograd Factory Committees in May, for example, which brought together more than 560 delegates from dozens of plants, Jacob Sverdlov, Grigorii Zinoviev, and Lenin himself led a blistering attack on the Menshevik minister of labor Skobelev and others, like Nekrasov, who insisted on a peaceful resolution of industrial conflict. Not surprisingly, Bolshevik railroaders echoed these sentiments on a number of lines, particularly those like the Nikolaev and the Moscow-Kursk, which served the capitals. Yet the sense of autonomy and disdain for outside authority that was coming to characterize the committees' outlook stemmed more from the very power and importance these organizations were acquiring in daily affairs. It made little sense to waste time appealing to government or even soviet agencies when crucial issues could and had to be decided on the spot. And particularly on the railroads, where workers' control had official sanction and seemingly broad government-soviet support, a syndicalist approach appeared to be precisely suited to Russia's revolutionary needs.

Second, these attitudes on the part of the committees intensified a growing friction between different categories of railroad workers themselves, a friction not readily apparent to those who tended to see all railroaders as a unified and harmonious labor "family," as it was often called. In fact, this family was highly stratified by profession, income, well-being, and a variety of social distinctions associated with rank. These divisions had a structural basis in the ten or so individual "services" into which all railroad workers were categorized. The two largest of these, the traction service (*sluzhba tiagi*) and the roadway service (*sluzhba puti*) included the largest numbers of shop workers and ordinary laborers; the operations, telegraph, supply, administration, and other services had relatively small percentages of the total railroad work force but had the majority of educated clerks and white-collar workers, "grey-collar" train personnel (conductors, trainmen), station masters, ticket sellers, and the like, many of whom prided themselves (with little obvious reason) on the importance and social distinction of their jobs, as "evidenced" by their fancy uniforms. Engine drivers in particular carried with them the aura of a labor elite—an "aristocracy" in the use of the term as popularized by the Bolsheviks. Comprising less than 4 percent of the total railroad work force, engine drivers earned on the average more than twice the wages of firemen, who worked with them in the cabs in a clearly subservient relationship, and almost five times the wages of greasemen, car cleaners, or ordinary watchmen. Along with shop and depot workers and ordinary laborers of the roadway service, personnel in these categories stood at the bottom of the railroaders' social spectrum and were often treated contemptuously by the "aristocratic" drivers and the officious petty "service intelligentsia" in ticket bureaus and administrative offices up and down the lines.[29]

The organization of workers' committees on the railroads reflected, and soon reinforced, these occupational and social divisions. The evidence indicates that most committees sprang up initially either among yard and repair workers in shops and depots or among clerks and other employees in administrative centers; but administrative personnel soon began to dominate the provisional and then the permanent central line committees—that is the *principal* organs of workers' control.[30] This dominance followed logically from the committees' administrative tasks, most of which required special skills and technical expertise not generally held by lower-level employees. Typically, the committees met three or four times a week to consider complex administrative issues: methods of improving traffic and productivity; the question of train lengths and their relationship to goods traffic and safety; technical deficiencies in line operations; and so forth. Like the soviets, they received a constant stream of delegations from various lower-level shop, depot, trade, and station organizations, which presented specific grievances and demands; and they generally responded either by forming special commissions or by taking various issues up directly with managerial personnel.

Yet, as rank-and-file workers organized themselves by shop and depot and as engine drivers and conductors held meetings to discuss specific professional problems (more often than not, incidentally, at the urging of the provisional central line committees and their "organizational-agitational" commissions), the question of the central line committees' own ability to defend particular workers' interests naturally came into question. This issue usually emerged first at the various congresses of line workers, which initially convened in April and early May. Here, more direct issues of pay rates for particular trades and services, hours, responsibility for line problems, personnel, and the like were raised along with political issues: support for the war and the liberty loan; elections to local dumas; and the questions of a Russian republic and the Constituent Assembly. Some delegates heatedly insisted these latter questions were not properly within the railroaders' provenance; others challenged the "territorial" (as opposed to "trades") principle on which central line committees were organized and urged their organizations to take a more partisan stance in defense of particular "professional" interests and, as a group of workers on the Moscow-Kursk line put it, to become something more than a "dead skeleton without a political soul."[31] On lines like the Moscow-Kursk and the Nikolaev, more radical committees responded by openly resolving to "strengthen ties with Russia's proletarians and peasants" and supporting the "equalization of the economic circumstances of all employees"; but committee members like those on the Alexandrovsk line, who early came to the realization that "antagonism between senior agents of the operations service and those on the traction service" was itself "one of the main elements" affecting line operations, clearly saw the dangers of "professionalism" at the expense of a more general, territorial, and intratrade approach to problems.[32]

Questions concerning the nature and limits of committee authority thus began to emerge in the spring of 1917 not only from above—in government and soviet circles—but also among railroad committee members themselves. In response to these "sectarian" pressures from below, moreover, main line organizations gradually began to press for an extension of their own power. Against management, they insisted on the right to discharge unpopular personnel (Alexandrovsk line, Chinese Eastern line, Moscow-Kursk line, and many others), although they generally accepted "suspension pending investigation" as a compromise solution. They also tried to respond to particular grievances (such as introducing a three-shift system for switching personnel and limiting the allowable running time for locomotive brigades), although here, too, there was a willingness to wait until the question was settled by the government.[33] More important, the committees also pressed against lower-level groups, insisting to the increasing number of professionally sectarian organizations along the lines that their own authority was, and had to be, paramount.

Consequently, new complaints soon began to be heard from below about central line committees "usurping" workers' prerogatives, "interfering with and ignoring the competency of local groups," or ignoring worker interests by failing, or example, to abolish piece rates in railroad shops.[34] In response to this growing unrest, moreover, central line committees themselves began to demand even greater unity and discipline. Some even insisted that they themselves had the right to levy fines and impose other disciplinary sanctions in the traditional way. And while conductors, ticket sellers, engine drivers, and various other categories of workers began to sense here the reaffirmation of prerevolutionary authoritarianism on the lines (a feeling that intensified in late spring and early summer when railroad performance again began to decline), a number of central line committees, for their part, pressed the government for an even further extention of their powers. As one committee spokesman declared to government officials who believed railroad committees should restrict themselves to welfare issues, "Open your eyes! You are blind! Life has already given us the power to organize and control railroad life, and you do not even see it!"[35]

— — —

To appreciate how troublesome these charges were for Nekrasov and other supporters of workers' control, who continued to hope that a regime responsive to popular interests could bring stability and order to revolutionary Russia, we need to recognize that democratization of the railroads still represented a "success" in the spring of 1917, in contrast to deteriorating situations elsewhere. In the countryside, peasants were refusing to cooperate with government-organized land committees and were seizing estates with increasing frequency and rapacity. The new socialist minister of labor Skobelev, whose post was established with the organization of the first coalition cabinet in early May, found it almost impossible to resolve critical industrial conflicts, particularly in the Don region and the Urals. By early summer, almost half of the metal-working and mining plants in these areas had closed.[36] On April 23, the provisional regime had officially recognized the right of workers to set up committees in industrial enterprises of every kind, but in many places factory owners responded with lockouts, blamed (with at least some degree of legitimacy) on the absence of materials and the increased costs of production. For those who valued the revolution essentially in terms of military victory and responsible, representative political institutions, these developments were ominous in the extreme. For those oriented as well toward popular interests, the growing syndicalist outlook of groups like the railroad line committees represented a challenge that had to be faced head on.

Together with his socialist colleagues, Nekrasov soon developed what was, in effect, a comprehensive response based implicitly on the soviet principles that workers had a right to participate in industrial administration, that workers' control on the railroads was both necessary and desirable for effective line operations, that cooperation between workers and management was crucial to Russia's political and economic future, and that serious efforts had to be made to diminish unjust wage inequalities and improve material conditions. Though not articulated as such, Nekrasov's program (and, hence, government policy) was essentially comprised of three interrelated parts: what might be called the "statization" of railroad workers' organizations; the limitation of committee authority; and the equalization of railwaymen's wages.

First, Nekrasov pressed the idea that the railroads, as Russia's lifeline and most vital industry, had an importance extending far beyond normal bounds and had to be regarded as institutions of "state competence and significance." This justified his extending state regulations to all private lines in late March and early April and using the transport ministry's administrative apparatus to facilitate the formation of an all-Russian railroad union, whose leaders would work closely with ministerial personnel committed "to revolutionary democracy"— whose "official representative," he declared, "I consider myself."[37] Hence Nekrasov circulated through the ministry's own network all declarations and appeals of the Petrograd Soviet's railroad commission. He brought Soviet representatives into its various committees, a move he thought "both logical and necessary"; and, in early April, he began to make funds available to the organizers of an all-Russian railroad union, supporting a provisional conference and funding the operations of the "Provisional Union Executive Committee," the forerunner of *Vikzhel'*. Thousands of rubles may have been spent for this purpose.[38] Despite attacks from other ministers and members of his own party, who accused him of "stabbing them in the back," Nekrasov argued enthusiastically for the role an "autonomous state union" could play in railroad affairs. As he told a huge gathering of workers at the

Bolshoi Theater in early May, railroaders would not follow traditional paths, since they were limited by law in terms of competence and activities. The All-Russian Railroad Union would be autonomous, "with state significance [*gosudarstvennoe znachenie*] acquired not because official state representatives participated . . . but because railroad workers themselves operate with railroads, which are the vital nerve of the whole country as well as national property, the property of the whole nation."[39]

Second, Nekrasov moved to delineate clearly the limits of workers' committees' competence, insisting on the need for "strict revolutionary discipline." In late May, he issued a special Circular Instruction 6321, comparable in the eyes of some observers to the Petrograd Soviet's famous Army Order Number One.[40] Circular 6321 officially sanctioned existing railroad workers' committees but only as individual units of the All-Russian National Railroad Union; specific powers were consequently left to the determination of that organization's national congress, scheduled for late July. Meanwhile, line committees were to continue to have broad competence, but they could not issue instructions or orders unless specifically authorized by law, which included dismissing railroad administrators and electing their replacements. Hundreds of administrators had been discharged from the lines in the first months of the revolution, and Nekrasov's circular was designed to end this process (although the minister himself felt that, up until May, these dismissals were justified in "ninety out of one hundred cases").[41] The circular thus officially sanctioned the committees, but within a limited range of action.

Finally, in addition to "statization" and the joint legislation and limitation of committee authority, Nekrasov and soviet leaders moved together to equalize railroad wages and to relieve the hardship of lower-echelon employees. Since early March, the joint soviet-ministry commission under George Plekhanov had been working on a comprehensive solution to the wage issue, but in early May it decided that the situation of many railroaders had become desperate and that a series of emergency interim measures was necessary—and possible under the law. These involved, essentially, the distribution of a new "war bonus" of not less than one hundred rubles in districts with the highest cost of living and not less than forty rubles in the least expensive districts, heavily weighted in favor of lower-paid workers. The commission recognized that these funds were quite "inadequate" but still expected that they would "provide immediate assistance to the most needy sectors of the railroad work force."[42] From some government and liberal quarters, the Plekhanov bonus brought howls of complaint about pandering to worker militance and the weakening treasury; but, to Nekrasov, Plekhanov, and other supporters of a responsive regime, wage equalization and pay increases were a necessary adjunct to "statization" and the limitation of committee competence as a means of bringing the whole issue of mass organizations on the railroads under firm leadership and control.

▬ ▬ ▬

With hindsight it is clear that these policies, though necessary from the standpoint of regularizing railroad committee activities, maintaining productivity, and responding to worker grievances, also intensified the broader pressures of social polarization that in the early summer of 1917 began to rip Russia apart. As the regime launched its ill-fated June offensive, and then found itself beset by the Bolsheviks' attempt to seize power in July and the collapse of the first coalition, attacks in the liberal press on peasant and worker anarchism were accompanied by growing unease in government and soviet circles alike about the continued efficacy of workers' control at a time of dwindling state resources, disaster at the front, and the simple inability of Russia to meet its pressing economic needs. In scores of worker meetings and line congresses, events prompted new questions about "whose railroads" and "whose revolution" railroaders were supporting, but members of Russia's liberal and socialist intelligentsia found themselves increasingly pressured both toward greater support for state authority and toward still further restraints on committees and other forms of mass participation. This brought soviet and government figures closer together, lessening the consequences of dual power at the national level (particularly with the formation of the second coalition under Kerensky in July), but intensifying the sharpening division between the "democratic" commitments and goals of ordinary workers and peasants and those of most national leaders. It also engendered an increasingly strong sense of betrayal among those who thought in March and April that their national leaders stood firmly behind workers' control.

This polarization can clearly be seen on the railroads in the dramatically harder line toward committees taken after the publication of Circular 6321 by such groups as the State Council on Transport and the Association of Private Railroads as well as in the attitudes of government and soviet officials themselves. In late June, for example, as administrators on the Nikolaev line were meeting with the line's central committee to "resolve questions of their mutual cooperation," the vice minister of transport Takhtemyshev suddenly "electrified" the gathering with a scathing attack on the "outrages" of the committee, its "rapacious, malicious attitude," and its unwarranted demand for "self-government."[43] In the State Council on Transport, the railroads were described as in "total chaos," "covered with Bolshevik propaganda," "oblivious to all authority," and "bent on seizing power"—charges that were, at best, grossly exaggerated. Some of the recent dislocation on the lines, in fact, was the result of demobilizing soldiers commandeering trains or of various officials insisting they had priority in the allocation of equipment—problems that line committees, in most places, were struggling valiantly to control.[44] In any event, the basic causes of railroad dislocation antedated the revolution, as transport officials had themselves recognized in February.

Yet, despite these attacks and the growing problems and dangers of day-to-day railroad operations, railroaders as a whole generally remained "loyalist" in the summer of 1917, supporting the war in their congresses and meetings, condemning the July Days, still pledging support for the Petrograd Soviet and the coalition regime. In some places contributions for the government's Liberty Loan were even deducted automatically from salaries and wages, with little or no protest.[45] Consequently, these broad patterns do not fully—or even primarily—provide an explanation for the transition from February to October on the railroads. Indeed, these developments suggest that railroaders might have supported to a greater extent the all-Russian union and Nekrasov's policy of "statization" as well as the coalition regime and its minister of transport.

But the results of Nekrasov's and the soviet leadership's efforts weakened, rather than strengthened, railroader support. Each of their "solutions" provoked not social or political harmony but new antagonism and new difficulties. And, in coping with these new problems, commitments to "democratization" in the sense of mass participation and control became fundamentally incompatible with efforts to establish a stable democratic political order, while Bolshevik rule for tens of thousands of "loyalist" railroaders became an acceptable, if not entirely desirable, alternative.

Let us first examine the problem of wage equalization. The ministry's policy here undoubtedly stemmed from a special concern about militant shop and depot workers. Wage levels for these positions were generally below those for comparable job categories in other industries. Shop workers were vocal in their demands for wage increases in March and April and repeatedly threatened to strike. Raising their wages, therefore, seemed politically prudent as well as compatible with socialist ideals.

   Yet the basis on which the Plekhanov bonus was calculated remained the piece rate. With increasing shortages of supplies, the
frequent absence of technicians and skilled workers (many of whom
were off as delegates to conferences and meetings!), and the influx of
returning workers from the spontaneously demobilizing army, new
declines in shop productivity occurred, and the real gains from
bonuses calculated on a piece-rate basis sharply decreased. Workers
most favored by the bonus consequently remained dissatisfied. They
demanded hourly or daily wages and an end to piece rates based on
output. Even socialist officials like Plekhanov, however, could not
support state interference in such a essential feature of shop administration as this without doing violence to principles of political democracy and the rule of law; now, as earlier, factory administrators remained convinced that the piece-rate system was the last best defense
against further disastrous declines in productivity. For those opposed
to piece rates, therefore, the only alternative was to attempt to change
fundamentally Russia's political and socioeconomic structure—in
other words, to take over completely shop administration and to establish, in effect, a socialist order, which was precisely what the Bolsheviks
wanted to do.
   The very effort to equalize wages and reduce differentials,
moreover, offended many skilled railroaders, who cherished their
various petty privileges and perquisites. The engine drivers in particular reacted angrily to news that unskilled assistants would get relatively greater increases than themselves. Their reaction on some lines
was to climb down from their cabs. Other workers and employees were
also indignant, especially about efforts to ameliorate the conditions of
road repair gangs, traditionally the lowest group in the railroad social
hierarchy.[46] On this issue, given the importance of skilled, upper-
echelon employees to railroad operations, the regime soon felt forced
to promise a new series of bonuses for skilled labor categories; but, by
mid-August, the situation had not been resolved, and a new series of
brief but crippling strikes by drivers occurred. By pressing wage
equalization, the left liberal-socialist leadership was thus pulling
threads in the railroaders' rather closely woven social fabric, kinking
one rank as another was tugged out of line. Hierarchy remained
important among many workers, despite radical revolutionary commitments and deepening animosity toward privileged "bourgeois"
society.
   One consequence of this was to reinforce particularistic tendencies among the railroaders' multifarious occupational groups, prompting different groups of workers to begin organizing their own "union

of conductors" or "union of locomotive engineers" to defend their special interests. These "ribbon unions," as they were called, had begun to proliferate like spring mushrooms in April and early May, much to the consternation of central line committees, ministry officials, and all-Russian union organizers alike. In early summer, with joint soviet-government efforts to equalize wages, they suddenly became a great deal more attractive as a means to satisfy special interests at precisely the moment when the regime was attempting to unite all railroaders in a single national union and bring order to committee activities by making them national union cells. And the popularity of the "ribbon unions" came, paradoxically, largely in response to sympathetic government actions.

A second result of these government efforts, however, was even more consequential. It centered on the question of limiting committee authority. In this instance, again paradoxically, although Plekhanov, Nekrasov, and others were convinced that the committees were still the best place to solve wage and productivity issues, the limitations placed on the committees' competence greatly affected their ability to do so. On the one hand, line administrators began immediately after the publication of Circular 6321 to by-pass the committees and reassert their personal authority. "Before 6321," a representative from the Riazan-Urals line told the railroad union leaders in July, for example, "the administration worked closely with us and came to discuss important matters. After the instruction was issued, attitudes changed completely. Administrators began to refuse to meet with us and regarded us with hostility."[47] Here and elsewhere, *nachal'niki* reasserted sweeping powers, relying on past traditions and laws. Orders "had to be obeyed without the slightest reservation"; committee members were "forbidden absolutely to interfere in the issuing of line directives" and were permitted "only to express their personal views" under threat of dismissal.[48] On the Northern railroad, *nachal'niki* who had continued in their positions after the February Revolution with the express approval of the line committee now issued orders forbidding any criticism of the provisional regime, any opposition to the military offensive, or "the incitement of one group of the population against another." All violators were to be "prosecuted for treason."[49]

On the other hand, many railroad workers properly understood the central line committees' declining authority in the eyes of soviet and government officials and, after 6321, began themselves to by-pass their own organizations in pressing their complaints. An "enormous number" of persons began coming directly to the transport ministry with their problems, according to the ministry's socialist secretary,

"ignoring the very basis of all-Russian railroad union organization."
Thousands more sent letters and telegrams. By mid-July, almost eight
thousand cables had been received from telegraph operators, asking
the ministry directly about such individual matters as when they would
"finally" be given a vacation.[50]

This circumvention of the line committees led, of course, to
additional fragmentation among railroad workers and accelerated the
growth of "ribbon unions," but it also pressed central line committees
to assert their authority further—by insisting on new powers of dismissal and other sanctions, which they did not legally possess. Here the
social position of most committee members came into play. Many
clerks, engineers, and even jurists and medical personnel among committee members were deeply concerned about Russia's national interests and identified with the intelligentsia generally, rather than with
ordinary workers. For them the question was not so much a reform in
the nature of authority on the lines and in the workplace but a determination of who should exercise this authority in order to produce the
highest level of transport efficiency. Yet such actions also pressed more
militant local committees into demanding further "democratization."

If the goals of wage equalization and the delineation of committee authority were thus contradicted by consequent particularization
and social antagonism on the lines, the third element of the "model"
government-soviet approach—organization of an all-Russian railroad
union with state or governmental significance (*gosudarstvennoe znachenie*)—generated still another range of problems. *Gosudarstvennoe
znachenie* was certainly not a clear expression. It appealed to syndicalist
attitudes among railroad committeemen by implying a union with
governmental powers or, at least, a union whose resolutions and decisions the government would implement into law with little discussion
or change; and the organizers of the all-Russian railroad congress
certainly understood it this way in March and April, when it was first
used. But Nekrasov's speech at the Bolshoi Theater in early May made
it clear that "statization" meant a good deal less than assigning a
national railroad union full governmental powers. Since state competence derived from the fact that railroads were "the property of the
entire people," Nekrasov claimed, railroad workers would acquire
through their union "a special state significance that, on the one hand,
will give their union special rights but, on the other, will impose special
responsibilities . . . *and the duty to fulfill special state tasks.*"[51] These "special
rights," Nekrasov elaborated further, included "autonomy" and the
determination of a broad range of welfare issues, such as wage rates, at

the union's all-Russian congress, but the "special responsibilities" clearly meant obedience to government directives.

In many ways, the response of rank-and-file railroaders to these dubious advantages of "statization" was predictable. No substantial powers were actually granted to union leaders that other trade unions did not enjoy, while "special state responsibilities" implied that railroaders could not oppose government policies. And, indeed, Nekrasov's speech was met immediately by a strong rebuttal from S. V. Dvumiantsev, the prominent SR chairman of the Moscow-Kursk central line committee and a leading Moscow labor organizer: state significance without state power, he argued angrily, meant simply that the union would become a government instrument.[52] This view was shared not only by militant shop and depot workers but also by the staunchly loyalist union of railroad engineers and technicians, one of the few professional associations allowed to function under the tsar. The engineers agreed that railroaders had to subordinate their professional interests to those of the state but could not see how this could be done effectively without union leaders becoming, in effect, state officials—a view shared by many of the provisional *Vikzhel'* members themselves. "Statization" meant to them, in other words, that the railroad union should become a state agency, something the government could not and would not allow.[53]

Assigning "government significance" to the railroad union, moreover, led directly to two further problems: one concerning the extent to which the union leadership (in its social and occupational composition) was representative, and one concerning the government's own policies. The provisional executive committee elected at the all-Russian union's April conference was not, in fact, a broadly representative body, any more so than were many of the railroad line committees. Its fifteen members included only two grey- and three blue-collar workers; and its five-man presidium was composed of three jurists, one engineer, and one high-ranking administrative office worker. But, as P. Vompe of the Nikolaev line argued in *Mysli Zheleznodorozhnika*, it behaved like a *khoziain* ("master"), sending telegrams and directives up and down the lines and acting like a governmental agency when, in fact, it was at best a consultative organ.[54] Indeed, in these circumstances various categories of railroaders could quite logically wonder whether their particular needs might better be served by ordinary trade unions not burdened with special state responsibilities. Similarly, the notion of subordinating railroad workers' interests to the state could quite understandably raise broad political questions. Minister Nekrasov's "solution" presumed an essential nonpartisanship in railroader outlooks, but this was no more realistic here than it was with the military; and, in fact, the government did not want a disinterested neutrality on the issues of the day, but active support.

Hence, "statization," which was also being pressed at this time by the socialist minister of labor Skobelev for other vital industries, necessarily injected politics into questions of union structure and organization, while it also greatly intensified already existing proclivities toward occupational professionalization. Discussions about the union's competence led to arguments about state policies and to the formation of Socialist Revolutionary, Menshevik, and other party caucuses in line congresses and committees—including, of course, caucuses dominated by Bolsheviks. On June 18, a conference of Socialist Revolutionary railroad workers convened in Moscow; in early July, other party organizations began to draft their own statements and proposals for presentation to the all-Russian congress.[55] Meanwhile, "ribbon unions" of telegraphers, shop and depot workers, engine drivers, conductors, and other railroad occupations expanded rapidly. The whole notion of an all-embracing national railroad union itself came under attack as these "sectarian" groups, despite competing interests, shared the conviction that all workers would best be served by professional unions in the traditional sense, with the government in the adversary role of "management." And, as line committee members and other all-Russian union delegates prepared for the first national railroad congress in July, the "professionalists" also gathered in their meetings and prepared to bring their case for aggressive shop unionism to the broader railroad work force.

- - -

The extended government crisis after the July Days and the collapse of the military offensive represented an important turning point in Russia's transition from February to October. Organized only after intensive negotiations among various leading social groups, the new coalition cabinet was committed both to reestablishing firm state authority and to retaining strong soviet support; but its socialist complexion and its commitment to soviet programs were hardly adequate grounds for building a strong popular base, and its concessions to those like General Kornilov, determined to restore military discipline and state authority, failed to restrain the deepening hostility of "bourgeois" and "privileged" Russia. Popular support for the Bolsheviks increased even as Trotsky and others were arrested and Lenin went into hiding; many liberals and others temporized their commitments to political democracy and began seriously to consider alternative forms of state power.[56] While Kerensky's new cabinet thus became even less identified with the popular meaning of February, it also became increasingly unacceptable to those who legitimized the revolution in terms of Russia's national interests, and this, in part, because of its very coalition character. In a phrase, the sociopolitical foundations of the civil war were being set firmly in place.

In these circumstances, and against a background of increasing disruption and disorganization on the railroads, of potentially catastrophic declines in transport operations, and of growing worker demoralization, the nature of committee control on the railroads came under new challenge from masses of workers and "privileged" elements alike, one for failing to meet popular needs and the other for contributing to "anarchy" and "chaos." Nekrasov soon resigned. Plekhanov retired from the scene with an ambiguous statement insisting that the transport ministry would not "for one minute fail to meet the just demands of railroad laborers."[57] As late as August, Nekrasov's successor as minister of transport, P. P. Iurenev, continued to argue publicly that the desperate situation on the railroads was not of recent or "accidental" origin but the cumulative result of "deep organic difficulties" in the way that the railroads had been run for years.[58] Yet confidence in the process of democratization, badly eroded on all sides, was undermined, most importantly, among many railroaders themselves. "I am practically starving, comrades," a bookkeeper wrote in Ausust to one railroad journal, for example:

I have exhausted all loans, and tomorrow will have nothing whatsoever even for a small scrap of bread. I won't discuss the causes of such conditions—they are known to all. I only want to point out that, as a bookkeeper, I am considered to be somewhat more privileged (at 150 rubles a month) than a majority of my fellow workers, and I am therefore not alone at the brink of starvation. . . . What is going to be done? I know very well that the government has gone through a ministerial crisis and that there is no chance of finding the means to increase my salary. . . . Yet all of us railroad workers desperately need food and fuel for the winter. I feel that catastrophe is upon us.[59]

Under such circumstances, "democracy" in the sense of mass participation undoubtedly retained its emotive content, as social polarization intensified in Russia at large, but its practical meaning either as a system of representative institutions or as a society committed to popular participation and welfare was increasingly unclear.

One dramatic consequence was the rapid increase in the process of professional sectarianism among railroad workers (*tsekhovshchina* ["shopism" or "craft consciousness"] was the term some used), accentuating social differences between different labor groups and highlighting material inequities. The "pernicious lure of professionalism," as one commentator called it, which had earlier given rise to scores of "ribbon unions," now became intense.[60] Organizations of this sort grew quickly. The strongest were unions of shop and depot workers in Moscow and Petrograd, which expanded with close Bolshevik support. When the All-Russian Railroad Congress opened in mid-July, these workers even refused at first to participate; and they were active in the massive protest against Kerensky's State Conference in August. In September, they developed close contacts with the Bolshevik-dominated metal workers. Some saw this process resulting essentially from Bolshevik "subversion"; but the relationship between workers' control on the railroads and professional particularism and the growing disillusionment over the ability of a responsive and popular government to satisfy worker demands were far more important. In some cases, labor sectarianism did not even mean antagonism to important government goals, even among "Bolshevized" shop workers. In early September, for instance, a congress of shop workers on the Southern railroad insisted without qualification on workers' control over all areas of production "as the only way to pull Russia out of its current morass," but among the other demands of the one hundred or so delegates was also the "immediate introduction of universal obligatory labor [*trudovaia povinnost'*]" as a means of increasing productivity.[61]

Other restricted and militant "ribbon unions" also expanded rapidly. Enrollment in *Madzhel'*, a new union of "lower-ranking railroad employees," increased dramatically in August.[62] Conductors and switchmen also organized, and they lodged strong protests with the Petrograd Soviet over the way national union leaders and government officials seemed to be ignoring their interests.[63] One of the most important and militant groups, seemingly disdainful of all authorities above them, remained the relatively well-paid engine drivers, the railroad "aristocrats," who strongly resented the government's efforts to reduce wage differentials. When a new bonus system was announced in August by the vice-minister of transport Ustrugov that again failed to meet engine-driver demands, the drivers threatend to strike all lines in the Moscow and Petrograd junctions.[64]

What appeared to many as political radicalism on the railroads was thus most of all an aggressive sectarian defense against the failure of "legitimate" authorities to protect diverse workers' interests. The response of many line committee and national union leaders in turn, however, was to emphasize the danger of "Bolshevism" and political fragmentation, to insist more forcefully than ever that they themselves represented Russian state interests, and that the all-Russian union as a whole had to enjoy official state competence. "There can be no doubt that railroad workers are possessed in the main with a concern for state interests, with state-oriented rationality," one of the all-Russian union leaders, Malitskii, argued in support of this effort. The all-Russian union could not, therefore, be simply a professional association but "a state organ, having tasks of a public-legal character . . . and bearing full responsibility for the operation of the entire railroad industry not only in the interest of railroad employees but in the interests of the entire nation."[65] The shop and craft orientation of rank-and-file railroaders, in other words, was being countered by an equally forceful syndicalist outlook on the part of leading committeemen and union activists.

These differences sharply divided railroaders during the early sessions of the All-Russian Railroad Congress in July, particularly as a parade of government and soviet officials alike stressed the importance of maintaining the war effort and postponing welfare benefits; but, by the time the sessions closed in August and a new executive committee, *Vikzhel'*, had been elected, the predominant view favored giving the union state powers. Editorial writers in *Birzhevyia Vedomosti, Rech'*, and the liberal press in general consequently saw the congress and *Vikzhel'* as a clear indication of the dangers of labor radicalism in 1917, the culmination of dangerous and destructive "anarcho-syndicalism." The railroads were cynically deemed an "independent republic."[66] In fact, however, what the congress epitomized was not a drive for labor independence so much as the problems and contradictions in the efforts of moderate socialists and left liberals like Plekhanov and Nekrasov to find a solution to the problem of revolutionary power in 1917, as well as to the disjunction between the "democratization" of Russian social institutions and the requirements of political democracy. *Vikzhel'* reflected essentially an instrument of the weakened coalition regime's last hopes to build some degree of institutional support among vital sectors of Russian labor rather than an aggressive new force of worker radicalisn. Its base at the all-Russian congress was overwhelmingly the upper levels of the railroad labor hierarchy, where "persons with administrative authority" constituted 25.5 percent of the delegates; office workers, 21 percent; jurists, teachers, engineers, and technicians, 19 percent; and line and shop workers, only 15 percent. Most important, the congress also firmly rejected the "professional" or "craft" principle of union organization. It refused outright to seat delegates from the twelve "professional" unions demanding admission (and representing more than one-third of the work force), and it adopted a formula describing itself as a *pravochno-publichno* ("public-legal") institution with state responsibilities, essentially echoing the government's view. With "stormy applause," it rejected as "legend" the idea that railroaders intended to by-pass the regime and take complete control of the lines, pledging full support to Kerensky's "government of national salvation."[67]

Yet in September, when it became apparent that Kerensky's government did not think it possible to implement the new wage scales adopted by the railroad congress and more militant employees at various levels increasingly threatened a nationwide strike, the syndical-ist orientation of committee members and *Vikzhel'* represented to many inside the government and out the complete collapse of state authority and national order. Again, *Vikzhel's* efforts were overwhelmingly aimed at gaining control over the "pernicious lure of professionalism" in order to contain strikers, at "taking over the leadership of the strike movement" in order to prevent a total strike on the railroads, which might include the termination of military and food supply transport, and at "conducting any strike with minimum ill effects."[68] As an edito-rial in the newspaper *Volia i Dumy Zheleznodorozhnika*, the organ of the Moscow-Kursk workers' committee, argued, it made no sense for rank-and-file railroaders to struggle against state authority, since the latter was, in effect, based in the all-Russian union: "to struggle with author-ities established by the people is to struggle with ourselves, and that would be absurd."[69]

- - -

Exactly such statements, of course, became the central arguments of Bolshevik authorities after October as they repressed worker inde-pendence, and the irony here illustrates rather dramatically how the democratization of Russia's railroads brought advantages to Lenin's followers. Even without exploring the question in detail, how the Bolsheviks' coming to power gained a degree of acquiescence far greater than their actual level of support becomes understandable: by attacking union leaders for identifying with state interests, by castigat-ing moderate central line committees for their close relations with government officials and for their "usurpation" of local committee powers, and, above all, by supporting the particularistic interests of diverse railroad labor groups, the Bolsheviks fostered dissatisfaction among all railroaders. Alone among party activists, Bolsheviks seemed well tuned to service and craft identities and seemed to understand better than others the importance of social hierarchy in the workplace. Leninist categorizations served well in identifying labor particularities. Their strongest base of support, of course, was among shop and depot workers, but party activists on the lines were also apparently able to identify with *all* craft unions in one way or another. They supported the "aristocratic" engine drivers in their work stoppages and at the same time found strong support within *Madzhel'*, the union of lower-level service personnel, whom drivers treated so badly. Even the lowly road-repair workers were approached by Lenin's followers, just as they approached hostile peasants in the local *zemstvo* election campaigns.[70] These patterns, obviously, were not unique to the railroads, but railroad workers potentially had real power, providing they were organized and they supported firm leadership. Had *Vikzhel'* actually controlled the railroad "army" and been able to commit it to the defense of political democracy, Lenin's rule might well have been short lived.

Vikzhel' was, however, far weaker than it seemed because democratization on the railroads, as elsewhere, meant mass worker participation in industry affairs rather than commitment to a democratic state order or support for those, like Nekrasov, who became increasingly identified with state interests. Professional sectarianism, localism, and committee members' concern to protect their own authority from outside encroachment engendered a growing disillusionment both with the soviet-liberal coalition regime, whose commitments to political democracy seemed increasingly irrelevant in terms of defending worker interests, and with the all-Russian union, which insisted it was a responsible state organ and struggled for its own "state competence." The expectations for material betterment that accompanied democratization were not, and probably could not, be met. When neither the government nor the union proved able to meet worker goals, when both attempted to restrain lower committee authority, and when Nekrasov, Plekhanov, and other responsive officials pressed wage equalization at the expense of traditional hierarchies and wage differentials, disillusionment turned to increased institutional fragmentation. On a number of railroads, particularly on the important Moscow-Kursk, Moscow-Kazan, and Nikolaev lines, where the influence of shop workers was quite strong, central line committees reacted to these developments by assuming even more authority on the eve of the Bolshevik coup, as institutional autonomy remained a last defense against unacceptable outside allegiances. (Shortly after the Bolsheviks came to power, in fact, the Nikolaev line became the first railroad in history to be fully managed by its own worker representatives.) Over these groups, without question, *Vikzhel'* remained power-less to implement any directives that were not specifically acceptable to the railroaders themselves.

The all-Russian union leadership was thus organically weak, de-spite the apparent radicalism of its syndicalist mentality and however otherwise it might have appeared to Lenin himself in October or to later historians and commentators. The solutions to the problem of revolutionary political power sought by Nekrasov and moderate soviet figures, based on close government-labor relations, therefore con-tained inherent frailties. Support for the process of democratization clearly brought little backing or political strength, and no gratitude. What was surprising about Circular 6321, in fact, was not the opposi-tion of those who felt it violated the premises of civil liberties and a rule of law but the anger of railroaders themselves, whose organizations and mass involvement it officially legitimized. Nekrasov unsuccessfully faced the problem of eliminating authoritiarianism from the work-place without disturbing social and professional hierarchies, a difficult task in the best of circumstances. But, more important, the opposition of many workers to what union leaders and many committeemen themselves recognized as reasonable and appropriate restraints on mass action showed there was increasingly little correlation in 1917 between mass participation, economic decentralization, popular psychology, and the procedures and institutions of democratic rule. So strong were the internal contradictions of Nekrasov's solutions, in fact, that political democracy might not have been able to survive in revolu-tionary Russia even under a democratic socialist regime; the logical outcome seems necessarily to have been one or another form of politi-cal authoritarianism, at least for the immediate future.

Finally, perhaps, prevailing conceptualizations of democracy de-limited its potential for success in the Russian revolution, creating the dichotomy between the dynamics of political difficulties at high levels and the achievement of "democratization" below. The experience of Russia's railroaders makes it clear how the Bolsheviks could, in the end, appropriate the emotive and psychological content of "democracy" as it was popularly understood, pledge themselves to defend proletarian class interests while acknowledging professional and craft differentia-tions, identify class and state interests, and be accepted even by non-Bolshevik workers as "democrats." In this sector, as in others, Russia's experience with democracy was itself prelude to the Soviet state.

Notes

I am especially grateful to David Bien, Heather Hogan, Ronald G. Suny, and Allan Wildman for their constructive criticisms and thoughtful comments. Much of the research was done with support from the Center for Russian and East European Studies, University of Michigan, and the Joint Committee on Soviet Studies of the American Council of Learned Societies.

1.   See especially Marc Ferro, *La Révolution de 1917: La chute du tsarisme et les origines d'octobre* (Paris, 1967); George Katkov, *Russia 1917: The February Revolution* (New York, 1967); Roger Pethybridge, *The Spread of the Russian Revolution: Essays on 1917* (London, 1972); Alexander Rabinowitch, *The Bolsheviks Come to Power* (New York, 1976); Mikhail Reiman, *Russkaia revoliutsiia, 23 fevralia–25 oktiabria 1917*, 2 vols. (Prague, 1968); and Allan Wildman, *The End of the Russian Imperial Army* (Princeton, 1980). For the best Soviet work on the revolution, see E. N. Burdzhalov, *Vtoraia russkaia revoliutsiia: Vosstanie v Petrograde* (Moscow, 1967), and *Vtoraia russkaia revoliutsiia: Moskva, front, periferiia* (Moscow, 1971). Important contributions have also been made by L. S. Gaponenko, A. Ia. Grunt, V. Ia. Laverychev, P. N. Pershin, and P. V. Volobuev, among others.

2.   Oskar Anweiler, *Die Rätebewegung in Russland, 1905–1921* (Leiden, 1958); John Keep, *The Russian Revolution: A Study in Mass Mobilization* (New York, 1976); Marc Ferro, "The Birth of the Soviet Bureaucratic System," in R. C. Elwood, ed., *Reconsiderations on the Russian Revolution* (Cambridge, Mass, 1976), 100–132.

3.   Maklakov, *Vlast' i obshchestvennost' na zakate staroi Rossii* (Paris, 1938), 451–453; and Kerensky, "The Policy of the Provisional Government of 1917," *Slavonic and East European Review* 31 (1932), 19.

4.   *Vikzhel' v oktiabr'skie dni* (Petrograd, 1918), 86. *Vikzhel'* was an acronym for *Vserosiiskii ispolnitel'nyi komitet zheleznodorozhnikov* ("All-Russian Executive Committee of Railroad Workers").

5.   Approximately 70 percent of Russian trackage in 1917 was state-owned. For general analyses of the condition of Russian railroads in this period, see I. D. Mikhailov, *Evoliutsiia russkogo transporta, 1913–1925* (Moscow, 1925), 64–75; and N. Vasil'ev, *Transport Rossii v voine, 1914–1918 gg.* (Moscow, 1939).

6.   Nicholas Vissarionovich Nekrasov had been mayor of Tomsk and a professor at the Tomsk Technological Institute before being elected to the Third and Fourth State Dumas. He was a member of the Kadet Central Committee and, despite his resignation in May, was reelected at the Eighth Party Congress. From July until the end of August, he served as minister of finance and deputy minister-president, and, for a brief time in September and October, he was governor general of Finland. He remained in Russia after the October Revolution and served throughout the 1920s in various minor administrative posts. On the Kadet party in general in 1917, see William G. Rosenberg, *Liberals in the Russian Revolution* (Princeton, 1974).

7. For a detailed discussion of these negotiations, see *Vikzhel' v oktiabr-'skie dni,* passim; and, for less extended treatments, see Pethybridge, *The Spread of the Russian Revolution,* 50–52, and Edward H. Carr, *The Bolshevik Revolution, 1917–1923,* 2 (New York, 1952), 394–397. Also see W. R. Augustine, "Russia's Railwaymen, July–October 1917," *Slavic Review* 24 (1965), 666–679.

8. M. V. Rodzianko (president of the Fourth Duma and chairman of the Temporary Duma Committee), Speech to the Preobrazhenskii regiment, as reported in *Izvestiia Revoliutsionnoi Nedeli,* February 28, 1917.

9. *Zheleznodorozhnik* (Petrograd) 211/30 (August 1, 1917).

10. *Vestnik Riazansko-Ural'skoi Zheleznoi Dorogi* 3 (January 20, 1917).

11. See Paul H. Avrich, "Russian Factory Committees in 1917," *Jahrbücher für Geschichte Osteuropas* 2 (1963), 161–182; D. A. Tseitlin, "Fabrichnozavodskie komitety Petrograda v fevrale-oktiabre 1917 goda," *Voprosy Istorii,* 11 (1956): 86–96; A. M. Pankratova, *Fabzavkomy Rossii v bor 'be za sotsialisticheskuiu fabriku* (Moscow, 1923); and the important collection of materials *Rabochii kontrol' i natsionalizatsiia promyshlennykh predpriiatii Petrograda v 1917–1919 gg.* 1 (Lenningrad, 1947). For a general discussion of the literature, see William G. Rosenberg, "Workers and Workers' Control in the Russian Revolution," *History Workshop Journal* 5 (1978), 89–97.

12. See, for example, the optimistic speech by A. I. Konovalov, minister of trade and industry, in *Vestnik Vremennago Pravitel'stva,* March 7, 1917; cabinet discussions reported in *Zhurnaly Zasedanii Vremennago Pravitel'stva* 14 (March 10, 1917); and the general reaction to the agreement on working conditions reached between a Petrograd Soviet committee and the Petrograd Society of Manufacturers on March 10 in, especially, *Rech',* March 11, 1917.

13. *Rech',* March 10, 1917; *Vestnik Putei Soobshcheniia* 11 (March 18, 1917); and *Rech',* March 29, 1917. Nekrasov communicated his views directly to the railroad workers by teletype; see, for example, Telegram 1788, *Vestnik Ekaterininskoi Zheleznoi Dorogi* 489/90 (March 4–12, 1917).

14. *Vestnik Putei Soobshcheniia* 11 (March 18, 1917), 49–50.

15. *Izvestiia Sobraniia Inzhenerov Putei Soobshcheniia* 1 (1917), 11; and *Proizvoditel'nyia Sily Rossii,* 9–10 (1917), 36–37.

16. Ronzhin, "Zheleznyia dorogi v voennoe vremia" (Palich, Yugoslavia, 1915), 15, MS in the Hoover Institution, Stanford, Calif.; and V. G. Izgachev, "Revoliutsionnoe dvizhenie zheleznodorozhnikov Zabaikal'ia v 1917 godu," *Chitinskii Gosudarstvennyi Pedagogicheskii Institut: Uchenye Zapiski* 3 (1958), 27.

17. *Izvestiia* (Petrograd), March 4, 1917.

18. *Vestnik Ekaterininskoi Zheleznoi Dorogi* (Ekaterinoslav) 489/90 (March 4–12, 1917).

19. *Vestnik Iuzhnykh Zheleznykh Dorog* (Kharkov) 13 (March 27, 1917); and *Vestnik Riazansko-Ural'skoi Zheleznoi Dorogi* (Saratov) 13–14 (April 12, 1917).

20. A. Taniaev, *Ocherki dvizheniia zheleznodorozhnikov v revoliutsii 1917 g.* (Moscow, 1925), 4.

21. *Professional'noe dvizhenie na Moskovsko-Kazanskoi zheleznoi doroge, 1917–1927* (Moscow, 1928), 8–9; *Vestnik Omskoi Zheleznoi Dorogi* 12 (March 25, 1917); *Vestnik Iuzhnykh Zheleznykh Dorog* 13 (March 27, 1917); *Golos Zheleznodorozhnika*, June 7, 1917; *Izvestiia Ispol. Kom. Moskovsko-Kazanskoi Zheleznoi Dorogi* 3 (June 13, 1917); and *Vestnik Riazansko-Ural'skoi Zheleznoi Dorogi* 23 (June 20, 1917).

22. *Golos Zheleznodorozhnika*, June 4, 1917.

23. The delegate congress of the Northwestern Railroad resolved on April 6, for example, to "recognize the Soviet of Workers' and Soldiers' Deputies as the sole representative of the interests of railroad workers" and at the same time pledged full support to the Provisional Government "while it enjoys the trust of the Petrograd Soviet"; see *Zemlia i Volia* (Moscow), April 12, 1917.

24. *Vestnik Ekaterininskoi Zheleznoi Dorogi* 489/90 (March 4–12, 1917).

25. Ibid.

26. *Izvestiia Izpolnitel'nago Komiteta Moskovskago Uzla, Moskovsko-Kazanskoi Zheleznoi Dorogi* (Moscow) 2 (June 6, 1917).

27. *Vestnik Iuzhnykh Zheleznykh Dorog* 13 (March 27, 1917). Also see *Russkiia Vedomosti*, May 30, 1917, June 6, 1917; and *Vestnik Riazansko-Ural skoi Zheleznoi Dorogi* 23 (June 20, 1917).

28. I. D. Mikhailov, *Transport: Ego sovremennoe sostoianie* (Moscow, 1919), 32–33; and *Ekonomicheskoe polozhenie Rossii nakanune velikoi oktaibr'skoi sotsialisticheskoi revoliutsii* 2 (Moscow, 1957), 226–228.

29. A. G. Rashin, *Chislennost' i sostav rabotnikov zheleznodorozhnogo transporta k kontsu 1920 g.*(Moscow, 1921), 5–11; and V. Rachinskii, *Zheleznodorozhnyi transport v 1913 g.*(Moscow, 1925), 146–150. Also see P. F. Metel'kov, *Zhelesnodorozhniki v revoliutsii* (Leningrad, 1970), 23–24. The role of engine drivers in the railroad work force elsewhere is discussed in two interesting essays: F. Caron, "Essai d'analyse historique d'une psychologie du travail: Les mecaniciens et chauffeurs de locomotive du Nord de 1850 à 1910," *Le mouvement social* 50 (1965), 3–40; and Margot B. Stein, "The Meaning of Skill: The Case of the French Engine Drivers, 1837–1917," *Politics and Society* 3–4 (1978), 399–428.

30. *Vestnik Ekaterininskoi Zheleznoi Dorogi* 489/90 (March 4–12, 1917); *Vestnik Omskoi Zheleznoi Dorogi* 12 (March 25, 1917); *Vestnik Iuzhnykh Zheleznykh Dorog* 13 (March 27, 1917); *Golos Zheleznodorozhnika* 4 (June 7, 1917); *Izvestiia Ispol. Kom. Moskovsko-Kazanskoi Zheleznoi Dorogi* 3 (June 13, 1917); and *Zhelezno-dorozhnaia Zhizn' na Dal'nem Vostoke* 26 (July 9, 1917).

31. *Volia i Dumy Zheleznodorozhnika*, April 28, 1917.

32. *Zemlia i Volia*, May 3, 1917; and *Vestnik Aleksandrovskoi Zheleznoi Dorogi* 17 (September 15, 1917).

33. *Golos Zheleznodorozhnika*, June 29, 1917; *Volia i Dumy Zheleznodorozhnika*, April 28, 1917; and *Zheleznodorozhnaia Zhizn' na Dal'nem Vostoke* 10–11 (March 15, 1917).

34. See, for example, the accounts of committee meetings in *Vestnik Aleksandrovskoi Zheleznoi Dorogi* 17 (September 15, 1917); *Vestnik Omskoi*

Zheleznoi Dorogi 12 (March 25, 1917), *Vestnik Ekaterininskoi Zheleznoi Dorogi* 504/28 (July 27, 1917); *Vestnik Riazansko-Ural'skoi Zheleznoi Dorogi* 13/14 April 12, 1917); and *Zemlia i Volia*, April 26, 1917.

35. *Volia i Dumy Zheleznodorozhnika*, April 28, 1917.

36. Z. Lozinskii, *Ekonomicheskaia politika vremennogo pravitel'stva* (Leningrad, 1929), 26–32.

37. *Volia i Dumy Zheleznodorozhnika*, May 14, 1917.

38. Nekrasov mentioned fifteen thousand rubles, but the actual amount may have been much larger; see *Vestnik Putei Soobshcheniia* 15 (April 15, 1917); and *Volia i Dumy Zheleznodorozhnika*, May 14, 1917.

39. *Volia i Dumy Zheleznodorozhnika*, May 14, 1917.

40. *Vestnik Putei Soobshcheniia* 25 (June 24, 1917), 270.

41. Ibid., 22 (June 3, 1917), 111–112.

42. *Volia i Dumy Zheleznodorozhnika*, May 26, 1917. Bonuses were to be distributed by local line administrations in agreement with central line committees, which reduced past bonus allotments to women by 15 percent and set limits of 25 to 50 percent on other categories of labor, particularly watchmen, employees entitled to railroad meals and lodging, teachers, and medical service personnel.

43. *Mysli Zheleznodorozhnika*, July 1, 1917.

44. See especially *Novaia Zhizn'*, June 3, 1917; and the report of E. V. Landsberg to the Special Council on Transport, July 13, 1917, in *Ekonomicheskoe polozhenie* 2:238–242.

45. *Vestnik Ekaterininskoi Zheleznoi Dorogi*, 510/34–36 (September 12–27, 1917).

46. *Golos Zheleznodorozhnika*, July 2, 1917. Also see D. M. Zol'nikov, "Stachechnoe dvizhenie zheleznodorozhnika v 1917 g.,"*Uchenye Zapiski Tomskogo Universiteta* 38 (1961), 28–42.

47. *Biulleten' Vserossiiskogo Uchreditel'nogo Zheleznodorozhnogo S"ezda* (Moscow, 1917), 2 (July 29, 1917).

48. *Vestnik Riazansko-Ural'skoi Zheleznoi Dorogi* 23 (July 20, 1917).

49. *Zheleznodorozhnaia Zhizn' na Dal'nem Vostoke* 27 (July 15, 1917).

50. *Volia i Dumy Zheleznodorozhnika*, July 16, 1917.

51. Ibid., May 1, 1917 (italics added).

52. Ibid.

53. Ibid., June 10, 1917. Also see *Russkiia Vedomosti*, June 18, 1917.

54. *Mysli Zheleznodorozhnika*, June 21, 1917; and Taniev, *Ocherki dvizheniia*, 23–24.

55. *Golos Zheleznodorozhnika*, June 25, 1917.

56. For a discussion of this hostility and the changes in the liberals' position, see Rosenberg, *Liberals in the Russian Revolution*, 170–195, 203–233. On the growing strength of the Bolsheviks, especially see Rabinowitch, *The Bolsheviks Come to Power*, 83–93, 111–112.

57. *Novaia Zhizn'*, June 22, 1917.

58. *Biulleten' Vserossiiskogo Uchreditel'nogo Zheleznodorozhnogo S"ezda* 11 (August 26, 1917).

59.   *Vestnik Ekaterininskoi Zheleznoi Dorogi* 507/31 (August 21, 1917).

60.   *Volia i Dumy Zheleznodorozhnika*, May 5, 1917. Thus, the Union of Junior Agents of the Operations Service, *Madzhel'*, organized in late April, represented by mid-summer some forty-five thousand workers; other "ribbon unions" grew with equal rapidity. See V. D. Gurevich, *"Madzhel'" (Soiuz mladshikh agentov dvizheniia zheleznykh dorol) 1917–1919 gg.* (Moscow, 1925); and Metel'kov, *Zheleznodorozhniki*, 119–134.

61.   *Vestnik Iuzhnykh Zheleznykh Dorog* 37 (September 11, 1917). On the shop workers, see especially *Volia i Dumy Zheleznodorozhnika*, May 5, 1917; Zol'nikov, "Stachechnoe dvizhenie," 31–42; and I. M. Pushkareva, "Vseobshchaia sentiabr'skaia stachka zheleznodorozhnikov v 1917," in *Rabochii klass i rabochee dvizhenie v Rossii v 1917* (Moscow, 1964), 181–190.

62.   Gurevich, *"Madzhel'*," 120.

63.   *Rabochaia Gazeta*, July 25, 1917.

64.   *Birzhevyia Vedomosti*, August 19, 1917.

65.   *Biulleten' Vserossiiskogo Uchreditel'nogo Zheleznodorozhnogo S"ezda* 2 (July 29, 1917), 6 (August 11, 1917).

66.   See, for example, *Rech'*, August 19, 1917, September 19, 21, 1917; *Birzhevyia Vedomosti*, August 19, 1917; and *Russkiia Vedomosti*, *September 23, 24, 1917*.

67.   *Biulleten' Vserossiiskogo Uchreditel'nogo Zheleznodorozhnogo S"ezda* 11 (August 6, 1917), 13 (September 2, 1917); and *Golos Zheleznodorozhnika*, August 2, September 7, 1917. The exact political complexion of *Vikzhel'* is unclear. The group was apparently almost evenly divided among left socialists (Left SRs, Bolsheviks, and Menshevik Internationalists), moderates (Mensheviks, SRs, and Popular Socialists), and nonparty people. See P. Vompe, *Tri goda revoliutsionnogo dvizheniia na zheleznykh dorogakh Rossiiskoi Sovetskoi Respubliki* (Moscow, 1920), 8–10; O. Piatnitskii, "Vikzhel'do, vo vremia, i posle oktiabr'skikh dnei," in *Put' k Oktiabriu* (Moscow, 1923), 175–177 and W. Augustine, "Russia's Railwaymen," 668.

68.   *Izvestiia*, September 24, 1917. Here also, perhaps, are clues as to why such relatively little effort was made after October to equalize wages or abolish social or professional hierarchies in the workplace. The principles of Bolshevik union organization immediately after 1917 corresponded neatly with the workers' own craft and professional identities.

69.   *Volia i Dumy Zheleznodorozhnika*, July 26, 1917. For a discussion of the September strike and subsequent events, see Pethybridge, *The Spread of the Russian Revolution*, 40–47.

70.   Gurevich, *"Madzhel'*," 16–18; and Metel'kov, *Zheleznodorozhniki v revoliutsii*, 119–133.

Chapter Ten

Workers' Control in Europe: A Comparative Sociological Analysis

Carmen Sirianni

As David Montgomery has noted, workers' control of production has represented a long historical struggle, a "chronic battle in industrial life which assumed a variety of forms."[1] From the beginning of industrial society, workers have devised a great variety of strategies—formal and informal, deliberate and spontaneous—to set their own pace and style of work, to define their own intragroup relations, and to resist the routine of the clock and the discipline of the boss. As much as the working classes have been transformed by the dynamics and rhythms of capital accumulation, they have resisted the very same driving forces of accumulation and redefined them.

During the First World War and the immediate postwar period, this perennial struggle took on new forms. For the first time the efforts of skilled workers to control their own jobs were transformed into mass struggles to wrest control of the production process as a whole from capitalist management and to lodge it in formal organs that were democratically constituted by the workers themselves. Those skilled workers who had previously been in the forefront of job control struggles began to develop organizational forms that promised to

This is a revised version of an article that first appeared in *Theory and Society* 9 (1980), 29-88.

transcend the boundaries of craft and to include the mass of less skilled workers in the general project of democratic management. For the first time truly mass struggles were waged to give specific institutional form to the socialist project of reappropriating the means of production and transforming the relations of production. The historic struggles for labor dignity received innovative institutional expression, and important aspects of the class division of labor were challenged.

It was during this period that "workers' control over production" became a significant part of the vocabulary of the socialist left. Even though certain rudimentary conceptions of workers' control could be found in the socialist, anarchist, and syndicalist writings of the previous half-century, it was not until the struggle over the control of production became a mass phenomenon during World War I that socialist theory was impelled to take serious recognition of the questions being raised—questions that went to the very heart of orthodox Leninist as well as Social Democratic conceptions about the nature of the revolutionary process and the socialist society that stood as its proximate goal. Nor was the impact of these movements limited to the socialist left. As Steve Fraser has noted, "workers' control" and "industrial democracy" represented complex metaphors whose meaning varied according to the social grammar and specific context of which they were a part.[2] The outcomes of these movements, no less than the specific industrial sectors and working-class traditions within which they emerged, engendered various interpretations, theories, and models of worker participation and control, which have subsequently been implemented in capitalist and socialist countries alike.

This essay makes a preliminary attempt to understand these movements—their emergence, development, and outcomes, their internal dynamics, and their relationship to the larger totality of social forces that simultaneously created and circumscribed their possibilities. The countries chosen for systematic comparison—Russia, Germany, Italy, Britain, and France—represent a broad enough range of experiences in the area of workers' control to permit us to draw certain tentative conclusions. On the one end we have the Russian case, in which limited control over the owners developed in stages into actual workers' self-management in many sectors of the economy. In France, on the other end, rank-and-file oppositional movements around such goals were very limited, although the ideals of democratizing industry had considerable resonance within established labor organizations.

While this study is not directly a test of sociological theory, it does draw very considerably on a resource mobilization approach to social movements.[3] In contrast to much previous literature, which stressed deprivations and beliefs,[4] resource mobilization theory focuses primarily on capacities and constraints. While it does not ignore ideologies and felt deprivations, it tends to make weaker assumptions about their role and seeks to situate them within contexts defined by organized structures. This essay is informed by such an orientation, without excluding the possibility of a much richer analysis of felt deprivations, cultural traditions, or ideological orientations. It does, however, focus on broad political and economic structures; the conditions for the mobilization of resources for struggle; preexisting and emerging organizational forms and networks and the degree and density of these; cooperation, competition, and canalization by and among organizations in the struggle for scarce resources (including legitimacy) and the rational calculation of risks and rewards; and the relation of constituency types and organizational forms. Of central concern throughout are the specifically political factors, such as the various roles of the state, political elites outside the state, the forms and degrees of state crisis, and the constraints and forms of leverage within the international state system. The latter, along with international economic factors, are of essential relevance to the study of movements in a period of war and postwar reconstruction and realignment. Finally, the temporal articulations of movement and organizational development are particularly important in the study of phenomena with both broad continuities and abrupt critical junctures such as characterized this period of total war.

Wartime Contradictions and Protest Potential

The industrial working classes in Europe experienced a noticeable decline in their overall living and working conditions during the war, a decline that contrasted sharply with the trend of the previous decades. Galloping inflation significantly reduced the real wages of most workers, though increased employment opportunities for women and children compensated for this among certain families. Only a very thin stratum of the most highly skilled workers in the war industries were able to achieve gains that kept pace with the constant rise in prices. General working conditions deteriorated as hours were lengthened and protective legislation (where it existed) was often suspended or ignored. Discipline at the workplace intensified severely, especially for those draft-age males covered by the various forms of labor mobilization and special exemption. Labor mobility was itself curtailed, though never completely or effectively. Shortages of food, housing, fuel, and other necessities became increasingly severe as the war dragged on.

Such shortages not only increased the absolute burden of the working classes, for whom the incidence of undernourishment and sickness rose considerably (Britain seems to have been the exception here), they also starkly revealed the differential capacities of the various classes, especially wherever the black market served as a supplement to official rationing policies. As Jürgen Kocka has noted of the German wartime experience, nothing more raised the level of class tensions than the manifest inequality in the supply of necessities, at a time when the working classes were being called upon to make incredible sacrifices for the "nation" as a whole. Under such conditions, rumors that the crown princess bathed in milk while workers' children went without were powerful instigators of class conflict. Awareness of the immense profits that were being made on the war also contributed to the increasing sense of unequal sacrifice and unequal reward and directly fed the antiwar sentiments that continued to grow as the initial patriotic enthusiasm wore off and the war came to be seen as both endless and senseless. Daily life became increasingly more disrupted and brutalized, as families were broken up, children with working mothers were inadequately cared for, and community life was dislocated by the massive population shifts away from the fronts and towards the centers of war production.

While the war dramatically reversed prewar trends toward a general betterment of conditions, it simultaneously led to an increase in expectations in regard to the role of the working classes in the national polity and also created labor market conditions favorable to working class protest. The nationalism used to mobilize the workers behind the state and the ruling powers was a two-edged sword that cut in the direction of increased popular participation and social reform as well as labor integration. Indeed, labor's cooperation in the war effort had been achieved only with explicit or implicit promises of reform, some of which were not to be postponed even until the war's end. And the war-induced labor shortage provided the leverage—particularly in war-related industries—for workers to press their demands in the face of the two major restrictive conditions: state repression (including dispatch to the front) and trade union opposition or lack of support. The threat that wildcat strikes posed to the war efforts of the respective governments, as well as to the inflated wartime profits of the owners, was responsible for the relatively high proportion of settlements favorable to the workers.[5]

The war proved to be the great accelerator of trends toward more rationalized production (including chronometry, price-rates and bonuses, and serial production). Taylor's ideas had already spread to

Europe before the war but had met with only very selective application by industrialists, as well as resistance by some of the workers affected. But the peculiar suitability of such methods to bulk repetition production required especially in munitions, the direct and indirect state support in the form of guaranteed markets and profits and preference for uniform standards, and the sudden and severe shortage of skilled labor as a result of the call-ups provided the impetus for a real "take-off" in this regard. The metal and machine industries in all the countries under consideration were most directly affected, but so also were selected other industries (chemical, optical) at least partially. Those industries producing for the war not only experienced a huge growth in their workforces but a disproportionate increase in the number of semi- and unskilled workers, mainly women, peasants, youth, and, in some cases, foreigners and prisoners of war. For many of these new recruits, work in the war industries represented increased opportunities, wages, and even skills.

The introduction and extension of rationalized production methods and scientific managerial techniques, however, represented a direct threat to the power and position of the mass of more highly skilled workers—those to whom the limited opportunities for advancement (into the supervisory hierarchy, or the tool rooms, for instance) created by the new methods did not extend. The relative monopoly on productive knowledge and technique that the skilled workers possessed had allowed them a certain degree of informal control over such factors as the process of production, the pace of work, the amount of output, and the training of new workers. Sometimes this informal control became formalized in union work rules, imposed unilaterally on the owners and not the subject of contract bargaining. The extent of such job control, however, varied considerably from industry to industry, and country to country. Even in the British engineering works most directly affected by the war, the dilution of skill had progressed considerably in the previous decades under the impact of new machinery. A long craft tradition and strong craft union muscle had been relatively effective in maintaining the old rates for diluted work, but the objective basis for such a response was being rapidly undermined by wartime transformations—transformations that received added ideological and political impetus from the presence of a foreign threat. In the war industries elsewhere on the continent, craft control had never been as strong as in Britain, and there was even less possibility of actually resisting the introduction of new methods. The expansion of the number of dilutees during the war tended to strengthen the hand of management vis-à-vis the skilled workers on questions of discipline and exacerbated the latter's fears of being expendable and hence subject to duty at the front. But most conflicts seem to have centered on wages—the wages of the skilled relative to those of the less skilled and the hoards of new recruits, and the establishment of acceptable piece rates for those who had been shifted off hourly scales. The *numerical rates* of piece and hourly wages were a constant issue of contention under conditions of steep inflation (which continued into the immediate postwar years in Germany, Italy, and France). The actual *process* of establishing the rates seems to have remained as much of an issue as it had been, for instance, when chronometry had first been introduced in the Renault factories in 1912 and the workers had insisted that their own delegates participate in its application (the famous *grève du chronométrage*). And to a certain extent, *piece work itself* was a focus of struggle. A prominent slogan of the Free Trade Unions in Hamburg, for instance, captured the widespread feeling: *Akkord ist Mord*—piecework is murder.[6]

Organizational Forms:
Old and New

The sacrifices imposed by the war on the working classes and the heightening of perceived inequalities and class tensions generated an increasing potential for mass protest and opposition. The organizational articulation of this potential for protest depended in the first instance on the behavior of the trade unions. The limitations in the unions' ability to adequately defend workers' interests had both political and structural causes, though these were interrelated. In those countries with legal and well-established (though unevenly developed) trade unions—Britain, Germany, Italy, and France—the political limitations were roughly similar. The major union federations had renounced class struggle tactics that might be disruptive to the war effort for the duration of that conflict. Their decisions had been conditioned by (1) pressure from above, i.e., the very real possibility of state repression of their organizations; (2) pressure from below (with the partial exception of Italy), i.e., pressure from the masses of workers themselves, whose own nationalistic feelings often ran very deep and whose antimilitarism was extremely vulnerable in the absence of an effective internationalist strategy for preventing the outbreak of war;[7] (3) the reformist politics of most trade union leaders, which had evolved in the prewar period of organizational growth and economic improvement for the working classes; and (4) the possibilities of significant concessions in exchange for official participation and collaboration in the war effort (i.e., on various war boards, arbitration commissions, and in relief work). In other words, the unions had not abandoned all aims of their own. In Germany, for instance, the unions not only achieved much greater recognition by the state, but also curbs on company unions, favorable statutes on wages and job mobility in the Auxiliary Service Law, and general treatment encouraging the growth in membership, despite restrictions on overt organizing. All four countries shared in this trade union growth in the second part of the war. But to maintain favorable government treatment and the possibilities of further growth and reform at the war's end, all the major union federations—the General Labor Union Federation (Allgemeine Deutscher Gewerkschaftsbund) (ADGB) in Germany, the General Confederation of Labor (Confédération Générale du Travail) (CGT) in France, the General Confederation of Labor (Confederazione Generale del Lavoro) (CGL) in Italy, and the Trade Union Congress (TUC) in Britain— renounced militant tactics like the strike, including the refusal of strike funds and, in some cases, reporting striking workers to the military authorities.[8]

The unions were also unresponsive to rank-and-file protest because of certain structural characteristics. In the prewar years unions had evolved into relatively stable, bureaucratic, and centralized organizations based primarily on craft association with geographical membership jurisdictions. Such organizations were seen as the only real alternative to the high degree of instability (in terms of membership and concrete gains) that characterized the low-dues, antibureaucratic, anticentralist, and class warfare practices of the syndicalist form of organization—a form of organization that presented a significant challenge to the CGL in Italy (in the form of the Italian Syndical Union [Unione Sindacale Italiana] [USI]) and had characterized many of the unions in the French CGT itself before the latter began to adopt more bureaucratic forms of organization in response to the increasing centralization of capital and the demands of the workers themselves for more stable and secure achievements.[9] Craft associations formed the core of the major union federations in these countries, with the exception of the CGT in France, which had made considerable progress towards industrial forms of organization by the time of the war and further progress during it. But even in France the actual organization of the unskilled and semiskilled workers proved extremely difficult before the war's end. In Germany, Italy, and Britain a multiplicity of craft associations in any given workplace was the rule, and the craft unions exercised hegemony in the labor movement as a whole and even in many unions with a significant number of unskilled workers.

Given the collaborationist, centralized, bureaucratic, and craft character of the trade unions, the rising protest over general economic and political issues and the conflict generated around changes in the production process in the war industries (particularly metals) warranted alternative forms of organization. These would have to be able to respond to the immediate problems arising in the workplace, rather than mediating these problems through sections based in geographical units outside the factory. They would have to be able to respond quickly to the ever-changing structure of wage rates, rather than through cumbersome bureaucratic processes. And they would have to cut across craft distinctions that production process changes were making increasingly outmoded and dangerously divisive. The pattern of organizational formation, however, varied considerably.

Britain In Britain, the country with the most profound craft tradition and the most persistent and rigid craft structure in industry and in the trade unions, the response of the Amalgamated Society of Engineers, the major union federation affected, to the dilution crisis was a highly conservative one. The ASE essentially sought to maintain its prewar policy of "following the machine," or accepting new types of work necessitated by the introduction of new machinery on the condition that jobs traditionally done by craftsmen should continue to be paid at the standard rate, that dilution be confined to war work, and that old practices be restored at the war's end. Such a policy, James Hinton has shown, "made no allowance at all for the technological dynamism of the industry."[10] It was a strategy based more and more on bluff as the objective skill basis rapidly declined, and it largely ignored the organization of the less skilled and the pursuance of an all-grades strategy. The national agreements between the government and the unions, however, helped open the way to local negotiation as well as conflict. The shop stewards' movement—a movement based on the direct representation of the skilled engineering workers and tending toward the creation of an all-grades organization rooted in the workshop—thus arose to fill the gap that most ASE locals could or would not. Because the ASE craft structure was so rigid, the stewards in most places existed *outside* the union organizations and often in direct antagonism to them. Their organizations became the basis for strikes not only around workplace issues but also around the war, the draft (i.e., of specially exempted skilled munitions workers), and food and housing shortages.

Germany The pattern in Germany and Italy was somewhat different. Many local sections of the German Metalworkers' Union (Deutsche Metallarbeiter Verband) (DMV), the major union in the metal works producing for the war, had evolved considerably towards an all-grades organization. Craft control had never been very strong to begin with, and craft organization was further weakened by the massive influx of previously unorganized and often unskilled recruits who began streaming into the union in the last half of the war. A new mass base was in the process of formation that had little tradition of trade union discipline and stable organizational work. But the normal channels of protest and leadership challenge within the unions were blocked for the duration of the war. There thus arose a new stratum of rank-and-file organizers to fill the leadership gap. As Peter von Oertzen has argued, in the larger factories and cities (especially Berlin) a stratum of trade union functionaries could develop and rise to responsible and influential positions without following the career path of permanently appointed secretaries, i.e., without getting quickly coopted into the union bureaucracy, as was usually the case in the smaller factories and cities. The revolutionary *Obleute* or shop stewards thus arose from *within* and drew upon the resources *of* the various metal workers' locals that had moved considerably towards an all-grades organization. Though invariably led by the more highly skilled turners and fitters, the organizations they constructed would become the basis in 1919 for a revolutionary factory committee movement involving broad masses, both skilled and unskilled.[11]

Italy The factory committee movement that arose in Italy at the war's end was centered largely in Turin, the major Italian industrial city producing for the war. As in Germany, the dominant metal union federation, Federazione Italiana Operai Matallurgici (FIOM), was formally structured along the lines of craft sections, with a fairly high degree of sectional consciousness among founders, coppersmiths, and so on. But, also as in Germany, the actual extent of craft control was not very great—not nearly so far-reaching as in Britain before the war. And this was especially true of Turin, a city whose recent breakneck development as an industrial center was based on a more extensive use of the latest production methods. There was thus very little hope of preventing or reversing the trend toward increased rationalization of production. But the issues raised by rationalization required an all-grades approach and a shop-based organization that could not be provided directly by the union. In the interstices of the union organizations there thus developed internal commissions (*commissioni interne*). These were usually elected on the shopfloor by all union members irrespective of craft distinctions (though they were sometimes appointed from above) and functioned essentially as grievance committees overseeing the application of wage agreements. Their functions were at first quite limited and their official existence tenuous, for the union was very suspicious of the increase in local initiative that they represented.

But there was considerable pressure from below for their official recognition, and rather than risk a breakaway movement or the loss of locals to the syndicalists, the union moved toward the end of 1918 to incorporate them into its structure. The February 1919 national FIOM agreement recognized the internal commissions as organs competent to negotiate directly with management on all collective and individual grievances arising out of the application of the agreement. Some in the union hierarchy seem to have honestly viewed the commissions as preparatory organs for workers' self-management, but prior to the revolution that few saw on the immediate agenda, they were to function to help raise productivity, ensure the smooth application of new methods, and maintain overall industrial peace. Indeed, FIOM had come around to the monopolies' program for industrial reconstruction and development, which was predicated on the unions' trade-off of all claims to control the labor process and discipline, and of the right to strike for the duration of the contract. In return for a free hand for increased rationalization, the owners conceded the eight-hour day and substantial pay increases. (A similar agreement in 1911 had been disrupted by rejection by the rank and file and syndicalist-led strikes whose defeat resulted in the loss of all concessions. FIOM leaders were determined not to let this happen again.) Thus, the 1919 agreement also established a cumbersome apparatus for the mediation of conflicts in order to avoid spontaneous strikes, and rather stringent penalties for the failure to pursue grievances through the proper channels.

Under the immediate postwar conditions, however, it was unlikely that the internal commissions would remain within this reformed trade union framework. Inflation rates requiring quick adjustments continue to focus wage disputes and negotiation at the local level. Piece rates remained a persistent problem, as many workers viewed them as simply a tool of capital for rationalizing production, speeding up work, lowering pay, and dividing the workers against one another. Disciplinary measures, which all had hoped would be relaxed after the end of hostilities, actually intensified in certain ways. And the eight-hour agreement was undermined by frequent mandatory overtime. Indeed, it was the introduction of daylight savings time—so reminiscent of the harsh wartime measures for raising production—that precipitated the momentous April 1920 strike (*'lo sciopero delle lancette'*) over the powers of the internal commissions. The continual influx of unskilled factory recruits and the enormous growth of trade union membership itself increased pressure for industrial unions, and the internal commissions quite naturally became a basis for this. When FIOM leaders were absent from Turin for an extended period in the late summer of 1919—they were leading strikes in Liguria, Emilia, and Lombardy— more radical conceptions of internal commissions as permanent factory council organs with extensive powers spread rapidly and began to present a major challenge to the economism and reformism of the traditional union leadership. The ground was prepared for the historic confrontation over workers' control in Italy.[12]

France In Britain the shop stewards' movement arose for the most part outside the framework of the unions largely because of their rigid craft structure, and in Germany and Italy the movements grew more from within the unions because of the greater congruency between the quasi-industrialized unions and the demands for all-grades representation at the shopfloor level by the *Obleute* and the *commissioni interne*. In France by contrast, a system of workshop delegates to handle questions of wage adjustments, manner of payment and working conditions developed primarily at the suggestion of the unions themselves after the passing of legislation regulating wages and mandating arbitration in January 1917. (Some did develop as a result of the spontaneous action of the workers, however.) The even greater degree of structural congruence between such a system of delegates and the rather extensively developed industrial organization of the French unions, particularly in metals (whence the proposal had originated), at least partially explains this difference. The Socialist Minister of Armaments, Albert Thomas, accepted the unions' suggestion, and against the original opposition of many important firms, workshop delegates were subsequently established. The union proposals went considerably beyond the scheme that was eventually put into effect, however. Aside from more inclusive criteria of eligibility for voting and office holding, the unions had insisted on broad functions covering all aspects of corporate order and workers' dignity and on the constitution of the delegates as a collective factory body under the overall authority of the union. The latter point represented the unions' fear that isolated delegates—the system that was finally approved officially (and later strengthened under the new minister) in order to palliate the owners— would come under the undue influence of the management and would thus undercut the solidarity and effectiveness of the union. Indeed, the latter seems to have been common, as the delegates functioned more to conciliate than to control, to make work more productive in line with the new methods rather than to change it. But fears of the delegates being used as a base of more radical opposition also no doubt played a part in the unions' proposals.

The institution of workshop delegates never became mandatory, however, and their development remained very uneven. They were most numerous in the metal firms producing for the war, and particularly in large and medium-sized companies. Most important firms in the Paris area had workshop delegates, although they existed over a wide range of cities. Aside from continued owner resistance in many areas, the diffusion of the institution was limited by a significant degree of worker opposition and apathy due to the innocuousness and conciliationist nature of the delegates' functions. Some local unions opposed them after the initial union schemes had been rejected, and this hostility increased after the war's end. As a result, only a small percentage of those created during the war continued into the postwar years, although a few dozen firms instituted new delegations in 1919.

In contrast to Britain, Germany, and Italy, there seems to have been much less tension between the workshop delegates and the unions. The overly conciliatory behavior of some delegates led to accusations by union militants that they had been bought off by the owners. Many delegates, however, violated the official restrictions against linking the affairs of their particular workshops with those of others, and the internal affairs of the factory with the syndical organization outside. They often presented collective reports to the syndicate, and many delegates were "loyal" union members themselves. In such cases the delegates served as a kind of workplace cell of the union. Some delegations, however, did constitute themselves as a kind of factory council independent of the unions and hostile to their moderate policies. The Russian Revolution and the Russian factory councils served them as a model, although their actual knowledge of the latter was quite limited. These delegations became the basis for radical strike action against the war and related political and economic grievances, though on the whole such action seems to have occurred outside both the union and the workshop delegate structures. It is unclear whether such radical delegates ever secured greater effective control over the production process itself. In any case, such radical factory councils remained fairly limited, partly as a result of effective repression by the state. They never became the basis for a more revolutionary movement (as in Germany, Italy, and, to a much lesser extent, Britain), even though rather intense revolutionary sentiments among significant sectors of the working class, especially in the Parisian metal industries, carried over into the postwar years and even though the mass strikes of 1919 witnessed some explicit demands for the nationalization and reorganization of production by the producers themselves.[13]

Two factors seem to account, at least partially, for the lack of development of a worker council movement with revolutionary goals. The first is the aforementioned structural congruence between the largely industrialized French unions and the institution of workshop delegates. This congruence largely undercut any struggle for recognition of the delegates as a means for creating an all-grades organization of workers. In Britain especially, but also in the only partially industrialized metal unions in Germany and Italy, the stewards' movements drew a good deal of their impetus from the need for all-grades representation. The struggle for recognition provided a common basis around which more radical demands and conceptions could be articulated. Two major British munitions centers, Coventry and Birmingham, highlight the distinction. In contrast with stewards in Glasgow and Sheffield, the shop stewards in these centers proved fairly easy to officialize and incorporate into reformed trade union structures in such a way as to isolate the revolutionaries. In both cases this was made possible by the much greater presence of the industrially organized Workers' Union, itself a result of the greater progress of dilution before the war. The wartime dilution crisis was thus not only less acute, but union structures capable of housing the stewards were available, thereby depriving the more revolutionary elements of leadership and a mass base in the struggle for recognition itself.[14] In France this pattern seems to have been the general rule.

The second factor was that the CGT itself, despite its opposition to the mass strikes in 1919 and to a strategy for immediate revolution, had a much more vigorous postwar reform program than the union federations in Germany, Italy, or Britain. From the start this program included demands for nationalization of the monopolies, which would be managed by representatives of both producers and consumers. Likewise, the national economic council, which the CGT called for and attempted to institute in direct opposition to the government's plans, contained representatives from the unions, consumer cooperatives, technicians, and civil servants.[15] This program bore the marks of the CGT's revolutionary syndicalist heritage, and it undoubtedly helped undercut more radical demands for workers' control. Indeed, it might be said that the CGT's far-reaching proposals preemptively achieved what the German and Italian unions' proposed reforms were able to accomplish only *after* the rise of more revolutionary council movements.

Russia The development of a movement for workers' control in Russia took a very different path from that in other countries. As in the other warring countries, struggles around wages, piece rates, increased discipline and hours, inflation, time studies, shortages, political issues including the war itself, and the increased leverage of the working class resulting from the severe labor shortages had led to workers' representation in the War Industries Committees (the elections for which were factory based), and some revival of the previously very paternalistic though potentially militant factory elder system.[16] But the economic and political crises engendered by the war were much more severe in Russia than in the other warring countries, and the organizational heritage was quite different.

On the eve of the February Revolution trade union organization in Russia was extremely weak. This was primarily the result of decades of tsarist repression, interrupted by a brief period of full legalization after the 1905 revolution and very sporadic and selective toleration thereafter. During the war only a few small unions in Moscow and the provinces maintained a semilegal existence. After full legalization again in March 1917, the unions experienced rapid, though somewhat loose and disorderly, growth. Most had little continuity with the preexisting legal or semilegal organs. Besides, their activity was at first disrupted by an intense struggle over job categories. As Marc Ferro has noted, their structures were often so complex as to represent a "veritable tower of Babel,"[17] and it was only later in the year that they began to iron out their jurisdictional conflicts and move towards more industrial forms of organization. Though the unions rather quickly enlisted a large proportion of the work force in industry, mining, and transport, they remained more bureaucratic shells than structures with organic links to the rank and file. Their weakness at the time of the February Revolution, their largely bureaucratic growth thereafter, and the persistence of craft distinctions in the crucial early months of 1917 all represented structural impediments to their ability to lead the struggles at the base—struggles that often demanded a rapid response and an all-grades strategy.

These structural impediments were exacerbated in the early months by the political outlook of the leadership of most unions. The Mensheviks, who had remained more intact during the war than their radical Bolshevik rivals as a result of the less severe police repression against them and their legal participation and leadership in the War Industries Committees, dominated most union hierarchies at first. Because they viewed the February Revolution as a bourgeois revolution ushering in a prolonged period of capitalist development and liberal democracy, they were opposed to any action by workers that fundamentally encroached on capitalist control of the production process. Regulation of production, where it was necessary, was to be exercised by the state representing all democratic classes. Because of their view that in the absence of a bilateral, negotiated, non-annexationist peace, the workers' movement must continue to support the Allied cause, the Mensheviks favored the limitation and restraint of workers' demands if these would further disrupt the economy and undermine the war effort.[18]

Thus, aside from the occupation and management of those factories temporarily deserted by their managerial staffs in the wake of the February Revolution, factory committees were formed spontaneously by the workers in the plant to fill the void left by trade unions. The rapidity and intensity of response, however, was determined by workers' prior mobilization, particularly in the factory-based forms of representation.[19] And although pragmatic concerns were foremost, the committees became the arena for asserting and defending the profound sense of dignity of workers against managerial abuse, including the protection of women from sexual harassment. The evolving urban working-class culture of pride and power received direct organizational expression in the factory committees.[20] The eight-hour day struggle in March was waged primarily by the committees, and the latter took up a whole range of questions that had traditionally been the preserve of the unions, such as wages, working conditions, and job security. Many strikes were called by the committees without the unions' approval and often without even their knowledge. The motivation behind the committees' actions was primarily defensive and pragmatic at first, even while their intervention and control (e.g., of company books, over the administrative staff) was often quite active, indeed belligerent. They looked toward improving labor's position within normalized, if reformed, capitalist relations of production, not toward transforming those relations fundamentally. Propaganda along the lines of the latter strategy began to have an effect only later in the year, as the economy spiraled downward and capitalist sabotage seemed to warrant the assumption of managerial functions by the workers themselves. The committees had the advantage over the unions of being able to take direct and immediate action unimpaired by distant and bureaucratic central offices, and with the highly unstable conditions beginning in June, marked by skyrocketing inflation and increasing layoffs and lockouts, this became more and more necessary. Control over hiring and firing, the supervision of administrative personnel, the organization of fuel and raw materials supplies, and even (though to a much lesser extent) the expropriation and management of the factories themselves became increasingly common as the year wore on. The October revolution would accelerate these trends even further. But that it occurred at all was due in no small measure to the fact that the Russian industrial scene had lacked strong and stable trade unions with a tradition of union discipline and collective bargaining that might have inspired a minimal degree of mutual trust between labor and capital. Under conditions of war-induced economic disintegration such unions had little chance of developing. The factory committees, which developed to a certain extent as surrogate unions, were too close to the rebellious and demanding rank and file and too unencumbered by craft distinctions and bureaucratic procedures to play the role of mediator between the two hostile classes. The attempts to incorporate them into the trade union structures showed only limited success in 1917.[21]

Crisis and Continuity: States and Movements in the Aftermath of War

The development and fate of the various movements for workers' control can only be understood in the context of the respective national and international state systems. In all the countries under consideration, it was the state that undertook the task of mobilizing national economic resources, financing industrial reorganization, and providing the rationalization projects with national-popular legitimation. Its actual or threatened repression, besides securing the coercive basis for the latter, set the limits for trade union activity and extraunion protest even as it intervened (often against business) to secure concessions for labor (and hence the consensual basis for that legitimation) in order to prevent the disruption of the war effort. State propaganda efforts had the unintended consequence of raising expectations concerning the role of labor in the polity even as its mobilization activities resulted in a decline in the general living and working conditions of most workers. And, finally, the relative degree and form of state crisis, along with the balance of international political and economic power as perceived and mediated by the elites of the most established political and economic organizations, profoundly shaped the final contours and outcomes of the various movements for workers' control. Relative ability to wage total warfare was the proximate determinant of political crisis, though this in turn reflects long-term structural characteristics of the respective state systems and national economies. These crises manifested themselves at the level of representation, administration, and legitimacy, but it was ultimately at the level of repressive force that the immediate crises were resolved. Their resolutions simultaneously determined and were determined by the relative balance of organized forces within the workers' movements themselves. These crisis resolutions established the limits of contestation and defined the relative costs and opportunities of alternative working-class strategies even as they were themselves partly determined by the organizational and ideological legacies that exerted their relative historical strength within the workers' movements.

Britain and France Serious political crises failed to materialize in either Britain or France after the armistice. Victory seemed to vindicate nationalistic rationales and legitimate political systems. Despite considerable discontent among certain sectors of the working classes, militant protest remained localized and contained by skillful combinations of concession and effective repression. Neither country was faced with a mass peasant movement threatening to link up with urban discontent, as in Russia and Italy. The repressive apparatuses, despite certain internal strains, remained intact and isolated from civilian protest. The armies were demobilized in relatively orderly fashion. And parliamentary majorities were firmly secured against the forces of socialism and revolution. This general bourgeois political stability even further delimited the already scant possibilities for an independent mass-based workers' control movement in France by reinforcing the reformist tendencies in the trade unions. In Britain, the lack of political space in which to extend the skilled engineers' demands for workers' control provided the general context for the strengthening of the unions, the isolation of the revolutionaries, and the restoration of craft structures and practices.[22]

That the struggle of the British engineers around the question of dilution was able to transcend to some significant degree the traditional exclusiveness of craft prerogatives was partially due to the influence of revolutionary Marxist and syndicalist ideas on the leaders of the stewards' movement. The DeLeonite Socialist Labour Party in particular worked to undermine the craftsmen's hope for the restoration of craft structures and craft privileges at the war's end by arguing that dilution was both inevitable and progressive. If dilution could not be prevented, then an all-grades organization was necessary. The move for unified organization also received impetus from the various syndicalist and industrial unionist movements and ideologies, as well as from the more intellectual and gradualist Guild Socialists around G. D. H. Cole. These various movements had been in the ascendancy in the immediate prewar period. Groups of active revolutionaries had formed in the centers where the shop stewards developed most strongly during the war. The influence of the different ideologies varied from place to place, but all developed important critiques of state socialism and stressed the need for workers' control over industry. Even the Guild Socialists had an important impact on the militant stewards' movement on the Clyde. Of course, these various ideologies were not the major impetus behind the movement as a whole. They helped to give that movement coherence and "to transform this narrow demand [for craft control] into a wider movement for workers' control."[23] As James Hinton has argued, the various ideas on workers' control helped provide the language, the ideological mediation that could bridge the gap between craft and revolutionary consciousness. But it was the actual struggles over job control by highly skilled craftsmen that provided the fertile soil and the popular base for these revolutionary ideas.[24]

The shop stewards' movement, however, failed to develop a fully coherent ideology or an effective organization. Its conceptions of workers' control remained, for the most part, excessively vague, especially concerning the higher levels of coordination. This was in marked contrast to the miners and railwaymen, who developed more elaborate conceptions of national coordination but tended to ignore the details of local control. If stewards' ideas on control were inadequate, their conception of how to achieve a socialism based on such control was even more so. Following the ideas of James Connolly and the Guild Socialists, the stewards believed that they could gradually extend workers' control in the various workplaces up to the point at which the capitalists would no longer have any function. An industrial republic would be constructed within the shell of the old political state, which would then crumble of itself. The struggle for political power need not be organized on its own terrain, for political power would automatically follow from the progressive conquest of control in the workplace. The program of the stewards thus remained largely confined to workshop and trade union questions and ignored the broader political problems with which the mass of the workers and other popular strata were concerned. Complementing this attitude toward political power was a distinct disdain for leadership and organization. In response to the bureaucratic politics of traditional socialism, many stewards came to see leadership itself as reactionary. They never developed any real national organization or elected a responsible leadership capable of taking action at decisive moments. The movement was thus condemned to rebellious isolation: the militant actions in different centers were each defeated in turn, and the movement as a whole failed to build links to other opposition groups. Their hostility to all forms of bureaucracy led the stewards to largely ignore even union politics, and thus they never had any real impact within the structures of their own unions. Though ideology acted as a brake on the development of organizational capacities, the conditions of organizing during the war, namely severe state repression and union antagonism, also hindered effective action.[25]

The limits of the revolutionary shop stewards' movement were set by the basic stability of the British state and the resiliency of the trade unions. Lacking the political space in which to extend their demands for workers' control, the skilled engineers reverted to their old exclusiveness. The partial transcendence of exclusiveness—reflected in demands for all-grades organization and in periodic solidarity (especially in the May 1917 to January 1918 period) with the less skilled on questions of wages, food, and the war—had always been tenuous, especially among the rank and file engineers. In the immediate postwar years the "ambiguous inheritance"[26] of the craft tradition resolved itself rather decisively away from the pole of incipient revolutionary workers' control based on the democratic representation of all workers and toward traditional craft exclusiveness. In the absence of a general political crisis and more vigorous pressure from less skilled and female workers (who remained organizationally weak and preoccupied with questions of pay, recognition, and numbers in their organizational struggles), the potentially expansive reinterpretation of craft control became increasingly confined to those skilled engineers who by now had developed an independent commitment to revolutionary Marxism. And with the success of the Bolsheviks and the rapid decline of their own movement, even many revolutionary stewards began to despair of workers' control as either a strategy for change or the organizational basis for a socialist economy.

The ASE, for its part, succeeded in reintroducing the old craft structures in many places, though it was itself radicalized to a certain extent by postwar unrest. Amalgamation with other craft societies never questioned the underlying principles of craft organization. Immediately after the armistice the unions in engineering and shipbuilding solidified their hold on the majority of their members by negotiating a reduction of the working week from 54 to 47 hours, with a corresponding increase in pay. Only on the Clyde was this resisted in the name of the 40-hour week, but protest there remained localized and basically unthreatening, despite the contrary appearance created by government overreaction. During the war timely concessions helped undercut the shop stewards' movement in some places (e.g., the

Tyne, where militance was so great as to force early concessions), while in other areas (Coventry, Birmingham) government proposals for official recognition of stewards exercising very limited functions as part of the trade union structure successfully contained militant demands for control and isolated the revolutionaries. The 1919 Shop Stewards' Agreement generalized this pattern. This, along with the decline in the high levels of employment that had been one of the major sources of strength of the independent shop stewards' movement in the first place, finally destroyed it as a mass-based phenomenon. The unions had survived the challenge of workers' control and had even resisted the pressure for all-grades organization. Now even the most radical stewards turned their attention to working within them.[27]

Italy The severe postwar political crisis in Italy was the context for the development of a factory council movement with revolutionary goals, a movement that made a spectacular if rather ineffective challenge to the capitalist industrial order in 1920. In Italy (in contrast to Britain and France) incredibly severe social strains produced by the war had led to intense popular discontent and polarization in both urban and rural areas, and this reflected itself at the parliamentary level. Universal male suffrage had been won in 1911, and for the first time since unification the liberals lost their absolute majority. It was the mass parties—the Italian Socialist Party (PSI) and the new Catholic Popular Party (Partito Popolare Italiano—PPI)—that showed the most dramatic increases. The insecure position of the bourgeois forces in parliament and the uncertain reliability of the armed forces after a victory markedly resembling defeat encouraged mass workers' and peasants' movements, including the movement for workers' control.[28] The political crisis, however, never reached the point of dual power (as it had in Germany and Russia), and hence the workers' control movement proceeded without the protection and encouragement of political and military organs favorable to its general goals. As a result, the degree of actual control over production remained very limited (especially compared with Russia), and the scope of the movement was limited to areas where class formation took highly exceptional forms and where particular grievances were most intense (compared with both Russia and Germany).

The most articulate theorization of the revolutionary role of the emergent factory councils was put forth by the group of young Turinese socialists around Antonio Gramsci. In May 1919 they set up the weekly *L'Ordine Nuovo* to assist in the creation of a new working-class culture. Such a project was necessary, they felt, if the workers were to become conscious of themselves not as mere passive objects of history or cogs in the capitalist industrial machine but as producers and creators of history, as the new ruling class that would abolish all classes in the struggle for its own liberation. This Hegelian emphasis on the transformation of culture and consciousness took a decisive step beyond Crocean idealism once the *Ordine Nuovo* group rooted it in the struggle to transform the relations of production in the workplace itself. The internal commissions, it was argued, were an expression in practice of the irreconcilable conflict between capital and labor, and at the same time represented *in nuce* the striving of the major productive force of capitalism—the working class itself—to reappropriate its powers of control in a conscious fashion. *L'Ordine Nuovo* set as its task the transformation of these still very limited commissions into full-fledged factory committees as autonomous organs of the entire working class. The trade unions were seen as organs suited to the struggle for more favorable terms for the sale of labor power as a commodity, but not to the abolition of the commodity form itself. Industrial legality, for which the trade unions had struggled and which they had begun to attain in increasing measure, was a great achievement for the defense of the workers' interests *within* capitalism, but one hardly suited to the movement of revolutionary offense *against* capital. Because of the unions' divisions by trade and because of their need to discipline the workers and enforce their side of the collective bargain, they had to distance themselves from the rank and file. They became bureaucratic organs rather than organs of proletarian democracy striving to institute full working class control over all aspects of production. The latter could be achieved only by factory committees, which built upon the solidarity incarnate in the production process itself and which were the very antithesis of industrial legality because they refused to trade off control for better wages and conditions. It was the factory councils that would be the material and organizational basis for the creation of a new consciousness, that would prepare the workers technically and spiritually to run society without the bourgeoisie. "All power to the workshop committees," the *ordinovisti* demanded. These were to be the basis of the new proletarian state. And many anarchists and anarcho-syndicalists, despite their rejection of any form of state and their more persistent warnings of the reformist pitfalls of the councils in a non-revolutionary situation, gave energetic support to councilist ideas and organization.[29]

It was the activity of these socialists and anarchists, nourished by the spontaneous struggle occurring on the shop floor around questions of control over discipline, piece rates, and the new production methods, that spread the revolutionary conception of the councils like wildfire throughout Turin in the fall of 1919. The *ordinovisti*, in alliance with Bordiga's "abstentionists," gained control of the local PSI, and even the Turin FIOM section and Chamber of Labor approved fairly radical conceptions of the councils and their relation to the trade unions (all workers and not just union members were to elect factory delegates, for instance). In November and December the election of Workshop Commissars (as council members were called) spread among the chemical and tire workers, coachbuilders, auto body workers, and even technicians in the metal plants, and in early 1920 among others as well. Although the *ordinovisti* played a crucial role in these developments, their ideas were never fully accepted by the movement, as Martin Clark and Giuseppe Maione have demonstrated. The workers themselves rejected the productivist criteria that Gramsci and others put forth, criteria that stressed the maintenance of discipline and order, and the workers' acceptance of all technical innovations designed to increase production, even *before* the workers had attained power. Likewise, many of the workers and even some of Gramsci's close collaborators rejected his conception of the relation between the unions and the committees, which opposed close organizational links directed at revitalizing the unions and reorganizing them on industrial lines. The unions, Gramsci felt, must exercise a certain degree of discipline over the councils and prevent them from acting capriciously in a situation not ripe for direct attack; and the committees, in turn, must help democratize and industrialize the unions. However, this reciprocal process should occur voluntarily, through the overlap in membership, not through hierarchical organizational links. This was a highly unrealistic conception in any but the most unstable situations. And to many workers, especially outside Turin, the syndicalist interpretation of the councils, which stressed their role in (often uncoordinated) factory occupations and sabotage, became prominent, despite the efforts of the *ordinovisti* to prevent this.[30]

The organizational and ideological limitations of the councilists manifested themselves very clearly in the two major confrontations of 1920. In April, the owners, supported by a massive deployment of troops, declared a lockout in response to the increasing tendency of workers and their factory councils to by-pass the arbitration machinery set up the previous year. The council leadership and their *ordinovisti* supporters helped organize a massive strike of some 500,000 workers in Turin and the surrounding province. But national support was not forthcoming from the PSI or the CGL. The councilists never had control of the situation, and local negotiations themselves quickly passed to D'Aragona, reformist secretary-general of the CGL. The settlement was a shattering defeat for the councils. The internal commissions were stripped of most of their newly claimed powers, and the provisions of the old FIOM agreement were reaffirmed. The workers were extremely embittered, not least by the deficiencies of council leadership. Gramsci and *L'Ordine Nuovo* were thoroughly discredited locally as well as nationally, and the movement that revived around other questions was never in their hands again. Indeed, it was Gramsci's former collaborator Tasca who now led the PSI Maximalist effort in Turin to unify the factory councils and trade unions, while utilizing the former to democratize and industrialize the latter. Control functions were not to be abandoned, but neither were specific demands made in this regard. Tasca's scheme, similar to that proposed in Milan by Schiavello, was approved in the Turin Chamber of Labor, though little was done to actually implement it. The scheme was opposed by only a handful of anarcho-syndicalist delegates, and it was they, not the former *ordinovisti*, who now led the struggle to revive the councils and to push the revolutionary movement forward both in Turin and elsewhere.

It was only the movement over wages led by FIOM against employer intransigence that brought about the major confrontation that the anarcho-syndicalists had been seeking all along. FIOM's tactic of a slowdown provoked lockouts in the metal industry nationwide, and a half-million metal workers responded by occupying their factories. In the process factory councils were revived to manage the various aspects of the occupation, not the least of which was maintaining production. And in Turin, where again factory councils were most vigorous due to the struggles over the previous year and the peculiar nature of Turinese industrial development and class structure,[31] an entire local economic network was soon established, managed by the workers and cooperating technicians and clerks. Overall coordination, however, was in the hands of FIOM and the Chamber of Labor. The CGL itself now pressed for workers' control (through the union) and the restoration of the pre-April powers of the internal commissions. But its National Council rejected the idea of a revolutionary political solution put forward (probably not seriously) by the PSI Directorate, which was unwilling to act without the support of the trade union leaders. As Terracini, a former *ordinovisto* and founding member of the Italian Communist Party, was to say at the Third Comintern Congress in 1921, "when the comrades who led the CGL submitted their resignations [in response to the PSI's proposal for a national movement to seize power], the party leadership could neither replace them nor hope to replace them. It was Dugoni, D'Aragona, Buozzi, who led the CGL; they were at all times representative of the mass."[32]

Though it underestimated the revolutionary impulses that guided a certain proportion of the workers, particularly in Turin, Terracini's statement underlines a basic fact of this period, namely, that the unions had weathered the onslaught of the factory councils and had maintained the leadership and allegiance of the majority of organized workers. Their structures and policies had been severely strained by the massive influx of new members after the war (representing a ninefold growth in two years), but they effectively resisted the factory council challenge. The relatively youthful workplace-based leadership of the council movement that had emerged over the past few years proved incapable of dislodging the veteran union functionaries from overall control, even as their activity helped democratize and industrialize some union structures themselves. To the great mass of organized workers, especially those not as directly affected by the employers' drive for increased rationalization and productivity, the traditional union leadership seemed capable of renewing the generally favorable trend that had been interrupted by the war. The negative example of Russia and the constellation of international forces further reinforced the unions' reformist tendencies. Trade union leaders, including Colombino of FIOM and D'Aragona himself, had been in Russia with PSI chief Serrati just that summer and were quite shocked at the harsh dictatorship and economic devastation that they witnessed. A revolution in Italy at this time, they felt, given the minority support for socialism even among the industrial workers and the inevitable blockade by other capitalist powers, would lead to conditions similar to those in Russia.[33] The overwhelming vote to return to work on September 24, though by no means an unambiguous proof of what the workers would have been willing to do two weeks earlier, testifies to the hold of the unions. Only in Turin was the vote even close. And the metal workers were the *vanguard* of the Italian revolutionary movement. Towards the end of the strike most workers were concerned primarily with getting paid for the time they had worked during the occupation. This, along with the reestablishment of the old functions of the internal commissions and promise of limited trade union control in industry, finally brought them back to work. The issue of control over production had not died, but neither had it decisively broken out of the framework of trade union legality. The momentum of workers' control stopped short of the revolutionary tasks set for it by its theorists. And as the *ordinovisti* had been discredited by the April strike, so now were the syndicalists, whose "favorite weapon—factory seizure—had been shown up as ineffective."[34]

Unobtrusive though it may have been throughout this conflict, the power of the Italian state stood firmly behind the normalization of capital/labor relations. This fact must not be forgotten. It certainly entered crucially into PSI and CGL decisions not to extend the movement into a national revolutionary seizure of power. A hastily armed workers' movement, still isolated from the rural classes, may have been able to defend the occupied factories, and even destroy them if provoked, as Prime Minister Giolitti warned the more militant employers. But it would hardly have been a match for an army that was still intact and extremely hostile to the antiwar socialist movement, as were the vast numbers of ex-combatants.[35]

Given this constellation of political and ideological forces at the end of the war, it is unlikely that even a more insurrectionary-minded party would have been able to tip the balance in favor of armed revolution. The anticapitalist posturing of the Giolitti government may have encouraged the workers and their unions to vigorously press their claims for higher wages and to have recourse to quite militant tactics when they were met with intransigent refusal. But the repressive apparatus was not immediately threatened, and the "old fox" Giolitti was able to skillfully force concessions from the owners. His triumph was ambiguous, since the government's apparent anticapitalism and its unwillingness to immediately suppress mass unrest gave further impetus to the fascist movement. But his strategy had halted the revolution and had contained the factory councils within sufferable limits. The recession that followed the September occupation, and increasing fascist and employer attacks, would soon destroy even the remnants of the movement for workers' control in Italy.

Germany The political crisis that had been developing in Germany in the later months of the war reached revolutionary proportions once it was clear that defeat was at hand. Thoroughly alienated from the Kaiserreich, its prosecution of the war and its meager attempts at political reform, the troops began to mutiny in early November. Workers all over the country moved decisively to take over local power once it was clear that the old repressive apparatus was crumbling. The workers and soldiers established councils (*Räte*) with the function of controlling the old authorities, maintaining food supplies and public order, and supervising demobilization. And military power was in the hands of the soldiers' councils. This relation of forces did not last long; but it was crucial to the extension of control in the workplace in

November and December 1918, since the councils gave official recognition and encouragement to the creation of factory committees that occurred in several important industrial regions. The workplace electoral base of most workers' councils no doubt facilitated this support. The Berlin councils' executive committee recognized the independence of the committees from the unions, and full co-determination rights for the committees in all matters affecting workers and white-collar employees (who were to be represented jointly). Even where the Workers' and Soldiers' Councils did not lend support to the extensive forms of control over the activities of the owners that were introduced by the more radical factory committees, they did not move directly against such committees either.[36]

Dual political power, however, was not resolved in a manner favorable to the extension of workers' control over production. Though the councils possessed revolutionary legitimacy in the eyes of workers, soldiers, and even certain sectors of the middle class and peasantry, they did not move to consolidate real administrative and military power. The relatively few exceptions to this in the early weeks were unsuccessful. Most councils saw themselves as interim organs for control and democratization, not as permanent substitutes for a democratic parliament as the highest state organ. The soldiers, councils, in particular, held a very moderate conception of their role. And demobilization undermined their power and prepared the way for the reconstitution of a new state military apparatus around an old officer corps that had not decomposed as a result of protracted mutinies and defeats (as happened in Russia). The First National Council Congress in December by an overwhelming majority approved of the early election of a National Assembly elected by universal suffrage, though it also registered itself in favor of thorough democratization of administrative and military organs and the initiation of orderly socialization measures.[37]

That the councils did not try to consolidate power in their own hands reflected both the lack of a practical and theoretical councilist heritage in the workers' movement and the dominance of the SPD. Under the peculiar conditions of social isolation, lack of access to the levers of political power under the constitutional monarchy and the Prussian three-class voting system, and a significant degree of toleration that permitted promising trade union gains and constant electoral advance, the German workers' movement had developed over the previous decades as a highly class-conscious movement with a strong subculture of its own, an avowedly revolutionary ideology, and a political and economic practice that was largely reformist and bureaucratic. The close links of the party to and dependence on the trade unions was the most important factor in the last regard, though the necessity to build an efficient organization to wage massive electoral campaigns and to appeal to middle-class voters on issues of political reform, the strong nationalism of its own constituency, and the deterministic brand of its own Marxian theoretical synthesis, also played significant roles in this as well. The wartime experience of collaboration with the government and with the bourgeois parties, and the achievement of definite political reforms and even greater promises just before the war's end, reinforced these tendencies. By November 1918 the party leaders were firmly convinced that socialist progress could be orderly, peaceful, and parliamentary, and that socialist democracy was consistent with no other way. And without the support of the SPD and the unions, the newly formed council structures could not maintain themselves on a national scale.[38]

An SPD heritage that had revealed profound, though weakened, sources of strength among the workers even during the sacrifices of war was now brought to bear on an immediate postwar situation fraught with severe, though perhaps overestimated, dangers: Entente opposition to radical political and economic measures, critical food shortages, immediate and long-term reparations, demobilization and reconversion of industry, secessionist movements, and opposition to the workers' movement by the vast majority of other strata. Under these conditions the moderate socialist leaders were largely able to maintain their hold on the working class, especially in the early months. Political and economic caution made much more sense to a working class with far more to lose than its chains, and the powerful negative image of Russian dictatorship and economic chaos continually reminded German workers of this. If military defeat produced the temporary crippling of the state apparatus in November 1918, it also circumscribed the possibilities for radical political and economic measures that did not threaten to wipe out the very real gains of the past and the immediate present. The SPD, mediating these concerns, lent its support to the establishment of a parliamentary democracy that would unite the nation, negotiate a peace, restore order in the economy, and forestall foreign intervention.[39]

The other organized political forces in the workers' movement were in no position in the early months to dislodge the SPD from its dominant role. The Communist Party (KPD) was extremely weak, had little presence in the daily work of the councils or the trade unions and tended to draw its support from the more marginal elements in the working class. The Independent Social Democratic Party (USPD) was able to achieve a leading position in only a handful of cities, and its national weakness was reflected in its 2.5 percent tally in the National Assembly elections. It was not only very loosely organized but was divided over major questions of power, councils, and parliament. The radicals, who were in the ascendancy throughout 1919, stood for a councilist dictatorship and immediate socialization but had little more than a vague program and no convincing strategy for achieving democratic socialism under the immediate postwar circumstances. The moderates, though committed to the councils as instruments of democratization, were much more cautious about preempting a universally elected parliament altogether. They wished to delay its convocation and present it with a series of radically democratic and socialist faits accomplis, but they shared SPD fears of a minority proletarian dictatorship. The burgeoning opposition bore within itself both the organizational and ideological weakness of its relatively recent emergence under wartime constraints and of the left's prewar incoherence, as well as the democratic parliamentarist heritage of the broader workers' movement itself.[40]

The hold that the SPD had in the workers' movement in the early weeks after November, however, began to loosen considerably as it became clear that its commitments for democratizing the state administration and military and initiating the cautious socialization approved at the First Council Congress were less than serious. From January to April 1919 a new phase of radical mass protest occurred. Despite the differences in emphasis in the three major areas of intense activity and confrontation (Berlin, the Ruhr, and Central Germany) and the variety even within these, the goals were basically the same: socialization based on extensive control by the workers at the point of production. Economic demands (wages, hours) and political demands (disarming of the Freikorps) played a significant part in the mass strikes that occurred, but so did a radical protest against the conditions of factory absolutism. The workers demanded respect and dignity and resisted authoritarian discipline even in those areas in which the old paternalistic traditions were strongest. Spurred on by the decisions of the First Council Congress on socialization, numerous council congresses in the various regions developed a series of demands that would begin the process of socialization by anchoring the factory councils in the workplace and in the constitution. Factory councils were elected and district and regional councils were formed out of them. In some places mines and factories were directly seized, but these were exceptions and were opposed by the regional organs. The councils wanted a firm commitment from the government on socialization and wanted the factory

councils to be given extensive rights of co-determination in the mean-
time. But the power of the owners would be directly and immediately
curtailed as well, for the higher council organs, composed solely of
workers' representatives, claimed overall authority over industry and
power to intervene in disputes between the temporarily retained owners and the councils in the factory. Socialization was seen as a process,
but one that would be guided by the workers' immediate appropriation
of overall economic control.[41]

The mass movement for workers' control and socialization in the
winter and spring of 1919 failed for several reasons. One of these was
certainly the continued deficiencies in leadership and ideology. The
KPD's influence was limited to a few places, and its attitude toward the
factory councils remained basically instrumental. Its putschist tendencies, however, were held in check wherever the mass movement was
strong and fairly unified. The German workers' movement had no
strong anarcho-syndicalist tradition upon which it might draw, and
where anarcho-syndicalist groups and unions did develop some limited regional strength in this period (e.g., in the Ruhr and Central
Germany), they remained antagonistic to overall coordination. The
lack of such coordination proved to be one of the main weaknesses, for
none of the major strikes in this period was linked up with the others,
and each was defeated in turn. Though the USPD dominated the
movement, it was itself divided and unable to provide general direction
and coordination. Its radically federalist and decentralist philosophy
and structure, shared by virtually all radical left groups in the period as
part of their rebellion against the bureaucratism of the SPD and the
trade unions, certainly contributed to this. The growth of the USPD in
1919 was tremendous, but, as one group of scholars has noted, it
remained more an expression of the spontaneous mass movement
than a political party in the real sense of the word.[42]

The mass movement on the shopfloor was unable to generate an
indigenous leadership to unify its activities soon enough to prevent
defeat. In November, when political power was still in flux and when
the Workers' and Soldiers' Councils could still have attempted to seize
the initiative, there existed no mass movement with a clearly articulated
ideology and vigorous leadership to press for the rapid extension of
workers' control as the real basis for the socialization that was being
demanded in the higher council organs. The revolutionary leadership
was too recently formed and theoretically undeveloped to be able to
lead the struggle both on the shopfloor around questions of control
and in the political council organs around basic questions of program
and power. Leadership and ideology developed further in the course

of the mass struggles themselves, though these remained either unclear or inadequate on many important questions (the relation of the
unions to the factory councils, of universal suffrage and democracy to
councilist dictatorship, on party pluralism and competition, and on
actual institutional levels and mechanisms for participation and control). But the development of a leadership with even a minimally
coherent ideology articulating the felt needs of the mass movement
and with the media to communicate it came too late. The effect of
council thinking on the mass of workers was thus very irregular, even
in the areas of most intense struggle. Not only was the council leadership unable to coordinate the movement to produce the maximum
effect, it was unable to adequately educate the movement to ensure
against its derailing by skillful yet meager concessions and vague promises by the government and the SPD. In November the coherent
leadership on questions of workers' control and socialization had been
lacking; at the height of the mass movement in early 1919 it was only
beginning to take shape.[43]

Skilled workers provided leadership in the council movement
and the mass strikes of early 1919. Extensive erosion of craft control
and significant progress towards all-grades organization in metals, plus
the greater opportunities apparently opened up by political crisis,
provided the basis for the translation of craft control conceptions into a
democratic and universalistic ideology of liberated labor that promised
to provide the institutionalized framework for participation of the less
skilled workers as well in the inevitably contradictory and conflictual
process of overcoming the unnecessary hierarchies in production.
There is little evidence for that interpretation that attributes the defeat
of the socialist revolution in Germany primarily to the sectoral interests
of skilled workers threatened by rationalization and striving to simply
eliminate the owners so as to place themselves at the top of a retained
hierarchical organization of production.[44] There existed no deterministic relation between skill or position in the division of labor, on the
one hand, and politics or workplace practice, on the other. Skilled
workers formulated demands with a good deal of appeal to the less
skilled. And the latter at times displayed considerable enthusiasm for
workers' control over production.[45] Local variations were extremely
complex. Nor is it possible to reduce the problems of fundamental
political transformation to that of skill composition within the working
class or its leading political organs. Less skilled workers were often
more reformist in their political and economic demands than skilled.
And the eventual "cooptation" of the latter was neither easy nor complete, as the huge demonstrations and mass desertion from the SPD in

the wake of the factory council bill and the continued use of the councils as a base of radical opposition were to show.

The major reasons for the failure of the movement in the spring of 1919, however, were that the reconstituted state apparatus proved too strong for a movement confined to a few geographical areas, however important, and the old trade unions, however strained, proved capable of resisting the onslaught of the factory councils. The Freikorps had little trouble containing and suppressing the uncoordinated strikes, feeble putsch attempts, and isolated council governments that lasted into May. The factory council leaders continued their activity, attempting by peaceful means to construct a council system within a hostile political environment that could no longer be challenged directly. But in July the SPD broke up the Berlin Council's General Assembly and its executive organ (*Vollzugsrat*). The radical councils (a majority in Berlin) were unable to maintain themselves as independent organs, however. In view of the impending moderate law on factory committees, the government declared their elections illegal and occupied their bureau.

That the movement was contained and then largely destroyed in its original sense was in no small part due to the fact that the trade unions were able to maintain themselves basically intact. Most unions, as previously noted, had developed into highly centralized, bureaucratic organs dominated by craft sections even where they embraced significant numbers of semi- and unskilled workers. Their reformist outlook had been further cemented during the period of the *Burgfrieden*, even though most of the gains were the result of government and military pressure rather than more tolerant attitudes of industry. The unions, believing that revolution and rapid socialization were out of the question and that any economic disorganization would destroy their organizations, looked toward the postwar period as one of harmonious collaboration between organized labor and capital (known officially as the *Arbeitsgemeinschaft*). Leading industrialists, for their part, had come to recognize by the war's end that the unions could be useful in limiting radicalism, maintaining labor discipline, and undoing the extensive system of government controls. Without a postwar reconstruction policy of its own, the trade union leadership agreed to follow the lead of capital in exchange for a series of very real gains: the eight-hour day (if implemented in other countries as well), full recognition of collective bargaining, industry-wide contracts, uniform wages and conditions, labor exchanges, and the end of employer support for yellow unions. These concessions helped promote the phenomenal growth of the unions to an extent entirely unimaginable before the war and in industries that had completely resisted unionization. In return, labor mediation on the basis of parity and trade union collaboration in the formulation of economic and social policy were to be institutionalized within the *Arbeitsgemeinschaft*.[46]

By the end of 1919 over eight million workers were organized into trade unions in Germany, compared with less than two million before the war. This massive growth shook the unions from top to bottom but did not fundamentally transform them. The old craft structures and leadership maintained themselves despite the huge influx of semi- and unskilled workers, and their hostility toward the factory councils was often very strong. They were not willing to risk their very existence and the concrete gains won over the last few years in premature and quixotic attempts to establish socialism. And, in any case, they saw the existence of unions as still necessary under socialism and hence saw the factory committees' attempts to displace them— which *was* a tendency in practice though not in the theory or policy of the council leaders—as highly dangerous. The unions were willing to permit worker representation on the shopfloor, but only with very restricted functions and only if strictly subordinated to the union hierarchy.

Large numbers of the trade union rank and file, however, were quite enthusiastic about council ideas. Those unions that were already more industrially-structured before the war (metals, mines, and rails) were more open to councilism and its stress on factory organization. Many saw the councils as a way of transforming the unions along industrial lines. Also, those unions with the most expansive membership (also metals and mines),[47] whose new recruits had little tradition of union discipline and stable organizational work, were more open to the councils, as were those who had not been previously organized at all (the new chemical industry, state workers, and clerks). In the mines and state factories and offices an especially oppressive patriarchal/authoritarian tradition existed which the council structure directly challenged, and in the state plants the demand for councils was itself partly a natural spin-off of political democratization. The large-city and large-factory union organizations had a particularly difficult time resisting demands for councils, but even the smaller craft bastions were not immune to council ideas. At the June 1919 ADGB Congress the opposition had perhaps a third of the votes, and this support increased over the summer as many SPD workers became increasingly disillusioned and embittered over party and union policy, especially vis-à-vis the spring strikes that had been resisted by the unions and denied strike funds. But the opposition was able to win control of only

one union, albeit the largest and most important—the metalworkers'
union (DMV). This victory, however, came only in October 1919 after
the movement as a whole had already reached its climax. The old
structures had resisted the attack. The ADGB had even increased its
centralized powers. It had helped capital weather the stormiest days of
the revolution and had helped normalize labor relations at least in
these crucial months. The inflationary policy that permitted such a
happy coalition between large industry and organized labor immediately after the war, as during it, would later tear at the very fabric
of German society. But in the 1918–19 context, which produced some
very significant gains for organized labor, the militant but disorganized
factory council leadership proved incapable of decisively undermining
the authority of the traditional leaders of German labor—the trade
union officials and functionaries. Until the crisis in 1923 it was the
unions, not the councils, that were in the forefront of labor's struggles
and the foundation of its united front.[48]

The mass strikes of the spring of 1919, it should be recalled, were
ended not only through effective and often ruthless repression but
through a skillful policy of concessions and promises of reform. The
idea of factory councils was incorporated into the Weimar Constitution, and much council activity occurred in the latter part of the year
around the final draft of the bill that was to be presented to the
National Assembly. A combination of pressures by owners, unions, and
the SPD, however, whittled down the bill to such an extent as to make
the councils virtually powerless. Blue- and white-collar workers were to
have separate councils, and delegates were to be elected at fixed intervals only, with no power of recall. The councils were strictly subordinate to the unions, and access to the owners' accounts was limited to
periodic official reports. They were not to have control over hiring and
firing or to interfere in production in any manner. Some participation
on questions of wages and conditions was granted, but in cases of
conflict the councils had no real power. At the higher levels, labor
representatives were to sit with those of the owners, since the stated
purpose of reform was cooperation in the interests of raising production. As Eberhard Kolb has expressed it, the factory council bill
approved by the Assembly in January 1920 was a first-class state fu-
neral for the economic council system.[49] For forty-two workers who
took part in the large demonstration outside the Assembly, that
metaphor became reality. The autonomous factory council movement
was dead, though militant activity was to occur periodically through the
legalized but disempowered councils. As many as 100,000 workers left
the SPD for the USPD as a result of the bill, but SPD and trade union

conceptions were approved at the first official National Factory Council Congress in August of that year. As Charles Maier has so neatly put it, "The councils could thus hold either old union beer or new revolutionary liquor. Bourgeois leaders were prepared to drain a glass if the workers agreed to a weaker potion."[50]

Russia Repeated military defeats and severe home front deprivations had thoroughly delegitimated the tsarist regime among the masses of workers, peasants, soldiers, and even large sections of the urban bourgeoisie and middle classes. And once the garrison in Petrograd came to the support of the huge strikes and demonstrations in February 1917, the fate of that regime was sealed. Lacking any real tradition of parliamentary democracy, workers and soldiers (and later peasants as well) established their own organs of political power in line with the revolutionary tradition of 1905. And despite their lack of officialization by the hastily constituted Provisional Government of liberal democrats and the dominant moderate socialist leadership that lent it support, the soviets remained the only truly legitimate political organs in the eyes of the popular strata. Continued participation in the war and the economic disintegration that ensued as a result only further enhanced their legitimative and administrative capacities relative to the legal government. The military apparatus itself continued to disintegrate under the dual onslaught of defeat and internal democratization. The troops in the rear, fearing service at the front, stood behind the soviets, and in place of the old police apparatus that had been shattered along with the court in February, local citizen militias arose to keep civic order. Workers' Red Guards, often the most influential elements in these, gave the factory committees direct protection to extend their powers in the workplace. By October the politico-military conditions existed for resolving dual power both in the factory and in the state apparatus. In no other country were the political, military, and economic crises so severe as to permit the decisive shift of forces in the popular movements themselves. Under these conditions the Bolshevik Party was able to achieve mass support, forge popular coalitions among workers, peasants, and soldiers, and establish the necessary degree of legitimacy for a revolution in the name of the soviets. Though far from being strictly disciplined and organizationally coherent, it was relatively well organized and decisively led, especially in contrast to the other important left-wing groups. The seizure and maintenance of power could hardly have been achieved otherwise.[51]

The Party also played a significant role in propagating workers' control. Although it certainly had not initiated the idea, the activity of many Bolshevik factory militants was quite important in the early spread of the committees. And after Lenin had officially come out for workers' control in May, the Party's role in the movement became even more pronounced. Leading Bolshevik factory committee militants took the initiative to call the first citywide Petrograd conference in late May, and these workers played the most prominent role in the Petrograd Central Council of Factory Committees that the conference elected. The Central Council, in turn, took an active part in spreading the committees nationwide.

The coordination of the movement, of course, was absolutely essential if individual committees were not to suffer the defeat that comes from isolation and if they were to serve as the cells of a unified *system* of economic self-management after the problem of state power had been resolved. With the aid of Bolshevik militants—whose activity was often as much an expression of the rank-and-file workers' movement as it was of Party organization per se, though the two were hardly dichotomous—the factory committee movement achieved a very noteworthy degree of coordination. There were innumerable instances of local solidarity that pointed beyond the corporativism embedded in continued competitive capitalist relations. Thus, despite the often strong factory identification of workers, for instance, as "Treugolniki" or "Putilovtsy," both the Treugolnik and Putilov factory committees, in collaboration with the Central Council, provided money and material to keep the Brenner plant from closing down. By October, municipal coordinating organs existed in the great majority of industrial centers and were complemented by several provincial and industrial branch organs as well. The Central Council in Petrograd functioned as a de facto national center until an all-Russian conference could be convened. After October, efforts at coordination intensified everywhere, and areas previously without such councils quickly developed them. The Petrograd Central Council was the most energetic and effective economic organ in the capital in the crucial weeks after the revolution, arranging for the procurement and transfer of fuel and raw materials among the committees on the basis of democratically agreed-upon criteria, instituting a system of industrial information and registration, disseminating technical advice, and aiding in the process of demobilization and, later, partial evacuation. Its activity, if not matched everywhere, was by no means an exception.

The committee movement was hardly without its contradictions in this regard, however. There were more than a few instances of parochial and competitive behavior among the committees, and even where municipal councils existed, they were not always effective in arranging for cooperation. Coordination at the provincial and regional levels was even less adequate, and the first (and only) national conference of committees was convened only a few days before the revolution. Political and military exigencies seem to have prevented the regular election of the national council that had been planned. Coherent proposals on how the economy as a whole could be coordinated on the foundation of workers' democratic control developed quickly, considering the recent origins of the movement in February and March, but not quickly enough, in view of the rapid development of the revolution, the economic urgencies of the post-October period, and the enormity of the task itself. The movement was never mobilized nationally around a coherent and detailed program of economic democracy and socialist construction, though there was great support for a system of control built from the bottom up and much resistance to statist conceptions of economic reconstruction.[52]

The evidence, however, does not point to the conclusion that particularism and economic fragmentation were *inherent traits* of the movement for workers' control that would necessarily lead to its undoing.[53] We can neither ignore or belittle the very impressive degree of coordination and solidarity achieved in the short and turbulent months between the February and October revolutions, nor the enormous amount of attention given to these issues by committee militants. As October approached, the committees were coordinating their activities at an accelerated pace, on an ever-broadening scale, and with increasing ideological coherence. What is important methodologically, however, is that we not impute tendencies *inherent* to the movement, as if that movement were not shaped by a complex set of institutional and organizational interrelationships within Russian society and the revolutionary process itself. The committees were, for the most part, hastily improvised in the wake of the February Revolution for pragmatic and defensive purposes. The weakness of the trade unions and their general hostility to workers' control deprived the committee movement of a preexisting organizational base from which to effect coordination. Although the committees generally recognized the need for close cooperation with the unions in principle, this was frequently disrupted in practice, and the continual organizational competition led to the dissipation of scarce resources, including potential organizational resources for coordinating economic activity. It is significant, for instance, that in the one region (the Urals) that did develop a relatively efficient and democratic system of workers' self-management after October, the unions seem to have cooperated with the committees for common goals—nationalization, control from the bottom up—even though the unions *as organizations* were excluded from the council system.

The committees were able to draw upon the preexisting networks and resources of the Bolshevik Party, and this undoubtedly aided the coordination of the movement. The great majority of factory committee centers were initiated by local Bolshevik militants, many of whom were in contact with factory committee leaders in Petrograd or local party committees in the more important industrial centers. But the Bolshevik Party was itself relatively disorganized at the intercity, provincial, and national levels. And Party leaders directed relatively few organizational resources to the development of the Central Council of Factory Committees into an effective economic center. The Council seems to have been used more for strategic political purposes than to have been the recipient of Party resources for its own pressing tasks of coordination. As a result, the workers' movement faced October without a coherent democratic strategy for economic reconstruction. As regrettable as such decisions may be in hindsight, we cannot overlook the fact that they occurred within the context of political struggle where time was a very scarce factor, power uncertain, and the Party's own resources incredibly strained. Virtually all Party committees and workers' organizations chronically complained about the shortage of competent and effective activists, not to mention material resources. The Bolsheviks were better organized than their major competitors for popular urban support. But their costs of mobilization were nonetheless considerable, relative to all the tasks they were confronted with and the competing claims on those resources. And some of the organizational conflicts within the Party overlapped with trade union/factory committee coordination and crisscrossed other lines of conflict. Where Mensheviks and Socialist Revolutionaries (SR's) predominated in local soviets or in the factory committees themselves, they often resisted the formation of separate coordinating councils for the committees.

Interwoven with these various organizational and political divisions was the fact that communication and transportation networks, always insufficient in this country of such vast size and geographically dispersed industrial centers, were increasingly disintegrating under the strains of the war, revolution, political animosity among workers, and, as William Rosenberg has shown, occupational divisions as well.[54] Under such conditions it became more and more difficult to convene delegates from scattered locales or for delegates elected to coordinating centers to maintain close contacts with their constituents. The dynamic between fragmentation and bureaucratization was henceforth in motion. Where industry was more geographically concentrated, as in Petrograd, committees could be more successful in rapidly developing coordination with their own resources. The smaller, more dispersed and variegated character of Moscow industry contributed to coordination difficulties. And in addition to these factors, a basic aspect of the revolutionary process cannot be forgotten, namely, that as long as political power remained in the hands of the Provisional Government and its Ministries and production continued under the incentive of private profit, the costs of coordination through independent factory committee centers could be as real as the benefits were uncertain. Short-term sacrifices, especially under the economic conditions of 1917, which provided such small margin for the misdirection of material and human resources, were so much more difficult to rationalize as long as the long-term payoffs were so unsure. Until these issues of political and economic power were resolved, there would remain a powerful impetus for committees and general assemblies to simply protect their own factories' economic interests and for individuals and occupational groups to do the same. That there was so much effort at coordination in 1917 testifies to both the contradictory demands of economic survival and an emerging consciousness of the requirements of reconstruction on new foundations. As Georges Haupt has argued, "it is the dynamic of mass mobilization in a period of social tension that renders the workers' movement, or more precisely the workers in motion, more susceptible to ideological considerations."[55]

However unfavorable were the organizational and political preconditions for factory committee coordination and coherent institutional formation, the role of ideology as a relatively autonomous historical determinant cannot be overlooked. As Theda Skocpol has argued, ideologies do not "provide *the key* to the nature of revolutionary outcomes."[56] But it is impossible to understand revolutionary outcomes simply by an analysis of the forms of political and structural crises and the organizational capacities available for their resolution, since ideological formations and the modes of their implantation in active historical subjects can determine in significant ways both the nature of crisis and the utilization of potential organizational and administrative resources. In the Russian Revolution, Bolshevik ideology both reacted and contributed to crises and selectively influenced immediate choices in a way that had short-run consequences as well as cumulative effects on urban and rural social development. Capacities for administration and organization were not pregiven, independent of the ideological orientations of the Bolshevik leadership and cadre. Those orientations, to be sure, reflected the conditions of struggle under tsardom, namely, the necessity for conspiratorial activity, relative isolation from

mass work, and the lack of prominence of control struggles in comparison to wages, hours, and basic union organization. But Bolshevik
ideological confusion and ambiguity in relation to workers' control, on
the one hand, and the emerging Leninist commitment to a conception
of "state capitalism under the dictatorship of the proletariat," on the
other, impeded coherent activity and coordination in the committee
movement before October. After October they directly contributed to
the economic fragmentation and disorganization that became the major rationale for bureaucratic centralization. The dual power in the
heart of the factory inherent in Lenin's formula was, under the conditions of struggle of 1917, bound to produce innumerable conflicts,
hinder the struggle against the sabotage of the owners and technicians,
and undermine the factory committees' attempts at instituting new
forms of worker self-discipline. Industry was further disorganized
when the regime initially failed to recognize the right of committees to
borrow money and failed to ensure that the banks would not financially
undermine the committees' attempts to continue production. Whereas
the Central Council of Factory Committees came up with a plan for
overall economic coordination on the day after the seizure of power,
Lenin rejected this as not immediately relevant, and the government
floundered through precious weeks without an adequate economic
center. The most effective one that existed at that point—the Central
Council itself—did not receive official authorization, thus making its
attempts to impose sacrifices on some committees in the interests of
others that much less effective. When official regulating organs were
finally constituted, their competencies were never clearly delineated
and conflict among them was constant. The factory committees, struggling to retain their work forces under the very difficult circumstances
of the initial transition, were thus faced with a set of highly bureaucratic, confused, and conflicting organs with little connection to the
workplace, little legitimacy among the workers, and not much effectiveness to compensate for these deficiencies. Is it any wonder that such
labyrinthine statist policies reinforced tendencies to particularism on
the part of workers' collectives? Party leaders could not understand
this, although Central Council leaders vigorously argued for overall
economic institutions that would possess both the transparency that
derives from clarity of functions and the legitimacy that derives from
democratic accountability.[57]

The administrative capacities represented by both local committees and their coordinating organs were not utilized or developed to
the extent that they might have been, even if, under the circumstances,
this would have inevitably fallen considerably short of their own aspira-

tions. But the ideological factors involved in this reflect a more basic aspect of the Russian Revolution that strikingly parallels both the Italian and German cases, namely, that even in situations of severe crisis where authority relations in production were directly challenged, the relative historical weight of trade union and party organizations made itself overwhelmingly felt in the resulting outcomes. Despite the active and very radical base of support in the committees and their increasing organizational capacities, especially relative to other organizations in regard to managing production, the Bolshevik Party—with the levers of state power in its hands—shifted its previously ambivalent support decisively toward the trade unions. Within a few months, factory committee activists were compelled to struggle on the organizational terrain of the unions rather than vice versa, though not without exerting a distinctive influence of their own. Political divisions within the Party and the need for Right Bolshevik, Left SR, and Menshevik support partly determined this response. Yet equally important, it seems, was the fact that even though prerevolutionary organizational networks were relatively attenuate and the new committee activists threw their support to the Party much earlier than did union leaders, the historical linkages between Party and union leaders proved most important. In the crucial discussions on the forms of economic reorganization, union leaders had much greater access to the Party hierarchy and provided the dominant definition of the economic situation. Lenin's own emerging ideology of "state capitalism under the dictatorship of the proletariat" had a definite affinity with that of many union leaders, but the organizational heritage of tsarism provided a distinct bias in the actual "production of knowledge" relevant for strategies of economic reconstruction.

In terms of social composition, factory committees were almost universally constituted by skilled male workers. In some cases delegates were even sent from outside the plant to guide the activity of workers' assemblies composed predominantly of so-called less "conscious" and less "disciplined" female workers. Patriarchal cultural patterns were quite pronounced. Women continued to be responsible for housework, childcare, and waiting on rationing lines, which made participation on committees much more difficult. (To what extent the nurseries and communal kitchens organized by factory committees and especially raion soviets helped reverse this pattern is unclear, though the committees did struggle against sexual harassment and the raion soviets intervened in family disputes to prevent wife abuse.) The general reasons for the dominance of the skilled in the committees are fairly clear. Within the working class only they had the requisite degree of technical and administrative skill necessary to control production. They were usually the most literate workers and also the most disciplined. Their general cultural horizons were broader, and they did not view their stay in the factories and the cities as merely temporary. They had the best sense of how production as a whole actually ran, and they had the greatest confidence in their own ability to manage it, if not without the technical experts, then certainly in conjunction with them.[58] It was also these workers who had the longest tradition of organizational work in the parties and the unions. Although they sometimes lagged behind the more politically explosive elements among the urban working-class women, youth, and recently proletarianized peasants that had swarmed into the factories during the war, the skilled workers dominated the organs exercising the functions of workers' control.

Despite the privileged position of skilled male workers relative to others within the industrial division of labor and within Russian political and cultural life, there is no evidence that they tried to formalize this privilege, or that they were able, to any significant degree, to informally use their positions of power in the factory committees to further their own corporate and sectoral interests against the less skilled. The informal jockeying behind the scenes for representation on the committees probably derived more from the traditions of party politicking in the workers' movement and the lesser degree of participation by the unskilled in the daily affairs of the assemblies and committees. The criteria used in the constitution of the formal organs of power were consistently universalistic and democratic: election by all, short terms of office, public meetings, availability of relevant information, instant recall. This was a distinct *tendency* in all the council movements under consideration. The predominance of skilled workers in the committees was not primarily the result of narrow corporativism or manipulation. The skilled were elected to the councils because the less skilled workers themselves put a high premium on advanced knowledge and skill when it came to running the factories. And there were numerous instances in which general assemblies with large unskilled and female participation asserted themselves against their elected delegates and rectified substantive positions and formal procedures.

It cannot be denied, of course, that skilled male workers often viewed themselves as superior not only to unskilled women but to the recently proletarianized male *chernorabochie*, who were often described as backward looking and superstitious, passive and fatalistic, crude and ignorant, and prone to drunkenness and wife beating. In fact, the evolving sense of urban worker dignity was defined very much against these perceived peasant-worker traits. The culture of superiority of skilled workers was thus not completely negative, especially in the context of diffuse egalitarian ideological influences from Marxists, populists, and anarchists alike. Internationalism among skilled veteran proletarians was very high, ethnic antagonisms minimal, and egalitarian and democratic political beliefs profound. Craft traditions were particularly weak as a result of the lack of a strong tradition of artisan guilds, late industrialization, and the political foreclosing of the craft union option under the tsar, among other factors. Industrial forms of union organization relatively quickly came to prevail over craft forms in 1917 with little resistance and a great deal of leadership from the skilled.[59] And the latter faced a mobilized mass of less skilled and less privileged workers who were militantly demanding their own share in political power and social rewards. They pressed these demands in the streets, in the neighborhood soviets, and in the factories. Indeed, the egalitarian elements in the behavior and thinking of the more privileged workers were no doubt encouraged by the constant pressure from the masses below them. There was much conflict between various categories of workers, and the unskilled often resented the skilled in the committees who enforced discipline and decided on layoffs when these became necessary. But although there was real potential for conflict over the question of wages, for instance, especially in a situation in which everybody's livelihood was threatened by inflation, lockouts, and the like, this conflict does not seem to have become overly intense. Some groups of skilled workers used the committees to foster their own claims, but the committee movement as a whole (in conjunction with the unions and soviets) seems to have been effective in narrowing the differentials. This no doubt resulted from the fact that the less skilled were able to effectively express their demands (which were predominantly around wages and job security) through the elected workers' organs, even if they did not enter those organs in large numbers themselves, although skilled workers also often vigorously supported a lessening of differentials.[60]

The position of the skilled Russian workers was an ambivalent one. Under conditions of political mobilization, of expansive political and social alternatives, of independent pressure from below, and of extensive egalitarian ideological influence, the skilled workers became a leading force—technically, administratively, organizationally, ideologically, and culturally—in the struggle for the liberation of all workers. Their initiative helped create and sustain an organizational framework within which the different sectors of the working class might fruitfully interact in the inevitably contradictory struggle to break down the relevant differentials in skill, knowledge, and effective power over the production process. But as the alternative of workers' self-management was closed off after October, as a top-heavy system of economic administration was created by the Bolsheviks and the trade unions, and as the mass of workers were demobilized in the workplace, many of these same factory committee militants began to narrow their horizon—though often not without a considerable degree of struggle both outside and within the new economic organs. Gradually they became entrenched in authoritarian factory management staffs or absorbed into bureaucratic state agencies. Their privilege, instead of being progressively undermined through democratic control and participation of the working class as a whole, was reproduced and reinforced on other levels.[61]

Despite whatever possibilities the factory committees might have had under more coherently democratic leadership, we cannot overlook the fact that some of the very conditions that helped bring about the October Revolution and the rapid extension of workers' control simultaneously circumscribed the subsequent development of an economic system based on workers' control over production. The extreme industrial disorganization and the disruption of exchange with the countryside not only fostered destructive centrifugal tendencies but led to a significant disintegration of the urban proletarian base itself. The severe undernourishment of those workers who remained in the factory sapped the vitality of the working class and undercut the very energetic attempts by the factory committees to create new forms of industrial self-discipline.[62] This would have been no easy task, even under more favorable conditions, for a working class with such a large proportion of recently proletarianized elements. The fragility of a state apparatus so radically removed from the life of civil society and so estranged from the forces of popular democracy made the seizure of power relatively easy, but it simultaneously necessitated a large transfer of politically reliable and administratively competent workers from the workplace to the new state organs and the Red Army—many of the latter never to return from the front. The already meager proletarian base for a system of political and economic democracy built upon active soviets and factory committees was thus even further weakened. The added economic devastation and deskilling of the working class that resulted from nearly three years of civil war made the extensive use of Taylorist and scientific management methods that much more attractive to a state leadership faced with the necessity of rapidly rebuilding industry, increasing productivity, and reintegrating Russia into the world market. The overall result of this was to further undercut the possibilities of workers' control.[63] The specific forms of "degeneration" of the democratic workers' organs spawned by the two revolutions may not have been predetermined, and alternative policies may have kept alive possibilities for their renewed development under more favorable conditions, but the immediate realization of their radically democratic content was severely circumscribed by some of the very conditions that allowed them to develop so far in the first place.

Conclusion

While it is impossible to briefly summarize the foregoing analysis or to draw attention to all of the distinctive contributions of the other essays in this volume, let me highlight several central concerns that have emerged in the study of labor insurgency and workers' control in this period, namely, temporal articulation, spatial (geographic/national) dimension, and movement composition and organization.

The development of movements for workers' control must be viewed in terms of the disjunctive articulation of several distinct time frames. Both the autonomist tendencies and the relative organizational weakness of councilist movements can be partly explained by their emergence during a period of relatively sudden wartime and postwar crisis that had followed upon a period of economic expansion generally conducive to cautious labor reformism and bureaucratic craft-structured organization. The preceding period of "organized capitalism" represented one of heretofore unknown prosperity, the end of chronic mass unemployment, and unprecedented growth in the rights and organizations of labor. To be sure, even before the war both the industrial and political dimensions of the dominant labor strategy revealed their limits, as inflation undermined gains, the unorganized waged fierce strikes, and revolutionary industrial unionism demonstrated a limited but noteworthy capacity for growth. Nonetheless, this period contrasted starkly with the Great or Long Depression of 1873–96, which had been characterized by high levels of unemployment, violent fluctuations in the labor market, and conditions generally unfavorable to trade union growth and consolidation. It was the contrast of these two periods, and the difficult transition from one to the other, that had deeply imprinted itself in the collective memory of many of the older workers, particularly those who had risen to responsible leadership positions in labor organizations, and set them apart from many of the younger workers. Karl Mannheim's conception (borrowed from Pinder) of the noncontemporaneity of contemporaries had a very definite organizational translation here.[64] The heritage of moderation in union officialdom was reinforced by the kinds of concessions that were or appeared realistically achievable during the war and immediate postwar period. The factory committees, on the other hand, had for the most part emerged relatively suddenly in the heat of local factory struggles during the war. As a result, they often lacked the organizational and agitational experience tested through years of struggle and constructive activity. Their factory constituencies were often quite unstable during the period of their ascendancy, thus disrupting the informal networks and solidary group relations that were often crucial to sustained activity. As a result of their recent emergence, they drew at best on quasi-coherent ideological conceptions of the means of their struggle and the institutional goals towards which they were striving, and this often reinforced organizational deficiencies. Finally, the factory committees were constantly constrained by state repression during the war, which limited their abilities to organize above the plant level. Under these conditions, factory committee movements had extreme difficulty providing the kind of broader organization and coordination necessary to make an effective challenge during the relatively short periods of political crisis when this was most possible. In short, the outcomes of worker control struggles reflect the complex articulation of several distinct time frames of struggle, whose contours were defined by broad socioeconomic and political factors and whose practical and organizational manifestations were often in conflict.

In view of these developments, the radical councilist perspectives developed by Antonio Gramsci and Anton Pannekoek appear seriously lacking. Both postulated a progressive autonomization of function and organization for the factory councils, though Gramsci at least believed that voluntary organizational cooperation with the unions was both necessary and possible.[65] But the resilience of the unions in the face of serious organizational strain was as noteworthy as the weakness of council structures that tended toward autonomy. The unions never really lost their dominant role, and the factory committees played more a part in revitalizing them than they did in displacing them. In fact, the distinct tendency that finally prevailed everywhere was that which favored the (re)incorporation of the committees into the unions. This was the case in Glasgow and Sheffield, where craft structures had been very strong and autonomism among shop stewards pronounced. Even in the limit case of Russia, where the unions had been very weak before the February revolution, where their loose and top-heavy growth thereafter gave great scope to autonomist factory committee development, and where the extreme severity of political and economic crisis facilitated shopfloor workers' control, the tendency toward integration of committees and unions prevailed, primarily on the terms of the latter. In Germany and Italy, where autonomism was less pronounced in practice and where the strengths of the movements for workers' control partly derived from the mobilization of preexisting union resources, (re)integration prevailed despite serious organizational strain within the unions. And the labor movement with the most continuous and profound ideological tradition of workers' control, namely France, was the very one that defined control least in terms of autonomous shopfloor action. Factory council organizations labored under what Arthur Stinchcombe has called the "liability of newness," which is particularly severe for new *forms* or organization.[66] They competed on unfavorable terms against the older, more powerful trade unions for scarce organizational resources and legitimacy, and on a terrain where collective bargaining had hardly outlived its usefulness in the eyes of the vast majority of workers or proved itself incapable of accomodating to issues of control. Under these conditions the radical separation of functions and structures in the Gramscian schema, or the even more total bifurcation in Pannekoek's, could hardly be expected to sustain itself for any period of time. Further advances in workers' control could only have been achieved with the support if not organizational preeminence of the trade unions. And if the limits of the councilist perspective are evident even for the period in which it emerged, they should be even more apparent today. This was a period marked by the strains of prolonged total warfare, of a relatively young union movement not nearly so organizationally established or buttressed by participation in state apparatuses as it is today. It was a period marked by a massive and sudden influx of new recruits into the old organizations, and one in which the specific struggles of highly skilled workers against accelerated wartime rationalization were most intense. The combination of such conditions facilitating autonomism are not likely to be repeated. Shopfloor struggles for control since the Second World War have largely remained within trade union frameworks or have been reintegrated into them after brief periods of autonomism. Even in Third World countries such as Chile and Peru this has been the case.[67] The movements of the First World War period reflected the growing pains of industrial unionism, magnified by the crisis of the war, more than they represented a viable alternative to trade unionism as such.

The international dimensions of workers' control in this period are also of utmost significance. Not only did movements develop on a broad scale across national boundaries in response to similar structural changes and specifically war-induced conditions, but Taylorism and its variants helped to alter the international conditions under which national labor movements could struggle to improve the position of workers. Once Taylorist methods had become so much more diffused during the war, labor movements were in a position where they could no longer hope to completely resist them and also achieve gains on other important fronts. The industry and currencies of the warring European countries had lost considerable ground to the United States, whose leading industries continued to set the pace for rationalized production. The pressure transmitted through the world market on corresponding European national industries was internalized by the unions, since resistance to such processes could only *weaken* the position of national labor in the *absence of an effective international strategy* against them. In a sense, the underlying premise was very similar to one often expressed in the debates of the Second International parties regarding the tactics to be used to prevent war—namely, that the stronger workers' movement, the one actually able to obstruct its government's military mobilization through militant mass actions, would suffer the most at the hands of those countries whose labor movements were less effective in this regard. The leaders of FIOM in Italy clearly recognized this dilemma as did German union leaders, for whom hyperinflation and war indemnities made rationalization of German industry appear that much more necessary. The economic devastation of the civil war and the "de-skilling" of the Russian working class as a result of death, migration to the countryside and to commercial occupations, and absorption into the new state apparatuses, generated strong pressures on Soviet leaders to adopt the latest production techniques. The international vulnerability of the revolutionary state had to be reduced and a rapid reintegration into the world market effected, since the proximate possibilities for indigenous technological development were very slim. Accomodation with Taylorism was a necessity, even if revolutionary state power may have provided objective possibilities for experimentation (workers' participation and education, job rotation, industrial democracy on the RAIC model). The ASE in Britain represented only a partial and temporary exception here, and one not without its own costs.[68]

The French case is most instructive in this regard. Leaders of the CGT in France, vigorous opponents of Taylorism in the prewar period, came to regard it as rational and necessary if the position of French industry in the world market was to be enhanced sufficiently enough to secure the increase in wages and the decrease of the working day to eight hours that were both central concerns of the French working class. Their ambitious reform program, which included extensive union participation in economic management, was specifically linked to the need for increased rationalization.[69] As Gary Cross has shown, this represented not passive accommodation, but an active strategy based on a critical reflection on past failures, a realistic recognition of the changing nature of the French working class, and a creative redefinition of workers' control that included broader possibilities for coalition politics (workers, consumers, and technical experts).[70] Basic aspects of craft control were sacrificed in this new conception, to be sure. But given the constraints of the world market, and the centrality—even among many skilled workers—of nonworkplace interests in material security and culture (the latter symbolized by the eight-hour day demand), the interest in craft control could no longer have been effectively represented by labor's organizations, nor could Taylorism have been effectively resisted. In the long-term struggle against Taylorism and rationalization throughout the industrial world, many if not most skilled workers were concerned more about wages, relative status and earnings, and forms of payment and calculation, than with integral skills and craftlike work. Rationalization for the less skilled often brought advances in terms of earnings, hours, physical strain, regularity of employment, and for some, genuine upgrading. The promise of the eight-hour day must be seen in terms of the value placed on culture, community, and family life—even if the terrain of leisure time would not remain an uncontested one. To interpret working-class struggles in this period primarily in terms of the fight against Taylorism would thus represent its own peculiar form of productivism. In the context of world market constraints, national options, credible strategies, and the relative priorities and varieties of actual or perceived working-class benefits, it becomes impossible to view the mass struggles for workers' control simply against the backdrop of "Frederick Taylor as Serpent"[71] or the trade unions as Satan's lieutenants.

The relations among various groups of workers were complex and shifting. Skilled workers predominated in worker control struggles as a result of their relative deprivations brought about by the impact of wartime rationalization, technical and administrative skills relevant to controlling production, organizational and cultural skills, and preexisting linkages to trade union and party networks. Women workers, who were predominantly semi- and unskilled, suffered multiple disadvantages in terms of participation in control struggles as a result of deeply embedded patriarchal patterns. Responsibility for home and child care, including long rationing lines during the war, made participation much more difficult and tended to preclude the formation of workplace recreational cultures and institutions that have often been the basis for sociability, solidarity, and protest. Communities, neighborhoods, and marketplaces, rather than workplaces, tended to be more central focal points for struggle.[72] And, in general, unskilled workers tended to be more instrumental in their attitudes towards work, and their demands centered not on control, but on wages, conditions, and treatment by supervisors. These divisions were neither wiped away by the mass movements for democratic control nor did they remain unaffected by them. Rather, in a complex and contradictory fashion, these movements drew upon and in certain ways reproduced inequalities that were challenged by the very forms of democratic representation developed in the struggle against managerial control. Gramsci's belief that solidarity was incarnate in the production process itself inadequately represented the divisions that existed. It reflected more the peculiar conditions of Turin as well as the limits of his own critique of the capitalist division of labor. He did not view as problematic large gradations in expertise but considered them functionally necessary and hence the basis for a form of solidarity rooted in the mutual recognition of indispensability. Nor, however, did there exist a deterministic and narrow relation between position in the division of labor and politics or workplace practice. The dynamic of struggle was not deterministically set by the privileges of skill or the interdependencies of productive functions but by a range of other political, organizational, and ideological factors that interacted with these. Such factors included the previous extent of rationalization, the strength of craft organization, the degree of mobilization of the less skilled workers, cultural and ideological formations in the working-class movements, the extent to which alternative forms of production and power appeared possible as solutions to crisis, and the forms of council democracy themselves. The consciousness of skilled workers was not narrowly fixed by corporativist interests but displayed a multivalent dynamism. Likewise, less skilled workers at times became quite receptive to workers' control. The differences between groups could be bridged in various ways, including those that did not rely solely on rational calculation of mutual benefit but appealed to solidarity and principle.[73] In all these council movements, however, the form of democratic participation played a relatively autonomous role. Despite the fact that all the movements drew upon (and hence in some ways reinforced) the inequalities of existing divisions of labor, democratic and universalistic forms tended to foster an egalitarian dynamic of their own.

Notes

1. David Montgomery, *Workers' Control in America* (New York, 1979), 10.
2. Steve Fraser, "The 'New Unionism' and the 'New Economic Policy,'" in this volume.
3. See, for instance, Mayer Zald and John McCarthy, eds., *The Dynamics of Social Movements* (Cambridge, 1979); Zald and McCarthy, "Resource Mobilization and Social Movements: A Partial Theory," *American Journal of Sociology* 82, no. 6 (1977), 1212–1241; Charles Tilly, *From Mobilization to Revolution* (Reading, 1978); Anthony Oberschall, *Social Conflict and Social Movements* (Englewood Cliffs, N. J., 1973); Michael Schwartz, *Radical Protest and Social Structure* (New York, 1976); and Theda Skocpol, *States and Social Revolutions in France, Russia and China* (New York, 1979).
4. For example, Ted Gurr, *Why Men Rebel* (Princeton, 1970); Neil Smelser, *Theory of Collective Behavior* (New York, 1963); Ralph Turner and L. Killian, *Collective Behavior*, 2nd ed. (Englewood Cliffs, N.J., 1972). Unlike some, however, these authors do not completely neglect structural and political factors.
5. On general wartime conditions for the working classes in Germany, see Jürgen Kocka, *Klassengesellschaft im Krieg 1914–1918* (Göttingen, 1973); Gerald Feldman, *Army, Industry, and Labor in Germany 1914–1918* (Princeton, 1966); Robert Armeson, *Total Warfare and Compulsory Labor* (The Hague, 1964); Reinhard Rürup, Eberhard Kolb, and Gerald Feldman, "Die Massenbewegungen der Arbeiterschaft in Deutschland am Ende des Ersten Weltkrieges (1917–1920)," *Politische Vierteljahresschrift*, 13 Jahrgang, Heft 1 (August, 1972), 87 ff.; for France, William Oulaid and Charles Picquenard, *Salaires et tarifs* (Paris, 1928); Roger Picard, *Le mouvement syndical durant la guerre* (Paris, 1927); Marjorie Ruth Clark, *A History of the French Labor Movement (1910–1928)* (Berkeley, 1930), 51 ff.; Val Lorwin, *The French Labor Movement* (Cambridge, 1966); 51 ff.; Max Gallo, "Quelques aspects de la mentalité et du comportement ouvriers dans les usines de guerre, 1914–1918," *Le mouvement social*, 56 (July–September, 1966), 3–33; for Italy, Martin Clark, *Antonio Gramsci and the Revolution that Failed* (New Haven, 1977), 5, 21 ff.; Gwyn Williams, *Proletarian Order* (London, 1975), 55 ff.; Luigi Einaudi, *La Condotta Economica e Gli Effetti Sociali della Guerra Italiana* (Bari, 1933), especially 99 f. and chapter 3; Giuseppe Prato, *Il Piemonte e gli Effetti della Guerra sulla sua Vita Economica e Sociale* (Bari, 1925), chapters 3 and 5; for Britain, Arthur Marwick, *The Deluge* (London, 1965); James Hinton, *The First Shop Stewards' Movement* (London, 1973), 33 ff.; Marion Kozak, "Women Munition Workers During the First World War with Special Reference to Engineering," Ph.D. dissertation, University of Hull,

1976; for Russia, S. O. Zagorsky, *State Control of Industry in Russia during the War* (New Haven, 1928), 51 ff., passim; John Keep, *The Russian Revolution* (New York, 1976), 42 ff., 16 ff. See Stanislaw Andrezejewski, *Military Organization and Society* (London, 1954), 28 ff., for an early statement of the hypothesis that increased popular participation in the war effort is conducive to democratization and the narrowing of class differences; see also Arthur Marwick, *War and Social Change in the Twentieth Century* (New York, 1974); Marc Ferro, *The Great War, 1914–1918*, trans. Nicole Stone (London, 1973), 170 ff.

6.   Peter von Oertzen, *Betriebsräte in der Novemberrevolution* (Düsseldorf, 1963), 273–274; Richard Comfort, *Revolutionary Hamburg* (Stanford, 1966), 94–95; Feldman, 205; Kocka, 12ff., 27–28; Heidrun Homburg, "Anfänge des Taylorsystems in Deutschland vor dem Ersten Weltkrieg," *Gesellschaft und Geschichte* 4, no. 2 (1978), 170–194; Hinton, 56 ff.; Lyndall Urwick, *The Development of Scientific Management in Britain* (London, 1938); Kozak; Eric Hobsbawm, "Custom, Wages and Work-load in Nineteenth Century Industry," in Peter Stearns and Daniel Walkowitz, eds., *Workers in the Industrial Revolution* (New Brunswick, 1974), 246 ff.; Clark, *Antonio Gramsci*, 26–27, passim; Aimée Moutet, "Les origines du système de Taylor en France. Le point de vue patronal (1907–1914)," *Le mouvement social* 93 (Oct.–Dec. 1975), 15–49; James Laux, *In First Gear: The French Automobile Industry to 1914* (Montreal, 1976), chapter 13; Patrick Fridenson, *Histoire des usines Renault* (Paris, 1972), 70 ff., 89 ff.; Oualid and Picquenard, 91 ff., 348 ff.; Picard, *Le mouvement syndical*, 109 ff.; Robert Wohl, *French Communism in the Making, 1914–1924* (Stanford, 1966), 119–120; Bertrand Abherve, "Les origines de la grève des métallurgistes parisiens, juin 1919," *Le mouvement social* 93 (Oct.–Dec. 1975), 75 ff.; Peter Stearns, *Lives of Labor* (New York, 1975), Part II; Chris Goodey, "Factory Committees and the Dictatorship of the Proletariat (1918)," *Critique* 3 (Autumn 1974), 31; Paul Devinat, *Scientific Management in Europe* (Geneva, 1927).

7.   On this whole problem, see especially Georges Haupt, *Socialism and the Great War* (Oxford, 1972). Also, Wohl, 54, for the vivid testimony of Merrheim, head of the CGT's Metal Federation, in this regard.

8.   The CGL, under the banner of "neither adherence nor sabotage," remained officially opposed to the war, however. See Daniel Horowitz, *The Italian Labor Movement* (Cambridge, 1963), 128–129.

9.   See Peter Stearns, *Revolutionary Syndicalism and French Labor* (New Brunswick, 1971). Both the Industrial Workers of the World (IWW) in North America and the National Confederation of Labor (Confederación Nacional del Trabajo) (CNT) in Spain were plagued by similar problems, and both developed reformist/bureaucratic tendencies as a result of mass pressure.

10.   Hinton, 68, 58 ff., passim; also Branko Pribićević, *The Shop Stewards' Movement and Workers' Control* (Oxford, 1959), 30–31, 35, passim.

11.   Von Oertzen, *Betriebsräte*, 271 ff., passim; Fritz Opel, *Der Deutsche Metallarbeiter-Verband Während des Ersten Weltkrieges und der Revolution* (Hannover, 1958); Comfort, 94–95; David Morgan, *The Socialist Left and the German Revolution* (Ithaca, 1975), 55–56.

12.   Clark, *Antonio Gramsci*, 36 ff., 80 ff.; Giuseppe Maione, *Il Biennio Rosso* (Bologna, 1975), 7 ff.; Mario Abrate, *La Lotta Sindacale nella Industrializzazione in Italia, 1906–1926* (Turin, 1966), chapter 8; Horowitz, 58 ff., 70 ff., 128–129.

13.   Picard, *Le mouvement syndical*, 116 ff.; Picard, *Le contrôle sur la gestion des enterprises* (Paris, 1922), passim; Oualid and Picquenard, 420 ff.; Gallo, 22 ff.; Nicholas Papayanis, "Masses révolutionnaires et directions reformistes: les tensions au cours des grèves des métallurgistes français en 1919," *Le mouvement social* 93 (Oct.–Dec. 1975); Abherve.

14.   Hinton, chapter 8.

15.   Clark, *French Labor Movement*, 66 ff., 80 ff.; Lorwin, 52 ff.; Picard, *Le contrôle ouvrier*, 24, 84 ff.

16.   Zagorsky, 86 ff.; Keep, 42 ff.; Oscar Anweiler, *The Soviets: The Russian Workers, Peasants and Soldiers Councils 1905–1920*, trans Ruth Hein (New York, 1974), 97 ff.; Paul Avrich, "Russian Factory Committees in 1917," *Jahrbücher für Geschichte Osteuropas* 11 (1963), 165.

17.   Marc Ferro, *La Révolution de 1917*, vol. 2 (Paris, 1976), 275. On the Russian unions, see also Isaac Deutscher, *Soviet Trade Unions* (London, 1950); Uwe Brügmann, *Die russischen Gewerkschaften in Revolution and Bürgerkrieg* (Frankfurt am Main, 1972); Keep, 96 ff.; Diane Koenker, "Moscow Workers in 1917," Ph.D. dissertation, University of Michigan, 1976, chapters 6 and 7.

18.   Brügmann, 59 ff.; Frederick Kaplan, *Bolshevik Ideology and the Ethics of Soviet Labor* (New York, 1968), 54 ff., 61 ff.; Leopold Haimson, ed., *The Mensheviks*, trans, Gertrude Vakar (Chicago, 1974).

19.   On this general feature of mobilization see Tilly, p. 141.

20.   See Haimson, "The Russian Workers' Movement on the Eve of the First World War," paper delivered at the annual meeting of the American Historical Association, New York, December 1971, 34 ff.; Avrich, 172; Anne Bobroff, "The Bolsheviks and Working Women, 1905–1920," *Soviet Studies* 26, no. 4 (1974), 554; Mark David Mandel, "The Development of Revolutionary Consciousness Among the Industrial Workers of Petrograd Between February 1917 and July 1918," Ph.D. dissertation, Columbia University, 1978, 188 ff., 492.

21.   On the rise and development of the committees in 1917, see Carmen Sirianni, *Workers' Control and Socialist Democracy: The Soviet Experience in Comparative Perspective* (London, 1982), chapters 2 and 3; Brügmann; Avrich; Richard Lorenz, *Anfänge der bolschewistischen Industriepolitik* (Köln, 1965); Benjamin Ward, "Wild Socialism in Russia: The Origins" *California Slavic Studies* 3 (1964), 127–148; Kaplan; Falk Döring, *Organizationsprobleme der russischen Wirtschaft in Revolution und Bürgerkrieg (1918–1920)* (Hannover, 1970); William Rosenberg, "Workers' Control on the Railroads and Some Suggestions Concerning Social Aspects of Labor Politics in the Russian Revolution," *The Journal of Modern History* 49, no. 2 (June 1977), reprint D1181-D1219; Robert Devlin, "Petrograd Workers and Workers' Factory Committees in 1917: An Aspect of the Social History of the Russian Revolution," Ph.D. dissertation; SUNY–Binghamton, 1976; Marc Ferro, *The Russian Revolution of February 1917*, trans.

J. L. Richards (Englewood Cliffs, N.J., 1972), 112 ff., 271 ff., passim; Ferro, *La Révolution de 1917*, vol. 2, chap. 6. The latter's contention that the factory committees had voluntarily decided to subordinate themselves to the unions is, however, mistaken.

22.   Charles Maier, *Recasting Bourgeois Europe* (Princeton, 1975), 91 ff.; Walter Kendall, *The Revolutionary Movement in Britain 1900–1921* (London, 1969), 187 ff.; Wohl, 114 ff.; Papayanis.

23.   Pribićević, 164.

24.   Hinton; Pribićević, 163–64; compare Jean Monds, "Workers' Control and the Historians: A New Economism," *New Left Review* 97 (May–June 1976), 81–100; see Hinton's response in the same issue.

25.   Kendall, chapter 8; Hinton, passim; Pribićević, passim.

26.   Hinton, 56. Iain McLean questions the representativeness of the leading stewards in the Workers' Committees in "Popular Protest and Public Order: Red Clydeside, 1915–1919," in R. Quinalt and J. Stevenson, eds., *Popular Protest and Public Order* (New York, 1974), 221.

27.   McLean; Hinton, chapter 8, passim; Pribićević, 37 ff., 102 ff.; Kozak, passim. Joint labor-management Whitley committees were established in response to rising worker protest during the war. But, despite the use of similar vocabularies, they were unable to perform the function of channelling labor demands in areas that were previously well organized, and their peak inclusion of 3.5 million workers lasted for only a short period of time. See Harvie Ramsay, "Cycles of Control: Worker Participation in Sociological and Historical Perspective," *Sociology* 11 (1977), 481–506.

28.   Maier, *Recasting Bourgeois Europe*, chapters 1 and 2; Clark, *Antonio Gramsci*, 4–5; Paolo Spriano, *The Occupation of the Factories*, trans. Gwyn Williams (London, 1975), 80; Antonio Gramsci, *Selections from the Prison Notebooks*, ed. and trans. Quintin Hoare and Geoffrey Nowell Smith (New York, 1971), section I.3; Adrian Lyttelton, "Revolution and Counter-Revoluttion in Italy, 1918–1992," in Charles Bertrand, ed., *Revolutionary Situations in Europe, 1917–1922* (Montreal, 1977), 63 ff.

29.   Antonio Gramsci, *Selections from Political Writings 1910–1920*, ed. Quintin Hoare, trans. John Matthews (New York, 1977); Clark, *Antonio Gramsci*; Williams, *Proletarian Order*; Carl Boggs, *Gramsci's Marxism* (London, 1976); Alastair Davidson, *Antonio Gramsci: Towards an Intellectual Biography* (London, 1977); Maione; Pier Carlo Masini, "Anarchistes et communistes dans le mouvement des conseils à Turin—première après-guerre rouge 1919–1920," *Autogestion* 26–27 (March–June 1974), 37–38, 43 ff.

30.   See particularly Clark, *Antonio Gramsci*, 69 ff. and chapter 4; Maione, chapter 1, passim; Gramsci, *Political Writings*.

31.   Due to its late development, firms there tended to be more technologically advanced, larger, and more concentrated. One industry (automobiles) dominated the city, and one company in particular (FIAT) stood above all the rest. The city possessed a very small middle class and virtually no artisan strata to distract from the basic polarity between owners and workers.

There was a high proportion of skilled workers yet with much less of a craft tradition and corporativist consciousness than elsewhere. See Giuliano Procacci, "La classe operaia italiana agli inizi del secolo XX," *Studi Storici* 3, no. 1 (Jan.–March 1962), especially the first section; Abrate 22 ff.; John Cammett, *Antonio Gramsci and the Origins of Italian Communism* (Stanford, 1967), 19 ff.

32.   Quoted in Spriano, 91, also 84; and Davidson, 147; Clark, *Antonio Gramsci*, chapters 5 to 9; Maione, chapters 2 and 3; Williams, *Proletarian Order*, chapters 8 to 10; Tasca in Gramsci, *Political Writings*, 239 ff. Maione, 11 notes that the original resistance of Fiat workers to the FIOM contract that most other workers felt favorable toward was due in part to corporativist motivations. These workers felt that their own better contract terms had been sacrificed for the benefit of the national contract.

33.   Albert Lindemann, *The "Red Years"* (Berkeley, 1974), 164, 181, 203.

34.   Clark, *Antonio Gramsci*, 179.

35.   Spriano, 152, n. 49, also p. 80 and 132 ff.; compare Williams, *Proletarian Order*, 256 ff.; Davidson, p. 148; Lyttelton.

36.   Eberhard Kolb, *Die Arbeiterräte in der deutschen Innenpolitik 1918–1919* (Düsseldorf, 1962), 71 ff.; Ulrich Kluge, *Soldatenräte und Revolution* (Göttingen, 1975); Von Oertzen, *Betriebsräte*, 80 ff., 134–135.

37.   Kolb, *Arbeiterräte*; Kolb, "Rätewirklichkeit und Räte-Ideologie in der deutschen Revolution von 1918/19," in Eberhard Kolb, ed., *Vom Kaiserreich zur Weimarer Republik*, (Köln, 1972), 170 ff.; Rürup, Kolb, and Feldman; Hans Schieck, "Die Behandlung der Sozialisierungsfrage in den Monaten nach dem Staatsumsturz," in Kolb, *Vom Kaiserreich*, 150 ff.; Henry Egon Freidlander, "Conflict of Revolutionary Authority; Provisional Government vs. Berlin Soviet, November-December 1918," *International Review of Social History* 7 (1962), 163–75. For some local studies, see Reinhard Rürup, ed. *Arbeiter- und Soldatenräte in rheinisch-westfälischen Industriegebiet* (Wuppertal, 1975).

38.   Guenther Roth, *The Social Democrats in Imperial Germany* (Totowa, N.J., 1963); Carl Schorske, *German Social Democracy, 1905–1917* (Cambridge, Mass., 1955); Robert Michels, *Political Parties*, trans. Eden and Cedar Paul (New York, 1962); Feldman, *Army, Industry, and Labor*; Ashok Desai, *Real Wages in Germany* (Oxford, England, 1968). As Rürup argues on the basis of the studies in *Arbeiter- und Soldatenräte*, the councils may have represented a realistic third way between Bolshevik-style dictatorship and the Ebert-Noske repression that was to follow. But the SPD and the unions would have had to lend decisive political and organizational support.

39.   Schieck; Helga Grebing, "Konservative Republik oder soziale Demokratie?" in Kolb, *Vom Kaisserreich*, 388–403; von Oertzen, *Betriebsräte*, 247 ff., 67; Kolb, "Rätewirklichkeit," 181–182; Rürup, Kolb, and Feldman; Arno Mayer, *Politics and Diplomacy of Peacemaking* (New York, 1967), 90 ff., 253 ff.

40.   Kolb, *Arbeiterräte*; von Oertzen, *Betriebsräte*; Gerhard Bassler, "The Communist Movement in the German Revolution, 1918–1919: A Problem of Historical Typology?" *Central European History* 6 (1973), 248 ff.; Morgan; Hartfrid Krause, *USPD* (Frankfurt am Main, 1975).

41.   Von Oertzen, *Betriebsräte*, chapter 5; von Oertzen, *Die Probleme der wirtschaftlichen Neuordnung und der Mitbestimmung in der Revolution von 1918, unter besonderer Berücksichtigung der Metallindustrie* (Frankfurt am Main, 1975), Part II (these two have since been combined in the 1976 edition of *Betriebsräte*).

42.   Rürup, Kolb and Feldman, 100. See also Morgan; Bassler; von Oertzen, *Betriebsräte*, chapter 8. It must remain questionable to what extent such a diffuse opposition, emerging during a relatively brief period of intense conflict and under considerable state constraints, *could* have developed a more coherent and effective organization *even if* the ideological barriers to this were less extreme.

43.   Von Oertzen, *Betriebsräte*; Rürup, Kolb and Feldman, 85; Morgan 245 ff.; Karl Korsch, *Schriften zur Sozialisierung* (Frankfurt am Main, 1969). The latter wrote in the council journal, *Der Arbeiterrat*, though he was not strictly a council theorist associated with the mass movement.

44.   Sergio Bologna, "Class Composition and the Theory of the Party at the Origin of the Workers' Councils Movement," *Telos* 13 (Fall 1972), 4–27. This is a full translation from the original *Operai e Stato*, by Bolgona et al. (Milan, 1972), and has been translated into German as well. More recently Karl Heinz Roth has tried to develop this argument, but with a new stress on the unskilled workers as historical subjects, in *Die "andere" Arbeiterbewegung* (Munich, 1974). Despite the rigidly evolutionistic character of the general schema and the often careless and superficial documentation of specific arguments, this thesis has been frequently repeated.

45.   See von Oertzen; Erhard Lucas, *Zwei Formen von Radikalismus in der deutschen Arbeiterbewegung* (Frankfurt am Main, 1976); Comfort, 96 ff.; Bassler, 258 ff.; and the essays of Peterson and Nolan in this volume.

46.   Gerald Feldman, "German Big Business between War and Revolution: The Origins of the Stinnes-Legien Agreement," in *Entstehung und Wandel der modernen Gesellschaft*, ed. Gerhard Ritter, (Berlin, 1970), 312–341; Feldman, *Army, Industry, and Labor,* 436 ff., 521 ff.; Schieck, 138 ff.; von Oertzen, *Betreibsräte*, 181 ff.; Comfort, 85 ff.

47.   In the expansive textile unions there was a high degree of radicalism but less councilism due, according to von Oertzen (*Betriebsräte*, p. 277), to the large unskilled, especially female component (which created personnel difficulties for co-determination), and the small and medium-sized plant structure.

48.   Von Oertzen, *Betriebsräte*, chapters 11 and 12, 189 ff.; passim; Rürup, Kolb and Feldman, 90 ff., 101 ff.; Comfort, 28, 37, 88 ff., 96 ff.; Lucas, 148; Morgan, pp. 129–130, 249–250, 270, 342; Maier, *Recasting Bourgeois Europe*, 61. Where the hold of the old unions was weaker, the *Obleute* often formed the basis of new revolutionary industrial unions. See Peterson, in this volume.

49.   Kolb, "Rätewirklichkeit," 165–166.

50.   Maier, *Recasting Bourgeois Europe*, 148, 160 ff.; von Oertzen, *Betriebsräte*, 153 ff., 256; Morgan, 233–234, 269, 312; Comfort, 98 ff.

51. Of the numerous general treatments of political developments in Russia in 1917, see especially Ferro; Anweiler; Keep; Rabinowitch, *The Bolsheviks Come to Power* (New York, 1976).

52. On the extent of coordination and the general problems associated with it, see especially Sirianni, *Workers' Control*; M. L. Itkin, "Tsentri Fabrichno-zavodskikh Komitetov Rossii v 1917 g.," *Voprosy istorii* 2 (1974), 21–36; Döring, especially parts 1 and 2; Brügmann, chapter 12.

53. This conclusion is shared by various historians, though to different degrees. John Keep (p. 158), for instance, concludes that " 'workers' control' was bound to create anarchy." Paul Aurich speaks of "the elemental drive of the Russian masses towards a chaotic utopia," in "The Bolshevik Revolution and Workers' Control in Russian Industry," *Slavic Review* 27 (1963), 63; see also Jean-Marie Chauvier, "Contrôle ouvrier at 'Autogestion Sauvage' en Russie (1917–1921)," *Revue des pays de l'est* 14, no. 1 (1973), 82.

54. William Rosenberg, "The Democratization of Russia's Railroads in 1917," in this volume. As Steve Smith has argued, however, the strength of shop and craft identities in the Russian labor movement should not be exaggerated. Nor, I would argue, did the Bolsheviks consistently use the factory and shop committees to encourage particularistic interests, and quite often did just the opposite. See Steve Smith, "Craft Consciousness, Class Consciousness: Petrograd 1917," *History Workshop Journal* 11 (Spring 1981), 33–56.

55. Haupt, 231.

56. Skocpol, 168, my emphasis.

57. The relationship of movement, leadership and theory is a central theme of Sirianni, *Workers' Control.*

58. It should be noted that although the committees exercised vigorous control over the technical and administrative personnel, to the point of dismissing those who proved overly recalcitrant, no general purges were undertaken.

59. Reginald Zelnik, "Russian Bebels: An Introduction to the Memoirs of Semen Kanatchikov and Matvei Fisher," *The Russian Review* 35, no. 3 (July 1976), 262–263; and Smith. Perhaps the strength of occupational parochialism on the rails, which Rosenberg emphasizes, was due to the complex coordination problems, the deep political divisions among different categories of workers, and the fact that the Central Line Committees were dominated by very highly skilled engineers and technical personnel. As Steve Smith points out, factory committee organization generally held "shopist" tendencies in check.

60. Keep, 71 ff., 258; Goodey, 30 ff.; Ferro, vol. 1, 114–116; Ward, 139 ff.; Koenker, part I; Heather Hogan, "The Putilovtsy: A Case Study of Workers' Attitudes during the Russian Revolution of 1917," unpublished paper, August 1974, University of Michigan; and especially Mark David Mandel.

61. It is this ambivalence and resistance which Goodey, in his very provocative article, fails to recognize.

62. Brügmann, 151 ff.; L. B. Genkin, "Rozhdeniye Sotsialisticheskoy Distsiplini Truda (konets 1917-leto 1918)," *Istoriia SSSR* 1 (Jan.–Feb. 1965), 3–27; A. Lomov, *Die Produktivität der Arbeit in Sowjet Russland* (Berlin, 1919).

63.   See Franciska Baumgarten, *Arbeitswissenschaft und Psychotechnik in Russland* (Munich; 1924); Kendall Bailes, "Alexei Gastev and the Soviet Controversy over Taylorism, 1918–1924," *Soviet Studies* 29, no. 3 (July 1977), 373–394; Anthony Sutton, *Western Technology and Soviet Economic Development, 1917–1930* (Stanford, 1968).

64.   Karl Mannheim, *Essays on the Sociology of Knowledge*, ed. Paul Kecskemeti (London, 1952), 283.

65.   In Pannekoek's postwar critique the unions no longer have any positive function and are viewed as "organs of domination of monopolist capital over the working class." The factory councils are completely different in both structure and function. See Serge Bricianer, *Pannekoek and the Workers Councils*, trans. Malachy Carroll (St. Louis, 1978); Anton Pannekoek, *Workers Councils* (Cambridge, Mass., 1970).

66.   Arthur Stinchcombe, "Social Structure and Organizations," in James March, ed., *Handbook of Organizations* (Chicago, 1965), 148 ff.; see also Zald and McCarthy, "Resource Mobilization and Social Movements," 1233–1234.

67.   See, for instance, G. David Garson, ed., *Workers' Self-Management in Industry: The West European Experience* (New York, 1977); Eric Batstone, Ian Boraston, and Stephen Frenkel, *Shop Stewards in Action* (Oxford, 1977); Evelyn Huber Stephens, *The Politics of Workers Participation: The Peruvian Approach in Comparative Perspective* (New York, 1980); Juan Espinosa and Andrew Zimbalist, *Economic Democracy: Workers' Participation in Chilean Industry, 1970–1973* (New York, 1978).

68.   Steve Fraser, in this volume; Roth, *Arbeiterbewegung*, 56 ff.; Devinat, passim; Charles Maier, "Between Taylorism and Technocracy: European ideologies and the vision of industrial productivity in the 1920s," *The Journal of Contemporary History* 5, no. 2 (1970), 48.

69.   Moutet, 39 ff.; Abherve, 79; Wohl, 120.

70.   Gary Cross, in this volume.

71.   The phrase is borrowed from Jean Monds, 85.

72.   John Sharpless and John Rury, "The Political Economy of Women's Work, 1900–1920," *Social Science History*, no. 3 (1980); Temma Kaplan, "Women's Networks and Social Change in Twentieth Century Petrograd, Turin and Barcelona," paper presented at Center for European Studies, Harvard University, March 1981.

73.   The latter is reemphasized in Bruce Fireman and William Gamson, "Utilitarian Logic in the Resource Mobilization Perspective," in Zald and McCarthy. Skilled workers' acceptance of narrower wage differentials was often expressed in terms of principle, ideology, and solidarity with those whose conditions were worse off.

Index